Eminent Economists

Eminent Economists

Their Life Philosophies

Edited by
MICHAEL SZENBERG

The right of the
University of Cambridge
to print and sell
all manner of books
was granted by
Henry VIII in 1534.
The University has printed
and published continuously
since 1584.

CAMBRIDGE UNIVERSITY PRESS

Cambridge

New York   Port Chester   Melbourne   Sydney

Published by the Press Syndicate of the University of Cambridge
The Pitt Building, Trumpington Street, Cambridge CB2 1RP
40 West 20th Street, New York, NY 10011, USA
10 Stamford Road, Oakleigh, Melbourne 3166, Australia

First published 1992

Printed in Canada

Library of Congress Cataloging-in-Publication Data
Eminent economists: Their life philosophies /
edited by Michael Szenberg.
p.   cm.
Includes index
ISBN 0-521-38212-2 (hardcover)
1. Economists – Biography.   2. Economics – Philosophy.
I. Szenberg, Michael.
HB76.L54   1992
330'.092'2 – dc20   91-3107
[B]   CIP

A catalog record for this book is available from the British Library.

ISBN 0-521-38212-2 hardback

B'H

To Avi
with fatherly admiration

Great men, taken up in any way, are profitable company.

Thomas Carlyle

We all have our philosophies, whether or not we are aware of this fact, and our philosophies are not worth very much. But the impact of our philosophies upon our actions and our lives is often devastating. This makes it necessary to try to improve our philosophies by criticism.

Karl R. Popper

The ideas of economists and political philosophers, both when they are right and when they are wrong, are more powerful than is commonly understood. Indeed the world is ruled by little else.

John Maynard Keynes

The physicist who is only a physicist can still be a first-class physicist and a most valuable member of society. But nobody can be a great economist who is only an economist – and I am even tempted to add that the economist who is only an economist is likely to become a nuisance if not a positive danger.

Frederick A. von Hayek

Contents

viii   *Contents*

Preface

The idea for this collection of essays came to me some time after 1983, when, on the occasion of the twenty-fifth anniversary of the *American Economist*, a new feature was introduced – reflections by some of our most eminent economists on their life philosophies. The series, inaugurated by Paul A. Samuelson, has generated extensive interest among the readers of the journal. Inspired by the dearth of autobiographical writings in economics, it certainly is a step toward constructing a biographical inventory of the creative minds among economists.

"The raw materials out of which science is made," according to physiologist René Dubos, "are not only the observations, experiments, and calculations of scientists, but also their urges, dreams, and follies."[1] Many in the profession assume that people act in accordance with the profession's constructs, which are abstracted from the psychological and political aspects of economic behavior. They neglect the role of personal and social factors in the formation of economic discourse. As Herbert Simon argues, they invent systems describing individuals without individuality. Joseph Schumpeter has observed, however, that the analyses and issues economists study are influenced by their personal experiences.

The contents of this volume – twenty-two autobiographical essays – give us an intimate view of some of the dominant economists of this century, scholars whose work has changed the direction of the discipline. Why twenty-two essays? The plan was to have a volume of seventy thousand words. Since the average size of the essays was limited to about three thousand words, this prescribed the arbitrary number of twenty-two essays. Fourteen of them are original pieces written for this volume. The others have appeared in the *American Economist*; they are reprinted here with minor changes.

The self-portraits offer us details about the economists' personal and professional lives that we might otherwise not have known, and they capture the significance of the total person. Moreover, they shed light

---

[1] René Dubos, *Louis Pasteur: Free Lance of Science* (Boston: Little Brown, 1950), 374.

on their writings, and as such, they change one's notions of what an economist can do or be.

There is in our culture a craving to share the lives of well-known individuals.[2] We are boundlessly curious about their accomplishments, their motives, and the resources they bring to their tasks. We also attempt to probe the inner landscape of scientists' lives. Our interest is in the how and the why, which can lead us to discover the wellspring of the creative impulse. Paul Samuelson asks, "What would we not give to learn" about the creative processes of artists and scientists and to read their autobiographical accounts?[3] Several years ago, there was much excitement in the scientific world in the wake of the news that the personal papers of Albert Einstein were being prepared for publication. A *New York Times* editorial, "Sources of Genius," declared that the papers were among this country's great treasures because of their potential for advancing our understanding of genius. Unfortunately, according to Myron Coler, our current knowledge of creativity has only reached a stage analogous to Tycho Brahe's preliminary investigation of planetary motion.[4] But as James Froude, the biographer of Thomas Carlyle, has said, "We must have the thing before we can have a science of a thing."

Some words concerning the editor's feelings about this volume are appropriate. Preparing it has been especially exciting, for I have been an elated reader of memoirs and biographies since my childhood. It has permitted me to travel to distant worlds, places, and periods and become acquainted with events and personalities. Many of the historical figures I have met have spoken to my heart and stirred me powerfully. As George Bernard Shaw observed, "I see biography rather like foreign travel. You go to a country quite unlike your own and you pick up something of that way of life, that language, and your life is changed by the experience."[5] In other words, we intensify our own lives by living a number of other lives at the same time.

[2] Biography has become an important literary form since World War II, but it has focused mainly on political and literary figures. Autobiographies of or biographies by scholars are not common. See Michael Szenberg and Eric Y. Lee, "Empirical Estimation of Demand and Supply of Books in the United States, 1966–1982," in Douglas V. Shaw, William S. Hendon, and C. Richard Waits (eds.), *Artists and Cultural Consumers* (Akron, Ohio: Association for Cultural Economics, 1987), 207–15. Also Eric Y. Lee and Michael Szenberg, "Analysis of Factors Determining Book Consumption in the United States, 1952–1985," in Douglas V. Shaw, William S. Hendon, and Virginia Lee Owen (eds.), *Cultural Economics 88: An American Perspective* (Akron, Ohio: Association for Cultural Economics, 1989), 129–36.
[3] Paul Samuelson, *Foundations of Economic Analysis* (Cambridge, Mass.: Harvard University Press, 1983), xv–xxvi.
[4] Myron A. Coler (ed.), *Essays on Creativity in the Sciences* (New York: New York University Press, 1963), xvii.
[5] Quoted by Kim Heron in "Did You Hear the One About the Fabians?" *New York Times Book Review* (Oct. 9, 1988). Interview with Michael Holroyd upon publication of

My love affair with biographical writings was stimulated when, as a child, I taught myself to read using the only book available to me – the biography of Felix Dzerzhinskiy, the infamous head of Cheka, the Soviet Security Service after the Bolshevik Revolution. I read and reread the book numerous times during the last two years of the Second World War, when I was hiding from the Nazis. For me, good biography became a synthesis of fiction, poetry, and history.

As the editor of this volume, I took the occasion to outline what I thought was appropriate ground to cover beyond the ideas implicit in the series title. The essays were not structured. Each contributor was free to determine his own approach and method of treatment. In several cases, I asked the authors to clarify, to shorten, or to expand on certain aspects of the discussion. The pieces thus differ not so much in length as in degree of analytical emphasis. I quote a passage from my letter to the authors to enable the reader to evaluate what was intended and to judge how well it has been realized:

Regarding the essay's content, contributors certainly have latitude in interpreting its title and in responding to it accordingly. Still, besides the usual biographical sketches, the essay should ideally be interspersed with philosophical issues, some perspective on the nature of life and of the universe, and the relationship between economics and other disciplines. Contributors are encouraged to probe and articulate – perhaps via personal anecdotes – how background and upbringing molded their attitudes, ethics, religion, and how these, in turn, affected choice of occupation, political preference, selection of original research areas, and the related methodology – the theorizing matrix. Also, teachers and colleagues play an important role in the process. There is strong reason to believe that these elements in the configuration are not entirely independent and mutually exclusive.

The rationale for the selection process was a simple one. It was based on the recognition accorded to the authors by the scientific awards bestowed on them and by their election to various learned societies. After all, as Paul A. Samuelson remarked in his presidential address to the American Economic Association, the scholar works for the only coin worth having – peer applause. Initially, I tried to select participants irrespective of age, but after some communication with several of the younger eminent economists, I decided to concentrate on the older generation. Otherwise, the selection of contributors from the younger members of the profession would have been idiosyncratic. The younger economists felt they were still too young to be considered for this honor, and they asked to be reinvited in five years or so. Perhaps they felt they could not write of their accomplishments without laying themselves open

vol. 1 of his three-volume biography of GBS: *Bernard Shaw: The Search for Love* (New York: Random House, 1988). Holroyd has so far spent fifteen years on Shaw, with two more volumes to come.

to the charge of egotism. The writing by and about oneself is not soft ground to plough for a young scholar with intellectual attainments. One young economist suggested that reaching celebrity status, such as being awarded the Nobel Prize, might be justification for him to elaborate on his life philosophy. He did not wish to bank on the award, however, even though he is so acclaimed as to be a shoo-in for the prize in the next decade. The story is told of Albert Einstein, the 1921 Nobelist, who was so confident about receiving the prize that he promised his estranged wife the Nobel Prize money in 1919, as alimony. Another young economist looked on the senior participants with such awe that he declined to be included in the same volume with them. He suggested that I edit a volume of similar essays for the younger eminent economists.[6]

To my surprise, only a few economists declined my invitation to contribute an essay. Several of them could not meet the deadline due to other commitments. One wrote that it was an honor for him to be invited but, as far as he knew, he did not have a life philosophy. This reminds me of John M. Keynes's famous remark at the end of his most important book,[7] about policy makers who claim that they do not subscribe to any theories. Keynes suggested that such persons are slaves of defunct theories. Another invitee felt that he would be in trouble if he ever tried to figure out his life philosophy. He related the famous anecdote about the bearded man who was asked whether he slept with his beard above or below the blanket – and was never able to get a good night's rest afterward. Advanced age prevented two economists from completing the task and another, known for his outspoken views on the direction of the discipline, argued that an elaboration of his philosophy would require more than five hundred pages.

One eminent Eastern European economist was invited to contribute to the volume. He enthusiastically accepted the assignment, but later contacted me while on a visit to the West to tell me that, with the changes Eastern Europe is now undergoing, it would be better from his standpoint not to express his life philosophy openly. He said that in Eastern Europe a life philosophy is a sensitive subject, and he preferred to avoid complications and conflicts that might interfere with his scientific work at this time. I am sympathetic to his plight. After all, there is a risk that the few flowers now allowed to bloom in the Eastern European garden might wither away. This should draw our attention yet again to the inevitable

---

[6] I am reminded of the admiration Marquis de L'Hopital felt for Isaac Newton, which prompted him to ask in seriousness whether the great Newton ate and slept as other humans.

[7] John M. Keynes, *The General Theory of Employment, Interest, and Money* (New York: Harcourt, Brace, 1936).

conflicts between the social role of the scientist and his or her value system.[8]

One midwestern U.S. economist requested a compensation of about $10,000 for his essay. To borrow George Stigler's opinion of Samuelson when the latter published his best-selling text, the invited economist, having achieved some fame, is now looking for a fortune. Since I considered the invited pieces priceless, I had to turn down his request and continue my search for an equally eminent but more generous author. Paul A. Samuelson requested that his fee from the publisher be donated to the Honor Society in Economics.

Clearly, there are omissions, and my selection will not satisfy every reader. Just how personal such selections are can be seen from a paperback[9] that came to my attention after completing this volume. The list of entries includes one hundred leading economists. Maurice Allais, the 1988 Nobel laureate, is not on that list.

[8] I was surprised to learn that even in the West such a seemingly innocuous reflective piece can be damaging to its author. In October 1989, the London *Financial Times* printed a passage from a life philosophy essay in the *American Economist* series written by Sir Alan Walters, at that time the economic adviser to British Prime Minister Margaret Thatcher. In the passage, Sir Alan expressed his opposition to the plan of the chancellor of the exchequer, Nigel Lawson, to integrate Britain into the European Monetary System. The disagreement was propelled onto the front pages of newspapers, which led to the resignation of both officials, a reshuffling of the cabinet, and what was considered by observers to be the worst political and economic crisis in the past decade (see Michael Szenberg, "The Walters–Lawson Affair and the Two Worlds of Communication: A Collision Course," *American Journal of Economics and Sociology*, July 1990, 293–6).
In the aftermath of the Walters affair, an eminent economist and a leading candidate for nomination to the Supreme Court of the United States decided not to publish his life philosophy essay in the *American Economist* series. The recent rejection by the Senate of Supreme Court nominee Robert Bork and the easy confirmation of Justice David H. Souter may very well justify the position taken by the U.S. economist. The existence of what is called a "paper trail" – publications containing personal opinions – is damaging to confirmation to high positions as bits and pieces from the articles are dragged into the mass media, where they are given instant rather than deliberative analysis and judgment. We are thus entering, unfortunately, an era of publish and perish.

[9] Mark Blaug, *Great Economists Since Keynes* (Cambridge University Press, 1989). The hardcover edition was published by Wheatsheaf Publishers, London, in 1985.

Acknowledgments

Editing a book is a social activity, not only because it draws on many people's ideas, but also because it depends on the support of colleagues, friends, and family. I have been fortunate in this area, and I am very grateful to my daughter, Naomi, serving as a medical resident, and to my son-in-law, Dr. Marc Kunin, for bringing much joy and happiness to my wife and mother. I would also like to mention my teenage nephew, Chaim Jonathan, who lives with us and exemplifies that rare combination of wisdom of learning and wisdom of life experience. Paul Samuelson is only partly right to point out that having children is the biggest kick in life. For me, a more exhilarating kick comes from watching the ball go over the goal posts, that is, seeing my children develop into productive members of society.

I have accumulated many debts in the preparation of this volume. I should like to acknowledge in particular the cooperativeness of the contributors. I thank them for their congenial partnership, and especially for the lessons in scholarship that working with them has taught me. To illustrate, in the case of one contributor's essay, getting the final version in order took about eight submitted drafts, fifty letters and cables, and numerous telephone calls. This is meticulousness of the highest order on the part of the contributor. I intend to show the many versions of the essay to my students so they understand that inspiration, in the words of Tchaikovsky, "is a guest that does not visit lazy people." Also, as Polanyi has pointed out, being brought in contact with an eminent mind "will reveal the way he chooses problems, selects a technique, reacts to new clues and to unforeseen difficulties, discusses other scientists' work, and keeps speculating all the time about a hundred possibilities which are never to materialize."[1] This certainly cannot be transmitted through formal schooling.

More than to anyone else, this book owes its existence to the members of the Executive Board of the Honor Society in Economics: Professors

---

[1] Michael Polanyi, *Science, Faith and Society* (New York: Oxford University Press, 1948), 29.

William D. Gunther, Alex Kondonassis, C. Louise Nelson, Charles F. Phillips, and Harold F. Williamson. Professor Alan A. Brown, a member of the Omicron Delta Epsilon Board of Trustees, gave me welcomed and needed advice. He read an earlier draft of the Introduction and made many suggestions for its improvement. I thank him for his very warm-hearted encouragement. I am also indebted to an outstanding past student of mine, Sherri Weiller, a Sorbonne graduate, currently president of Sherri Weiller Associates, for her translation from the French of Maurice Allais's essay, and to my assistant, Lynn Von Salis. I owe a special debt to Diana Powell Ward, editor, Center for Applied Research and the *Lubin Letter*, who offered her editorial talents with unfailing grace, dedication, and good cheer. Her assistance to me, to use a term that goes beyond economics, has been invaluable.

Colin Day, past editorial director of Cambridge University Press and currently director of the University of Michigan Press, favored me with helpful comments at the initial stage of this project. Mary Racine, production editor of this volume, deserves accolades for her professionalism. Thanks are extended to my colleagues at Pace University: William C. Freund, chair of the Economics Department; Elayn Bernay, director, Center for Applied Research; Arthur Centonze, dean, Lubin Schools of Business; and Joseph M. Pastore, provost of the university – all provided support and an atmosphere that was both encouraging and stimulating.

I wish to thank the anonymous referees of Cambridge University Press for their enthusiastic support of this work and Dr. Abraham Goldstein, managing director, InterEquity Capital Corporation, for helpful comments and friendship. To them all, I am profoundly grateful.

Finally, I would like to express my appreciation to Professor Frank Genovese, editor in chief of the *American Journal of Economics and Sociology,* Professor Pascal Bridel, chair of the symposium entitled "Editing Economists and Economists as Editors" organized by the Center Walras-Pareto, Université de Lausanne, and the editors of *Revue Européenne des Sciences Sociales* for permission to use material published in article form.

It is to my son Avi, who was studying in Yeshivat Mir in Jerusalem while this volume was being written and is currently attending the University of Pennsylvania Law School, and his bride Tova that I affectionately dedicate this book. They are learning that the purpose of our existence in this world is not simply to raise our intelligence quotient, but primarily to ennoble our moral character.

As I write these words, I must record with sorrow that one of the contributors, Karl Brunner, died on May 9, 1989, of cancer. I regret that he did not live to see this volume, in which he showed deep interest.

Introduction

Rabbis of ancient Israel tell us, when speaking of a House of Learning, that a thousand come in and only one goes out. The meaning is that, of the thousand who enter the house, we are lucky if even one attains elite status in the learning establishment. An interesting custom existed in those ancient Talmudic academies. Their back benches were occupied by the weaker scholars. As they were able to manifest their intellectual gifts, they moved closer to the front bench. The front bench was occupied by only the brightest and most creative of the scholars, referred to as the "mountain movers."

The economists presented in this volume are among the older generation of principal movers of their discipline. Keats's description of artists as "God's Spies on Earth" is applicable to our group because, like artists, they not only see but notice, perceive, and inspire. These are individuals who are consumed by what V. S. Pritchett calls "spiritual greed" because of the "incessant activity of the mind."

To me, one of the joys of reading these essays has been to think of the manner in which scholarship is nurtured, molded, and enhanced and to observe parallels in the lives of the authors, despite their diversity. If one thing emerges clearly from the pages of this volume, it is that the paths of many of the contributors have so often joined or crossed since their student days. It indicates the virtue of intimate contact among scientists. Edward Gibbon's view that solitude is the "school of genius" is highly exaggerated. The mathematician Leopold Infeld, who collaborated with Albert Einstein at the Institute for Advanced Study in Princeton, relates how scientists laughed when Einstein said that the ideal job for a scientist would be that of a lighthouse keeper.[1]

---

[1] Leopold Infeld, *Quest: The Evolution of a Scientist* (New York: Doubleday, 1941), 280. In this regard it is worth relating a Talmudic story about Rabbi Elazar Ben Arak. His teacher, Rabban Yohanan Ben Zakkai, described him as an ever-surging spring. He also used to say that, if all sages of Israel were on one side of the scale and Elazar Ben Arak were on the other, he would outweigh all of them. The Midrashic commentary relates that, on the advice of his wife, Elazar Ben Arak moved away from Yavne, the prominent learning center, after the destruction of the Second Temple. As a result of his isolation

1

There is increasing recognition of the significance of face-to-face interaction, interpersonal communication, and cooperation among scientists.[2] A scientist can no longer work alone, given the complexity of the subject matter.

David Hull, a science philosopher, suggests that success in science arises from the tension prevailing between the need for simultaneous collaboration and competition among scientists. But then he argues that "the behavior that appears to be the most improper actually facilitates the manifest goals of science. . . . As it turns out, the least productive scientists tend to behave the most admirably, while those who make the greatest contributions just as frequently behave the most deplorably."[3] This leads one to associate aggressiveness and selfishness with high productivity by scientists. Similarly, Alexander Solzhenitsyn in his novel *The First Circle* argues that "you could never have two top engineers or scientists on the same project — one would always oust the other in the fight over who

from the other scholars, there is little left of his genius in the Talmudic literature. See *Ethics of the Fathers*, ch. 2, v. 12, and *Masehet Shabat*, 147b.

   A not dissimilar fate befell the great Renaissance artist Leonardo da Vinci. His notebooks include original contributions to many branches of science, such as anatomy, physics, engineering, geology, and botany, but since he kept them private and never communicated his research results, his contributions had to be independently discovered by others several decades after his death. Therefore, he lost priority to other scientists. As Oscar Wilde used to say, "To be intelligible is to be found out."

[2] The Nobelist James D. Watson has shown the connection between personal and social factors and the discovery of the structure of DNA. See his *Double Helix* (New York: Atheneum, 1968). Two British sociologists reveal the role that personal conversations play in any scientific discourse. See Michael Mulkay and Nigel Gilbert, "Accounting for Error: How Scientists Construct Their Social World When They Account for Correct and Incorrect Belief," *Sociology* (May 1982), 165–83. More recently, Arjo Klamer, in a fascinating book, *Conversations with Economists* (Totowa, N.J.: Rowman & Allanheld, 1984), conveys the importance of rhetoric in economics. See also A. Klamer, D. N. McCloskey, and R. M. Solow (eds.), *The Consequences of Economic Rhetoric* (Cambridge University Press, 1988). For a candid look at the human side of modern physics – the indiscretions, clashing egos, vitriolic squabbles, high-pitched emotions, competition, and cooperation – and the importance of informal communication, see S. Glashow with Ben Bova, *Interactions: A Journey Through the Mind of a Particle Physicist and the Matter of This World* (New York: Warner, 1988), and R. M. Hazen, *The Breakthrough: The Race for the Superconductors* (New York: Summit Books, 1988). Ben-Ami Scharfstein, in *The Philosophers: Their Lives and the Nature of Their Thought* (New York: Oxford University Press, 1980), gives interesting insights into leading philosophers' ideas based on biographical details of their lives. Also, the history of warfare indicates that superiority on the battlefield is determined not only by the types of weapons used or by strategic and tactical decisions, but by what is referred to as the "G Factor" – the rivalries, moods, loves, and hates among the generals.

[3] David L. Hull, *Science as a Process: An Evolutionary Account of the Social and Conceptual Development of Science* (Chicago: University of Chicago Press, 1988), 32. For an examination of the most visceral drives of an eminent physicist and the intriguing hostility between two Nobelists, Ervin Schrodinger and Werner Heisenberg, see Walter Moore, *Schrodinger* (Cambridge University Press, 1989). See also Paul Johnson, *Intellectuals* (New York: Harper & Row, 1989).

was to get all the credit." In prison, however, collaboration can exist. "You can have a dozen academic lions living together peacefully in one den, because they've nowhere else to go."[4]

WHO ARE THE CONTRIBUTORS?

Among the economists whose essays are collected here, we find a high sense of cooperation; continuing collaborative contact in the form of dual and multiple authorships of books and articles, joint teaching assignments, and review and support of one another's writings; single-mindedness; and hard and deep immersion in work, even passion,[5] but very little of the intensive, relentless competition that Hull speaks of regarding natural scientists. I would venture to say that the difference stems not so much from the fact that economics is a "soft" science, but rather from the degree of maturity of the discipline. The economists presented here were fortunate to enter the field at a time when it was ready to take off. As Paul A. Samuelson says, "It was like fishing in a virgin lake: a whopper at every cast, but so many lovely new specimens that the palate never cloyed."[6] Thus, this generation of economists consists more of collaborators and mutual supporters than of competitors.[7]

[4] Alexander I. Solzhenitsyn, *The First Circle* (London: Collins, Fontana Books, 1970), 82. It is worth noting that, even though two German chemists, Otto Hahn and Fritz Strassmann, discovered nuclear fission, the Americans were first to build the atomic bomb. One of the main reasons for the German failure to construct the bomb had to do with the separation of German physicists between theoreticians and experimentalists. In contrast, on the U.S. side there was cooperation between the two groups. J. Robert Oppenheimer, the director of the program at Los Alamos, had done work in experimental as well as theoretical physics. McGeorge Bundy, "Hitler and the Bomb," *New York Times Magazine* (November 3, 1988), 47.

[5] James M. Buchanan recalls the succinct advice Earl J. Hamilton gave him for finding success in academia. "Keep the ass to the chair" is a rule that he has followed and passed along to several generations of students; see "Better Than Plowing," in *Banca Nazionale del Lavoro Quarterly Review* (December 1986), 364. Charles Kindleberger speaks about cultivating *sitzfleisch*, "the capacity to put your tail in the chair and leave it there for hours at a time." A. Kekule quotes J. Liebig's advice to him, "If you wish to be a chemist, you must be willing to work so hard as to ruin your health," in Hans Krebs, "The Making of a Scientist," *Nature* (September 30, 1967), 1443. Several of our contributors, notably James Buchanan and Paul Samuelson, acknowledge the importance of luck in their professional careers. But as Louis Pasteur once insightfully remarked, "Chance favors only the prepared mind."

[6] Paul Samuelson, *Foundations of Economic Analysis* (Cambridge, Mass.: Harvard University Press, 1948), xv–xxvi.

[7] For example, the intellectual partnership of Samuelson and Solow is considered one of the most fruitful relationships in the history of economics. Each man provided a testing ground for the ideas of the other. "From MIT's point of view, nothing so powerfully held each of them to the Institute as the presence of the other." See the citation from the 1977–78 MIT James R. Killian, Jr., Faculty Achievement Award conferred on Robert Solow. This can be compared with what A. J. Ayer said to John Austin, famous for his ferocious attacks on fellow philosophers: "You are like a greyhound who does not want

Most of the contributors to this volume are Americans, by birth, by adoption, or by education. Nine, so far, have won the supreme accolade, the Nobel Prize. Of these, seven are Americans.

Many contributors have clustered together in the elite scientific institutions since their student days. In the second half of the 1930s, the magical places to be were Cambridge University, Harvard University, and the University of Chicago.[8] These were the schools where lasting contributions to the growth and vigor of economics were made.[9] The three institutions were home not only to luminous teachers, but also to equally brilliant students, who admit they learned as much or more from fellow students as from their professors. It may not be a coincidence, then, that outstanding minds appear in batches, as shown by our group of economists. The presence of some classmates of great originality pro-

to run himself, and bites the other greyhounds so that they cannot run either." I. Berlin, *Personal Impressions* (Oxford University Press, 1981), xviii.

[8] Columbia University and the London School of Economics were also strong economics centers at that time. Their student bodies, however, were weak in comparison with those of the other three universities. The Nobel laureate in chemistry, Sir Hans Krebs, in his article "The Making of a Scientist," 1442, reports on a chart exhibited in the Munich Museum of Science and Technology summarizing the teacher–student genealogy of the Nobel laureates descended from Justus Von Liebig, the founder of organic chemistry. The chart contains sixty individuals, all with important discoveries, and includes over thirty Nobel Prize winners. As Krebs states, "Distinction breeds distinction." That certain creative habits can be acquired can also be observed in the world of physics. The 1906 Nobel laureate J. J. Thomson, the discoverer of the electron, trained nine Nobel Prize winners and thirty-two fellows of Britain's Royal Society. However, one should note that eminent scientists are in a position to be highly selective in choosing distinguished students. The Nobel Memorial Prize in economic science, funded by the Central Bank of Sweden to commemorate its three hundredth anniversary, was established only in 1968 (Nobel awards began in 1901). And already one can trace a family tree of laureates in economics. Paul A. Samuelson was awarded a Nobel Prize in 1970. His teacher, Wassily Leontief, received the prize in 1973, while Samuelson's student, Lawrence R. Klein, won it in 1980. Thus, Samuelson's advice to students is very appropriate: "If you have any reason to think you are good, beg, borrow, or steal money to come to the top place." P. Samuelson, "Economics in a Golden Age: A Personal Memoir," in G. Holton (ed.), *The Twentieth Century Sciences* (New York: Norton, 1972), 163. Krebs feels that a distinguished teacher transmits attitudes to students, among the most important being humility, because it nurtures a self-critical mind. Illustrative of this is Kenneth J. Arrow's account at an MIT luncheon after he won the Nobel prize that, in his first years as a graduate student, he felt himself lacking in true originality (private correspondence with Samuelson).

[9] *The Economist* (December 24, 1988), 91–94, reviewing the work of eight of the world's best young economists, finds that they moved the spiritual home of twentieth-century economics from Cambridge, England, to Cambridge, Massachusetts, which contains two elite institutions of learning – Harvard and MIT. Four of the octet are associated with Harvard, two with MIT, and one each with Chicago and the University of Pennsylvania's Wharton School. This is a belated admission by the staff of the weekly magazine of a process that had begun in the 1940s. Since the 1950s, MIT has become the dominant institution in macroeconomics. Its faculty currently includes three Nobel laureates: Paul Samuelson, Franco Modigliani, and Robert Solow. All three are considered legendary teachers.

vides support and stimulus that allows others' dormant scientific prowess to emerge.

The topic of a life philosophy is a very broad one. Some of the contributors have taken an autobiographical approach; others, a philosophical, moral, or practical outlook; still others have concentrated on their professional lives. Although they come from different countries and have different specialties, there are some common strands. Most did not intend to be economists at all, but started out in other disciplines, especially physics, math, or chemistry. They found in economics, however, an intellectual challenge they could find nowhere else. C. P. Snow speaks of the divide in the Western world's two cultures – the humanistic and the scientific. Economics is unique among the various disciplines in that it bridges the two.

Many of the contributors are of humble circumstances, but financially only, since their parents showed breadth of interest and intellectual inclinations that furthered the authors' intellectual abilities.[10] They come from left-wing or liberal family backgrounds, and their voices are of liberalism and reason.[11] The 1930s was a period of leftist ideals, and many of the contributors shared in them.[12] Tsuru was jailed for Marxist activities; Klein had to leave the United States for Oxford University during the McCarthy era; Tinbergen was a member of the Labour Party; Baumol's parents were Marxists, and Rostow's were democratic socialists. Scitovsky, a member of the middle class, left Hungary to escape its social inequalities. Each of these economists expressed a desire to make the world a better place and to work in areas of importance to the solution of human problems.

A FRAMEWORK

In compiling this collection, I have been guided by Joseph Schumpeter's view of the progress of the science of economics as effectuated by the vision and technique of the scientists involved. It will therefore be appropriate to examine our contributing economists from the perspective of their vision and technique. This will provide a good framework for

[10] The 1944 Nobel laureate in physics, Isidor Isaac Rabi, relates how his mother greeted him daily upon his return from public school with the same query, "Did you ask any good question today?"

[11] It is worth noting that, according to a recent article, graduate students in economics at elite institutions during the 1980s considered themselves predominantly liberal. David Colander and Arjo Klamer, "The Making of an Economist," *Journal of Economic Perspectives* (Fall 1987), 95–111.

[12] C. P. Snow reports that by the mid-1930s, the sympathies of almost all physicists under forty were with the Left. See "The Age of Rutherford," *Atlantic Monthly* (November 1958), 80.

the reader to place, compare, and evaluate the philosophical ideas of the contributors to this volume.

Vision

Our twenty-two scholars operate from various perspectives and from divergent points on the ideological spectrum. Paul A. Samuelson's ideological and ethical views advocating the virtues of a mixed economy can be placed at the very center. Buchanan's libertarian or individualist position is at one end, while Tsuru's Marxist beliefs are at the other.

It is also worth reflecting on the contributors' conceptions of human nature, society, and justice. Kenneth Arrow quotes in his contribution Hillel, the Talmudic master's timeless expression of the ongoing and enduring condition of humanity: "If I am not for myself, who is for me? And when I am for myself, what am I? And if not now, when?"[13] The statement, offered with a sense of urgency, articulates the moral dimension of the relation between the individual and society, one that is crucial, since it concerns the nature of a just society. It touches our hearts because it tries to balance what ultimately are the two irreconcilable motives: selfishness and selflessness.

Hillel's account has been reformulated throughout history. Karl Brunner summarizes the human condition in terms of the eighteenth-century Scottish and the French schools.[14] The first school extols the significance of self-interest, while the second, influenced by the Enlightenment, articulates the acceptable role of society and the state.

Irrespective of ideological orientation, with perhaps one exception, the economists included here appreciate the centrality of the marketplace in the organization of the economy.[15] This position is based on their recognition of human nature as being driven by several motives, self-interest and rationality being just two of the most important ones. They also recognize that markets do not always function efficiently, as even James

---

[13] *Ethics of the Fathers*, ch. 1, v. 14.

[14] For an incisive study of the philosophical anticipators of Adam Smith's ideas on the importance of self-interest, see Milton L. Myers, *The Soul of Modern Economic Man, Ideas of Self-Interest, Thomas Hobbes to Adam Smith* (Chicago: University of Chicago Press, 1983). For a modern interpretation, see Robert Nozick, *Anarchy, State and Utopia* (New York: Basic, 1974), and the novels of Ayn Rand, especially *The Fountainhead* (New York: Bobbs-Merrill, 1943).

[15] Kenneth Arrow and Gerard Debreu jointly produced a mathematical proof of the existence of a general equilibrium solution. See their "Existence of an Equilibrium for a Competitive Economy," *Econometrica* 22 (July 1954), 265–90. In general equilibrium analysis, one considers the interrelationships among different markets. Frank Hahn introduced money into the general equilibrium analysis and has shown that competitive markets provide order rather than chaos. See Kenneth Arrow and Frank Hahn, *General Competitive Analysis* (San Francisco: Holden-Day, 1971).

Buchanan would admit. Among those factors that undermine the market efficiency are externalities, monopoly, public goods, and public bads, which require what Boulding calls "other coordination processes" to try to reconcile the different preferences of different individuals. These include the state and persuasion.

In order to obtain some sense of the landscape of these substantive ideas, it is worth exploring several key positions. Buchanan's belief is based firmly on the calculus of individual choice. For him, individual liberty is the cardinal moral conception. Buchanan makes the distinction between what he calls the organismic and the individualistic theories of the state.[16] The first considers the state an "organic entity." As such, it leads to the establishment of the social welfare function.[17] The function purports to represent an aggregation of the desires of different individuals in the country. For an individualist, there can be no such function for collective action unless the state's leaders feel they represent the interests of the citizens, in which case it becomes an authoritarian regime. Thus, Arrow's proof of his impossibility theorem is an outcome Buchanan could have predicted.[18]

[16] See James Buchanan's articles, "Man and the State" and "Market Failure and Political Failure," in his *Explorations into Constitutional Economics* (College Station: Texas A&M University Press, 1989). See also "Mueller on Buchanan," in Henry W. Spiegel and Warren T. Samuels (eds.), *Contemporary Economists in Perspective* (Greenwich, Conn.: JAI Press, 1984).

[17] Abram Bergson was the first to formulate what is called a "social welfare function." By incorporating human welfare and social evaluation into the function, he showed how ethics has a role in political economy. See Bergson's classic article "A Reformulation of Certain Aspects of Welfare Economics," *Quarterly Journal of Economics* (February 1938), 310–34. Paul Samuelson notes that he could not make sense of the literature on welfare economics until Bergson's contribution "came like a flash of lightning." "Bergsonian Welfare Economics," in S. Rosefielde (ed.), *Economic Welfare and the Economics of Soviet Socialism* (Cambridge University Press, 1981), 223–266.

[18] Carl Christ relates that, when Arrow began work on his *Social Choice and Individual Values* (New York: Wiley, 1951), he attempted to devise a social welfare function that would include several desirable conditions. He proved it impossible to construct such a function. *American Economist* (Spring 1990). Dale Jorgenson manages to escape the dictatorship conclusion, having "introduced a class of social welfare functions capable of expressing a variety of ethical judgments." See his "Efficiency versus Equity in Economic Policy Analysis," in Michael Szenberg (ed.), *Essays in Economics* (Boulder, Colo.: Westview Press, 1986), 118. Samuelson continually refers to the "Ethical Observer" in his "Bergsonian Welfare Economics." He rejects the idea that the necessity of the "Ethical Observer" implies that "*one* single person's tastes must rule dictatorially." In fact, Samuelson invokes the spirit of numerous religious authorities to demonstrate that ethical judgments in no way imply dictatorship (236). The issue is controversial and has been the subject of much discussion. R. P. Parks shows that all Bergson–Samuelson social welfare functions based on ordinal preferences make one individual an ethical dictator. "An Impossibility Theorem for Fixed Preferences: A Dictatorial Bergson–Samuelson Welfare Function," *Review of Economic Studies* (October 1976), 447–450. For a review of the terrain, see Dennis C. Mueller, *Public Choice II* (Cambridge University Press, 1989), ch. 19 and 20.

Buchanan's second theory holds the state as the sum of its citizens acting collectively. In this case, "the state has no ends other than those of its individual members."[19] Freely chosen collective activity is assumed to be of mutual benefit to all participants in the exchange process. The only test of mutual benefit is consensus. Obviously, unanimity satisfies the Pareto principle, since it involves changes that benefit someone while harming no one.

Since consensus is required for any activist policies, it in effect accepts the status quo regarding the present income distribution and imposes constitutional constraints on government intervention. The functions of the state are then minimal, since the state's authority is limited. As to justice and the perfectibility of human beings, these can be achieved through the competitive marketplace, which Buchanan views as an exchange mechanism encouraging bargaining among participants.[20] The results of such voluntary bargaining are expected to improve the position of the parties to the deal. In other words, markets guiding individuals driven by self-interest naturally also secure the interest of society as a whole.

Similarly, Kenneth Boulding holds to a set of beliefs in which the individual and the individual's conscience supersede the will of the majority. His position stems from his early Quaker education and the Quaker practice of following the "Light Within" each person. Hence, group decisions are made by consensus, and disagreement over an action means that no decision can be reached. The majority does not rule, and while Boulding would accept the power of persuasion to change the individual viewpoint, he would not accept coercion by a larger group such as the government. Boulding believes that the perfectibility of each human spirit and its direct access to religious experience are what make the individual conscience unbending in its acceptance of outside coercion. One might label him an anarchistic social democrat.

Maurice Allais's and Karl Brunner's views regarding the importance of the individual fall somewhere between Samuelson's and Buchanan's.

The alternative viewpoint, that each individual is constrained by the needs and rights of other individuals – that individual autonomy cannot be unlimited – is expressed by Paul A. Samuelson and held by the majority of our economists. Samuelson is a proponent of the mixed economy,[21]

---

[19] James M. Buchanan, "The Pure Theory of Public Finance: A Suggested Approach," *Journal of Political Economy* (December 1949), 498.

[20] See Buchanan's presidential address to the Southern Economic Association, "What Should Economists Do?" *Southern Economic Journal* (January 1964), 213–222, for a criticism of interpreting the market in terms of an optimizing mechanism that encourages manipulation of human behavior.

[21] Jan Tinbergen is credited with being among the first to discuss the convergence over time of the socioeconomic and political systems of communism and the West toward

in which there is a combination of public, private, individual, and social endeavors. As Samuelson himself stated in private correspondence with the editor:

Redistributive welfare transfers are not coercions on people by an external State; but rather, in the fashion of John Locke and John Rawls, are part of a social contract in which each person, operating under a veil of ignorance concerning chance's draw for him/her, opts voluntarily to set up rules of the road designed by us to be binding to us. Arrow's Impossibility Theorem, in this view, applies to and cannot be escaped by the Buchanan–Hayek view of sacred property rights in the Smithian *status quo*. A rule of unanimity would freeze Stalin's totalitarianism into perpetuity, and thus represents Humpty-Dumptyism in its attempt to legitimize an historically extinct Whig *laissez faire*.

The proponents of a mixed economy recognize that an individual is a product of his or her culture and society, just as the society is shaped by its individual members, and emphasis on the overriding importance of either individual or societal ends results in a "monstrosity."

Samuelson would applaud Anatole France's pithy statement – "The law in its majestic equality permits both rich and poor alike to sleep under the bridges at night and to beg in the streets" – as an illustration of how coercive and unjust elements are found not only in state arrangements. The lesson is clear. Individual property rights and freedom to act in the marketplace must be constrained by concern for the general social welfare.[22]

It is preferable that individuals reach shared ethical values voluntarily through persuasion, but if that fails, then the government has a social obligation to assume a greater role in redistributing income to the poorer segments of the population and even occasionally to regulate industries directly.[23] Governments should be evaluated and changed on the basis of the effectiveness of the functions they perform.

Further along this continuum we find Shigeto Tsuru, who, following Marxist analysis, does not separate economics from politics and values. He advocates governmental planning as a result of the failure of the competitive market mechanism. But the planned economy should incorporate a comprehensive price system as a tool for efficient resource allocation. He finds American belief in the inherent power of the individual unjustified since, to him, society develops in accordance with objective

forms of "mixed economy." See his "Do Communist and Free Societies Show a Converging Pattern?" *Soviet Studies* (April 1961), 333–41.

[22] For a trenchant examination of the liberal principles of justice, see John Rawls, *A Theory of Justice* (Cambridge, Mass.: Harvard University Press, 1971).

[23] Richard Musgrave elaborates on the trichotomy of allocative, distributive, and stabilization state interventions in his classic *The Theory of Public Finance* (New York: McGraw-Hill, 1959).

laws. For a Marxist, one can resolve the failings of the capitalist system only by changing it, even if this change requires violent means. Tsuru, however, practicing his teacher's philosophy of "realistic idealism," might not go that far. One would have to look to younger, radical economists to find the revolutionary view expressed. Some of these radicals would even adopt the view of Michael Bakunin who proclaimed in the "Revolutionary Catechism" that a revolutionary "knows only one science, that of destruction."[24]

Technique

In the space available, I am compelled to be selective rather than comprehensive in discussing Schumpeter's second criterion for the progress of economics as a science. My emphasis is on three sources of controversy: the question of normative valuation, the open-endedness of economic behavior, and the overmathematization of the discipline.

John Kenneth Galbraith's claim three decades ago that many of the economic issues that once divided liberal and conservative economists had been settled[25] is highly exaggerated. True, there is now a larger body of economic principles about which consensus among economists of diverse persuasions exists, but this has been coupled with a substantial increase in the normative component of the discipline in the form of different ethical norms, value judgments, and philosophical orientations. Since these cannot be quantitatively measured, they continue to serve as a source of disagreement. What has changed is that, as Samuelson points out, economists are now able to delineate quickly the contours of their disagreements.

To paraphrase Lord Rutherford's oft-used cry, the 1930s marked the beginning of the heroic age of economics, for the discipline was shaken by the Keynesian revolution in macroeconomics and the monopolistic – imperfect competition model in microeconomics. Not only did the "New Economics" provide new theoretical constructs. It was also a reorientation of social thought toward greater state intervention and public policy.

In the 1930s the contributors to this volume were young men maturing in a time of theoretical and actual upheaval, as the classical model with its self-adjusting features failed to explain adequately the unfolding events. They studied classical economics by day and met in small groups by night to read and discuss the latest Keynesian writings. Austin Rob-

---

[24] Quoted in Lee Congdon, "The Marxist Chameleon," *Intercollegiate Review* 23 (Fall 1987), 23.

[25] John K. Galbraith, *Economics and the Art of Controversy* (New Brunswick, N.J.: Rutgers University Press, 1955).

inson was a member of the "Cambridge Circus," which played an important role in the evolution of Keynes's ideas and those of his wife, Joan Robinson.

Furthermore, the historical background of the period – the Great Depression and World War II – shaped and inspired these economists' philosophical outlooks and their careers. Taken together, these developments and the public's demand for explanations brought the economists of the era into the corridors of power and the center of the policy-making arena. Our contributors, with some exceptions, have evolved into a more action-oriented and policy-oriented group, serving in the postwar period as advisers to political figures, as well as to private and governmental agencies.

The dominant position here is that a mere positivistic economics discipline standing by itself, and devoid of ideology and social involvement, would have little impact on the major problems affecting our society. In this respect the liberal economists in our group are allied with Tsuru. James Buchanan, however, argues that such a position leads economics to lose its stature as a science.

An interesting aspect to observe in these accounts is the personal growth of the authors. This touches on the second source of controversy since it concerns their attitudes toward the boundaries of the discipline. For example, while Samuelson is wary of economics invading other fields of endeavor, Boulding seeks to integrate all social sciences, and Nicholas Georgescu-Roegen attempts to formulate the principles of bioeconomics. Maurice Allais is still active in the field of physics, and Herbert Simon has moved beyond economics to psychology and artificial intelligence.[26] The issue is not merely an expression of the intellectual interests of the contributors. A widening of the traditional boundaries of economics must affect economists' conclusions and policy decisions. Thus, the bases for disagreement are likely to grow in importance.

As to the third source of controversy, since the 1930s the new theoretical apparatus has been merging ever deeper with mathematics, and most of our contributors, led by Samuelson, played a decisive role in this process. They showed great enthusiasm for the role of quantitative rigor in rendering economic models more predictable. Samuelson, whose *Foundations of Economic Analysis* has elevated economic analysis to a scientific level, reasons that, until the appearance of mathematical models, Keynes himself did not truly understand his own analysis. But today a large number of our economists, notably Maurice Allais, William Bau-

---

[26] It is worth noting that Norbert Wiener, the distinguished pioneer in cybernetics, predicted that the largest scientific advances would be made in the interstitial areas between the various disciplines.

mol, Kenneth Boulding, Evsey Domar, and Nicholas Georgescu-Roegen, join the critics who are discomfited by the increasing trend toward over-mathematization of the discipline and the elevation of technique over substance.[27] Many researchers show little regard for relevance. Kenneth Boulding feels that the mathematization of economics has been premature owing to its limited empirical background. Some would warmly agree with Robert Kuttner in summarizing Wassily Leontief's views that "Departments of Economics are graduating a generation of idiot savants, brilliant at esoteric mathematics yet innocent of actual economic life."[28] They would be equally dismayed at the relative decline of economic history and empirical studies.[29]

Robert L. Heilbroner, in his best-selling book,[30] argues that the work of leading contemporary economists is not in the tradition of the past. He deplores the absence today of great visionaries in the Smithian or Marxian sense who would be inclined to construct grand models of economic development.

Katherine Paterson, a writer of novels for children, relates that children

[27] Maurice Allais reminds us that the faculty of Ecole nationale superieure des mines expressed opposition to his 1944 candidacy for full professorship because of its hostile attitude toward the use of mathematics in economics. In astronomy, in the nineteenth century, the academic attitude was different. Augustus De Morgan tells us in his memoirs (London: Longmans, Green, 1882) about the unjustifiable resistance of English astronomers to publishing John Couch Adams's 1845 discovery of the planet Neptune based on mathematical calculations. About a year later a Frenchman, Urban Jean LeVerrier, supported by the French establishment partial to mathematics, published his simultaneous discovery of Neptune, and thus "scooped" Adams. The dispute between the two over priority of discovery was harsh and intense. Nicholas Georgescu-Roegen, a true Renaissance man whose 1971 American Economic Association Distinguished Fellow citation says, "No American economist has more successfully combined in his training and publications the fields of economics, mathematics, and statistics," also feels that many economic aspects of our lives cannot be quantified. Evsey Domar once confessed at the American Economic Association meetings that "my principal, if only periodic bond with the econometricians consists of the eight dollars I pay each year for their incomprehensible journal." Michael Szenberg (ed.), *Essays in Economics* (Boulder, Colo.: Westview Press, 1986), 132.

[28] Typical of this trend would be a comment made by the Cambridge University economist John Eatwell, "If the world is not like the model, so much the worse for the world." See Robert Kuttner, "The Poverty of Economics," *Atlantic Monthly* (February 1985), 74–84. This position is to be contrasted with that of Jan Tinbergen, who has never been interested in theorizing for theory's sake. Will Durant's poignant observation that "every truth is tempted to expand until it becomes a falsehood, and every virtue is made a vice through excess and nothing fails like excess" is an apt description of how far the overmathematization of economics has moved. Still, scientists feel that reducing complicated phenomena to several equations represents beauty similar to that found in poetry. Its parallel can be found in the words of William Blake, for whom poetry is like "seeing the universe in a grain of sand."

[29] See Theodore Morgan, "Theory Versus Empiricism in Academic Economics: Update and Comparisons," *Journal of Economic Perspectives* (Fall 1988), 159–64.

[30] Robert L. Heilbroner, *The Worldly Philosophers* (New York: Simon & Schuster, 1986; 1st ed., 1953), 322.

need the hope that fairy tales provide. It cannot be provided by realistic stories because, as Bruno Bettelheim reminds us, "unrealistic fears require unrealistic hopes. By comparison with the child's wishes, realistic and limited promises are experienced as deep disappointment, not as consolation."[31]

Heilbroner is thus expressing a childlike wistful yearning we all share for a "happily ever after" ending to the economics story. Likewise, there are economists who, disappointed by the diversity of methods within the discipline, would like economics to have a paradigm. They believe that, once the proper method is found, all important questions will be answered.

What Heilbroner bemoans, however, other economists extol. The late economic historian Alexander Gerschenkron once observed: "There is a deep-seated yearning in social science to discover one general approach, one general law valid for all time. But these primitive attitudes must be outgrown."

As I read these essays, I had the feeling that, for the contributors to this volume, knowledge not only has been tempered over the years, but has been transformed. What they know in the early 1990s they did not know in the 1930s or 1940s. They help us realize not only how far economics as a science has advanced, but also its limitations and failures. Being witness to the most extreme form of human bestiality in the history of humankind, I know all too well the destruction that visionaries with their paradigms have wrought upon societies. In this light, Robert Solow's suggestion that economists should aspire to be competent technicians, "like dentists" as Keynes once remarked,[32] appears very attractive. Economists would then have to be satisfied with marginal gains in theory and policy because they would be realistic about the world and the nature of its inhabitants.

Early last year I was invited to attend an intimate dinner in Washington on the occasion of the selection of the 1989 recipient of the Frank E. Seidman Distinguished Award in Political Economy.[33] At the conclusion of the dinner, those attending were asked to discuss the current problems affecting the U.S. economy. Mary Keyserling[34] opened the discussion by urging those present to exert pressure on Congress to pass legislation increasing the minimum wage. Others followed in the same general gov-

---

[31] "Hope Is More Than Happiness," *New York Times Book Review* (December 25, 1988), 19.

[32] Leonard Silk, *The Economists* (New York: Basic, 1976), 250. This is an exceedingly delightful biographical treatment of five famous economists.

[33] The 1989 selection committee consisted of James Buchanan, Irving Kristol, C. Louise Nelson, Donald Ratajczak, and James Tobin. The award director was Mel G. Grinspan.

[34] The late Leon Keyserling was chair of the first Council of Economic Advisers established during the Truman administration.

ernment interventionist direction by urging increased federal spending. Toward the end of the round-table discussion, I observed that the preponderance of approaches suggested that far too much attention in our academic institutions is given to the macroeconomic aspects of society. Microeconomic issues (such as survival of the family unit), even though they may be far more important to society in the long run, are often neglected because they are more complex and intractable and have therefore produced less statistical information. The tendency of academicians to deal with what is large and easily accessible statistically and to neglect the particular and the difficult suggests an area of weakness in our current critical thinking.

Walt Rostow, like many of the contributors, urges economists to explore particular and individual phenomena. In the words of Boulding, "The survival of this present civilization depends on the solution of certain serious intellectual problems in the social sciences."[35] In this connection it is worth reflecting on the tale of a famous sixteenth-century moral preacher, Judah Ben Samuel of Regensburg. He relates that when he was a teenager his youthful idealism made him want to liberate the whole world. With advancing age and after much soul-searching, his political passions and infatuations slowly began to dim. He began to lower his sights. He thought about reforming the country, the city, then the neighborhood only. When he reached a very old age, he again critically assessed his thoughts and beliefs. Judah Ben Samuel concluded that he could understand and improve the human condition most effectively by concentrating on the individual and applying the process of self-understanding. Psychologists today are well aware of how difficult it is to change a single character trait in an individual.[36] Perhaps this is the reason so many idealistic people find it easier to love humankind than their next-door neighbor.

I will conclude by reflecting on the inescapable trade-off between equality and efficiency. Arthur Okun felt that since the two are a most improbable combination, they need one another "to put some rationality into equality and some humanity into efficiency."[37] Samuelson calls the resultant compromise "economics with a heart." He adds that it is his dream to keep it also "economics with a head."

The head is instrumental in the vast expansion of knowledge, which

---

[35] Kenneth Boulding, "Is Economics Necessary?" in his *Beyond Economics* (Ann Arbor: University of Michigan Press, 1968), 12.

[36] Today even communist-oriented countries have a much more sober view of human nature and no longer parade so openly the notion of creating a "New Man." Dictatorships of the Left or Right have failed to create a new social and psychological man because, as Plato remarked in *Politicus*, man is merely a biped without feathers.

[37] Arthur M. Okun, *Equality and Efficiency* (Washington, D.C.: Brookings Institution, 1975), 120.

is of itself neutral. It can be used for evil just as for good purposes. In the words of Albert Einstein: "Knowledge and skills alone cannot lead humanity to a dignified life. Humanity has every reason to place the proclaimers of high moral standards and values above the discoverers of objective truth."

Thus, while knowledge sets the intellectual tone of a society, it is wisdom that sets the moral one. According to the Bible, the heart is the source of wisdom. It shapes human character, refines the sensibilities, increases generosity of spirit, and makes the individual receptive to change. As the author of the Proverbs states, "The wise of heart choose good deeds."[38] The wise of heart are sensitive to the ills of the world because the heart is capable of evoking a climate of helpfulness and consideration of the needs of the poor and suffering.

Samuelson, like many other of the contributors on both the right and left of his ideological position, wants economics to remain a moral science[39] and its practitioners to aspire to be wise of heart, even as they pursue the domain of scientific knowledge. This, I feel, is a very noble objective.

---

[38] Proverbs, ch. 10, v. 5. In this regard it is worth noting a famous observation made by Herbert Simon: "You do not change people's opinions by defeating them with logic."
[39] In the past economics was listed as a moral science at English universities, and Adam Smith, the so-called father of modern economics, was professor of moral philosophy at the University of Glasgow.

MAURICE ALLAIS

The Passion for Research

At first sight Michael Szenberg's invitation, in the name of the *American Economist*, to write a twenty page essay on "my life philosophy" seemed very tempting. To give an overview of my economic, social, and political ideas, together with my career and scientific works, and to finish with my views on the nature of life and the physical world, appeared to be a fascinating task. So I accepted, probably very rashly.

In a first draft, in fact, I strove to respond to this idea, and to connect my life philosophy to the influences that determined it and which are inseparable from it: my social origin, the education I received, my professional experience, the para-political activities I was involved in, my works in fundamental and applied economics, my parallel interests, my conceptions of the physical world – all closely interdependent.

But just as this general conception was simple to define, just as it appeared easy to carry out, provided an entire book were to be devoted to it, so it became apparent that even in thirty pages it would be impossible to respond to this general conception, so vast was the subject. I would have been forced into difficult and certainly very arbitrary choices and over-simplifications, which truthfully are incompatible with the many and relatively complex aspects of my life philosophy, and therefore completely unacceptable.

I have limited myself, therefore, to a brief analysis of the factors determining my scientific vocation, the main philosophical lines of the original contributions in my works, and the philosophy of my conception of science and economics.

I have deliberately avoided presenting and analyzing my views on political fundamentals of life in society, on the different aspects of national and international political economics, and finally on the physical universe, all fascinating subjects which I have analyzed and worked on for over forty-five years, and which have resulted in many publications.

I do realize the regrets that these limitations may cause for any reader interested in knowing all aspects of my personality, but essentially, my life has been identified with my scientific work, and it is this which seems most important to me from the viewpoint of my life philosophy.

THE DETERMINING FACTORS IN MY SCIENTIFIC VOCATION

My youth

I was born May 31, 1911, in Paris. My parents owned a small cheese shop, and my maternal grandfather was a carpentry worker. I thus came from what is commonly known as the working class.

In August 1914 my father was called to war, and then taken prisoner. He died in captivity in Germany, on March 27, 1915. My youth, indeed my entire life, was deeply marked by this, directly and indirectly.

Albeit in often difficult conditions, I was nevertheless able to pursue my secondary studies. I received my high school baccalaureate diploma in Latin and Science in 1928, then my two baccalaureate diplomas in mathematics and philosophy in 1929. Throughout my college career I was generally first in my year in almost all subjects, including French and Latin as well as mathematics.

Fascinated by history, I wanted to apply to the Ecole des Chartes, but on the insistence of my mathematics teacher I entered the special mathematics class in order to prepare for the Ecole Polytechnique, which I entered in 1931. I graduated first in my class in 1933, which is commonly considered to be as a "*summum*" in France. Indeed the Ecole Polytechnique, together with the Ecole Normale Supérieure, are the top of French education in the sciences.

My choice of administration agencies upon graduation was the Corps National des Mines, not because of any particular vocation, but simply because each year the top graduates of the Ecole Polytechnique (three in my class) always chose this government service because of the career possibilities it opened up in the country's large industrial enterprises.

After a year of military service in the Artillery School first at Fontainebleau, and then in the Alpine Army, and two years at the Ecole Nationale Supérieure des Mines in Paris, I started as an engineer in the Mines public service in October 1936.

My professional career

In 1937, at the age of twenty-six, I found myself in charge of the Nantes mines and quarries service, which included five of the eighty-nine French "departments,"[1] and also put in charge of a number of controls, in particular that of the general and local railway system.

In 1939 I was called back to the Alpine Army on the Italian front, and was given command of a heavy artillery battery in the area of Briançon. But the real war only lasted two weeks, from June 10, 1940, when Italy declared war on France, until June 25, 1940, the date of the armistice.

Released from service, I took up my old position in Nantes in July 1940 in the German occupation zone. From October 1943 to April 1948 I was director of the Bureau of Mines Documentation and Statistics in Paris.

From January 1941 to April 1948 I simultaneously carried out my administrative functions and published my first works: two fundamental works, *A la Recherche d'une Discipline Economique* (In Quest of an Economic Discipline) (1943) and *Economie et Intérêt* (Economy and Interest) (1947); and three minor works, *Economie Pure et Rendement Social* (Pure Economics and Social Efficiency) (1945), *Prolégomènes à la Reconstruction Economique du Monde* (Prolegomena for the World Economic Reconstruction) (1945), and *Abondance ou Misère* (Abundance or Misery) (1946), as well as various topical articles. Throughout this period I worked very hard, at least eighty hours per week.

From April 1948 on, I was relieved of all administrative duties and was able to devote all my time to teaching, research, and writing for publication. I was professor of economic analysis at the Ecole Nationale *Supérieure* des Mines in Paris from 1944 on, and director of a research unit at the Centre National de la Recherche Scientifique (C.N.R.S.) from 1946 on. At various times I have also held teaching positions at other institutions, such as the Institute of Statistics at the University of Paris

---

[1] A department is a French administrative district.

(1947–1968), the University of Paris-X (1970–1985), the Institute of International Studies in Geneva (1967–1970), and the Thomas Jefferson Center of the University of Virginia as a Distinguished Visiting Scholar (1958–1959).

I retired from the civil service on May 31, 1980, but have been able to continue to work very actively in teaching, research, and writing.

I have received many awards for my works (fourteen scientific prizes from 1933 till 1987). The most important was the Gold Medal of the National Center for Scientific Research (C.N.R.S.), the most distinguished honor in French Science. It was awarded to me in 1978 for my lifetime work, the first and so far the only time an economist has ever received this honour.

My involvement in applied economics and politics

In addition to the above activities I have undertaken economic studies for both private and nationalized firms, and for the European Economic Community.

Throughout the years following World War II and until the formation of the European Economic Community in 1958, I was very active as a national or international rapporteur at many of the international conferences aiming to establish a European Community. I worked also for the foundation of an Atlantic Community and I was a rapporteur at the "NATO in Quest of Cohesion" international conference organized in 1964 in Washington by the Center of Strategic Studies at Georgetown University.

Finally, from 1959 to 1962 I was also founder and general delegate of the Movement for a Free Society, a liberal (in the European sense of the term) para-political organization.

My two parallel interests

During my entire career, since 1936, I have been actively involved in two fields: physics and history.

In physics, on the theoretical level, I have worked at different times on trying to develop a unified theory of gravity, electromagnetics, and quanta. On the experimental level, and as a by-product of this theoretical research, I conducted research from 1952 to 1960, at first in a small private laboratory, then in a laboratory which was specifically assigned to me at the Steel Industry Research Institute, on the anomalies of the paraconical pendulum whose existence I proved. The workload of this research, conducted in addition to my work as an economist, was as heavy at it was fascinating. For these experiments I received the Galabert

Prize in 1959 from the French Astronautical Society, and I was laureate in 1959 of the Gravity Research Foundation in the United States (on these experiments see the Appendix).

In history, I wrote from 1961 to 1966 the first version of a book: *Essor et Déclin des Civilisations – Facteurs Economiques* (Rise and Fall of Civilizations – Economic Factors), which I have continued to improve and develop at different times over the past twenty-five years. This work, as ambitious as it is daring, tries to draw out permanent regularities, particularly quantitative, from the history of civilizations, dealing with economic systems, standards of living, technology, monetary phenomena, demographic factors, inequality and social classes, the respective influences of heredity and environment, international relations, exogenous physical influences on human societies, and political systems.

My scientific vocation

My vocation as an economist was not determined by school; it was the economic reality I faced in the first years of my working life that decided it: my career as a state engineer, the intellectually shocking and socially dramatic Great Depression, the stress of social problems, and the conviction that objective economic analysis could contribute to their solution.

However, during these past forty-eight years, the evolution of my thinking has been very similar to Pareto's. I am now more concerned with understanding what men do than with convincing them. I still believe that certain policies are better than others, but more and more I think that men are motivated by their interests, their prejudices, their passions, and that logic, even scientific, really has no hold over what they do.

The inspiration for my scientific works derived simultaneously from: meditation upon the works of Leon Walras, Irving Fisher, and especially Vilfredo Pareto, three great masters who deeply influenced me; reflection on the economic and social history of recent centuries; thorough study of the applied economic questions I had been asked to investigate; and forty-five years of courses and seminars, an incomparable source of fruitful discussions.

I was involved in my two parallel interests much earlier than in my activities as an economist. During my secondary school studies, I was fascinated by history. This fascination has never left me. My involvement in physics dates from my reflections on physics, mechanics, and astronomy courses at the Ecole Polytechnique. Had the National Center for Scientific Research existed in 1938, I would have devoted myself to the study of physics and would not have become an economist. And in fact, over the past fifty years, I have never stopped reflecting and working on the problems involved in the elaboration of a unified theory of physics.

My scientific career was certainly determined by my basic nature, but, in fact, outside factors determined the directions it took, and what is commonly known as chance always played a large part: the element of chance in life's circumstances, in those we meet, in the authors we discover through reading and on whose work we reflect. It is this very complex chain of inter-connected multiple causes which really led to my researches and publications.

THE PHILOSOPHY UNDERLYING MY WORKS ON THE ESSENCE OF ECONOMIC PHENOMENA

What I have tried to do

All my researches, all my works on fundamental and applied economics, have been dominated by the concern to understand concrete reality and elaborate a theoretical synthesized analysis capable of helping, if not bringing about, this understanding. In the beginning, my desire to understand was associated with a profound desire to act, with the concern of influencing opinion and politics; progressively, however, this motivation became of secondary importance, far behind my desire to understand.

In the final analysis, everything I have done has been motivated by the need I felt to answer questions suggested to me by the obscurities, contradictions, and gaps in existing literature as regards observed reality. It has thus been a long and often laborious effort on my part to detach myself from the established tracks and dominant ideas of my time.

My approach has never been to start from theories to arrive at facts, but on the contrary, to try to bring out from facts an explanatory thread without which they appear incomprehensible and elude effective action. I have always established a close interdependence between theory and application; for me the only purpose of economic theory is the explanation of concrete phenomena and the analysis of conditions likely to assure maximum utilization of limited resources to satisfy practically unlimited needs.

Whether dealing with theoretical economic analysis or applied economics, consideration of human psychology has always appeared fundamental to me. What are the factors which determine it, and to what degree does it determine the evolution of the real world? These are the two essential questions that I have always endeavored to analyze, searching for the invariant relations that characterize them.

The fundamental structure of the economy

As regards the functioning of the economy, I have tried to bring out the fundamental factors of any economic system, and my contributions have essentially been aimed at five *highly interdependent* fields in which I have worked continuously since 1941: the theory of maximum economic efficiency, the theory of capitalistic intertemporal processes, the economic theory of uncertainty, the theory of monetary dynamics, and the theory of chance and exogenous physical influences. In each of these fields I think I have freed myself from currently accepted ideas, introducing new concepts and formalizing new theories likely to give a better representation and understanding of reality.

The achievement of an economic situation of maximum efficiency. First of all, in my first book in 1943, *A la Recherche d'une Discipline Economique*, I demonstrated with great generality the equivalence of situations of general economic equilibrium and situations of maximum efficiency. This analysis is based on the consideration of three new concepts: the concept of *surface of maximum possibilities* in the hyperspace of preference indexes; the concept of *distributable surplus for the whole economy*, a concept fundamentally different from the concept of surplus usually considered in the literature; and the concept of *economic loss* defined as the maximum value of the distributable surplus for all the modifications of the economy which leave the preference indexes of the operators unchanged.

From 1966 on, breaking away totally from the generally accepted theories and the Walrasian model on which they are based, I developed a new theory which bases the whole of economic dynamics in real terms *on the search for, achievement of, and distribution of surpluses*. The associated model is the model of the economy of markets.[2] This theory is free of any unrealistic hypothesis of continuity, derivability, and convexity. As regards the quest for situations of maximum efficiency, this approach replaces the search for a certain price system – the same for all operators – by the search for a situation in which no surplus can be achieved. The concept of price becomes secondary in the analysis and no longer plays but a subsidiary role. *It is the concept of surplus which plays the primary role in the new formulation.*

Not only does this theory, which generalizes the classical marginal approach to the most complex cases while simplifying its principles, give a realistic representation of economic dynamics in real terms, free from any artificial and useless hypothesis, but it allows a better understanding of both the profound nature of economic calculus and the true significance of the functioning of the economy under its twofold aspect of management and distribution, which it presents in a completely new light. This theory lends itself as well to analysis of international exchanges as it does to analysis of national economies, as well to the analysis of Eastern

---

[2] "Markets": in the plural.

bloc countries and the Third World, as it does to the analysis of Western economics, and as well to the economies of the past as it does to the economies of today.

I think that this formulation constitutes considerable progress by comparison with all preceding theories. In any case, it allowed me to overcome the major difficulties which faced me from 1940 to 1966 in my works on applied economics.

Capitalistic intertemporal processes. As regards the *theory of capital* I developed in 1947, and later generalized, a theory of capitalistic processes and maximum capitalistic efficiency which is based on three new concepts: the *primary income,* the *characteristic function,* and *maximum capitalistic efficiency.*

In *Economie et Intérêt* published in 1947, I presented, to my knowledge for the first time in the literature, a rigorous demonstration of the existence of a situation of *maximum maximorum* (i.e., assuring a maximum real consumed income per capita) for a stationary process. Such a situation corresponds to a zero rate of interest.

I later generalized the theory of maximum capitalistic efficiency to the case of a dynamic process, and showed in 1960 that in this case the *maximum maximorum* is reached when the interest rate and the rate of growth of primary income are equal (*the golden rule of accumulation*). I think I have given the first general and rigorous demonstration of this theorem.

To my knowledge, of all the theories of dynamic capitalistic processes, the one I have presented is *the only one* which lends itself to numerical applications. And it is *entirely confirmed by observed data.* An application of this analysis is given in my study of the influence of capital on the difference in average productivity between the United States and France in the 1950s.

The economics of uncertainty. The analysis of the fundamental factors underlying uncertainty of the future led me to: a critical analysis of the neo-Bernoullian theories of choice under uncertainty generally accepted after von Neumann–Morgenstern, Marschak, Samuelson, and Savage, and in fact contradicted by the behavior of people in the neighborhood of certainty; the elaboration of a positive theory of choice under uncertainty in conformity with observed data; the definition and application of a direct method allowing the existence of cardinal utility to be demonstrated and its measurement; and finally, the generalization of the theories of general equilibrium and of maximum efficiency to the case of risk.

One of the counter-examples to the neo-Bernoullian theories that I presented in 1952 became famous under the denomination of the *Allais Paradox*. In fact, this Paradox is only paradoxical in appearance, and it simply corresponds to a very profound reality, the preference for security in the neighborhood of certainty.

In my 1955 memoir *Method of Appraising Economic Prospects of Mining Exploration over Large Territories – Algerian Sahara Case Study,* I applied my theory of choice under uncertainty. The guiding principle was to offer the Mining Research Office of Algeria a reasonable compromise between the mathematical expectation of gains that might be expected and the probability of ruin. For this memoir I received the Lanchester Prize 1958 of the Johns Hopkins University and the Operations Research Society of America.

Monetary dynamics. My analysis of the fundamental factors underlying monetary dynamics has essentially dealt with: the general theory of monetary dynamics; the theory of economic fluctuations; the hereditary and relativistic theory of demand and supply for money, and of the psychological rate of interest; the analysis of the structural links between growth and inflation, especially as regards the capitalistic optimum; and finally, the implications of the creation of money and purchasing power through the credit mechanism.

My major contribution has been the development of the *hereditary and relativistic theory of monetary dynamics*. This theory is based on four pillars: the fundamental equation of monetary dynamics and the three hereditary and relativistic formulations of demand and supply of money and the psychological rate of interest. It is essentially founded on new guiding ideas applicable in numerous fields – economics, psychology, sociology, and political science: the hereditary process of forgetfulness, the fundamental analogy between forgetfulness and interest, the consideration of psychological time, the hereditary conditioning of men by past events, the hereditary propagation of monetary phenomena with a progressive weakening through time, and the existence of a lagged regulation generating limit cycles.

This theory is based on the introduction of new concepts which have no equivalent in the prior literature: the concepts of the *rate of forgetfulness and the time of reaction,* for which the values vary according to the economic situation; the concept of the *coefficient of psychological expansion* representing the average appraisal of the economic conjuncture by all economic agents; the concept of *psychological time,* the frame of reference of psychological time being such that the laws of monetary dynamics remain invariant therein.

The empirical verifications of the new theory of demand for money are remarkable; indeed they are the most extraordinary that have ever been found in the social sciences, and this in a field essential to the life of societies. In fact, observed reality is represented in an almost perfect manner by the formulation to which this theory leads, whether it is applied to, for example, the United States during the Great Depression, the German hyperinflation of December 1919 to October 1923 during which period the price index reached a value comparable to the speed of light measured in centimeters per second, or Soviet Russia from January 1922 to February 1924. *These results demonstrate the underlying existence of structural regularities in social phenomena* which are as striking as those we observe in the physical sciences.

I believe this is the only case in the whole history of econometric research where a model which utilizes only *one explanatory variable,* and which generally includes only *two arbitrary parameters, or even only one according to the approach considered,* has been able to provide such results in so numerous and so different cases.

By revealing the existence of *invariant effects of a hereditary and relativistic type* in social phenomena, the new approach opens up wide perspectives, almost unsuspected up until now. The results obtained show that *everything happens as if,* irrespective of the institutional framework, contingent historical situations, and their particular aspirations, people react in the same way, as it were mechanically, to identical complex sequences. *They show that we are conditioned by our past,* and they open up new perspectives in the general debate over determinism and free will.

Chance and exogenous physical influences. The reflection on the theory of random choices and the search for the fundamental factors underlying the fluctuations in time series led me at the same time to a critical analysis of the concepts of chance and the theories of probability, to the demonstration of a new theorem, the *T Theorem,* and to the consideration of a new concept, the *X factor,* representative of the exogenous physical influences on time series.

Actually, the mathematical theories generally designated as *mathematical theories of chance* do ignore chance, uncertainty, and probability. The models they consider are *purely deterministic* models, and the quantities they study are, in the final analysis, no more than the mathematical frequencies of particular configurations, among all equally possible configurations, the calculation of which is based on combinatorial analysis. In reality, no axiomatic definition of chance is conceivable. The axiomatic theory of *probability* makes absolutely no use of the concept of chance, and it is inconceivable that it could do so. The concepts of probability and chance *are only creations of the human mind,* and are unknown to both nature and mathematics. They are totally absent from the currently accepted theories of probability, as can be clearly seen as soon as we examine *the substance, and not the semantics* that they use in an absolutely unjustified manner.

According to the hypothesis of the X factor the fluctuations in time series that we observe in phenomena occurring in the physical, biological, and human sciences result in some part from the influence, through effects of resonance, of countless vibrations which are scattered through the space in which we live, and whose existence is by now a certainty. Thus we can explain, at least partially, the structure of the fluctuations, at first sight so incomprehensible, that we observe in a large number of time series, such as, for example, those in sunspots or in stock exchange quotations. In fact, these fluctuations present all the aspects of an almost periodic structure.

To such a structure there corresponds an almost periodic function, defined as the sum of sinusoidal components of which certain periods are incommensurable. It follows from the T Theorem that under very general conditions, the successive values of an almost periodic function are asymptotically normally distributed. It is thus established that the deterministic vibratory structure of the universe can bring about seemingly random effects, and that determinism can engender what is commonly referred to as chance.

With regard to this analysis, the interest in the search for hidden periodicities which at one time dominated a large part of the literature now reappears under a new light. For this research I developed a test generalizing in the case of auto-correlated series, the *general case in observed reality,* the classic Schuster test, whose application is limited to the case of time series with independent terms.

The confrontation of theories with empirical evidence and the quest for invariances

Taken as a whole, all my research into the structural regularities underlying observed reality has been marked by a growing concern with numerical applications using data provided through observation. I believe that the only source of knowledge is, and in fact has to be, experience. A theory which applies to a quantitative area can only be valid if it can be verified quantitatively.

Numerical applications, more and more numerous, crowned with success, especially in the theories of surplus, capital, choice under uncertainty, monetary dynamics, and time series, have progressively convinced me that there is a very great internal coherence and an underlying invariant structure in observed data, and that this offers extremely valuable guidance to the economist.

Implications of economic analysis for economic policy

During all my career, I have always been motivated by the conviction that a scientist cannot remain disinterested in the fundamental problems of his time. Indeed, I have never ceased to believe that whether he advises or teaches, the economist *as such* should not take a position on individual aims which for the most part are not compatible. The aims to be pursued belong to the political field, and in fact, it is the essential task of political systems to define them through general compromises. But precisely, in economics, the role of the economist is to examine whether the aims defined through these compromises are in fact compatible with each other, and whether the means used to achieve them are actually the most appropriate.

On the whole, in theoretical analysis as in applied economics, I have endeavored in my work to rethink the role of economic freedom and of the market economy as regards the attainment of economic efficiency and the achievement of the ethical objectives of our time, and to contribute to a thorough study of the questions arising from the economic organization of societies.

How can economic efficiency, which conditions the success of any social policy, be achieved? Can it be achieved without compromising an equitable distribution of production? What is the connection between inflation and the creation of money? Can inflation be considered as a condition for growth, or not? What are the causes of unemployment? For any given country, which conditions would be most likely to bring about maximum per capita real income? Is it, or not, in the interest of a given country to protect its economy from foreign countries? Can deflationary or inflationary economic fluctuations, which tend to destabilize the very foundations of our society, really be avoided? What are the monetary conditions of an economy of markets?

Can the changes implied by technical and economical progress – which conditions all improvements in our life – be made socially and humanly acceptable? What are the factors which determine inequality and social classes? What is the respective influence of heredity and environment? What kinds of income transfers are desirable, and under what form? What should taxation be? What role should the State play in the working of the economy?

From the point of view of economic analysis, historical lessons, and the observation of contemporary facts, how can one judge economic systems which are founded on liberty, decentralization of decision making, and private property, as against centralized economic planning and collectivist property? Which institutional economic framework appears to be the most favorable to social progress and human advancement? Can an international economic order be achieved which would contribute to the development of all countries and to the creation of international peace?

In the light of these different analyses, what measures or reforms appear most suited to each case? These are the questions to which I have endeavored to give *precise reasoned-out answers* in the field of applied economics, through theoretical analysis and the study of observed data.

For any question in applied economics, the analysis of a given situation is *always very complex*, because of the interdependence of numerous factors, multiple chains of cause and effect, specific historical conditions, and social and political implications. The inevitable result is that any applied economic analysis contains, *explicitly or implicitly*, a share of value judgments, a characteristic which is even more marked when the analysis leads to normative recommendations.

From this viewpoint my thinking has unquestionably been greatly influenced by a philosophy of liberal (in the European sense of the word) inspiration, along the lines of Alexis de Tocqueville, Leon Walras, Vilfredo Pareto, and John Maynard Keynes, to name but a few. But whatever this influence was, I always endeavored to keep my applied economic analyses as scientific as possible, following two principles: first, to constantly found them on in-depth theoretical investigation; second, always to provide accompanying quantitative estimates.

On a national level, my work in applied economics has dealt with economic management, income distribution and taxation, monetary policy, and, in energy, transportation and mining research policies.

At the international level, my work has examined comparative standards of living and productivity; development factors; the monetary conditions for the efficiency of international trade; and also, economic unions and liberalization of economic relations.

Finally, together with my works in applied economics I have tried to study the meaning and the implications of the different political systems, and published various studies on the sociological and political aspects of life in society, on liberalism and socialism, on democracy and totalitarianism, on inequality and social classes, especially with regard to the respective influences of heredity and environment. These works analyze the general framework and the structural conditions in which the economy functions, and strive to clarify the interaction between political and economic systems.

The contributions of my parallel interests to my economic philosophy

My research on the history of civilizations. My research into the economic and social factors of the history of civilizations was for me extremely illuminating. Nothing is more instructive than the history of facts, doctrines, and economic thought. Whether it be economic systems, the evolution of real incomes, monetary phenomena, demography, international relations, ideology, or the interaction between these factors and their chains of cause and effect, nothing is more significant.

I cannot but side with Schumpeter here. If, *in order to understand economics*, one had to choose between mastering economic history or mastering mathematics and statistics, there is no doubt that one must choose the former. But the best for an economist, of course, would be this dual mastery. This was the case for Vilfredo Pareto, the greatest economist the world has produced to date, who was able to bring together with penetrating intelligence a wide command of the mathematics of his time and a truly extraordinary command of the history of societies since Greco-Roman antiquity.

My work in theoretical and experimental physics. My studies in theoretical and experimental physics, which at first seem so far removed from my main activity as an economist, in reality enriched me with extremely valuable experience.

These researches, which constantly presented all kinds of very great difficulties, led me to reflect on the nature of our knowledge, the nature of experience and theory, the difficulties of experimentation and interpretation of results, and the scientific method in general. More than ever, I am convinced that the only source of knowledge is experience, and that any theory is worthwhile only insofar as it forms a usable condensed synthesis of experience.

I was particularly struck by the *identity* of problems relating to model building, and the meaning of experimental data in economics and physics. One of the major problems that I had to solve in my experimental research in physics was to test the reality of given periodicities in the anomalies of the movement of the paraconical pendulum, the structure of which seems to be almost periodic. This problem is, in fact, identical to the one dealt with by economists in their works on economic cycles and their research into "hidden periodicities." This example has general validity: all econometric studies present methods of analyzing time series which apply equally to geophysics. Likewise geophysicists have studied analogous problems, and the methods they have developed can only be of the greatest benefit to economists.

Nothing was more instructive for me than this confrontation between the two sciences, apparently so dissimilar. I think that the very deep, and indeed invaluable, influence that my experimental and theoretical physics research had on me considerably improved my work and my teaching in economics, by helping me better to understand the nature of economic science, and contributing to an improved presentation of all my work.

My preoccupation with synthesis

Taken as a whole my work has covered very different fields, but has always been inspired by the *same conception*. During the course of my whole career, my dominant concern was with synthesis: to bring together into one comprehensive view the study of real and monetary phenomena; to closely associate theoretical analysis and applied economics, to link economics to the other social sciences, psychology, sociology, political science, and history. Just as physics requires a unified theory of universal gravitation, electromagnetics, and quanta, so do the social sciences need a unified theory of human behavior.

First of all, on the purely economic level, I have always endeavored to develop a comprehensive theory of economic phenomena which presents their different aspects coherently, connects deductions to principles logically and rigorously, and allows a constant linkage between theory and application. All my works are closely interdependent and complementary. Theoretical analysis led me naturally into applications, and the study of concrete economic questions led me to consider the theoretical foundations which bring satisfactory answers within reach.

Moreover, I have been guided always by the principle that Economics is but a part of a whole, and that any concrete economic decision not only has a quantitative character, but also a human aspect, and is part of a historical context. In numerous studies, I emphasized that no valid solution to economic problems can be found solely using economic theory and quantitative aspects of social life. Analysis of societies obviously requires a synthesis of all the social sciences: political economics, law, sociology, history, geography, and political science, and I specifically tried to bring out certain essential aspects of this synthesis in several studies on the working of democracy, the balance of the different powers and the decentralization of economic power, and the competition for power, and the essential role of elites and of social mobility.

I believe that this concern with a synthesized conception of all economic and social phenomena constitutes the very basis for all my thinking, and the close connection between my works in theoretical and applied economics. This concern explains what, it seems to me, constitutes the deep underlying unity in all my work.

MY PHILOSOPHY OF SCIENTIFIC METHOD AND ECONOMIC SCIENCE

The fundamental criterion of experience

The essential condition of any science is the existence of regularities which can be analyzed and forecast. This is the case in celestial mechanics. But it is also the case, for a great part, of social phenomena, particularly economic phenomena, which, when analyzed thoroughly, display the existence of regularities which are just as striking as those we find in the physical sciences. This is why economics is a science, and why this science rests on the same general principles and methods as physics.

All science is based on models, whether descriptive, explanatory, forecasting, or decision making, and every scientific model entails three distinct stages: start with well-specified hypotheses, deduce from these hypotheses all their implications and nothing but these implications, and confront the implications with observed data. Of these three stages, only the first and the third – establishing hypotheses and confronting results with reality – are of interest to the economist. The second stage is purely logical and mathematical, that is tautological, and is of mathematical interest only.

The model and the theory it represents are accepted, at least temporarily, or rejected, depending on the agreement or disagreement between observed data and the model's hypotheses and implications. *When neither the hypotheses nor the implications of a theory can be confronted with the real world, that theory is devoid of scientific interest.* Mere logical, or even mathematical, deduction remains worthless in terms of the understanding of reality if it is not clearly linked to reality.

Submission to experimental data is the golden rule which dominates any scientific discipline. It explains the extraordinary success of Western thought in the last three centuries. This rule is the same in economics as in physics. No theory whatever can be accepted unless it is verified by empirical evidence.

Abstraction plays an essential role in the construction of theories and their models. The role of science, in fact, is to simplify and to choose: to reduce facts to significant data and to seek their fundamental dependences. A mass of facts does not constitute a science. However, if abstraction is necessary, how we set about achieving it is not a matter of indifference. We can simplify reality without danger and with advantage, if this is not likely to change the actual nature of phenomena. But under no circumstances should the concern for simplification change the essence of reality.

The legitimacy of abstraction can only be justified *a posteriori*. *A priori* all abstraction can legitimately be considered inadmissible. Reducing planets to points in order to study their movements is a shocking abstraction, but it works successfully, and this very success makes it legitimate. It is thus with all abstraction. This principle is valuable in economics as in any other science.

All science is a compromise between the concern for simplification and the concern for resemblance. Great simplicity is convenient, but carries the risk that the picture which emerges does not sufficiently resemble the facts; a more exact resemblance makes the model too complex and unusable in practice. What can be said is that for any given level of approximation, the best scientific model is the one which is most convenient to use.

The claim that theory and practice are opposed is completely unjustified, because a theory is valid only insofar as it constitutes a condensed synthesis of reality. If it does not, it is purely a creation of the mind, totally artificial, and of no value from the scientific viewpoint. If, however, a theory is actually a condensed synthesis of reality, it is extremely useful, because it represents in succinct and easily usable form a vast amount of information of all kinds on the real phenomena of which it treats.

In science the notion of *truth* is, in fact, relative. No theory, no model, can claim to represent *absolute truth* and, if there is such truth, it will certainly always remain inaccessible to us. There are only models which are more or less well verified by observed data, and of two models, the "best" will always be the one, which, for a *given degree of approximation*, will provide the simplest representation of observed data. Whatever its empirical verification, the most we can ever say about a theory is that *everything happens as if* its hypotheses actually correspond to the real nature of phenomena concerned.

These are the general principles of the method that long ago Henri Poincaré commented on so pertinently with respect to physical sciences, that Vilfredo Pareto so appositely extended to the social sciences, and which I have continuously observed in all my work.

Pseudo-theories

The criterion of confronting theory with experimental data is merciless. Easy as it is, with only a pen, to work out a purely literary analysis or an abstract mathematical theory as long as no empirical application is made, it is equally difficult to elaborate an analysis that is effectively verified by observed data. This doubtless explains the propensity of so many authors to avoid numerical confrontation, except in vague and general terms.

  To test the logical coherence of a theory and to bring out its real content when it deals with magnitudes linked to each other in a somewhat complex manner, mathematics is certainly an instrument without equal, indeed *irreplaceable*. But in examining certain contemporary theories in terms of the two requirements of scientific method − logical coherence and conformity with observed data − we find two kinds of deviation: logical inconsistency and neglect of real phenomena.

Literary theories. The defects common to many literary theories are the continual use of non-operational concepts, vague and undefined words, whose meaning changes constantly within the analysis and varies from author to author; the absence of rigor in the analysis; the abundant use of more or less metaphysical expressions, which, having no precise meaning, can mean anything one wants, and are thus sheltered from objections; the use of expressions charged with emotional content which, while they may ensure the popularity of their authors, cannot lend themselves to rigorous reasoning.

"Mathematical charlatanry." While many literary theories cannot be considered scientific, the same can be said of a great number of theories, purely logical, with no real link to facts. While mathematics is an instrument whose mastery is extremely precious, it is, and can only be, an instrument. One cannot be a good physicist or economist simply because one has some ability and skill in mathematics.

  For almost forty-five years contemporary economic literature had developed too often in a totally erroneous direction with the construction of completely artificial mathematical models detached from reality; and too often it is dominated more and more by a mathematical formalism which fundamentally represents an immense regression.

  Certainly, it is no longer necessary today to justify the necessity and the utility of rigorous building of models on the basis of perfectly specified axioms. However, one must be very careful not to consider that it is enough to base a theory on a rigorous axiomatization for it to be scientifically valid. Axiomatization may be necessary, but it is secondary to the confrontation of its implications in relation to experimental data. Paradoxically, from the scientific viewpoint, incomparably more care is brought today to the mathematical elaboration of models than to the discussion of their structure, their hypotheses, and their results from the viewpoint of analysis of facts.

  The contemporary literature offers us countless examples of

aberrations which flow from neglect of the essential principle that a theory is valid only if it is in agreement with observed facts, and that the only source of truth is experience. Indeed a large part of the contemporary theoretical literature has progressively come under the control of pure mathematicians who are more concerned with mathematical theorems than with analysis of the real world. A new scholastic totalitarianism has arisen based on abstract and apriorist conceptions, detached from reality; this kind of "mathematical charlatanry" had already been denounced by Keynes in his *Treatise on Probability*.

It cannot be repeated too often: for the economist, as for the physicist, the essential objective is not to use mathematics for its own sake, but as a means of exploring and analyzing concrete reality, and consequently never to dissociate a theory from its applications.

Unsound econometrics. But the abusive use of mathematics is unfortunately not the only failing in contemporary literature, which too often has generated a crop of pseudo-theories based on the mechanical application, devoid of any real intelligence, of econometrics and statistical techniques. All these theories have the same characteristics: the elaboration of models of linear correlation which are in reality only *pseudo-models*, accompanied by a mathematical – statistical panoply of *untamed*, totally unjustified econometrics which seem to the naive to be scientific theories whereas they are generally just empty shells; the *blind and brutal* application of linear correlation programs and the tests associated with them, although these *tests generally are not applicable to the cases studied*; and the use of models, too often applied to a single country and for a short period, where the number of explanatory variables and the number of arbitrary parameters *are such that the fittings can have no real meaning*.

Excessive specialization. Finally, a very regrettable tendency continues to develop in the world of economics: *excessive specialization*. It is too often forgotten that only through a vast effort of synthesis can social sciences achieve significant progress. What is needed are economists with a broad perspective of history, sociology, and political science, historians skilled in economic analysis and the study of sociology, and sociologists who also have training as economists and historians.

One cannot help but be reminded here of the portrait of the master economist painted long ago by J. M. Keynes:

Yet good, or even competent, economists are the rarest of birds. An easy subject, at which very few excel! The paradox finds its explanation, perhaps, in that the master-economist must possess a rare combination of gifts. He must reach a high standard in several different directions and must combine talents not often found together. He must be mathematician, historian, statesman, philosopher – in some degree. He must understand symbols and speak in words. He must contemplate the particular in terms of the general, and touch abstract and concrete in the same flight of thought. He must study the present in the light of the past for the purposes of the future. No part of man's nature or his institutions must lie entirely outside his regard. He must be purposeful and disinterested in a simultaneous mood; as aloof and incorruptible as an artist, yet sometimes as near the earth as a politician.

New ideas and the tyranny of dominant doctrines

In the development of science, that is, in building theories and their models, *creative intuition always plays the determining role.* It is thanks to intuition that, from knowledge already acquired, the selection occurs of concepts and the relationships between these concepts that allow the essential structure of reality to be represented, that is, the choice of hypotheses. Deductive reasoning draws out all the consequences of these hypotheses, which are then confronted with the facts. Thus, creative intuition, logical deduction, and confrontation of the consequences of hypotheses with observed data are the three basic stages in any scientific endeavor. The history of science can be characterized by the indefinite repetition of these three stages in a process which leads towards increasingly comprehensive and well-verified models.

Indeed, only through the blossoming of new ideas suggested by creative intuition and empirical evidence can science truly progress. But all real scientific progress comes up against the tyranny of the dominant ideas generated by the "establishment." The more such dominant ideas are taken for granted, the more they become rooted in the psychology of men, and the more difficult it becomes to gain acceptance of a new conception, no matter how fertile it may later turn out to be. The dominant ideas, however erroneous they may be, end up, simply through continual repetition, by acquiring the quality of established truths which cannot be questioned without confronting the active ostracism of the "establishment." The examples of Copernicus, Galileo, Pasteur, Wegener, and so many others demonstrate the obstacles encountered by discoverers of genius. It is this resistance to new ideas that explains why in economics we had to wait so long to discover the major contributions of Dupuit, Walras, Edgeworth, Pareto, and many others. The successful scholar is always the one who adds some marginal improvement to the dominant theories everyone is already accustomed to. If, however, a new theory falls outside of customary channels, it is certain to face general opposition whatever its empirical justification.

In science, the action of the "establishment" and pressure groups is often exercised insidiously, sometimes moreover for reasons entirely foreign to science, and in recent years a dangerous tendency to politicization has developed in science and scientific research, based on ideological ideas of all kinds.

For all of these reasons, today just as yesterday, it is essential to constantly subject admitted "truths" to critical analysis without complaisance, always keeping in mind Pareto's statement: "The history of science boils down to the history of errors of competent men."

The major principle of scientific discipline is always to doubt what is considered true, always to be open to examine opposite opinions favorably, and to foster research which might disprove propositions one believes in. Doubt of one's own opinions, and respect of those of others, are the first condition of any real progress in science. Universal consent, or even majority consent, cannot be considered a valid criterion for truth. In the final analysis, the essential condition for progress in science is a complete surrender to the teaching of experience, the only real source of knowledge. There is not, and there cannot be, any other test of the truth of a theory than its conformity, more or less perfect, with concrete phenomena.

MY PASSION FOR RESEARCH

Whatever the field of application, my whole life has been dominated by the thirst to know more, by the passion for research. I have felt this passion since my early youth; it has since formed the very foundation of my entire existence, and without any doubt, will remain so until the end.

Of all my experience, it is basically research, considered as an exploration of the unknown and totally detached from any concern with success, which appeared to me in itself as the most enlivening, the most exciting, because in this field any thorough investigation can only widen perspectives. It is this passion for research which, throughout my life, formed my major motivation.

Research is a sort of adventure full of risks, but a fascinating adventure. When a researcher undertakes some research, he is never sure of success. Very often he fails: reality is contrary to his expectations; and if he carries out an analysis and discovers some new regularity, what he finds is generally not exactly what he was looking for. Sometimes the results may even be more or less disappointing, but also, sometimes, at the end of an often painstaking effort, he discovers under the extreme complexity of the facts new regularities whose reality cannot be doubted. Sometimes, too, his findings can surpass his expectations. Such moments are rare, but they exist, and they compensate for the rest.

As the geologist Pierre Termier, a figurehead of scientific thought, put it long ago in an incomparable style on the borderline of science and poetry:

> The Joy of knowledge! Many scholars have experienced it. Some several times during their lives; some even in a lasting and persistent manner.... The joy of knowledge has marvelously consoled them from mediocrity, from incomprehension, from contradiction, from hostile silliness.... Knowledge is one of the reasons of our life and there is no satisfaction comparable to the one scientific research gives.... The researcher knows immense joys that others do ignore.... The joy of the scholar or philosopher, the joy of the artist or poet. It is somewhat impossible to speak about. It is indescribable.

In fact, there is hardly any greater satisfaction for the researcher than that which follows from the achievement of a vast synthesis between elements which at first seemed disparate or contradictory, or the display of new relationships between facts which seemed to have no connection, of regularities previously unrecognized, of invariant relationships in space and time.

However, such a synthesis can only result from patient and often unrewarding effort. Research in any subject must begin by first exploring its particularities, its differences, its varieties. Only by starting with details can an overview of a subject be reached. Only slowly, after lengthy effort, does the intimate interdependence between parts begin to reveal itself. Slowly, the difficulties subside, the whole becomes clear and limpid, like the countryside viewed from the top of a high mountain.

The ultimate goal of such an approach is the attainment of a reciprocal and coherent symbiosis between theory and observed data. This process is based on a twofold conviction: the conviction that without theory knowledge remains unavoidably obscure, and that an accumulation of facts only constitutes a chaotic and inevitably incomprehensible aggregate; and the even stronger conviction that a theory which cannot be confronted with facts or which has not been verified quantitatively by observed data is of no scientific value.

Certainly, nothing is comparable to the inextinguishable passion for research; to the unquenchable desire to know, understand, clarify, explain; to the constant will to persist in overcoming every difficulty wherever it is encountered, never to be content with approximation; to the permanent concern to never lose sight of the whole; to constantly think about the synthesis. In reality, nothing comes close to the satisfaction of this construction, the ineffable euphoria of innovation and discovery.[3]

---

[3] Text written in French in 1986, before the 1988 Nobel Prize.

APPENDIX: ON MY EXPERIMENTS IN PHYSICS,
1952–1960[4]

1. I believe it is very desirable to state explicitly what was the origin of all my experiments in physics.

I have always held the conviction that the propagation of the gravitational and electromagnetic actions implies the existence of an intermediate medium, the "ether" of Fresnel and the 19th century physicists, but without there being grounds to believe, as was generally considered in the 19th century, that all the parts of that medium are perfectly motionless in relation to fixed stars.

This conviction led me to consider that a magnetic field corresponds to a local rotation of this intermediate medium.

From this, I inferred that a link could be established between magnetism and gravitation by observing the effect of a magnetic field on the movement of a pendulum consisting of a glass ball suspended on a thread of a length of approximately two meters.

2. In order to detect such an effect I began by observing the movement of such a pendulum in the absence of any magnetic field other than that of the earth. *To my great surprise,* I found out that this movement did not reduce itself to the Foucault effect, but displayed *very significant anomalies* in relation to this effect. It was these *totally unexpected anomalies* which made up the essential object of my experiments from 1953 to 1960.

3. Of all the *very limited number* of observations made in 1952 and 1953 of the movement of a glass ball oscillating in a magnetic field of the order of a few hundred Gauss, *I was not able to draw any definitive conclusion.* With certain experimental devices, I found positive effects, while with others, I obtained no effect whatsoever.

However great, *indeed very crucial,* the importance of these experiments, I was led, given the difficulties to realize a much stronger magnetic field, to interrupt them in order to devote all the resources at my disposal to the study of the anomalies in the movement of a short pendulum the existence of which had been demonstrated *indisputably* in 1952 and 1953.

4. In order to study the anomalies detected in the movement of a short pendulum, I made use mainly of a paraconical pendulum, approximately one meter in length, consisting of a vertical bronze disc attached to a bronze rod suspended from a stirrup resting on a steel ball.

Indeed, outside any magnetic field other than the earth's magnetic field,

[4] Appendix added on December 16, 1988.

I observed, on the basis of *uninterrupted* observations realized over periods of a month between 1954 and 1960, *very remarkable* anomalies in the movement of the paraconical pendulum. A key finding was the existence of a significant periodicity of the order of 24h 50mn.

Identical results were found in June and July 1958 in two laboratories, some 6 km away from each other, one in a basement at Saint-Germain, the other in an underground quarry at Bougival 57 meters below ground.

Indeed, such a periodic *lunisolar* effect is quite *inexplicable within the framework of the currently accepted theories.*

5. The existence of the anomalies observed in the precision levelling and triangulation operations, compared with the anomalies observed in the movement of the paraconical pendulum, led me to realize, in parallel with my pendulum experiments at Saint-Germain and Bougival in 1958, a series of North–South and South–North optical sightings on fixed sighting-marks. As a result of technical difficulties, it was not possible to realize these optical sightings satisfactorily until the second half of July 1958.

Indeed, I found, in the second half of July 1958, a *remarkable correspondence* between the anomalies of the paraconical pendulum and the anomalies corresponding to reciprocal optical sightings of two theodolites on two sighting-marks borne on the same supports as the theodolites. In any case, these optical anomalies, considered in themselves, are *inexplicable within the framework of the currently accepted theories.*

6. Finally, during the total eclipse of the sun on June 30, 1954, a remarkable deviation of the plane of oscillation of the paraconical pendulum was observed. This deviation is *quite inexplicable within the framework of the currently accepted theories.* An entirely *similar* deviation was observed once again during the total eclipse of the sun on October 2, 1959.

7. These various anomalies appeared to me to be closely connected to the very many anomalies observed during the 19th and 20th centuries in mechanical, optical, and electromagnetic experiments, which have remained *unexplained*, and of which I presented an overall analysis in a paper in 1958 (published in English in 1959) (see References).

8. To conclude this very brief survey of my experiments, I believe I can make a prediction. If, *without interruption, for at least a month, at the same place and simultaneously*, observations were made of the movement of the paraconical pendulum, together with optical sightings such as those I made in 1958, and a repetition of the experiments of A. Michelson and A. Morley (1887) and E. W. Miller (1925), the purpose of which was to display the movement of the earth relatively to the ether, it would be found that the effects observed by Miller in 1925 correspond

to the anomalies of the movement of the paraconical pendulum and the anomalies of the optical sightings observed in July 1958.

Maurice Allais is Professor of Economics at the Ecole Nationale Supérieure des Mines de Paris and the 1988 winner of the Nobel Memorial Prize in economic science.

REFERENCES

References to my main works can be found in "Maurice Allais: Principaux Ouvrages et Memoires, 1943–1984" (about 300 titles) as well as some "Données Biographiques" in the collective volume *Marchés, Capital et Incertitude: Essais en l'honneur de Maurice Allais,* Marcel Boiteux, Thierry de Montbrial, and Bertrand Munier, editors, *Economica,* 1986 (pp. 225–257). This book also contains a general presentation of my work by the editors (pp. 5–44).

An English version of this book will be published soon by Kluwer Academic Publishers, Dordrecht, Netherlands, under the title *Markets and Risk: Essays in Honour of Maurice Allais,* edited by Bertrand Munier.

The main references to my experiments in physics are given in Boiteux, Munier, and Montbrial, *Marchés* (pp. 253–254). See especially: Allais, 1959, "Doiton reconsidérer les lois de la gravitation"; and Allais, 1959, "Should the laws of gravitation be reconsidered" (*Aero-Space Engineering,* Sept. 1959, no. 9, pp. 46–52; Oct. 1959, no. 10, pp. 51–55; and Nov. 1959, no. 11, p. 55).

References to my main works can be also found in *Les Prix Nobel* (The Nobel Prizes), *1988,* Almquist and Wiksell International, Stockholm, Sweden.

KENNETH J. ARROW

"I Know a Hawk from a Handsaw"

The world we live in and my inner world are both complex entities, not describable in simple formulas – in fact, not by any set of words that I could write down during a lifetime. I have therefore always been skeptical of the dictum "An unexamined life is not worth living"; it is part of my life philosophy that no life can ever be examined fully and that attempts to do so are never free of self-deception. There is therefore a paradox in my attempting to set forth a life philosophy. Yet we are faced with paradox everywhere, whether it be about our knowledge of the external world, as David Hume showed, or even about our own modes of thinking, as we have learned from Bertrand Russell and Kurt Godel. Like the state in which I live, we plan and build on ground that may open beneath us.

Here, then, are some partial statements, not completely consistent and no doubt partly self-flattering. I have interpolated some quotations. I do not necessarily mean that the writings quoted had a major impact on my thoughts, though some did, but rather that they express my attitudes with force and concision.

"THE PROXIMATE CIRCUMPRESSURE OF HISTORY"
(JOHN TANNER)

In some ideal sense, life philosophies, like economies, may be refined by successive adjustments through reflection, experience, and intellectual interaction with the past and the present until they come into an equilibrium independent of initial conditions. In fact, neither is ever independent of history.

I was born in 1921, and the history of my family echoed that of the country: prosperity followed by poverty. Even in prosperity, my family was politically and socially liberal. The ideals were concern for the poor, here and abroad, honesty, efficiency, a vague but not strident suspicion of entrenched wealth and of power based on status rather than accomplishment.

I early displayed an analytic bent. By the usual tests, I was unusually intelligent, and my parents knew and were proud of this. I also developed a critical attitude toward social conventions, wanting to know why they were to be followed and what good they served. My talents were directed, especially in secondary school and college, toward mathematics with a special fondness for mathematical logic. However, this bent was accompanied by a great love for history and for literature: after Edgar Allan Poe and A. Conan Doyle came Shakespeare, then Dostoyevski, Hardy, the Greek dramatists, later Proust, Joyce, Kafka, and the English poets, Milton, Browning, Shelley, and Keats.

The major intellectual currents of the time were an everyday part of our life at college. One strand was the demand for clarity of thought and suppression of meaninglessness, as we saw it, in scientific, political, and ordinary life: logical positivism, behaviorism in psychology, the "semantics" movement, particularly that represented by C. K. Ogden and I. A. Richards, *The Meaning of "Meaning,"* and, at a deeper level, Wittgenstein's *Tractatus Logico-Philosophicus*. Its stripped-down version of thought was parallel to another enthusiasm of mine and of many of my colleagues, the International style of modernist architecture. Some doubts about the extreme self-denial in the logical positivist program were created in my mind by the sensible observations of City College's pride and joy in philosophy, Morris Raphael Cohen. In the field of scientific method, he insisted that scientists in fact followed the "hypothetico-deductive" method; hypotheses were freely invented and only tested against observations, not induced by them. Now, under the influence of Karl Popper and others, this is the orthodox viewpoint.

Beyond the ways by which we understand the world, there were the even livelier questions of social and personal life, represented by Marx and Freud. The Freudian theory in particular was almost axiomatic in my circles. The predominance of unconscious motivation and the depiction of conscious activities and especially speech as rationalization were completely taken for granted. Recondite ideas like the threefold classification of personality into id, ego, and superego were thought to be somewhat suspect from a positivist viewpoint, and the universality of the sex drive was felt to be exaggerated, though no doubt an important correction to what we took to be Victorian suppression (the Victorian period looks a great deal better today than it did in the 1930s).

The economic determinism derived from Marx, but something of a vulgarization (e.g., Charles Beard on the Constitution), was another powerful influence. It fitted in with the "unmasking" tendencies of both positivism and Freudianism and suggested the possibility of a scientific understanding of social and economic behavior. Though many of my friends (some of them leading conservatives today) were fully involved in Marxism, I always found the complete apparatus of successive stages of history and the simple class struggle uncogenially schematic. I did not doubt the reality of class conflict, but there seemed to me many other conflicts as well.

Marxist theory is, of course, always related to practice, and the late 1930s were a heyday of making connections between them. There were repeated splits among Marxist factions, in which theoretical interpretations shifted in accordance with the various factional disputes and current political situations. I found myself staying aloof from what I took to be an intellectually shallow argument. But the fundamental political question on which one had to take a stand was one's attitude toward the Soviet Union. The trial of the Old Bolsheviks (Bukharin, Radek, and others) in 1935–6 was decisive for me, as it was for many other socialist sympathizers, such as John Dewey and Sidney Hook; it was inconceivable that the charges were true, and if it were true that the Old Bolsheviks would betray the Revolution when it was successful, it must be very rotten indeed. Having taken an anti-Stalinist position early, I was spared the necessity felt by those disillusioned later for accepting McCarthyism.

I found myself at once a systematizer by talent and inclination and an agnostic in my perception of the world. I had and have an all-pervading sense of the uncertainty of life and of the world. During my college years, I discovered the perfect Hegelian synthesis of this thesis and antithesis: the then very new discipline of mathematical statistics. For institutional reasons, this scholarly concern led to the study of economics at Columbia, which was dominated by an ultra-empiricist approach, embodied for me by the formidable intellect of Arthur F. Burns. I came to a partial reconciliation of my analytic skills with the chaotic demands for checking with reality. Economic theory had two roles: as the needed basis for empirical inquiry using the tools of theoretical statistics and as the basis for a better economic world, possibly embodied in a democratic socialist system.

FOR WHOM?

If I am not for myself, then who is for me? And if I am not for others, who am I? And if not now, when? (Hillel)

Nothing is more seductive for man than his freedom of conscience, but nothing is a greater source of suffering. And behold, instead of giving a firm foundation for setting the conscience of man at rest forever, Thou didst choose all that is exceptional, vague and enigmatic.... Instead of taking possession of man's freedom, Thou didst increase it. (F. Dostoyevski, "The Grand Inquisitor," in *The Brothers Karamazov*)

The basic element in my view of the good society is the centrality of others. This has two aspects, distinguishable but certainly coherent and even complementary: concern for others and respect for others. Concern without respect is at best paternalism and can lead to tyranny. Respect without concern is the cold world of extreme individualism, a denial of the intrinsically social nature of humanity.

Respect for others is, to me, based on a certain degree of mystery about them. Others are different in ways that are not completely reducible to our understanding. Of course, there is a large degree of mutual comprehension; otherwise, no genuine society would be possible. All I mean is that there will always be a degree of incomprehensibility, of unpredictability, that is an intrinsic element of individual autonomy.

These principles imply a general commitment to freedom. One aspect is a radically libertarian attitude toward freedom of speech. Stalinists and fascists are entitled to the expression of their views. Indeed, the variety and unpredictability of others imply that simple labels are never adequate. Academic freedom is one essential manifestation of freedom of expression, and though it is fair to say that it is not a live issue now, it has been in the recent past and could easily become so again.

Equally important is the freedom of the individual and the family in local spheres of action. Here it is low income and poverty that are the constraining forces. Improving economic status and opportunity therefore is a basic component of increasing freedom, of increasing the extent to which each individual can realize his or her own autonomous goals. It is for these reasons that I disagree with the alleged conflict of equality and liberty; equality of income and of political and expressive power are essential to freedom.

Respect and concern for others give rise to a critical attitude toward authority as such. At times, it has given rise to anarchist and pacifist views, but I understood early the contradictions between these views and the fulfillment of social obligations. I have in fact considered myself obliged to devote time and effort to contributing to the work of the organizations I have been affiliated with, learned societies, universities, and the government, without, however, being taken up with full-time authority with which I would be most uncomfortable.

The possibility of melding these strongly held feelings with the necessary intellectual discipline to incorporate them into meaningful structures was exemplified to me by Harold Hotelling and then by Tjalling Koopmans. Both had strong commitments to social welfare, but both emphasized the importance of formal analysis for preventing degeneration into wishful thinking.

HOW MUCH DO WE KNOW?

It struck me, what quality went to form a Man of Achievement . . . I mean *Negative Capability*, that is when man is capable of being in uncertainties, mysteries, doubts, without any irritable reaching after fact & reason. (From a letter by John Keats)

Someone must have been telling lies about Joseph K., for without having done anything wrong he was arrested one fine morning. (Franz Kafka, *The Trial*)

The great God whose seat is at Delphi neither reveals nor conceals but gives tokens. (Heraclitus)

It is my view that most individuals underestimate the uncertainty of the world. This is almost as true of economists and other specialists as it is of the lay public. To me our knowledge of the way things work, in society or in nature, comes trailing clouds of vagueness. Vast ills have followed a belief in certainty, whether historical inevitability, grand diplomatic designs, or extreme views on economic policy. When developing policy with wide effects for an individual or a society, caution is needed because we cannot predict the consequences.

These convictions came early to me, and certainly my exposure to the ultra-empiricist National Bureau school, the theoretical controversies over imperfect competition, and the failure of neoclassical economics to comprehend the Great Depression all reinforced the view that our knowledge of the economy was very limited. Experience during World War II as a weather forecaster added the news that the natural world was also unpredictable. An incident, which I have been fond of relating in my classes, illustrates both uncertainty and the unwillingness to entertain it. Some of my colleagues had the responsibility of preparing long-range weather forecasts, i.e., for the following month. The statisticians among us subjected these forecasts to verification and found they differed in no way from chance. The forecasters themselves were convinced and requested that the forecasts be discontinued. The reply read approximately like this: "The Commanding General is well aware that the forecasts are no good. However, he needs them for planning purposes."

The dangers of excessive certainty are, of course, far more borne out in the fields of war and international relations than in the economy or the climate; examples will come immediately to the mind of the reader. Within economics, one is struck by the certainty with which positions are held, though over time they change very considerably.

As I have already noted, one of the attractions of statistical theory has been the possibility of making definite statements about our uncertainties. No doubt there is some illusion here, but it is at least a step forward in recognizing the limits of knowledge and incorporating them into human action, social or individual. My professional interest in the economics of uncertainty and, subsequently, of information follows as an immediate corollary.

The sense of uncertainty is active; it actively recognizes the possibility of alternative views and seeks them out. I consider it essential to honesty to look for the best arguments against a position that one is holding. Commitments should always have a tentative quality. As may be supposed, I have always enjoyed satire and irony, as well as logical paradox; Swift and Russell are favorite authors.

WHAT IS KNOWLEDGE?

Wovon man nicht sprechen kann, daruber muss man schweigen (Whereof one cannot speak, thereof one must be silent). (L. Wittgenstein, *Tractatus Logico-Philosophicus*)

In addition to excessive certainty, the fragility of our knowledge often has another consequence: the utterance of nonsense. So much of our communication apparently conveys meaning but in fact does not. It is in no way informative. Everyday discourse is, of course, filled with empty statements. Even in a realm like the analysis of securities or other organized asset markets, where an economist would suppose that rationality prevails, there is an active market in which the commodity sold, information, contains a large fraction of statements of the form "The market will either rise, remain the same, or fall." In scholarly discourse, these views put a premium on definite results, mathematical or empirical, as against vague expressions of opinion whose consequences cannot be sharply defined.

Among other implications, this acceptance of logical positivism and operationalism made me sympathetic to behaviorism in psychology and especially to its counterparts in economics. I was very receptive, therefore, to the ordinalist view of consumer behavior; in fact, I could not really understand the cardinalist position, since it had no empirical significance. Similarly, the revealed preference approach of Samuelson was still a further step in the direction of operationalization; not only were market (and political) decisions in complex situations reducible to preferences, but the latter were in turn reducible to consistency in pairwise choices. My work on social choice and related concepts of individual choice clearly assimilated these influences.

I think now that these arguments were a bit simple-minded, and indeed positivism is in general at something of a discount these days. Accuracy of prediction is a desirable aim, but it is not the only use of economic theory. As in meteorology, understanding is possible, desirable, and useful even when predictability is very limited. Our present understanding of measurement, influenced to a considerable extent by the development of expected-utility theory, has shown that some cardinal structures may have a privileged position even though in principle they are equivalent to monotone transformations of them. What formally is mere convenience in theoretical statement turns out to be very valuable in our ability to comprehend.

Nevertheless, the need to insist on some sort of refutability as a condition of meaning is still with us, to avoid pseudo-questions and pseudo-answers. But the demarcation line is not as simple as it appeared earlier.

KNOWLEDGE OF THE SELF

The existence of consciousness ... is necessary because the data of consciousness are exceedingly defective. ... All ... conscious acts remain disconnected and unintelligible if we ... claim that every single mental fact performed within us must be consciously experienced; on the other hand, they fall into a demonstrable connection if we interpolate the unconscious acts that we infer. ... Experience shows that we understand very well how to interpret in others ... those same acts which we refuse to acknowledge as mentally conditioned in ourselves. Some special hindrance evidently ... interferes with our obtaining true knowledge of ourselves. (Sigmund Freud, "The Unconscious")

Cecil Graham: What is a cynic? *Lord Darlington*: A man who knows the price of everything and the value of nothing. *Cecil Graham*: And a sentimentalist ... is a man who sees an absurd value in everything and doesn't know the market price of any single thing. (Oscar Wilde, *Lady Windermere's Fan*)

Troilus: What's aught but as 'tis valued? *Hector*: But value dwells not in particular will. (William Shakespeare, *Troilus and Cressida*)

Caution in interpreting the world extends to interpretation of oneself. Our knowledge of our own motives and actions is also subject to error – error that is perhaps more insidious because more motivated. Each individual has a unique opportunity for internal observation, but this is not to be confused with error-free observation. I am, in particular, distrustful of moral conclusions drawn by introspection, because the desire to please the self must powerfully alter *expressed* morality. Most discussions of social justice, even or perhaps especially those with which I most agree, have a certain degree of smug piety about them. Actual behavior in critical moral situations is more revealing. We may get farther in moral analysis by trying empathetically to understand the apparently repellent behavior of others than by evolving axioms of justice from reflection.

Moral and ethical principles derived from idealized views of the self are likely to lead ultimately to cynicism about others, an easy but ultimately unrewarding way of thinking. Consciousness of imperfection in self-analysis should lead to realistic but not cynical appraisal of others.

Degree of self-knowledge is also important in the development of positive or descriptive economics. The fact is that our theories of rationality in economic behavior rest upon introspection. We are as apt to deceive ourselves about the prudence and rationality of our plans as about their moral worth. Since positive economics implies (hypothetically) refutable propositions, there is a somewhat better chance that we will find the inapplicability of our propositions; we have indeed been discovering the limitations of rational expectations formation in securities markets, for example. But if introspection is the source of our fruitful insights into economic behavior, it will not be easy to develop hypotheses other than those based on rationality.

UNITY AND BEAUTY

Euclid alone looked on beauty bare. (Edna St. Vincent Millay)

"Beauty is truth, truth beauty," – that is all / Ye know on earth, and all ye need to know. (John Keats, "Ode on a Grecian Urn")

Mathematics is certainly a source of aesthetic pleasure. Over and over we have the sense of symmetry, of elegance, of an abstract and pervasive unity of seemingly disparate parts. My mathematical skills and taste for abstraction led me to emphasize the aesthetic aspects of mathematics. As with many others, this aesthetic bent found its place in my scholarly work.

It also led me to particular likes and dislikes in the arts. Music is the usual preference of the mathematically inclined, and I was no exception, though my musical tastes were not always the most intellectual. (Many of my friends cannot understand my early and continued love of Wagner.) In painting, my early preferences were strongly toward abstract art, especially of a geometric variety, as in Mondrian. While no one can be insensitive to the Renaissance master, I tended to "read" them, along with Cezanne and the Impressionists, in formal terms of abstract patterns, rather than expressive content.

It is impossible to read literature in a purely formal way. I was in fact drawn first to Dostoyevski and Hardy, novelists whose realism was driven by a perception of the demonic and the irrational, a world very different from the abstract beauty of mathematics or music, as well as to the all-encompassing Shakespeare. I did, after a bit, also seek the more ordered worlds of who we then thought of as "modern" writers: Joyce and Eliot. But violence and disorder are close to the surface in them also.

My general sense of beauty has shifted with time, like my early literary tastes. Even in mathematics and in scholarly work, I am more interested in the struggle for knowledge than in elegant systematization. Simple symmetries are not as satisfying as they were, and I look much more for a sense of openness, of incompleteness and stretching out toward an unknown, than for closed forms. Research should have not only results, but also pointers toward the incomplete; who should know better than the author the limits of the work?

Kenneth J. Arrow is Joan Kenney Professor of Economics at Stanford University and the 1972 winner of the Nobel Memorial Prize in economic science.

WILLIAM J. BAUMOL

On My Attitudes: Sociopolitical and Methodological

My goals for society have always derived from the left. However, they have nothing in common with the totalitarian persuasions of those who have hoodwinked society into believing that theirs are the only true antitheses of reactionary values.

I believe deeply, with Shaw, that there are few crimes more heinous than poverty. GBS, as usual, exaggerated when he told us that lack of money is the root of all evil. But he did not exaggerate by much. Perhaps barely second to the battle against poverty in my list of priorities is the struggle for human rights, the guarantee against arbitrary arrest, mutilation and murder either by officialdom or by terrorist groups, even those convinced that the nobility of their purposes exempts them from any constraints on their methods. To these objectives add the civil liberties which the late Senator McCarthy sought so hard to subvert and civil

51

rights – freedom from discrimination on the basis of race, sex, nationality or beliefs.

It is quite fashionable to claim allegiance to these causes. Politicians who are prepared to cut expenditures on the poor before touching any other items in their budget show no shame in proclaiming their concern over hunger. Advocates of dangerous extensions of police powers and censorship trumpet their dedication to traditions of freedom. But such friends of these goals only underscore how difficult it is to achieve tangible progress toward their realization or even to prevent erosion of the progress that has already been achieved.

W. Arthur Lewis once remarked to me that throughout the world the veneer of civilization is very thin. It takes little to stimulate an outbreak of genocide; the Bill of Rights is an extremely recent phenomenon in human history – one which still encompasses a very limited portion of the globe, and even there it is often threatened.

My orientation toward the left (as I interpret the left) is come by honestly. My parents, Jewish immigrants from Eastern Europe, were part of the radical intellectual group engendered by the despotism of their homelands. My father was a devoted Marxist and remained pro-Soviet until the Hitler–Stalin Pact. My mother had had serious doubts much earlier and as a teenager I had already been revolted by the brutality of the Soviet government. But though divorcing myself from that totalitarian regime and its supporters I never lost faith in those ideals which had moved so many of the radicals who had populated my childhood world. I believe those are the objectives which I consider important still.

There is an opinion of a second sort which I also attribute to my Marxist upbringing. I feel a strong antipathy to acts whose only valuable consequence is likely to be the sense of virtue felt by those who undertake them. I have always interpreted Marx's quarrel with the "Utopian" socialists to have reflected similar concerns – the view that where an objective requires substantial and disquieting changes, few things are likely to be as damaging to the cause as an empty gesture. The opportunity cost is simply too great. That is why, for example, I have often opposed efforts to force *universities* to sell their stocks in firms which do business in South Africa. Such programs are unlikely to influence to any substantial degree the policies of the firms in question and cannot usually be expected to lead them to withdraw their investments. Moreover, even if some of them did withdraw, the effects on South African government policies would surely be minimal or may even drive them, in desperation, in an even more racist direction, with the bulk of the damage borne by the black population. True, those who worked hard for this cause must have felt more at peace with their consciences as a result. But the time and effort they spent on it might much better have been devoted to other approaches which might really have made a substantial contribution in the battle against discrimination. I know one case in particular in which a very promising opportunity to force increased hiring of blacks in a trade formerly largely barred to them was consciously neglected in order to throw all the available resources into the attempt to cleanse the universities' securities portfolios.

In sum, the causes I espouse face opposition from three sources: the forces of the right, the totalitarian left and what I term left-wing romantics.

What has all this to do with the discipline of economics? In my view, a great deal. There is a long tradition among economists of dedication to social causes. Frank Fetter's study of economists in Parliament in the nineteenth century suggests strongly on the basis of their attendance and voting records that they were responsible, dedicated and overwhelmingly supported what for their day were the radical causes – the secret ballot, enfranchisement of Catholics, extension of the suffrage. These causes were consistently supported by a far greater proportion of the economists than of the remaining members in Parliament. And they were supported by economists who stood to lose from the adoption of the measures at issue.

Yet economists have earned opprobrium by seeking to expose proposals for change which seemed to promise social benefits cheaply and easily but which they considered dangerous delusions. They have opposed rent control, believing that it is an incentive for neglect and abandonment and an obstacle to construction. For this they have been suspected of lacking sympathy for the ill-housed. Hoping to achieve substantial improvements in the environment they have advocated that polluters be required to pay for the damage they cause. For this they have been accused of espousing the sale of "licenses to pollute."

In short, given my orientation and my goals, I feel quite at home with those of a considerable number of my colleagues, particularly those who feel that a good deal must yet be done to provide work for the jobless, to raise the living standards of the homeless, to prevent the poisoning of our atmosphere and the degradation of our environment, who, in sum, are anxious to use our discipline to improve the circumstances in which people live.

ON POLITICAL POSITIONS BY PROFESSIONAL ORGANIZATIONS

While I am strongly predisposed toward colleagues who speak out on political and social issues and who are prepared to act on their convictions, I have always felt very differently about educational institutions and professional associations. I avidly opposed attempts to get the universities to take a stand on the Vietnam War or to induce the American Economic Association to take a public position on ratification of the Equal Rights Amendment, holding to this course even where I felt strongly that the cause for which endorsement was sought was just. There are two reasons for my opposition. First, any institution of the sort in question, precisely because it is not organized about any set of political opinions, is certain to encompass people whose views are diverse. If the organization then commits itself to some special political stand it must, consequently, misrepresent the views of at least some of its constituents – it must, by implication, distort such minority views, presenting to the world a spurious appearance of unanimity.

Second, the adoption of institutional positions imperils the organization and impedes pursuit of the purposes for which it was formed. If a professional organization which follows such a course drives away those members who differ from the "official" positions or, worse still, seeks to suppress their views, it loses its ability to promote the exercise of professional activities, the purpose for which it was founded. In an educational institution an official position is even more serious because it becomes a threat to academic freedom. True academic freedom is not merely a matter of willingness to listen to those with whom we disagree mildly. It requires the institution to offer a forum even to those whose opinions we vehemently detest. Official institutional positions are no encouragement to this principle, whose defense is apt at times to require considerable courage and tenacity.

It is sometimes suggested by those who advocate the adoption of organizational positions, particularly on critical public issues, that universities are repositories of wisdom, and that in times of crisis, it is a special responsibility of educational institutions to speak out. Fritz Machlup used to point out in reply that history does not support this conclusion – that with the onset of the Nazi regime the German universities *did* choose to speak out, but the position they adopted does them little credit.

In saying all this, I am not arguing against all political activities by universities and professional organizations. I have more than once urged the American Economic Association, or rather, the members of its executive committee, to do what they could for economists in other countries who had been imprisoned for the economic doctrines they held or advocated (I may add that the executive committee was in general quite willing to act in such cases). Similarly, I think it is quite appropriate for an educational institution to act on behalf of academic freedom whenever and wherever it is threatened. But that is because such a stand is entirely in line with its purposes, and constitutes no threat to its ability to function.

ON METHOD

My convictions on proper methodological approaches for economic analysis are relatively weak. Indeed, in the area of method I am not sure I have any deep convictions – I am quite happy to see a thousand flowers bloom. Mathematical economists, institutionalists, econometricians, economic historians, neoclassicists, followers of the Anglo-Italian path have each and all made valuable contributions. Yet none of them has found the philosopher's stone, and any of them that sees fit to denounce the others is apt to seem just a bit ridiculous. Economics *is* a difficult subject and we cannot afford to dispense with the services of anyone who has an approach that promises to provide any new light on the workings of the economy.

Having just trumpeted my unbounded forbearance on methodological issues, let me admit that there are some bounds to my tolerance. Indeed, I do have strong dislikes. I am particularly turned off by construction of models for their own sake or by painstaking attempts to complicate already available models, ostensibly for added realism.

A well-designed model is, after all, a judiciously chosen set of lies, or perhaps more accurately put, partial truths about reality, which have been chosen so as to permit us to reason more effectively about some issue than we otherwise could. The model *must* be an oversimplification if it is to be tractable analytically. Optimality in model construction must be based on the trade-off between these two desiderata – accuracy of representation of reality and usability in analysis.

Two conclusions follow from these observations. First, increased realism is not necessarily a virtue. Indeed, if it complicates the model to a degree that effectively precludes its use in analysis, it deserves to be treated as a mortal sin.

The second conclusion that follows is that a particular model can neither be judged good nor bad in the abstract. Only when related to the issue for whose analysis it is meant to be used can one judge its quality. A model which is admirably suited for the analysis of one such issue may be ill-adapted to another.

To make my point here let me give my favorite example. Models of the demand for cash can be said to be of at least three broad types. There are the macroeconomic models such as the liquidity preference or loanable funds constructs. The second type is the more microeconomic inventory theory model associated with Tobin's work and my own. The third type, generally unknown to economists, is based on the work of the psychologists. For example, there is one such construct in which the intensity of an individual's demand for money is related to his age at toilet training.

Whatever one may think of any of these models, it is clear that each of them is totally useless in dealing with some particular types of problem for which one of the others may be appropriate. For example, if one is asked to testify before the Joint Economic Committee of the U.S. Congress about the demand for money and the danger of increased inflation, the inventory theory model of the demand for cash will contribute little and the toilet training model probably even less. Here, only some one of the macro models offers any prospect of help.

Second, suppose an economist is hired as a consultant by the financial vice-president of a large corporation who seeks help in coping with the interest burden of the firm's cash reserves. Here, no macro model seems particularly promising, while the inventory theoretic model may conceivably be just what is needed.

Finally, imagine a distraught wife who seeks help because her wealthy but miserly husband is unable to part with cash and is keeping the family in penury. Here, what can be contributed by an analysis using either a macro model or one based on inventory theory?

The point is that each of the models is a highly specialized oversimplification – a set of partial truths which renders it fit only for use for the study of certain types of issues. What, then, can be the point of constructing a model for its own sake?

For these reasons, in building models I always prefer to work backwards, starting, if possible, with some hypothesis, some question I want to answer. Then I try to judge from this question and the range of possible answers what elements the model will have to contain and what features one can dispense with. That, to me, is the most effective way to try to make sure that the model is pertinent. It may seem as though this way of going about the process is likely to bias the result, predisposing it toward confirmation of the author's preconceptions. However, I have often found myself surprised at the results that emerged. Indeed, on a number of occasions the model's implications were completely opposite from my initial conjectures, and forced me to rethink the entire subject. I suspect that some of my most interesting articles emerged from surprises of this sort. The very fact that the result was unexpected meant that it was likely to suggest new ideas to some others beside myself. Moreover, it meant, at least sometimes, that the required analysis was more complex and subtle than I had anticipated.

ON SCIENCE AND ART

The fact that I spend a considerable amount of time working on painting and sculpture (I teach a course in wood sculpture at Princeton University) has forced me to think a bit about the relations between my two activities.

I put the matter that way because my preconceptions incline me to resist treating creative activity in the arts in a rigidly analytic manner. I like to approach the creative process in the arts as something that is best driven by feelings rather than systematic analysis. Art that emerges from a systematic intellectual process often seems to be threatened by sterility. Yet on a number of occasions I found myself forced to go beyond this purely negative statement.

The position I have arrived at over the years[1] is that ambiguity is perhaps the indispensable feature of a work of art, while it is at the same time the enemy of effective scientific work. There are at least two parts to the role of ambiguity in art. First, it seems to me that when a message can be transmitted rather unambiguously, any attempt to decorate it with an artistic superstructure is all too likely to degenerate into surface embellishment. I am not arguing that art should always have a message. When it has none, it is by definition all ambiguity. But where art *is* used to convey messages it seems appropriate to do so in cases where words fail the messenger – where it cannot be phrased in a manner that is direct and bears a unique interpretation. Allegory, poetry and other indirect communication media may then convey such imperfectly expressible messages more effectively than direct assertion.

There is a second reason why art must not avoid ambiguity. In a significant sense the artistic experience (whatever that term may connote) is produced by its audience as well as by its creator. Thus, the same work may evoke very different responses in individual A and individual B because the work and A together may involve a chemistry very different from the combination of that same work and person B. This is fortunate because otherwise a work of art could not long endure. A medieval altarpiece cannot possibly have had the same meaning for a fourteenth century monk that it does for a twentieth century observer from Japan. Without its ambiguity, its ability to be transmogrified as the members of its audience change, a work of art could not move different cultures or different ages. Without ambiguity, it can only attain the lifeless status of Soviet proletarian art or the art of the National Socialists.

Contrast this with appropriate standards for writing in our discipline. Anyone who has ever worked on the history of economic ideas is painfully aware of the extent to which ambiguity pervades our literature despite repeated attempts of economists to remove it from their writings. The persistence of discussions about what Ricardo or Marx really meant shows how imperfect is the economist's ability to preclude diversity of

---

[1] In arriving at this formulation of my views I have been helped enormously by the perceptive analysis of Louise M. Rosenblatt in her writings on literary criticism. See, for example, her *The Reader, the Text, the Poems*, Southern Illinois University Press, 1978.

interpretation of what they have written. Mathematical notation can, perhaps, help, but it is no panacea; witness, for example, the protracted and convoluted discussion of the meaning of the von Neumann–Morgenstern axioms on cardinal utility measurement which, while it has somewhat petered out, has still not come to an end.

Yet, while full success is out of the question, it is surely still part of the economist-writer's task to make the contents of his writings as clear and as unambiguous as possible. This is one of the reasons I have always stressed clarity of exposition and its importance as part of the student's training.

Though it is a disgression, I may add that it is by no means the only reason. I have often found that in the process of trying to rephrase a relatively difficult and obscure argument of my own, elements emerge of which I myself had previously been unaware, and sometimes the process even reveals errors or gaps in my analysis. Thus, exposition became not just an end in itself but a useful step in the creative process, one which is capable of generating ideas and of contributing even to more rigorous analysis.

ON APPLIED ECONOMICS

My rather strong views on social and political goals apply also to the work of economists. In line with many of my colleagues today, as well as their predecessors, I am particularly interested in what the discipline can contribute to improvement of the state of social welfare. To me the success of the discipline is to be measured primarily in the extent to which it can help to reduce unemployment and poverty and to improve the quality of life.

However, in arguing this I should not be taken to be questioning the value of "pure" economic research. I agree that additions to the state of knowledge are valuable in themselves. Veblen did have a point when he described the main motive for research as "idle curiosity." That, after all, is the primary business of the academic researcher – to achieve some reduction in the degree of our ignorance.

Moreover, at least occasionally, application is best approached by indirection. It is sometimes the purest of research which ultimately makes the greatest contribution to the social welfare. The only caveat I would address to those who are engaged in very abstract research is to urge the utmost caution before hastening to apply its results to the complex issues of reality. I suppose we are all prone to sin in that regard, ready to leap in with advice to the makers of public policy which is based on no more than an abstract analysis resting on obscure and unverified premises. That useful policy prescriptions may eventually derive from such work is true, but beside the point. Before completion of a careful process of testing and modifications to adapt it to the complications of reality, such a proposal might well be required to bear a label asserting, "This policy may prove dangerous to economic health."

William J. Baumol is Professor of Economics at Princeton and New York universities.

ABRAM BERGSON

Recollections and Reflections
of a Comparativist

I

I became an economist rather fortuitously. Only sixteen years of age, I enrolled as a freshman at Johns Hopkins, in September 1930. With the Great Depression already underway, I had only the vaguest ideas as to how in such a world I might make a suitable career. When my older brother, Gustav, who was already an upperclassman majoring in physics, urged me to concentrate in that discipline I was quite amenable.

According to a rule that the dean of the college held to be inviolable, however, a freshman was not eligible to take courses in physics. Still in close consultation with my brother, I turned instead to economics. In my sophomore year, when I was eligible to take physics, I somehow felt no inclination to do so.

I cannot honestly say that I immediately found economics to be a captivating discipline. After graduating from Johns Hopkins, however, I had no hesitation to take advantage of an opportunity that presented itself to become a graduate student in economics at Harvard in September 1933.

At Harvard, I took what was at the time a usual menu of courses, in theory, statistics, economic history and money and banking. But probably the most decisive course for me was a seminar that I did not get around to taking until 1935–36, Economics 18: "Price Theory and Price Analysis." Under that heading, the then Assistant Professor Wassily W. Leontief offered a rigorous and notably lucid mathematical exposition of core aspects of microeconomics: consumer demand theory, theory of the firm and so forth.

The seminar in effect provided an introduction to mathematical economics, and that was quite opportune for me. I wrote two papers for it, one on externalities in consumption, which I now regret not heeding Leontief's advice to submit for publication, for the MS has long since been lost; and the other, a paper on Ragnar Frisch's methodology of marginal utility measurement. The latter paper was published (Bergson, 1936), and has often been cited. Unexpectedly, a utility function that I analyzed had a form that has since come to be widely known and of much theoretical interest as the CES function.

Leontief's seminar was small (besides me, only three students were enrolled for credit), and a not so incidental attraction that it had for me was that Paul A. Samuelson attended it. He did so as an auditor, rather than as a credit student, but, apart from an auditor's being relieved of formal requirements, the distinction is usually insubstantial in a Harvard seminar. As no one who knows Samuelson will be surprised to hear, that was certainly true in his case.

Samuelson and I became friends at that time, and have remained so ever since. We also found then that our common interests as fellow students extended well beyond the subject of Economics 18. It was thus only natural that, when in the year after we attended the seminar I began working extra-curricularly in the area of welfare economics, I should discuss my progress with Samuelson. His thoughtful reactions, always constructive, were especially appreciated since at Harvard at the time most of the faculty that I was in touch with seemed to have only limited interest in welfare economics. The result of my efforts appeared in due course as a journal article (Bergson, 1938). While I thought the piece was illuminating, I have been most agreeably surprised at the extraordinary attention that has been paid it. For that outcome, though, Samuelson's persistent championship of the article has clearly been in no small part responsible.

II

I have often been asked how it was that, after working with some success in pure theory, I turned rather abruptly, while still a graduate student, to research on the Soviet economy. The short answer, I suppose, is that in the mixed-up world of the time, how socialist planning functioned in the one country where it was being applied on any scale seemed a rather momentous matter. It was also a matter on which at the time there had been remarkably little serious, scholarly work. For me, the subject was doubtless made the more interesting by the ongoing theoretic debate on socialist economic rationality, and by the fact that, in the course of that debate, an analytic structure was being created that might serve as a point of departure for empirical inquiry. Finally, I recall discovering some voluminous Soviet statistical data on wage differentials, which apparently had never been exploited in available Western writings on the Soviet economy. I quickly concluded that the data might provide the basis for the Ph.D. thesis, which I had still to write.

Having decided to do such a thesis, I did not really envisage devoting myself professionally to the study of the Soviet economy to the degree that I have. And I must not fail to record that the commitment I have made has not been exactly without its frustrations. In the face of official secrecy and disinformation, even ascertaining the most basic facts about the Soviet economy has often been extraordinarily difficult. Both the tone and substance of encounters and exchanges with Soviet scholars are inevitably affected by the repressive nature of the society in which they must function. Even for a tourist, the pleasures of travel in such a society are apt to be mixed.

Granting all the difficulties, though, I have never regretted in any serious way my professional involvement with the Soviet economy. As a scholar, I have found that involvement particularly rewarding since I have felt able to go beyond mere description to deal with problems of interest analytically, drawing where appropriate on contemporary Western economic theory. At an early stage, I wrote Sidney Webb in order to obtain his advice on whether such an approach to the Soviet economy might be fitting. As I came in time to realize, the inquiry was rather footless, and there was no reason to be surprised that a scholar, who hardly made use of any economic theory even in studying a Western economy, should reply negatively.

In any event, I happily did not allow myself to be discouraged on that account. From the beginning, I have been able, I think with some success, to organize my research in the light of contemporary neo-classical analysis. Should that not have been possible, I doubt that I would have persisted in working on the Soviet economy in any substantial way.

It would be quite wrong to infer, though, that the relation between my empirical work and economic theory has been unidirectional. My novel research interest was in itself stimulating theoretically. If I had any motive at all, beyond mere scholarly curiosity, for turning as a graduate student to the foundations of welfare economics, I believe it was primarily to clarify for myself the concept of optimal resource use, so that it might serve as a basis for inquiry into socialist planning. In working on my Ph.D. thesis on the Soviet wage structure, I found it necessary, I think in an interesting way, to go beyond Lange's treatment of income distribution in his famous 1936–37 essay on the theory of socialist planning (see Bergson, 1944, Ch. 2).

In applying myself to the task that occupied me for many – perhaps too many – years, the compilation of economically meaningful measures of real national income in the USSR (Bergson, 1961), I had to grapple with the valuation problem posed by the strange Soviet system of administered prices. The problem is probably in a degree intractable, but the Adjusted Factor Cost Standard that I concocted may represent a sensible "second best" solution, and has come to be widely accepted as such.

In trying in a 1973 essay to provide an alternative to Harberger's well-known treatment of monopoly welfare losses, I recall being inspired in part by misgivings as to a paradoxical corollary of his provocative contention that such losses are almost negligible: the mixed-up system of socialist prices should then not have been nearly as economically wasteful as was usually supposed. The question of how to assure an appropriate attitude towards risk-taking on the part of socialist managers, already raised at an early stage in the debate on socialist economic rationality, came to seem rather crucial in the light of the Soviet experience, and in due course became the subject of a separate theoretic inquiry (Bergson, 1978).

I referred to the USSR as socialist. That is in conformity with the conventional, though admittedly controversial, usage, according to which a country is socialist where ownership of the means of production is predominantly public. Numerous countries other than the USSR have in the course of time become socialist in that sense. In doing so, they tended initially to organize their economies in the well-known Soviet way, that is, through application of planning of the centralist sort, stressing bureaucratic, as distinct from market, coordination of production units. Despite numerous so-called reforms, such a scheme continues to prevail not only in the USSR but often elsewhere. Consequential defections from it have nevertheless occurred in three outstanding instances, Yugoslavia, Hungary and China. Where the centralist scheme still persists, pressures to revise it substantially seem to mount as time passes.

In brief, for the Western student of socialist economies, there is now quite a variety of experiences to explore. For me and, I am sure for others as well, the field of socialist economics has also been made more appealing since, while the political systems of all the countries in question are authoritarian, they are not always as much so as that of the USSR.

Another welcome development has been the further progress of theoretic work. This has sometimes materialized as an extension of earlier exchanges on socialist economic rationality (as for example in Bergson, 1948, 1967), and sometimes more or less independently of those exchanges. Among the more notable writings of the latter sort have been the burgeoning analyses of the labor managed economy, inspired initially by the seminal articles of Ward (1958) and Domar (1966), and much advanced by others, especially Vanek in his 1970 treatise; and the continuing efforts of Kornai, as in his 1980 opus, to probe in his own way the more decisive factors in socialist economic conduct.

III

In economics, comparative systems seems to be a rather amorphous area which might be delineated in more than one way. As I see it, a cardinal feature is the concern with economic institutions other than those that predominate in the mixed economies on which most Western economists focus. Such institutions are conspicuously prevalent under socialism. As a scholar who has long been concerned with socialist economies, therefore, I think of myself as a comparativist.

In the same capacity, I have inevitably pondered from time to time the question of what research styles and methods might be appropriate to inquiries in such a field. The answer obviously must be that, as in any branch of economics, there is room, in fact a need, for diverse approaches. Here as elsewhere, it is likely to be all to the good if many flowers bloom.

On a basic aspect, though, the use of theory in empirical work, my personal inclination must be evident. In engaging in such work, I have sought, where possible, to take relevant theoretic principles explicitly as a point of departure. For me, one of the appealing features of the study of socialist economics has been the opportunity it has afforded to employ just that sort of approach.

I should regard it as unfortunate, however, if that mode of work or anything like it were considered canonical. Other practitioners have often proceeded otherwise, and clearly have accomplished much on that basis. Granick and Berliner, for example, organized their early (1954 and 1957, respectively) monographs on the Soviet industrial enterprise to a great extent in only a relatively informal way analytically. But we learned from those studies a good deal of what we know even now about the behavior of the industrial firm under Soviet centralist planning. Berliner's similarly organized 1976 sequel on the Soviet innovation process has been similarly informative. Grossman's and Nove's always insightful writings have also contributed in the same way.

It may be argued that such work has been so fruitful because Western research on socialist economies has generally been at a very early stage. Now that it is relatively advanced, are not efforts at more formal modelling very much the order of the day? Such efforts are increasingly frequent, and that is a welcome development. But it is much too soon to suppose, as some seem inclined to do, that studies of a less formally structured sort no longer have their place. On the contrary, they probably can continue for long to contribute importantly.

In socialist economics, as might be expected, more or less formal modelling has often been accompanied by use of econometrics. Partly for that reason, use of econometrics is now a familiar feature. As in economics generally, the results have sometimes been disappointing, but the technique is often indispensable and obviously here to stay. Any practitioner worth his salt, however, will give careful attention to the nature and limitations of his data base. Such limitations may or may not be reflected in confidence intervals, so the latter cannot be relied on to disclose them. The caveat is in order always, but particularly in socialist economics, where the underlying data are again and again problematic. It is also a caveat which seems to me often insufficiently heeded.

As one who has given particular attention to the data base, I must also express my concern at a fairly prevalent view: While university scholars formerly had to devote a substantial effort to scrutinizing official data, and where necessary making independent calculations on the socialist economies, such work has largely been taken over by the US federal government, particularly the CIA, so there is little need for academics to trouble themselves with it any longer.

In reporting in an unclassified way many results of its massive researches, the CIA has doubtless made an invaluable contribution to Western study of socialist economies. Even the CIA's resources are limited, however, and how it uses them must reflect its own priorities. We must see in that light the fact that available quantitative data on the socialist economies still leave much to be desired. Among the countries on which I am relatively informed, the deficiencies are particularly noteworthy for Eastern Europe, but even for the USSR we are not nearly as well equipped statistically as might be thought.

Ultimately, official secrecy must limit what can be accomplished by Western scholars in quantitative work on the socialist economies, but much still could be done. Unfortunately, where gaps in Western quantitative research remain, a corollary of the "leave it to the CIA approach" is the inclination to employ, with minimal scrutiny, available socialist official statistics. Experience to date shows that to be a treacherous procedure.

Data compilation can be a dreary task, and younger scholars, now highly trained in theory and econometrics, understandably shy away from it. But at any sophisticated level, where the concern is to relate the data to relevant analytical categories, such work can also be challenging intellectually. So it has seemed when I have been involved with it, and many others who have been similarly engaged no doubt would testify similarly. The task seems especially challenging where the concern is with socialist economies, and one is seeking to compile in such a strange context conceptually meaningful data such as are often problematic even in the West, e.g., on real national income, the cost of living, capital stocks, etc.

IV

I have been asked to discuss my philosophy of life. I do have some beliefs that may be relevant to that theme and of interest to others. I have already expatiated somewhat on one of them: my sense of the scientifically intriguing nature of socialist economics as a field of scholarly study. For me, such a vocation has also had no little appeal because of the opportunities it provides to try to gain perspective on the comparative economic merit of socialism. That is a rather important issue in a world where proponents of that system seek actively to extend its reach, and hold its asserted economic superiority over its older Western rival to be a ground to consider such extension inevitable.

Regarding that contention, the reader is able to judge for himself what to think of the underlying Marxian dogma as to the decisive nature of material forces in history. As for the comparative economic merit of the competing social systems, the task of appraising that issue is unfortunately as formidable as it is important. Given the predominance of one kind of property ownership or the other, each system has assumed diverse specific forms and imaginably might assume still other rather different ones. Yet how a social system performs necessarily depends on the form in question. Beyond that, associated historical and cultural circumstances presumably are also relevant.

Granting such complexities, Western research has been illuminating, and I should at least record my impression that socialism is probably much less potent economically than many once assumed. If it can match capitalism in the more successful manifestations of the latter, that fact has yet to be demonstrated.

I refer particularly to socialist performance in respect of efficiency, as understood in the light of familiar Western norms. At least until recently, socialist countries have usually been able to achieve quite respectable rates of growth, but that apparently tends to reflect an inordinate reliance on costly capital and labor inputs, as distinct from technological advances. Under socialism, as thus far experienced, income inequality is difficult to gauge because of the substantial extra-market rewards and privileges, and usually also because of official secrecy. Income inequality probably has often been greater than commonly supposed.

While economic merit is of much interest, so too is political merit as manifest above all in the status of democratic political institutions, i.e., due process of law, civil liberties, and public dismissibility of responsible officials through free elections. From that standpoint, socialism, as thus far experienced, hardly scores at all. It is only by adopting another and quite different concept of democracy that proponents are able often to urge otherwise. I am among those who find it difficult not to view the socialist record to date in a Hayekian way as illustrating the inherent antinomy between more or less inclusive public ownership and democratic political processes, as conceived in the West.

I have been discussing comparative economic and political merit without explicit reference to my own ethical values. Perhaps I can repair that deficiency if I explain that in my personal social welfare function (SWF), one of the arguments, with a high value indeed, is a vector representing the status of the diverse institutions of political democracy, i.e., due process of law, etc. For the rest, I still find the oft-maligned principle of consumer's sovereignty to be quite appealing, though not inviolable; which is to say that, in respect of material arguments, my SWF has essentially the well-known individualistic form. In the realm of equity, there are, I think, recognizable minimum material levels which an economically advanced society should seek to assure for all. I regard it as an egregious and distressing flaw that such an imperative often fails to be observed. Otherwise, though, egalitarian income redistribution does not seem to me intrinsically very urgent. I recognize, however, that the degree of inequality and how it originates are factors which could affect the viability of democratic political institutions.

One's ethical beliefs are apt to have complex and elusive sources, but my parents came to the United States around the turn of the century as Jewish immigrants from Tsarist Russia. Such a family background seems almost naturally to predispose one to a deep commitment to democracy and often to an enduring concern for the lot of the under-privileged. My personal SWF probably is best understood in that light.

Writing the foregoing in 1986, as is abundantly clear, I hardly anticipated the extraordinary events in the USSR and the East more generally that immediately followed. Where these developments will finally lead is not apparent, but the prospects for socialism in those countries, especially in its authoritarian, centralist form, are dim indeed. Granting that it was not predicted, however, this abrupt denouement is perhaps not altogether surprising in view of results of much Western research, including my own, briefly adumbrated here, on the malfunctioning of the economies in question.

Abram Bergson is George F. Baker Professor of Economics, Emeritus, at Harvard University.

REFERENCES

Bergson, Abram. "Real Income, Expenditure Proportionality, and Frisch's 'New Methods of Measuring Marginal Utility,' " *Review of Economic Studies*, 4(1), Oct. 1936, pp. 33–52.

"A Reformulation of Certain Aspects of Welfare Economics," *Quarterly Journal of Economics*, 52(2), Feb. 1938, pp. 310–334.

The Structure of Soviet Wages. Cambridge, MA: Harvard Univ. Press, 1944.

"Socialist Economics," in Howard Ellis, ed., *A Survey of Contemporary Economics.* Philadelphia: Blakeston, 1948.

The Real National Income of Soviet Russia since 1928. Cambridge, MA: Harvard Univ. Press, 1961.

"Market Socialism Revisited," *Journal of Political Economy*, 75(5), Oct. 1967, pp. 655–673.

"On Monopoly Welfare Losses," *American Economic Review*, 63(5), Dec. 1973, pp. 853–870.

"Managerial Risks and Rewards in Public Enterprise," *Journal of Comparative Economics*, 2(3), Sept. 1978, pp. 211–225.

Berliner, Joseph. *Factory and Manager in the USSR.* Cambridge, MA: Harvard Univ. Press, 1957.

The Innovation Decision in Soviet Industry. Cambridge, MA: MIT Press, 1976.

Domar, Evsey D. "The Soviet Collective as a Producer Cooperative," *American Economic Review*, 56(4), Sept. 1966, pp. 734–757.

Granick, David. *Management of the Industrial Firm in the USSR.* New York: Columbia Univ. Press, 1954.

Kornai, Janos. *The Economics of Shortage.* Amsterdam: North-Holland, 1980.

Vanek, Jaroslav. *The General Theory of the Labor-Managed Economy.* Ithaca, NY: Cornell Univ. Press, 1970.

Ward, Benjamin. "The Firm in Illyria: Market Syndicalism," *American Economic Review*, 48(4), Sept. 1958, pp. 566–589.

KENNETH E. BOULDING

From Chemistry to Economics and Beyond

Perhaps the most general principle of the universe is that "everything is what it is because it got that way" or, more elegantly, "every structure is the result of past processes."[1] What I am today, therefore, certainly goes back to my conception in Liverpool in the spring of 1909, which gave me my genetic inheritance. As far as I know, all my ancestors were fairly humble people, and I am probably the first member of my family ever to go beyond the eighth grade. I came essentially out of the Methodist working class. My father was self-educated and a working plumber who had a little business of his own in Liverpool. He was a "local" – that is, lay – preacher in the Methodist Church, and Sunday School superintendent for many years. My mother and her parents were also Methodists. Her father was a blacksmith in a little town in Somerset. By today's

---

[1] I have sometimes called this "D'Arcy Thompson's Law" in honor of the great Scottish biologist whose book, *On Growth and Form*, influenced me greatly in the 1950s.

standards they were very poor, but they did not think of themselves as such. Life was often hard. My mother read widely, wrote some charming poetry. I had a very happy and supportive childhood living in downtown Liverpool in what might easily have been called a slum. It was really rather an exciting neighborhood – Jewish, Irish, Belgian, and one black family.

Our life centered around the downtown Methodist Church. As an only child, and indeed an only grandchild, my life at home was very much in an adult world – relations, visiting ministers, and so on, always coming in, and long conversations around the dinner table. In the street, my only playground, at the age of nine I published a newspaper with six or eight carbon copies, which I found made me leader of the gang, the typewriter being much mightier than the fist.

At that age also my parents transferred me from a crowded little Church of England school at the top of the street to a much better school, originally Unitarian, about a mile away. Here I was usually at the top of the class or close to it. I was very carefully groomed for scholarship examinations to the local high school, Liverpool Collegiate. Of course there were no girls in the Collegiate School and I studied very hard for six years. I spent three years doing almost nothing but mathematics, physics, and chemistry; got a scholarship in chemistry to New College, Oxford, in 1928; read chemistry for a year, found I could not stand it. The College allowed me to keep my scholarship and do politics, philosophy, and economics.

The late Lionel Robbins was then the tutor at New College, just before he went to his professorship at the London School, so I went to him and asked him what I should read in economics during the summer of 1929. He said, "You might read Marshall, *Principles of Economics;* Pigou, *The Economics of Welfare;* Cassel, *The Theory of Social Economy;* and Hawtrey, *The Economic Problem."* I had never heard of any of these books, so I got them out of the library and went back to Liverpool (too poor to go anywhere else) and spent the summer reading them. That is how I became an economist.

I went back the next October to find Henry Phelps Brown was my tutor. He gave me a little examination in which I got an "Alpha," so that convinced me that economics was what I should concentrate in. The next year Phelps Brown went off to America, oddly enough to the University of Michigan in Ann Arbor, to learn some economics, and I had Maurice Allen at Balliol as a tutor. He became, I believe, economist at the Bank of England, on the grounds, the story was, that as he had never written anything, he must be discrete. I think, however, I learned something from him.

After getting my first class honors in 1931, I did a year of so-called graduate work, simply because there was nothing else to do, and I had a little University scholarship. Graduate work at Oxford consisted in going to my adviser, Maurice Allen, once every two or three weeks. He would say, "How are you getting on?" and I would say, "Fine," and that was about the end of it. I did write a thesis on international capital movements which, probably fortunately, has become one of my lost works. I never actually took a higher degree.

In 1932 I got a Commonwealth Fellowship to the University of Chicago. The then Prince of Wales was a patron of the Fund, so all the outgoing fellows had to be blessed by him individually. I told him I was going to Chicago and he said jovially, "Oh, don't get bumped off!" and I did not. Chicago was a wonderful experience, even though it was in the depth of the Great Depression. I remember a headline in the Chicago Tribune: "No Construction in Chicago This Week." There was a busted bank on every main street. The University, however, was enormously exciting. Robert Hutchins had just come in as president, and the whole place seemed fantastically alive after Oxford. It did not seem to worry anybody that I was not a gentleman.

I discovered, however, somewhat to my dismay, that I was expected to take courses and know something. My advisor was Jacob Viner, and he suggested that I take a Ph.D. I asked him what I should have to do and he told me, and I said, "Well, if I do that, I will be a broken man." At that time, of course, I did not realize I was going to settle in the United States. In my "first" at Oxford I had, of course, my "Good Housekeeping Seal of Approval" for British academic life. At Chicago I studied mainly with Frank Knight and with Henry Schultz, almost the first econometrician, from whom I learned a great deal. I recall him once coming around the stat lab where we were grinding out coefficients of correlation on mechanical calculators. He sympathized with us and said, "I know this is very boring, but you *are* getting familiar with the data." Today, of course, a computer gets familiar with the data and nobody else does.

Part of the Commonwealth Fellowship was a summer of travel around the United States. At the Grand Canyon I got a cable that my father had died, and I went back to Liverpool and spent ten days trying to wind up his business, at which I think I learned more economics than any of my teachers had taught me. I found he had been insolvent for at least twenty years, but the bank and his suppliers had kept him going in the hope of better times.

That fall I went to Harvard to work with Joseph Schumpeter, whom I had met on the boat coming across to America the year before. I worked with him on capital theory, and discovered what I thought was a fundamental flaw in Böhm-Bawerk. I cannot quite now remember what it was, and I seem to have lost the paper. My mother joined me at the end of the year, and we went back to Chicago for six months.

Here I should backtrack a little – when I was still an undergraduate at Oxford I wrote a paper (a little note) on what was then called "displacement costs" (today it is what we call "alternative costs"), and sent it to Keynes as the editor of the *Economic Journal*. He accepted it for publication, but wrote quite a long critique of it, an extraordinary act of kindness on the part of a very busy man, as the result of which I revised it. When I got to Chicago I sent a reprint of this article to Frank Knight, who sent back a note saying, "Professor Knight thanks Mr. Boulding for his paper, which he thinks is as wrong and confused as it is possible to be." That got our relationship off on a very good level, and I became very fond of him. I am sure my thinking has been much influenced by his teachings. Another important influence in Chicago was a fellow graduate student, Albert Hart, a man of extraordinary fecundity of ideas, a great many of which I am sure I must have stolen.

In June of 1934 my mother and I went back to Liverpool. We each stayed with a different relative – we had no home to go back to – and just as our savings were about to run out I got a job at the University of Edinburgh as a very humble assistant at 250 pounds a year. After Chicago, Edinburgh really seemed like the Middle Ages, and I did not get along too well with the Scots, but I did have a lot of time to think, and became good friends with a colleague of about the same age and status, William Baxter, who later became professor of accounting at the London School of Economics. He introduced me to accounting theory, and I read William Paton's book on the subject, which had a great impact on my economic thought. For the first time in my life I began to understand what a balance sheet was, which nobody had ever told me at Oxford, or even at Chicago.

Life is often a set of parallel streams. Parallel to my academic experience there runs a strong stream of religious experience. This starts from my Methodist upbringing. In my teens I went to two or three conferences of the Methodists at which I met some of the major intellectual figures of the Methodist Church in England and was persuaded that one could be an intellectual and still a follower of Jesus and a member of a kingdom not wholly of this world. Even before this, at the age of about fourteen, I had an inner experience which convinced me that I could not participate in war. I was thinking about my experiences as a child in the First World War: my uncle coming back from the trenches with an expression on his face I have never forgotten; my Jewish playmate's older brother who was killed, his mother hysterical with grief; my magnificent Australian cousin who was killed in two weeks. I absorbed, even as a child, the endless propaganda of hatred. Behind all this was my commitment to Jesus and the Sermon on the Mount. I decided I could not reconcile loving my enemies with the demand of the national state that I should hate and kill them. The Methodist Church, I felt, was too compromised on this issue, and somehow I heard about the Quakers. I went over to the Quaker Meetinghouse, which was, again, only ten minutes' walk from the house, and immediately felt at home in the silent, contemplative worship.

I joined the Society of Friends during my first year at Oxford, although my main contacts at Oxford were still with the Methodists, who were much more of my own class. But in Chicago I found the Friends' Meeting on 57th Street very congenial, and at Edinburgh my religious life was tied up with the "New Meeting" there. I found also in the Society of Friends, in its lack of creedalism, tolerance of diversity, and, again, strong sense of transcendental community, a spiritual home in which I could reconcile my religious and my scientific experience. For my whole life, wherever I have lived, the community of the local Friends' Meeting has been the quiet center of a very busy, worldly, and occasionally stormy, life.

Now, however, to get back to economics. My appointment at Edinburgh was not renewed in 1937. My professor there, Alexander Gray, told me he thought I would never make a teacher, especially as I had a speech defect. Then in August of 1937 I went to Philadelphia, where Friends had a world conference, as a delegate from Scotland. While I was there an old Chicago friend phoned me and told me about a job opening at Colgate University in upstate New York. After the conference I went up there; they looked me over and I looked them over, and I never went back to Britain. I emigrated unexpectedly with one suitcase and a return ticket, a single event that changed my whole life.

I was very happy at Colgate. My mother joined me after a year and also found a very happy home there in the village of Hamilton, where she lived almost all the rest of her life. It was a very hectic teaching schedule – nine hours of classes and twelve hours of tutorials – but I had the summers free. I could not afford to go anywhere, so I spent two summers writing *Economic Analysis*, my first major work. Like many textbooks, this came out of my lecture notes in a course in intermediate theory. I forced myself to write it by setting up a little chart above my typewriter showing how many pages I was going to do by what date, writing ten pages a day all through the summer. I saw economics as a kind of landscape, indeed in the first drafts I had a little introductory paragraph of a chapter about the nature of the scenery, which the publisher made me take out. It is interesting that the first edition of *Economic Analysis* in 1941 essentially followed Irving Fisher rather than Keynes' *General Theory*, which I had read by then but had not really assimilated.

The second edition in 1948 was thoroughly Keynesian. I learned a lot of economics from my colleagues at Colgate, especially from Charles Phillips, under whose guidance I had to teach a seminar in marketing, a subject that nobody at Oxford ever told me existed, and I got very excited by it.

In the meantime, the clouds of the Second World War were rising. We could all see what was coming, and tension between my Arcadian environment, my deep commitment to nonparticipation in war, and the agonizing fear of Hitler created a tension which I relieved by writing verse. I had written a little juvenile verse at Oxford but did not really start writing until those years at Colgate.[2]

Then in 1941 I met Elise Biorn-Hansen at a Quaker Meeting in Syracuse. We were engaged in eighteen days and married in three months, and went down to Princeton. I worked for the League of Nations' Economic and Financial Section, which had moved to the Institute of Advanced Study in Princeton after the fall of France. I worked under the Estonian economist, Ragnar Nurkse, on a study of what had happened to European agriculture between 1913 and 1928 as a result of the First World War. This was part of a larger study of the reconstruction after the First World War which had, I think, a substantial impact, in the sense that the United Nations Relief and Reconstruction Administration came out of it, and a great many mistakes that were made after 1919 were avoided after 1945, again, perhaps in part due to the extraordinary influence of Keynes. My experience with the League of Nations was my main experience with data. We made maps of Europe by small divisions, showing what had happened to agriculture yields, production, and things of this kind, which were remarkably revealing. I became convinced that geography was a lot more important than correlation.

After Princeton we had a year at Fisk University in Nashville, Tennessee, where I was a one-man department, and so found myself teaching labor economics and other things that I had not known much about before. Robert Park, the sociologist, was there that year and had a great influence on me. I recall a half-hour conversation with him about social ecology which I think quite changed my life, beginning my interest in ecological and evolutionary theory.

From Fisk we went to Iowa State College (as it was then called) at Ames, at the invitation of Theodore Schultz. He felt they ought to have a labor economist there among the cornfields. He had the idea of getting a general economist to convert himself to the field, so he offered me a

---

[2] Kenneth E. Boulding, *There Is a Spirit: The Nayler Sonnets* (Nyack, N.Y.: Fellowship Publications, 1945), and Kenneth E. Boulding, *Sonnets from the Interior Life, and Other Autobiographical Verse* (Boulder, Colo.: Colorado Associated University Press, 1975).

year off to convert myself into a labor economist, an opportunity I could not resist. My old Chicago friend, Albert Hart, was there at that time and I am sure had something to do with the invitation, although he left to go to Columbia before I arrived. Iowa State had a remarkable department of economics; it was an extraordinary institution, which, starting off as a "cow college" of agriculture and mechanical arts, had become a great university in virtually all departments simply by the logic of education and scholarship. My year at becoming a labor economist I spent reading up on the field, which did not take long in those days, and visiting the head offices of eighty-five different unions. I also went to all the labor conventions, and visited virtually every local union in Iowa. Today this would certainly be called "casual empiricism," but I felt I learned an enormous amount.

I have often said that the study of labor was my undoing as a pure economist, as I became convinced that if one were going to study any particular segment of the real world, like the labor movement, one had to do this with the skills not only of the economist, but of the sociologist, the political scientist, the anthropologist, and even the philosopher and the theologian. I became convinced that all the social sciences were studying the same thing – the social system – only from different vantage points. This got me interested in the integration of the social sciences, which eventually led to my becoming one of the founding fathers of what is now the International Society for the Systems Sciences, and a lifelong continual interest in the unity of human knowledge.

However, I by no means gave up economics. It was at Ames, indeed, that I wrote the *Reconstruction of Economics*,[3] which I still think is my major unrecognized contribution to the field. This, going back to Edinburgh days and my introduction to accounting, was an attempt to reconstruct economics around the concepts of the balance sheet rather than the income statement, which I regard as essentially a dynamic derivative of changes in the balance sheet. This led to certain modifications of the theory of the firm and household, built on the old marginal theories. It emphasized the importance of possible alternative balance sheet structures, particularly the tremendous importance for the labor market and the demand for labor of the gap between interest and profit, which has been astonishingly neglected by economists. When labor is hired by a firm, money stocks diminish, stocks of something made by the work increase. Unless the structure of the balance sheet can be restored by sale of the product, which restores the money stock, the purchase of labor will soon grind to a halt. This seemed to me an essential element in the

---

[3] Kenneth E. Boulding, *A Reconstruction of Economics* (New York: Wiley, 1950).

Keynesian insight on unemployment, virtually forgotten by the "Keynesians."

Reconstructing economics around the balance sheet, however, led also to a macroeconomic theory of distribution, which was hinted at in Keynes' *Treatise on Money*, in what he called the "widow's cruse" theory – that the distribution of profits to householders recreates new profits as these householders buy products from firms, in addition to those products bought by wage earners. I have sometimes called this the "K Theory," as it was expounded by Keynes, Kalecki, in a rather strange form by Kaldor, and, of course, by Kenneth Boulding, although my contribution never was recognized. Certainly nobody in Cambridge, England, ever read my *Reconstruction of Economics*. There were some mistakes in the *Reconstruction* which were pointed out in a very able review by Ralph Turvey,[4] which I later corrected.[5]

I still think, however, that my basic concept is sound and is absolutely crucial to understanding the future of capitalism, which cannot exist without profits. Furthermore, there is a tendency for interest to gobble up profit, which we saw very dramatically in the Great Depression, when in 1932–33 real interest rates were still on the order of 3 percent and average profits were something like minus 3 percent. Under these circumstances, anybody who hired anybody was either a philanthropist or a fool, and the only reason why the economy did not disintegrate completely was habit and irrational expectations. We see something of the same thing happening today in a very ominous fashion.

It is one of the mild sorrows of a very happy life that while I have received an enormous amount of recognition and rewards, I still feel that nobody has paid any attention to the important things I had to say, of which the macroeconomic theory of profits is one. About the only treatment of this, as far as I know, is by Martin Bronfenbrenner and his excellent work on income distribution.[6] How economists could continue to believe in the distribution theory of the Cobb–Douglas production function completely baffles me in the light of what happened in the Great Depression. We would have had to explain the disappearance of profits on the thesis that all of a sudden capital became almost inconceivably plentiful! What has deceived economists is the absurd belief that profit and interest are prices, which they are not; they are rates of growth,

---

[4] See *Economica*, New Series 18 (1951): 203.

[5] Kenneth E. Boulding, "Economic Theory: The Reconstruction Reconstructed." *Segments of the Economy–1956: A Symposium* (Cleveland, Ohio: Howard Allen, 1957) (reprinted in Kenneth E. Boulding, *Collected Papers*, Vol. II, Fred R. Glahe, ed. [Boulder, Colo.: Colorado Associated University Press, 1971]).

[6] Martin Bronfenbrenner, *Income Distribution Theory* (Chicago: Aldine-Atherton, 1971), p. 411.

something of a totally different dimension. Profit and interest are both affected by the relative price structure, but they are not part of it. This delusion has persisted for fifty years.

In 1949 I went to the University of Michigan, perhaps because the chairman of the department, Leo Scharfman, a man who inspired great affection among his colleagues, was on the committee of the American Economic Association that awarded me the John Bates Clark medal. I was in a fairly good bargaining position, as I was very happy at Ames, so I said I would come if I could teach a seminar on the integration of the social sciences, which I did for several years. It was out of this that my interest in general systems developed. The social scientists did not want to be integrated very much and the seminar turned into an exercise in integrating anybody who was willing, including physicists, engineers, and especially biologists. This was where I first got really interested in biology.

The year 1954–55 I spent at the new Center for Advanced Study in the Behavioral Sciences at Stanford, set up by the Ford Foundation. That year in Palo Alto with my growing family (four children by this time) was perhaps one of the most creative years of my life. I associated with a remarkable group of people. I learned a great deal from them, and I think that what happened that year at the Center dominated the next ten years or so of my life. Four of us around a lunch table that fall founded what is now the International Society for the Systems Sciences, which is still going strong. A little group of us in the spring met to consider how we could mobilize the social sciences in peace research, war and peace being the most threatening problem of the human race. We decided we would start a journal, which we got underway as The *Journal of Conflict Resolution* when we got back to the University of Michigan the following year. It also is still going strong.

Then in the last nine days I was at the Center, in August of 1955, I dictated *The Image*.[7] Learning to use a dictaphone that year also had a profound effect on my subsequent career; I sometimes say it may have doubled the quantity of my output, and I have some hesitations about what it did to the quality. *The Image*, however, is, I think, perhaps the most influential book I have written, though its influence has been felt in rather odd places. Some of it can be interpreted as what I have sometimes called "economics imperialism," the attempt on the part of economics to take over all the other social sciences, a movement that I never really joined but which is also still alive and well. The book was a somewhat disguised attack on behaviorism and what I felt was a

---

[7] Kenneth E. Boulding, *The Image: Knowledge in Life and Society* (Ann Arbor: University of Michigan Press, 1956).

pseudo-scientific approach to the study of the human race. It emphasized that behavior was a function of the image of the world of the be-
haver, rather than of any immediate stimulus, and that we did have
access to our images of the world through the phenomenon of consciousness, which is a legitimate source of increase in human knowledge. In a way, *The Image* represented an attempt to integrate the
humanities with the sciences, an ambitious task in which I am afraid I
have not been very successful. My position still is that human knowledge
has an essential unity which is, however, characterized by great diversity
of methodologies of learning and testing, and that our images of value
are just as much part of this unity as our images of what we think of as
fact.

In the 1950s and early 1960s I was a member of the General Committee
of the Department of the Church and Economic Life of the National
Council of Churches, a fascinating, remarkably heterogeneous body of
people whose only common interest was the attempt to find applications
of Christian principles to economic life and institutions. In connection
with this I wrote *The Organizational Revolution,* the general theme of
which was that there was an enormous expansion of the scale of organization after about 1870, mainly as a result of a transformation in
communication systems, like the telephone, which pushed back the point
at which diminishing returns to scale began. This was part of a larger
study directed by Howard Bowen, and the manuscript was sent out to
about thirty people for their comments. Reinhold Niebuhr was so out-
raged by the book that he wrote a whole chapter in reply, to which I
wrote a chapter in reply to him. The other twenty-nine commentators,
I am afraid, I mostly quoted against each other. Niebuhr at that time
was a quasi-Marxist. I think perhaps the contrast in our philosophies
could be summed up in a sentence at the end of my reply to him, where
I say that "Niebuhr is afraid of freedom, seeing always behind it the
specter of anarchy, whereas I am afraid of justice, seeing always behind
it the specter of tyranny."[8] The problem of the definition and meaning
of justice has been a constant concern for me, because the pursuit of
inadequate ideas of justice seems to me to have caused so much human
misery.

We spent a year at the University of the West Indies in Jamaica (1959–
60). This, again, was a remarkably productive year. It is odd how my
years away seem to have been so important. It was there that I wrote
Conflict and Defense, an attempt to lay the foundations of what I believe
is a somewhat new and very necessary discipline of conflict studies.[9] It

[8] Kenneth E. Boulding, *The Organizational Revolution* (New York: Harper, 1953), p. 254.
[9] Kenneth E. Boulding, *Conflict and Defense* (New York: Harper, 1962). Since then, I

was there, also, that I began to develop my trichotomy of social systems into threat systems, exchange systems, and integrative systems, which has become increasingly important in my thinking.

The third great year away was 1963–64, which we spent at International Christian University in Tokyo. I look back on this year also as one of the most creative years of my life. It made me realize what an ignorant Westerner I was and how my education had been neglected, and what an extraordinary stream of human life and experience had come out of Asia. Japan is a great cultural broker between the two great streams of human life and experience. My students were mostly Marxists, perhaps because the Teachers' Union in Japan at that time was very Marxist. These students seemed to come up to college believing that intellectual history started with Hegel, went through Feuerbach, and virtually ended in Marx, with an appendix in Lenin, which seemed to me very limited. So I kept asking them, even if there were dialectical elements in human history, what about the nondialectical ones? At the end of my year in Japan I gave some lectures which I called "Dialectical and Nondialectical Elements in the Interpretation of Human History," which ended up as a little book called *A Primer on Social Dynamics*[10] and was later expanded into my *Ecodynamics*.[11] Nondialectical processes, of course, are mainly the evolutionary ones of mutation and very complex selection through ecological interaction.

I taught summer school at the University of Colorado at Boulder on my way back from Japan in 1964 and I finished up the revision of the fourth edition of *Economic Analysis*, a work which, I think, sums up my contributions to pure economics. The book was a failure, both as a textbook and as a contribution to the field. I do not believe it ever got reviewed in any of the major economic journals. However, I did fall in love with Boulder, which eventually led to our coming to the University of Colorado in 1967. In the interim my wife Elise got her Ph.D. at the University of Michigan. In 1965 I played a fairly crucial role in the first "teach-in" at the University of Michigan, which started off the whole wave of events that eventually ended the Vietnam War.

The years at Boulder have been very happy and productive, thanks in no small measure to an almost perfect setting for creativity – a half-time teaching, half-time research appointment, a full-time secretary, funds for research assistants, and a small suite of offices at the Institute of Behav-

have published a good deal in the Peace Studies field. See Kenneth E. Boulding, *Collected Papers*, Vol. 5, Larry D. Singell, ed. (Boulder, Colo.: Colorado Associated University Press, 1975), and *Stable Peace* (Austin: University of Texas Press, 1978).
10 Kenneth E. Boulding, *A Primer on Social Dynamics* (Glencoe, Ill.: Free Press, 1970).
11 Kenneth E. Boulding, *Ecodynamics: A New Theory of Societal Evolution* (Beverly Hills, Calif.: Sage, 1978; revised paperback edition, 1981).

ioral Science. My secretary, or administrative assistant, Mrs. Vivian Wilson, has been with me now since 1967 and has been a tremendous asset.

In the middle 1960s I got into grants economics – that is, the serious study of one-way transfers – and helped to found the Association for the Study of the Grants Economy. Curiously enough, this came out of my interest in conflict management, for as I puzzled as to why some conflicts were fruitful and some were not, I decided that the main clue to this problem was the study of integrative systems – that is, those aspects of social life and relations that involve love and hate, community and enmity, legitimacy, and so on. Being an economist I looked around for a possible measure of integrative structures and hit on the grant or one-way transfer. I got a little grant from the Ford Foundation to study grants and took on a young man, Martin Pfaff, to help me with this. He turned out to be an extraordinary entrepreneur who, together with Janos Horvath, helped organize the Association, meetings, volumes, and so on.

The grants economy idea was not well received at first. When we presented it, indeed, at the International Economic Association seminar at Bled, Yugoslavia (1970),[12] we almost created a riot, but it has gradually come to be regarded as moderately respectable, and the International Economic Association itself organized a seminar on the subject in Cambridge, England, in 1979.[13] Grants are an increasingly important part of the economy. They are extremely important in the household. They follow rather different principles from the market, although there are some similarities, and it is very important to study them because they are capable of very severe pathologies and often do more harm than good, even when well-intentioned. The importance of grants in the household was brought out very dramatically by Nancy Baerwaldt and James Morgan in two articles in which they estimate that grants within households amount to something like 30 percent of national income.[14]

This encouraged another theme in my thought, the neglect of households by economists, who tend to regard them as a black box just with inputs and outputs. There is no more important institution than the household, for the character of a society is determined more by the

[12] Kenneth E. Boulding and Martin Pfaff, "The Grants Economy and the Development Gap," in *The Gap Between Rich and Poor Nations*, Gustav Ranis, ed. (London: Macmillan Press, 1972).

[13] *The Grants Economy and Collective Consumption*, R.C.O. Matthews and G. B. Stafford, eds. (London: Macmillan Press, for the International Economic Association, 1982).

[14] Nancy Baerwaldt and James N. Morgan, "Trends in Intra-Family Transfers," in *Surveys of Consumers, 1971–72*, Lewis Mandell, ed. (Ann Arbor: Survey Research Center, Institute for Social Research, University of Michigan, 1973). James N. Morgan, "Intra-Family Transfers Revisited: The Support of Dependents Inside the Family," in *Five Thousand American Families: Patterns of Economic Progress*, Vol. 6, Greg J. Duncan and James N. Morgan, eds. (Ann Arbor: Institute for Social Research, University of Michigan, 1978), pp. 347– 366.

character of its households than by anything else. The household, indeed, is the only organization that produces people. The absurd identification of consumption with household purchases, which extends even to Keynes, I think has done a lot of harm in economics. A household purchase is an exchange of money for some good of varying length of life, of course, from furniture to groceries on the shelves, just like a purchase by a business. Irving Fisher (I think, the greatest economist America has produced) knew this! A balance sheet approach to economics would make this very clear. A purchase diminishes money in the balance sheet of the purchaser and increases something else. What that something else is, of course, is very important. Even though information on household capital is spotty, there is a good deal of evidence that it is now about as large as industrial capital and a crucial element in the dynamics of an economy.

Perhaps the most important product of my Boulder years has been *Ecodynamics: A New Theory of Societal Evolution.*[15] This is, in a way, my manifesto about the universe. It identifies three major dynamic processes in the universe. Physical and chemical evolution began, presumably, with the "big bang" and culminated on this planet with DNA and life, although Mr. Crick thinks that this must have come from somewhere else! Physical and chemical evolution are dominated by the phase principle, which defines a boundary between different states of the physical world. With life comes ecosystems – that is, systems of interacting populations of different species, a species being defined very broadly as any set of objects that are similar enough to make the set interesting. Species include not only biological species, like robins, but physical and chemical species, like water molecules, hydrogen atoms, no doubt quarks, and also species of human artifacts, like scissors and automobiles.

Biological evolution is dominated by *selection,* coming out of ecological interaction, which makes some species grow in population and some decline; and by *mutation,* which is a change in the parameters of the system. Genetic mutation, of course, is of great importance in biological evolution, but changes in climate, soils, and so on, are also very important in changing the parameters of the system. With the first *Homo and mulier sapiens,* Adam and Eve, evolution again went into a new gear because of the extraordinary capacity of the human race for producing images of the world and artifacts. The ecosystems of the earth almost without exception now contain human artifacts as part of their species structure.

In *Ecodynamics,* also, I developed the tripartite structure of human interaction into threat systems, exchange systems, and integrative systems. I also developed a genetic theory of production, arguing that all

---

[15] Kenneth E. Boulding, *Ecodynamics: A New Theory of Societal Evolution* (Beverly Hills, Calif.: Sage, 1978; revised paperback edition, 1981).

production, whether the chicken from the egg or the automobile from the blueprint, comes from the genetic structure of "know-how," but that the potential of the genetic know-how is limited by four categories of limiting factors: materials of many different kinds, energy in many different forms, space, and time.

This is in sharp contrast to what I call the "cookbook" theory of production, which is that we mix land, labor, and capital and out comes a product. Land, labor, and capital, I argue, as factors of production are hopeless heterogeneous aggregates of genetic and limiting factors and have all the scientific validity of earth, air, fire, and water. The theory of production has been the Achilles' heel of economics, for which, I am afraid, Adam Smith has to take some of the blame, much as I love him, and which was in part responsible for the human disaster of Marxism, which I have described as "Ptolemaic social science," hopelessly inadequate to deal with the complexities of the modern world.

I also argue that the species of human artifacts can also have a tripartite classification into things, like automobiles; organizations, like the Federal Reserve Bank; and people. People are partly biological artifacts from their genetic structure, but also, to a very large extent, social artifacts from the human learning process. I also stress the fact that there are two genetic processes in evolution: one I have called "biogenetics," which is DNA and all that; and the other, "noogenetics," which is the learned processes that are transmitted from one generation to the next by a learning process. In the human race, noogenetics has become of overwhelming importance, and biogenetics has been relatively unimportant, as there has been very little change in the human gene pool, as far as we know, in the last 50,000 years. Human biogenetics gives us the extraordinary potential of the human organism, but this potential has to be realized through a learning process.

Another very significant thing we have learned from evolution is that it is a highly indeterministic process, not at all like celestial mechanics. I argue that celestial mechanics was only successful because the evolution of the solar system had virtually ceased and it is a totally inappropriate model to describe even biological systems, much less social systems, which is why I am very skeptical about simple econometrics. Evolution, however, is dominated by stochastic processes and by the actual date at which extremely improbable events happen. It has been a great tragedy that economics and the other social sciences have been so obsessed by the success of celestial mechanics that they have tried to force what is a totally different kind of system into this Newtonian, Laplacean, straitjacket.

A young man came up to me at the American Economic Association annual meeting a few years ago and said, "My professor warned me about you – you sold your soul to the biologists." I was tempted to reply, "Well, I didn't sell it cheap!" Indeed, I have had very good terms of trade and learned a lot from the biologists, and from a lot of other people, too. My little book, *Evolutionary Economics*, is a plea to the economics profession to learn from anybody they can learn from.[16]

I have long been interested in welfare economics and in the last decade or so my interests have expanded to what might be called a general "normative analysis": what do we mean when we say that "things" – that is, a particular set or subset of the world – are going from bad to better rather than from bad to worse? The idea that human evaluations cannot be studied by scholarly methods seems to me ridiculous.[17] They are an extremely important part of the social system. No decision is possible without them. Their formation and dynamics should be treated very seriously. I have just finished a little book on the subject of human betterment which has still to find a publisher. A prominent publisher with whom I have published a number of books said they thought it was a subject in which nobody had any interest. If so, it is a sad commentary on our times.

If my life philosophy can be summed up in a sentence, it is that I believe that there is such a thing as human betterment – a magnificent, multidimensional, complex structure – a cathedral of the mind – and I think human decisions should be judged by the extent to which they promote it. This involves seeing the world as a total system[18] (the title of another book I have just finished, tied into my interest in general systems). It involves seeing economics as an important part of the total social system, but certainly no more than a third of it, for we have to deal with threat systems and integrative systems. On the whole I think the threat system, beyond a certain necessary minimum, is inimical.[19]

Kenneth E. Boulding is Distinguished Professor of Economics, Emeritus, and Research Associate, Institute of Behavioral Science, at the University of Colorado at Boulder.

[16] Kenneth E. Boulding, *Evolutionary Economics* (New York: Praeger, 1981).
[17] Kenneth E. Boulding, *Human Betterment* (Beverly Hills, Calif.: Sage, 1985).
[18] Kenneth E. Boulding, *The World as a Total System* (Beverly Hills, Calif.: Sage, 1985).
[19] Kenneth E. Boulding, *Three Faces of Power* (Newbury Park, Calif.: Sage 1989).

KARL BRUNNER

My Quest for Economic Knowledge

The topic I have been asked to write about may invite an elaboration of a "philosophy," in the sense of an explicit and encompassing orientation. But another sense expressed by the road I have travelled in life seems more relevant for my purpose. The ideas and decisions that shape the meandering of one's path reveal, beyond the circumstances encountered, the basic attitudes and orientations of one's life.

The origins set at least the initial segment of one's life and affect some of one's attitudes and ideas. My parents descended from the "lower orders" of society. My mother was born into the family of a peasant and factory worker in the western Jura Mountains along the Swiss–French border. My father grew up in the Toggenburg, a mountain valley in eastern Switzerland, as the tenth child of a very small textile merchant who travelled around the villages and little towns in the hill country. Both parents emigrated as teenagers to Russia in order to escape their local poverty and confinement. My father eventually managed to study mathematics and astronomy at the Swiss Institute of Technology in Zürich. Astronomy had already attracted his interest as a teenager and dominated his dreams and hopes. Confrontation with reality destroyed those dreams. Still, late in life, he was appointed professor of astronomy at the Swiss Institute of Technology. My love of books and ideas I derived from my father, who encouraged my reading at an early age. Resilience, persistence, and determination I inherited from my mother.

After an indifferent performance in high school, I entered the university in 1934 with a sense of liberation and joy. Thus began a very new phase in my life. It was a time of intellectual awakening and growing intellectual excitement. It was also a time of wondering and questioning what to do with my life. I searched for an avenue that would always remain a challenge. Concern about a safe career was overshadowed by my dream of being involved in the pursuit of ideas. It was entirely unclear to me how this could be achieved in the severely confined circumstances of Swiss society. My immediate problem was a choice of fields. Essentially by chance, I encountered economics. That settled my course. This choice was not motivated by any concern for solving so-called social problems by appeal to God, History, or the State. The major social and political influences in my family reflected a tradition committed to individual liberty with opportunities to shape one's own life. My move to economics expressed an entirely different and deep urge. The "human animal" and human society attracted me with an overpowering fascination. The events evolving north of the Rhine River stirred me and many other young Swiss, and I pondered and worried about it. It was my desire to understand the human riddle, considered in the context of human society, that made me eventually settle upon economics as my lifetime pursuit. I do not really know why I felt that economics could satisfy my dominant urge. At the time there were no good grounds for my belief or my decision. But in retrospect, I do know that my belief turned out to be correct and my decision right. The same urge also shaped a good part of my professional interests to the last segment of my life. At the same time, I made the second of the two fundamental decisions. I met my future wife and from that moment on evolved a close companionship for fifty-one years. The loving but not uncritical support that I received from my wife decisively shaped my life.

In the winter of 1936–37 I registered for one year at the London School of Economics for wider exposure. A new world opened up as I encountered books and names I had never heard about at the University of Zürich. I spent most of my time in the library reading widely. This was my first experience of modern economic analysis and I enjoyed it. It made me feel that I might be on the right track. But it also posed a problem. After resuming my studies at the University of Zürich in October 1938, with a delay resulting from military service, it gradually occurred to me that I could not expect to acquire an understanding of economics from the professors at the university. This recognition convinced me that I had to lay out my own course of learning. For this purpose I had to rely on library books. My ignorance and the absence of any guidance, however, created some difficulties. Much of my time was wasted with irrelevant or poor selections of literature. Early in 1939 I approached one of the professors to discuss a topic for my doctoral dissertation. In order to impose on myself the task of digging deeply into mainstream English and American literature, I proposed "Investigations in Anglo-Saxon Theory of International Trade." Progress on my thesis was much delayed by the war. But I managed to finish it by the end of 1942.

At this stage a new phase opened in my life. A job had to be found. My ultimate dream confronted its first hard test. There were long arguments with my father. I tried, and failed, to explain to him why I did not care for just any safe job. There were at the time no avenues for young people to pursue academic or intellectual interests. The faculty consisted only of full professors (ordinarius) or associate professors (extraordinarius). Those with a teaching appointment of any sort had to be independently wealthy or employed full time in the government or private sector. They had, quite generally, no time or opportunity to engage in serious intellectual pursuits.

The issue was ultimately resolved when I took a job in the Economics Department of the Swiss National Bank. Within a few months I understood that this department was a blind alley where one grew old peacefully by not ever writing or saying anything substantial, particularly not about monetary problems. The job gave me an opportunity, however, to acquaint myself with some interesting policy problems. Special assignments from the president's office allowed me to study in detail the minutes of the policymaking group and other internal documents. This information contributed to the evolution of my thinking on matters of economic policy. An examination of the detailed policy record with the supporting arguments convinced me that self-declared practical men of affairs frequently are, without seeming to realize it, ardent theorists. The minutes showed that evaluations and actions resulted from a dominant conception about monetary affairs. In order to understand the responses of policy to specific events and problems, we need first to understand the "theory" guiding that policy, i.e., the policymakers' ruling conception or vision of their segment of the world. I applied this recognition twenty years later in a study of Federal Reserve policymaking developed jointly with Allan H. Meltzer. During the 1930s and 1940s, the Swiss National Bank managed to combine a real bills doctrine, enlarged to admit Treasury bills, with an emphatic commitment to a gold standard with a large gold reserve and a quantity theory based on note circulation.

There was more to learn, however. This experience initiated a slow erosion of my implicit faith in the public interest theory, or goodwill theory, of public agencies. The final result of the process, interrupted for many years by other work, surfaced to extensive and explicit attention thirty years later. The question arose in my mind why Central Bankers held to their particular beliefs and why they generally avoided pondering and assessing the problems associated with their conceptions. A study of the crises and problems confronting these policymakers over time revealed that no serious attempt had ever been made to understand the issues in some relevant mode beyond the clichés of the public market.

Late in 1944 it was time to move on. A short interlude followed. In April 1945 I joined a research institute at the University of St. Gall. I was also appointed lecturer. This appointment could have been the basis of a permanent career at this university leading from the habilitation thesis to "Privat-Dozent" and finally professor, provided that I would play the game right. But I did not. The problem centered around the quality of our work. It seemed to me, and in retrospect I still maintain this position, that our endeavors at empirical research remained, at the very best, very amateurish and journalistic, with a very meager and dubious economic content. I recognized the problem, but because of my inadequate experience I failed to offer a solution. My suggestion to invite an experienced scholar from the United States was coldly received. It was unavoidable that I disrupted the prevailing sense of satisfaction and posed a problem. My discharge came in March 1948. Thirty-five years later I received an honorary degree from the same university.

The prospects of following my dreams seemed at this stage very somber indeed. There simply appeared no avenue for my hopes. But I rather quickly found a position at the Watch Chamber of Commerce in La Chaux de Fonds, the center of the Swiss watch industry. Some interesting and real problems required my attention: the two-tier exchange rate system prevailing at the time in Switzerland and the Trade Charter, a forerunner of GATT, under discussion at an international conference in Havana.

Amid the uncertain pressures and murky future, some friends banded together for systematic learning and discussion. We met every Saturday afternoon in a quiet coffeehouse in Zürich. We discussed chapter by chapter, section by section, Keynes' *General Theory*. These discussion prepared me for a critical reexamination of Keynesian theory some years later. The important point, however, was that this study group helped me to maintain my hope of finding some way out, somewhere. By the end of the war I was wondering whether I should emigrate to the United

States. The thought grew while I was in St. Gall and became definite with my dismissal. I applied to the Rockefeller Foundation, which offered a special program for European scholars. A fellowship was granted, and in September my wife and I moved to the United States. We sensed the beginning of a new life, and so it was. After one semester in Harvard, we stayed for one and a half years at the University of Chicago, interrupted by a long summer's visit to the University of California at Berkeley. The two years under the fellowship were a turning point. They were also years of confusion and search bearing on the nature of my work in economics.

I joined the (then) Cowles Commission for Research in Economics as a guest. My purpose was to acquaint myself with econometrics and the application of mathematics to economic analysis. I enjoyed a good working relation with Carl Christ and Harry Markowitz. Carl Christ and I worked together through Samuelson's *Foundations of Economic Analysis*, and subsequently Harry Markowitz and I studied von Neumann–Morgenstern's *Theory of Games*. These sessions, occurring over many months, were very useful. There were also regular seminars at the commission with an increasingly mathematical flavor. Beyond the commission, of course, was the Department of Economics – a somewhat different world. I became exposed to a group around Aaron Director, Frank Knight, and Milton Friedman. The group met with some regularity for discussions ranging over a wide array of problems. The thrust of these differed radically from that of the seminars at the Cowles Commission. They emphatically advanced the relevance of economic analysis as an important means of understanding the world, in a manner that I had never encountered before. I received a clear sense of economics as an empirical science beyond the formal exercises and statistical apparatus of econometrics, which in my experience often obscured the basic cognitive problem. I found this both confusing and strangely appealing. In contrast, many papers presented at the Cowles Commission seminars and their discussion puzzled me deeply. What the criteria of a good paper and an interesting problem really were remained quite obscure.

The issues raised in my mind during this period were not resolved by the time I left Chicago and joined the faculty of UCLA in September 1951. One question, however, became clearer: What is the nature of the intellectual game we actually play or might pursue in economics? So my search for an understanding of how to understand the world continued. Two things ultimately contributed clarity. The first was my many discussions with Armen A. Alchian, who, engaged in a similar search, was strongly conditioned by his prior basic training in statistics. The second was my encounter with Reichenbach's *Prediction and Experience*, which I read avidly. There followed a period of substantial investment in logic and the philosophy of science. I began to feel more at ease with a growing understanding of the only meaningful purpose of my intellectual activities in economics. The nature of the cognitive process gradually emerged in clear lines. This included an understanding of the structure of hypotheses and theories, the search for a useful and adequate formulation, the role of a formal apparatus, the evaluation of the intellectual product and the relevant criteria, and finally the relation between econometric practice and the relevant cognitive procedure and criteria.

The immediate victim of this phase of understanding the cognitive process was my Keynesian conviction, which I had developed by the mid-1940s. There seemed to me very little ground for accepting this theory. It failed miserably, most particularly its basic version expressed by the Keynesian cross, to explain the postwar transition and the longer-term postwar experience. My "liberation" from Keynesian conceptions revived my earlier interests in monetary analysis. In the past thirty years, I have allocated a substantial portion of my time and effort to work in this field. This phase opened with a project investigating the money supply process. This period also marked the beginning of a long and fruitful association with Allan Meltzer that continues to be an important part of my life. Our innumerable discussions on wide-ranging subjects have shaped my thinking over the almost thirty years we have worked together and sharpened my sense of the issues. It should come as no surprise that, to a large extent, our views have merged into a similar pattern. Our collaboration began with my suggestion that Allan examine the French money supply process. It appeared to me that this topic offered a good choice for a doctoral dissertation. My interest in money supply actually awoke in 1953–54. Reviewing the literature and a large number of textbooks, it struck me that there was no coherent hypothesis of the money supply process. The usual story of bank credit expansion was, of course, standard material. But it failed to satisfy the requirements of a useful hypothesis. It offered no propositions about the determination of the money stock or the interaction between money, credit, and interest rates with a full account of the nature of the process.

This failure was somewhat remarkable in view of the many assertions concerning the money supply process advanced by the profession and in the public market. My attention was increasingly directed toward developing some empirical hypotheses about the money supply process. It seemed particularly desirable to construct an analysis yielding empirical propositions about the relative importance of the monetary authorities, as well as the public's and the banks' behavior in the short- and long-run evolution of money stock and bank credit. A completely specified framework would also clarify the nature of "reverse causation," i.e., the conditions under which the observed correlation between money and income expresses a causal direction from income to money. It seemed rarely understood that this is not inherent but results from specific institutional choices. Once the conditions of reverse causation were elaborated, its relevance could be systematically assessed. More generally, a useful money supply theory would facilitate our understanding of different institutional arrangements. We would wish to know whether a shrinking membership of commercial banks in the Federal Reserve system actually impaired the efficacy of monetary policy, as was asserted by the Federal Reserve authorities over many years. Similarly, we would expect that an adequate money supply theory would offer useful answers to questions bearing on financial regulation and deregulation. Finally, we would wish to determine the degree of controllability of money stock and monetary growth. These problems motivated my work in money supply theory pursued jointly with Allan Meltzer. The framework we developed over the years offered answers to all these questions.

In the summer of 1963 Allan and I were approached to prepare a study on Federal Reserve policymaking for Congressman Patman's Committee on Banking and Currency. We gladly accepted an obligation that seemed closely associated with our projects. This work very much influenced my subsequent views and thinking about the behavior of the Central Bank. The examination of monetary policymaking revived an idea I had developed during my short association with the Swiss National Bank. In order to understand the behavior of the Federal Reserve authorities, we need to know their dominant conception, i.e., their theory about the process they wish to influence. This knowledge, even though not sufficient, is certainly necessary to understand the Fed's policymaking behavior. It needs to be supplemented, however, by some knowledge of the Fed's objectives. This second dimension was not included in our study and captured our attention much later. We still were influenced at the time, as were most economists in my experience, by a goodwill, or public interest, theory of government. We were inclined to believe that the Fed would act in the correct way once it properly understood the nature of the process confronting it. Our work made us realize that the Fed's views exhibited little resemblance to economic analysis and were actually in conflict with it. There was no trace in the professional literature, particularly in the textbooks, that prepared us for the encounter with the Fed's view. This view centered at the time on free reserves, i.e., the difference between excess reserves and bank borrowing from the Fed. Free reserves formed the centerpiece of the causal nexus linking monetary policy with bank credit. An increase in free reserves meant, in this view, an expansionary event raising the rate of expansion of bank credit. A reduction in free reserves was interpreted as a contractive move.

This conception determined the choice of free reserves as an indicator guiding the interpretation of monetary affairs. Its frequent use as a target guiding the authorities' actions also followed from this basic conception. We showed that this conception had emerged in the 1920s and had prevailed with some evolution into the 1960s. It explains the puzzlingly large increase in reserve requirements in 1936–37. We also demonstrated that the Fed's policy pronouncements, according to the Record of Policy, were significantly positively correlated with the movement of free reserves. In contrast, these policy pronouncements were significantly negatively correlated with actual behavior. Viewing free reserves as a crucial link between monetary policy and bank credit caused a systematic misinterpretation of monetary affairs and monetary policy. Restrictive policies were frequently sold to the public as expansionary moves, as in the early 1930s, in 1949, and in 1960, and expansionary policies metamorphosed into restrictive policies. To a large extent, the failure of the Federal Reserve can be attributed to such misinterpretations. By the late 1960s, the ruling conception was modified. Elements of a possible transition became visible in the early 1960s among the policymakers. But important fragments of the older ideas have reemerged in the past eleven years, particularly the contractive interpretation of "borrowed reserves" in contrast to non-borrowed reserves.

The Federal Reserve study alerted me to an important policy problem rather neglected in the professional literature, i.e., the indicator and the target problem. The indicator problem involves the optimal choice of a one-dimensional scale guiding the interpretation of policy actions in terms of their consequences on the pace of output. In contrast, the target involves the optimal choice of an observable magnitude guiding the regular adjustment of policy actions. Neither problem is contrived. Any careful observer of the Fed's tactical procedures necessarily encounters these problems. We also encounter them as an inherent component of all discussions, which typically characterize policies in classificatory terms (easy, tight) or in comparative terms (easier, tighter). In the first case we need to determine a unidimensional binary classification and in the second case a unidimensional ordinal scale (Brunner and Meltzer, 1967). The problem was generally neglected. Many economists argued that we need to look at "many things" or "everything." Both classificatory and comparative statements presuppose, however, a unidimensional scale. In the absence of a scale there is no justification for the statements typically made.

The nature of monetary transmissions caught my attention by the late 1950s. My concern about the nature of the transmission mechanism made me recognize the limitations of the IS/LM model. This paradigm telescopes the array of assets into two groups, money and "bonds." Three interpretations of this paradigmatic approach are possible. The first asserts that money substitutes only with "bonds." Real capital remains beyond the substitution nexus surrounding money. This means that the interest rate on financial assets forms the crucial link between monetary impulses, on the one hand, and economic activity and price level, on the other. The second interpretation accepts that money substitutes over the whole range of assets. This array is reduced to two assets in order to fit an analysis with a single portfolio equation. The reduction is achieved with the assumption that financial and real assets are perfect substitutes. The third interpretation also accepts the general substitution nexus of all assets but denies the perfect substitutability assumption. This assumption is replaced by a restriction on the range of admissible applications of the analysis. It needs to be confined to events and episodes with small variations in relative market conditions between financial and real assets compared with the movements of the major phenomenon under investigation. The first two interpretations involve hypotheses that I always judged to be quite untenable on empirical grounds. The third interpretation involves no potentially falsifiable hypothesis. It offers a rule guiding the domain of useful application of the paradigm. The problem encountered here bears on the limited range of use, which excludes all but extraordinary events. Moreover, the monetary system occurs in a severely emasculated form. Issues bearing on the interaction between money and credit market, or problems of deregulation and regulation of the financial industry, cannot be subsumed under the paradigm and cannot be effectively clarified within this framework. Any policy analysis executed with the aid of this framework could hardly expect to cope usefully with the relevant problems encountered. The Federal Reserve cannot control interest rates. It faces a whole structure of interest rates exhibiting different responses to shifting mixtures of perceived transitory and permanent shocks. In my judgment we clearly required an alternative view of the transmission mechanism.

The theme was initiated around 1960 and was subsequently elaborated in a long series of papers mostly written with Allan H. Meltzer. My review of the report prepared by the Commission on Money and Credit (Brunner, 1961) offered an outline of the alternative analysis. The broader view of the transmission mechanism emphasizing an imperfect substitutability between all assets, between assets and their services, and between assets and output substantially modifies major propositions of the IS/LM model augmented with the Phillips relation. In particular, this analysis changed the nature of monetary shocks influencing output or price level. Money stock and accustomed monetary growth exert little effect on output. Both are mostly absorbed by the price level. However, perceived deviations from accustomed growth affect current output. Unavoidably, such deviations remain more or less transitory events. Persistent deviations induce revisions of the accustomed growth rate.

Among other issues in monetary theory that attracted our attention were the impulse or shock problem, the interpretation of normal output, and the use (or existence) of money in transactions. Twenty years ago we accepted the thesis of a dominant shock pattern in the form of monetary shocks. In contrast, today we accept a thesis emphasizing unpredictably shifting combinations of shocks.

Until recently the use of money was taken for granted. Monetary analysis offered no explanation for the existence of money. Long discussions with Armen Alchian in the early 1960s contributed to our thinking. We understood that information and transaction costs are necessary conditions for the phenomenon to occur. The basic idea was subsequently developed in a paper (Brunner and Meltzer, 1971). This work initiated a more general interest bearing on the emergence and role of social institutions.

Several issues attracted my attention over the years as a result of my continued interest in the philosophy of science and logic. Milton Friedman's (1953) article questioning the emphasis on the "realism" of assumptions generated some heated objections. Friedman's logical instincts led him on the right track. But his arguments concentrated on metaphors and illustrations and neglected the core of the essentially logical issue. The objections also missed the logical issue. This situation motivated my attention (Brunner, 1969). The term "assumption" was used by economists in very different ways. The precise logical characterization of these different uses of the term showed, moreover, that in no case was it possible to infer the confirmation of a hypothesis (or theory) from the confirmation of "its assumption."

The cognitive process represented by econometric practice presented another important issue. I felt increasing concern about questionable logical aspects of much of our practice. The language used to convey the results of an empirical investigation was frequently quite misleading. Categorical conclusions or objections were offered that required highly corroborated hypotheses for justification. Such hypotheses were sometimes not even formulated and many times not evaluated against serious alternative contenders. The large-scale econometric models presented some special problems. The degree of freedom problem typically confronting such models was usually resolved by resorting to a set of instrumental variables. But each choice of such a set imposed an implicit class of unspecified hypotheses. Such an intellectual game was, in my judgment, more nearly numerology than science (Brunner, 1973).

Finally, most of our disputes involve systematic alternative hypotheses, but much of our work seems satisfied to show significant inconsistency with the null (i.e., chance) hypothesis. There is, of course, a deeper layer of questions bearing on possibly inherent difficulties in developing real tests. I leave this aside and consider some methodological issues posed by the emergence of the new classical macroeconomics. Rational expectations analysis generalized Marshak's rationale for structural formulation and estimation. The sensitivity of the structure to changes in policy regime suggested the need for a deeper level of invariance. "Technology" represented by a production function and tastes seemed to offer the required anchor. Thus emerged the methodological theme that all analysis should be derived from such "first principles." This position, however, involves two major fallacies. First, we should recognize that there are no "first principles." This is a Cartesian illusion. There is no rock bottom, neither of certainty nor of invariance. The general point has been effectively made by Sir Karl Popper. Jensen and Meckling (1979) demonstrated in our particular case that the production function is not invariant with respect to institutional changes. Moreover, the production function involves more than technology. Optimizing behavior is already at work shaping its form. Second, the methodological thesis seemed also to have convinced new classical macroeconomists that all work need start from "first principles," anything else being unacceptable. Such methodological legislation is a travesty of science. We possess much useful knowledge, particularly in medicine and even in economics, about empirical regularities without an adequate underlying theory. The advice of new classical macroeconomists to throw this knowledge away makes no sense. The methodological thesis supplemented with the requirement of full "rigorization" may cause them to box themselves into a corner that omits the most relevant problems.

Some unattended issues inherited from the Federal Reserve study kept surfacing off and on. They centered around the questions: Why do Central Banks behave the way they do, why do they accept the strategies and tactical procedures actually observed, why do they generally oppose any pre-commitment, and why do they generally exhibit a high level of determined ignorance about the processes addressed by their activity? These questions generally destroyed the more or less unconsciously held goodwill theory of political institutions. In the early 1970s, these questions led to some deeper questions. It occurred to me that we could explain the major differences in our approach to political institutions in terms of two alternative hypotheses about man supplemented by two alternative conceptions of justice. Two traditions compete in the social sciences for our attention (Brunner and Meckling, 1977; Brunner, 1987). Both traditions originated in the eighteenth century, one in Scotland with Mandeville, Ferguson, and Smith, the other in France with the Enlightenment. The first evolved into the core of economic analysis with the hypothesis of a resourceful, evaluating, and maximizing man. A crucial element of this hypothesis is the proper interpretation of self-interested (not identical with egotistic) behavior and the biological basis of this behavior. This approach implies in particular that the "human animal's" basic disposition, his self-interest, operates independently of specific institutions. They operate in commercial contexts and in contexts of political institutions without private property and profits. Differences in institutional arrangements imply very different specific expressions of self-interested behavior. The French tradition became in the hands of Marx and Durkheim the sociological model of this century, which probably influences most of the intelligentsia and also a number of economists' thinking about social problems.

The sociological model sees man as a passive agent of society. Basic human nature is quite malleable and can be shaped by social engineering. The two hypotheses yield very different implications about the working of political institutions. The "Scottish hypothesis" generally determines a constitutionalist approach to government imposing clear and severe constraints on the government's agenda. The sociological model encourages and justifies an open-ended agenda for the state and its agencies, including the judiciary. It appears that much of the detail of our disputes bearing on questions of political economy can thus be explained in terms of the two competing hypotheses. They are, however, not quite sufficient. They are reinforced by suitable notions of justice, the outcome patterns, and the process view. The criteria of justice in the first case pertains to a particular pattern of outcome of the social process (e.g., some preferred income distribution). The criteria refer in the second case to characteristics of the social process. There is an important relation between the perception of man and the conception of justice. The Scottish hypothesis cannot be reconciled with the outcome pattern view, whereas the sociological model offers a rational underpinning justifying the choice of an outcome pattern as criterion of justice.

These issues also bear on two fundamentally different approaches to economic policy. The conflict between the two approaches covers a wide range including monetary and regulatory policy. One approach emphasizes the choice of institutional arrangements and general rules of procedures. The other, in contrast, addresses detailed and contingent actions specific to time and place. The dispute is clearly visible in the field of monetary policy. Discretionary policy and pre-commitment directed to longer-term consideration and predictability continue to be argued. The central issue in this debate often seems somewhat obscured. It involves the hypothesis about man and the information he may command. Human nature and the reliable information at hand crucially condition the working and consequences of different political institutions. Advocacy of activist and discretionary policy is a rational consequence of the sociological model of man supplemented with full and reliable information about the structure of the relevant processes. For many years I have argued that these conditions do not hold. I had concluded that the sociological model, particularly in its form as the public interest, or goodwill, theory of government, is empirically untenable. Moreover, the information requirement imposed by an activist policy can never be satisfied. The social process continuously generates and disseminates new information. The resulting modification of perceived opportunities induces revisions of optimal behavior patterns, and thus variations in the economic structure over time. The best we can achieve is the choice of institutional arrangements that minimize uncertainty and offer as many women and men as possible a chance to shape their own lives.

The human spirit is a remarkable phenomenon. The soaring spires and vaults of a Gothic cathedral may be seen as a pure and beautiful expression of this spirit. They seem also to symbolize the human search for knowledge. But we should remember that these beautiful expressions of an aspiring spirit were frequently motivated by less than noble motives. The Bible tells us that grubby life persisted even around the holiest place of ancient Israel. We are thus reminded that our intellectual pursuits are not separated from "society" in the purity of a monastery or in Hermann Hesse's world of the "Glassbead Game." Intellectual life remains embedded in a social and political context. Temptations and incentives reaching beyond purely cognitive criteria thus shape the behavior of all participants in the intellectual game. It also follows that intellectual pursuits are tied to institutional arrangements that condition its character. It occurred to me in the early 1960s that it would be interesting to examine the effect of different arrangements on the patterns of intellectual life, and I observed the role of institutions in our profession. This observation motivated me to develop a regular series of conferences. The idea was initiated in 1964 at UCLA. This endeavor evolved by 1973 into a joint venture with Allan Meltzer: the Carnegie–Rochester Conference on Public Policy. The Konstanz Conference on Monetary Theory and Monetary Policy began in 1970, and in 1974 the annual Interlaken Seminar on Analysis and Ideology. The latter was deliberately planned as a forum for the "imperial" application of "economic analysis" over the whole range of the social sciences. The development of two professional journals, the *Journal of Money, Credit, and Banking* and, subsequently, the *Journal of Monetary Economics*, was similarly motivated. One consideration, among others, was the desire to offer alternative opportunities to younger, not quite established professionals and to prevent a closed shop. The Shadow Open Market Committee, jointly founded in 1973 with Allan

Meltzer, was deliberately set in another mode. It is a small, homogeneous group designed to articulate publicly our concerns about the drift in monetary, fiscal, and international economic policy. Though it had no direct effect on policymaking, we were gratified to see the interest it stimulated.

The problem of creating a "good society" was not at the forefront of my search in life: a search for understanding and insights. But in the last stretch of my path it has become a natural consequence of the work and ideas I have pursued over many years. It will occupy my mind as long as it continues to function and my body supports it. My fascinating search, initiated more than fifty years ago, was greatly influenced by many people from whom I learned many things. Life offered me thus a singular chance.

Karl Brunner, at the time of his death, was Fred H. Gowen Professor of Economics, and Director, Center for Research in Government Policy and Business, William E. Simon Graduate School of Business Administration, University of Rochester.

REFERENCES

Brunner, Karl, "The Report of the Commission on Money and Credit," *Journal of Political Economy*, 69, December 1961, pp. 605–20.

" 'Assumptions' and the Cognitive Quality of Theories," *Synthese*, 20, No. 4, 1969, pp. 501–25.

"Review: Economic Models of Cyclical Behavior (Bert G. Hickman)," *Journal of Economic Literature*, 11, No. 3, 1973, pp. 927–33.

"The Perception of Man and the Conception of 'Society': Two Approaches to Understanding Society," *Economic Inquiry*, 25, July 1987, pp. 367–88.

Brunner, Karl, and William H. Meckling, "The Perception of Man and the Conception of Government," *Journal of Money, Credit, and Banking*, 9, No. 1, Part 1, February 1977, pp. 70–85.

Brunner, Karl, and Allan H. Meltzer, "The Meaning of Monetary Indicators," *Monetary Process and Policy: A Symposium*, George Howrich, ed. Homewood, Ill.: Irwin, 1967.

"The Uses of Money: Money in the Theory of an Exchange Economy," *American Economic Review*, 61, No. 5, December 1971, pp. 784–805.

Friedman, Milton, "Methodology of Positive Economics," *Essays in Positive Economics*. Chicago: University of Chicago Press, 1953.

Jensen, Michael C., and William H. Meckling, "Rights and Production Functions: An Application to Labor-managed Firms and Codetermination," *Journal of Business*, 52, No. 4, October 1979, pp. 469–506.

JAMES M. BUCHANAN

From the Inside Looking Out

INTRODUCTION

In the early 1970s, I received a short and strange note from a woman whom I had met at a European conference. In the note she asked me, quite straightforwardly, to outline my philosophy of life in a single paragraph not more than a half-page in length. The challenge was sufficient to make me respond, and my outline summary was expanded into, first, a lecture and, later, a brief chapter in a book.[1] I now interpret that response to be an adequate statement of what I should call my "public philosophy," a statement that requires little or no emendation after a decade's ripening. In this essay I respond differently. Partly in order to differentiate the product and partly to meet what seem the particular

[1] See James M. Buchanan, "Criteria for a Free Society: Definition, Diagnosis, and Prescription," in *Freedom in Constitutional Contract* (College Station: Texas A&M University Press, 1977), pp. 287–99.

98

desires of the editor of this project, I shall here offer a statement of my "private philosophy" or, rather, a set of statements about separate attributes of my personal stance before my own gods.

I shall limit the autobiographical narrative, because I have traced out portions of my life story in two previous papers.[2] This essay is personal rather than autobiographical. That is to say, I shall describe how I look out at the world beyond, and not attempt to look on myself as an object of narrative exposition. There is a sense in which this sort of private or personal statement of a philosophy is almost the intellectual opposite of autobiography.

I hope to treat several distinct features of my window on the world. In the next section, I discuss my approach to scholarship and its responsibility. In the third section I move on to examine the mixture of scientist and artist that I have always felt myself to be. A natural follow-on involves the issues of normative and positive analysis, which I examine in the fourth section. The section following is more autobiographical and surveys my role as an outsider. Finally, I respond to questions of current motivation as well as more general questions of ultimate purpose.

IS IT MY TASK TO SAVE THE WORLD?

I shall commence this section with a citation from Frank H. Knight:

> It is intellectually impossible to believe that the individual can have any influence to speak of,... on the course of history. But it seems to me that to regard this as an ethical difficulty involves a complete misconception of the social–moral problem.... I find it impossible to give meaning to an ethical obligation on the part of the individual to improve society.
>
> The disposition of an individual, under liberalism, to take upon himself such a responsibility seems to be an exhibition of intellectual and *moral* conceit...; it is *un*ethical. Ethical–social change must come about through a genuine moral consensus among individuals meeting on a level of genuine equality and mutuality and not with any one in the role of cause and the rest in that of effect, of one the "potter" and the others as "clay." ("Intellectual Confusion on Morals and Economics," *Ethics*)

I have long felt a strong affinity for Knight's position. But I have found it difficult to go beyond affirmation of agreement and to mount a persuasive supportive argument. We face squarely the question: If no individual assumes responsibility for improving society, how can society ever improve, other than through the forces of evolutionary change? I

---

[2] See my "Better Than Plowing," *Banco Nazionale del Lavoro Quarterly Review*, 159 (December 1986), pp. 359–75; and my "Born-Again Economist," in W. Breit, ed., *Lives of the Laureates: Ten Nobel Economists* (Cambridge, Mass.: MIT Press, 1990), pp. 163–80.

am on record as rejecting acquiescence before the forces of a cultural evolution. I have stated, on numerous occasions, that we have a moral obligation to think that we can constructively design and implement reform in social arrangements.

Any appearance of paradox vanishes if care is taken to read and to understand what Frank Knight says in his statement. He is not advancing a logic of rationally grounded abstention from discussion about changes in the rules of social order. He is defining the limits or constraints under which any individual must place himself as he enters into such discussion. The moral conceit that bothers Knight arises when any individual, or group, presumes to take on the responsibility for others, independently of their expressed agreement in a setting of mutuality and reciprocity. The underlying principle is indeed a simple one: Each person counts equally. And even if this principle counters observed empirical reality in terms of measurable criteria, adherence to the principle must remain relatively absolute, even on an acknowledged "as if" basis.

This principle has been a central element in my own approach to political economy. I have always thought it my task to develop and create ideas and to enter these ideas into the discussion matrix. Once this step is taken, my task is done. I have felt, and feel, no moral obligation to promulgate my own ideas, or those of others. In this, I differ sharply from many of my colleagues in economics. I have never been didactically motivated, despite reasonable success in teaching, especially at the graduate level. For me, utility enhancement stems from working out ideas for myself and with sufficient clarity that enables me to present a coherent and aesthetically satisfying argument. Ultimate publication reconfirms initial judgments in this respect. If my ideas succeed in persuading others to view the social world in a fashion similar to my own, I secure secondary utility gains. But if my ideas fail to persuade, and the implied reforms in social arrangements do not occur, my private utility losses are no greater than those of persons who do not enter the discussion. I do not, in any sense, accept responsibility for the results of the interaction in which I am only one among many participants. I cannot, as Knight suggests, move the world unaided, and it is morally arrogant of me to imagine myself in a position of power sufficient to enable me to act unilaterally.

Respect for the individual, as one among many participants in the social network of interaction, imposes a necessary humility on the social scientist. This humility is a stance that must be deliberately maintained. The natural scientist faces no comparable choice; he works within the constraints imposed by the almost total exogeneity of the subject matter that he explores. The social scientist must acknowledge the endogeneity of the structure of social interaction, at least within broad limits. But the endogeneity applies to the whole community of participants, including the scientist. Imagined, and potentially realizable, structures of social interaction that are alternatives to that which is observed to exist are within the set of those that are made feasible by physical and natural limits, including human nature. The social scientist defaults on his duty if he fails to model structures of interaction "that might be." As the social scientist makes predictions about the working properties of imagined alternative structures, he becomes both internally and externally vulnerable in a manner unknown to the natural scientist. Precisely because the direct linkage between observed reality and theories about that reality is abandoned, the discipline imposed by potential testability (falsifiability) is weakened. The social scientist is internally tempted to bias his argument toward structures that reflect his normative values. And even if he succeeds in thwarting this temptation, his critics will charge that he has not done so.

The fact–value distinction so beloved by second-rate methodologists confuses rather than enlightens. The social scientist who predicts "what might be" is not working within the realm of facts that may be observed in historical reality. The often-observed pitiful efforts to milk empirical data to reinforce hypothetical predictions reflect misunderstanding of the whole enterprise.

SCIENCE OR ART?

I have never been attracted to enter the sometimes complex upper reaches of the philosophy of science, and particularly the discussion of "economics as a science." I have not shied away from presenting my own methodological position, which does, indeed, ensure that I remain an outsider in this as in so many other aspects of my endeavors.[3] But discussion among philosophers of science, per se, has always seemed to me to use the natural sciences as a model and to embody a failure to appreciate the distinguishing features of social science, only some of which I noted in the preceding section.

It is precisely because of my conviction that social science is different from natural science that I find myself more sympathetic to the interpretist critique than most of my economist peers, save for a few who locate themselves among modern Austrians. Yet while I am more sympathetic to the criticism, I should insist that the social scientist hold fast to the truth-directed morality of his natural science counterpart.

I can perhaps clarify my position by comparing and contrasting the

---

[3] See my "Positive Economics, Welfare Economics, and Political Economy," *Journal of Law and Economics*, 2 (October 1959), pp. 124–38; and my "What Should Economists Do?" *Southern Economic Journal*, 30 (January 1964), pp. 213–22.

scientist and the artist, with the former described in the role normally assigned to the natural scientist. I return to the exogeneity of the subject matter with which the natural scientist works, the reality that is, independently of his own understanding of its inner workings. The behavior of the scientist is *discovery*; he finds that which exists, and his imaginative talents are deployed in a search process. There is, and should be, no pretense that something new is created.

Consider the artist, however. He is, of course, constrained by the physical limits of his medium, be this paint or stone. But it is totally misleading to model the artist's act as discovery. The artist creates something where there was nothing. Both the act of scientific discovery and the act of artistic creation are intensely private as they are carried out. But the products divide sharply along the public–private dimension, once the acts are done. Scientific discovery is public in the classical sense; once made available to anyone, it can be available to everyone. Artistic creation is available to everyone once it is done; but that which is created may be privately interpreted in many and varied ways.

This comparative sketch should suggest that social science, as an activity, falls somewhere between the two models. Because the social scientist must explore the working properties of imagined alternatives to that which is observed, constrained only by the natural limits of the material with which he works, his activity has elements that are more akin to those that inform the artistic process than the scientific. However, his ultimate motivation matches that of the scientist, not the artist. The social scientist works in the hope that improvement in the processes of social interaction will finally emerge upon agreement both on diagnosis and on effective reform; aesthetic experience plays little role.

My own subdisciplinary prejudices should be evident. Within economics, I look on the efforts of the general equilibrium theorists, even if these efforts are sometimes extended to unnecessarily rarefied abstraction, to be potentially more productive than the works of those empiricists who behave as if the reality of social interaction embodies an exogeneity comparable to that of the physical world.

NORMATIVE AND POSITIVE POLITICAL ECONOMY

Critics have charged that my work has been driven by an underlying normative purpose, and by inference, if not directly, they have judged me to be mildly subversive. As I noted earlier, anyone who models interaction structures that might be is likely to be accused of biasing analysis toward those alternatives that best meet his personal value standards. Whether or not my efforts have exhibited bias in this sense is for others to determine. I shall acknowledge that I always work within a self-imposed constraint that some may choose to call a normative one. I have no interest in structures of social interaction that are nonindividualist in the potter–clay analogy mentioned in the earlier citation from Frank Knight. That is to say, I do not extend my own analysis to alternatives that embody the *rule* of any person or group of persons over other persons or group of persons. If this places my work in some stigmatized normative category, so be it.

The individualist element in my vision of social reality, actual or potential, has been an important component of my substantive criticism of the work of others in political economy. I have remained unable either to share in the enthusiasm for the social welfare function of formal welfare economics or to participate putatively in proffering advice to a presumed benevolently despotic government. There are at least three distinguishable sources of my criticism of orthodox political economy. First, I have been influenced by Frank Knight and by F. A. Hayek in their insistence that the problem of social order is not scientific in the standard sense. Second, I was greatly influenced by Knut Wicksell's admonition that economists cease acting as if government were a benevolent despot. Third, I rejected, very early in my thinking, the orthodox economist's elevation of allocative efficiency as an independent standard of evaluation.

These three sources seem internally consistent, and properly combined, they have provided me with my own window on the political economy. From this window, I found it relatively easy to mount criticism of much of the conventional wisdom. There seemed to be no shortage of matters to be straightened out, and I have been quite happy to leave to others the classification into normative or positive categories.

Wicksell's was perhaps the most significant influence, but without Knight's teaching and without my conversion to a catallactic perspective, Wicksell's message might not have been so compelling to me. However, once Wicksell's advice is heeded, once we acknowledge that governmental or political decisions are themselves produced by an interaction of persons acting in various roles, the political economist necessarily must extend analysis to the process of interaction and to the relation between process and patterns of results. The theory of public choice, at least my own version of this theory, was an almost natural consequence of my absorption of the Wicksellian message.[4]

Conceptualization of political reality as emergent from the interaction of many persons immediately suggests that patterns of results depend on the rules or institutions within which behavior takes place. Constitutional

[4] The relationship between the precursory ideas of Wicksell and later developments in public choice theory was the subject of my Nobel Prize lecture in December 1986. See "The Constitution of Economic Policy," *American Economic Review*, 77 (June 1987), pp. 243–50.

political economy, in both its normative and positive variants, replaces the political economy of policy at center stage. The shift of focus to rules comes quite naturally to the economist who has been exposed to the approach of modern game theory. But concentration on processes rather than outcomes does not fit well within the orthodoxy of political science, the pre-modern origins of which involve idealizations of parliamentary regimes. Despite our expressed intent to model the logical foundations of constitutional democracy, roughly corresponding to the Madisonian enterprise, Gordon Tullock and I found a very mixed reception to our book, *The Calculus of Consent* (1962).

There seemed to be a surprising reluctance by modern social scientists, economists and political scientists alike, to accept the two-stage decision structure that constitutional understanding requires and that all game theorists necessarily adopt. For over a quarter-century, I have found myself trying to clarify the constitutional perspective on policies, and on the economy as well, with demonstrable but quite limited success.

AN OUTSIDER COMES INSIDE

Nonetheless, the dialogue has shifted. "Constitutional economics" or "constitutional political economy" has emerged as an entry in *The New Palgrave*. My own emphasis on the importance of the rules of the social–economic–political game was recognized in the Nobel Prize citation in 1986. No longer could I claim status as a genuine outsider whose efforts continue to be largely ignored by my peers in the academy. Within limits, and despite my stance of relative indifference noted earlier, my ideas are beginning to have consequences. I do not yet know how I shall react when and if specific changes in rules are more or less directly traceable to my influence. I do not welcome becoming an "insider" in any sense, and my own efforts over four decades can be understood only in terms of the outsider image of myself that has been an integral part of my personal luggage.

The outsider appellation explains the somewhat singular type of self-confidence that I have always had to a degree and that has been reinforced over four decades. I have been academically successful, far beyond any plausibly predictable range, more or less "in spite of" my limitations rather than "because of" my capacities. I would never have been really surprised had my work failed to prove acceptable for publication, had my published work been neglected for more than it was, had my career advancement been less rapid, had there been no series of alternative opportunities in the competitive academic environment of the United States, had I not been awarded the Nobel Prize in 1986. I have never felt, nor do I feel today, that there is much that is unique or special about what I have done or what I do, write, and say. My surprise, and this surprise has continued to exist for four decades, is not at all that my own work is relatively neglected; my surprise is, instead, that other economists have failed to acknowledge the simple and the obvious, which is all that I have ever claimed my work to be. In a sense I have felt embarrassed at being placed in the role of telling my far more clever peers that the king really has no clothes.

Why was it my task to point out that economists should postulate some model of policies before proffering policy advice? Why, among the many critics of Arrow's important work in the general impossibility theorem, did it fall on me to point out that the satisfaction of his plausible conditions would amount to political tyranny rather than effective democracy? Why was it necessary for me to demonstrate that classical public debt theory was logically valid, in the face of the Keynesian macroaggregation absurdities? Why was it required to show that genuinely sacrificed opportunities must be measured in a utility dimension? These and other "contributions" attributed to me might not have been made had I worked as an "insider" involved in the complexities of analytical discussion along the heated cutting edges of economics. Such an insider might have been unable to take the comprehensive perspective that my outsider position allowed me to assume, almost as a matter of course.

It is in this respect that I do not especially welcome the increasing academic respectability and popularity of my own ideas. As a critic of prevailing orthodoxies, I had no reason to back up and respond to critics of my constructions, which seemed, in any case, to be triturations of the obvious. As my ideas approach mainstream, at least in some aspects, I find myself being challenged to defend foundational normative sources that I had long considered to be widely shared. The fact that my own acknowledged normative starting points do not seem so widely accepted as I should have expected may possibly account for the apparent oversight of propositions that seemed so obvious to me. In other words, my normative mind-set may be more important than I have ever realized.

WHY NOT SIT IN MY ROCKING CHAIR?

I resist, and resist strongly, any and all efforts to pull me toward positions of advising on this or that policy or cause. I sign no petitions, join no political organizations, advise no party, serve no lobbying effort. Yet the public's image of me, and especially as developed through the media after the Nobel Prize in 1986, is that of a right-wing libertarian zealot who is anti-democratic, anti-egalitarian, and anti-scientific. I am, of course, none of these and am, indeed, the opposites. Properly understood, my position is both democratic and egalitarian, and I am as much a scientist as any of my peers in economics. But I am passionately individualistic, and my emphasis on individual liberty does set me apart from many of my academic colleagues whose mind-sets are mildly elitist and, hence, collectivist. And to these colleagues, I can never be forgiven for having contributed to the development of a subdiscipline, public choice, that has exposed the operation of collectivist political institutions to serious scrutiny for the first time in well over a century.

Why do I continue to work? Why do I not retire gracefully to my mountain farm in Virginia, sit in my front-porch rocking chair, bemused at the follies of the world? Since I have acknowledged that I do not presume to move the world unaided, and that I have no urge to do so, what inner forces drive me? My answer, as adumbrated, is simple and straightforward. I work because I enjoy it! I get utility in ideas, in thinking, in organizing my thoughts, in writing these thoughts in coherent argument, in seeing my words in manuscript and in print. In some real sense, I am a writer who enjoys living in his own world, a world that some critics claim to be fictional but that I defend as feasibly attainable territory. I am also a lecturer, perhaps a century out of date, and I get utility from the receptive feedback for an intellectually competent audience. Here again, my ultimate purpose, either in writing or in lecturing, is not so much to convince readers or listeners of the merits of my argument, but to engage them in ongoing discussion.

Above all, perhaps, I am an intellectual reductionist who seeks to cut through the complexities of argument and to understand points in simple terms and homely examples. As noted earlier, much of my work has been in the form of exposé, and hence of a sort that is rarely welcomed by those who are natural obscurantists.

When all is said, I have faced few genuine choices between work and play because there is really no distinction. My work is my play, and I am surely among the fortunate in this as in so many other aspects of a happy and well-ordered life. I have not been plagued by psychological hangovers that make me try to respond to the "whys" of existence or the "whats" beyond. I hope that I seem what I think I am: a constitutional political economist who shares an appreciation for the Judeo-Christian heritage that produced the values of Western culture and institutions of civil order, particularly as represented in the Madisonian vision of what the United States might have been and might still become. Am I grossly naive to think this definition is sufficient unto itself?

James M. Buchanan is Harris University Professor and Advisory General Director of the Center for Study of Public Choice, George Mason University, and the 1986 winner of the Nobel Memorial Prize in economic science.

GERARD DEBREU

Random Walk and Life Philosophy

I

As a particle performs a random walk in a high-dimensional space, an observer may discover a subspace in which the projection of its path approximates a straight line. The observer may then be tempted to anthropomorphize the particle and to believe that it has "a system which a person forms for the conduct of life."[1] In an inversion of roles, a scientist or a humanist who is asked to expound his life philosophy must feel inclined to identify with that particle if he is aware of the many chance events that shaped his career and of the inchoate system that he formed for its conduct as it began.

That very beginning I owe to a high school teacher who gave me my first glimpse of the austere beauty of mathematics and my first mathe-

[1] *A New English Dictionary on Historical Principles*, vol. 7, pt. 2, James A. H. Murray, ed., "Philosophy, 9.a" (Oxford: Clarendon Press, 1909).

matical experiences. For several years, Jules Dermie challenged the in-
genuity of my class with the geometric puzzles that were then at the core
of the French curriculum. A seductive subject presented by a dedicated
master at a critical time in my intellectual development pointed me,
unaware, toward a career of scientific research. Chance intervened again
when, in my last year at the high school I had been attending in Calais,
an uninspiring teacher of mathematics and an inspiring teacher of physics,
Albert Javelle, shifted my allegiance from the first subject to the second
and when, at the end of that year, my school sent me to participate, in
the field of physics, in one of the national competitions of which the
French are fond. In 1939, the Concours Général was a venerable institution dating back to the first half of the 18th century, but a year before,
Louis Mandel, after becoming minister of colonies, had added munificent
awards to the symbolic value of its prizes. Thus in late August 1939, in
Bordeaux, I boarded a liner heading for Dakar. The travel program was
to include a rail trip from Dakar to Bamako, a journey by more primitive
means to Abidjan, and a return sea voyage to Bordeaux. So exotic an
experience and the sudden perception of the unimagined possibilities that
the future held would have elated an adolescent brought up in a provincial
town if his joy had not been tempered by the storm that was about to
break over Europe. By the time the liner reached Dakar, World War II
had started for France. Passenger ships were commandeered as troop
transports, and the return voyage was made on a mixed freighter slowly
steaming for Marseilles.

The next step in my walk, as I began to study for admission to one of
the Grandes Ecoles, was not random. But the conditions for that first
year of study would have been unpredictable a few weeks earlier. An
improvised curriculum had been set up in the small town of Ambert in
the Massif Central. There, Joseph Coissard, a retired teacher called back
to active duty, communicated his enthusiasm to his students as he initiated
them into college mathematics. The isolation of the Ambert novitiate
often made it possible to forget that France was at war. It also made the
defeat that brought the school year to an end stunning.

Entering the Ecole Normale Supérieure in the fall of 1941 meant another initiation, this time into living science. The three years during which
I studied and lived at the Ecole Normale were rich in revelations. Nicolas
Bourbaki was beginning to publish his *Eléments de Mathématique*, and
his grandiose plan to reconstruct the entire edifice of mathematics commanded instant and total adhesion. Henri Cartan, who represented him
at the Ecole Normale, influenced me then as no other faculty member
did.

The student body of some one hundred and fifty men formed a mi-
crocosm that the pressure of the dark outside world of Paris under Ger-

man occupation contained in a state of permanent implosion. Daily interaction and the diversity of their fields of study in the humanities and the sciences helped to create a charged intellectual atmosphere that I did not experience again elsewhere with the same intensity. Another experience remained unique, that of living in a totalitarian state that does not concede any right to its subjects. It made walking through Paris in 1943–44, with papers that were not in perfect order, a game of evasion with a high payoff.

The new levels of abstraction and of purity to which the work of Bourbaki was raising mathematics had won a respect that was not to be withdrawn. But, by the end of 1942, I began to question whether I was ready for a total commitment to an activity so detached from the real world, and during the following year I explored several alternatives. Economics was one of them. In 1943–44 the teaching of the subject in French universities paid little attention to theory, and the first textbook that I undertook to read reflected this neglect. The distance between the pedestrian approach I was invited to follow and the ever higher flight I had been riding for several years looked immense, perhaps irreducible. Reason counseled retreat to a safe course. What kept me on an unreasonable heading? The formless feeling that the intellectual gap could be bridged? The wishful thought that the end of the war was near and the perception that economists had a contribution to make to the task of reconstruction that would follow? An improbable event brought my search to a close. Maurice Allais, whose *A la Recherche d'une Discipline Economique* had appeared in 1943, sent copies of his book to several class presidents at the Ecole Normale. One of them, Jacques Bompaire, knew of my interest in the application of mathematics to economics, an interest that, as a Hellenist, he did not share. In the copy that he gave me in the spring of 1944, I discovered the theory of general economic equilibrium, and found a scientific vocation.

But several years would elapse before an observer of my wandering course could reasonably believe that it would not take yet another direction. As the war was nearing its conclusion, the French army gave me the opportunity, unrepeated to this day, of experiencing life outside the academic cocoon. Then in 1945–46, I had to go through the scholastic exercise of the *agrégation de mathématiques*, rendered specially pointless by my new heading. After that, the way was clear for the conversion from mathematics to economics, which the Centre National de la Recherche Scientifique made possible by its tolerance of the absence of results of one of its research associates. In 1948, at a critical bifurcation point, chance occurred in its purest form. The Rockefeller Foundation had earmarked a fellowship for a young French economist. Maurice Allais, whose recommendation was to be decisive, brought together in

his office the two candidates, Marcel Boiteux and me, and suggested that
a coin choose between us. The winner would spend the year 1949 in the
United States and the loser the year 1950. The coin rotated on a table
for a long time and eventually decided that I would leave Paris at the
end of 1948. But before that, my visit to the United States was prepared
by a summer at the Salzburg Seminar in American Studies. From Wassily
Leontief and Robert Solow I learned about developments in economics
from which France had been cut off, and in the Schloss Leopoldskron
library I started reading *Theory of Games and Economic Behavior.*

The Rockefeller Fellowship I had won in a game of heads or tails took
me on a discovery tour of American universities in 1949, and to Uppsala
and Oslo in the first four months of 1950. It led my path to another
pivotal point in Chicago in the fall of 1949 when Tjalling Koopmans,
then director of research of the Cowles Commission, invited me to join
his group.

II

Shortly after my association with Cowles began on June 1, 1950, the
methodology that became explicit a few years later started to delineate
itself. A central tenet was respect for mathematical rigor in economic
theory.

In the early fifties, the tolerance of mathematical economists for approximate rigor in their field strongly tempted one to overlook bother-
some, apparently insignificant technical points, and *Econometrica*
published articles then that would not go past its referees now. In that
climate, it was easy to stray from the narrow path that I had followed
until my formal study of mathematics ended in 1946. In contrast,
the Cowles Commission, by welcoming strict intellectual discipline,
prompted one to look at economic theory from the viewpoint of a mathematician. An even more compelling motivation came from the nature
of two problems on which I began to work. The first was the existence
of a utility function representing a preference relation. The second was
the existence of a general economic equilibrium. In either case, the proposed solution would be pointless if an irremediable defect invalidated
the argument claiming to prove that its assumptions ensured existence.

The rewards of allegiance to rigor were many. It helped one to choose
the mathematical tools most appropriate for a particular question of
economic theory. Taking the uncompromising stance of a mathematician,
one also shared in his insights into the behavior of mathematical objects,
in his drive for ever weaker assumptions and ever stronger conclusions,
and in his compulsive quest for simplicity.

The studies of welfare economics by means of convex analysis that

Kenneth Arrow and I separately published in 1951 had already left a lasting personal imprint on these points. By 1950, the characterization of Pareto optima had been the subject of an extensive literature whose reliance on the differential calculus had several drawbacks. The differentiability assumptions on which it rested did not allow, for instance, for consumers who do not consume some commodities. Nor did they allow for producers whose technologies are generated by a finite number of elementary processes. The alternative analysis by means of convexity showed that those disturbing assumptions were superfluous, in a proof of the second theorem of welfare economics that can be summarized in two steps. Given a Pareto-optimal allocation of the resource-vector e of an economy, define the set E in the commodity space by adding the preferred sets of all the consumers and by subtracting the production sets of all the producers. A hyperplane H through the point e supporting the set E yields an intrinsic price vector orthogonal to H. The derivation so obtained was at the same time simpler and more insightful, more general, and more rigorous.

Powerful reinforcement was provided by the two existence problems, whose solutions did not tolerate fudging of rigor. The former gave rise to the first of a series of articles on preference, utility, and demand theory. The aim of that initial paper was to give topological conditions on the space of actions of an agent implying that a closed preference relation can be represented by a continuous utility function. The latter eventually led to the article on the existence of a general equilibrium that Kenneth Arrow and I published jointly in 1954, after having worked independently on that question until Tjalling Koopmans brought us together. The paper is based on the presentation of a general equilibrium as a Kakutani fixed point. But first the concepts of an economy and of a general equilibrium had to be defined with the precision that an existence proof requires. The reexamination of the theory of general equilibrium that was entailed must be credited to the pursuit of rigor.

The developing mathematization of the theory of general equilibrium was giving it an axiomatic form in which the structure of the theory could be entirely divorced from its interpretations. The value of that axiomatization was illustrated when Kenneth Arrow conceived the idea of a contingent commodity whose delivery is conditional on a specified state of the world. In a paper I wrote at Electricité de France in 1953 and elaborated as the last chapter of my *Theory of Value*, a theory of general equilibrium under uncertainty, formally identical to the theory under certainty, was obtained by the reinterpretation of the concept of a commodity along this line.

The Cowles Commission provided an ideal environment for research on each one of those problems. The work of any member was of interest to all. Opportunities for interaction arose every week in staff meetings and every fortnight in seminars. The compact cluster of offices, some of which were shared, created many other occasions for exchanges of ideas. But the state of the economics profession in that period also helped. The small number of working papers to read, and of colloquia to attend, and the general lack of interest in exacting mathematical approaches gave one freedom in choosing problems and time to work on them.

III

As the fifties drew to a close, Edgeworth's contract curve was retrieved from a neglect of nearly eighty years by an article of Martin Shubik that set off the contemporary theory of the core of an economy. After Herbert Scarf had proved a first extension of Edgeworth's limit theorem, we were given a chance to collaborate on another generalization in the winter of 1962 when I moved from New Haven to Berkeley and before he left Stanford for Yale. From this brief overlap resulted the article that we published in 1963. The study of the core did more than elucidate the function of prices in bringing about allocations of the resources of an economy that are stable relative to coalition formation. It led to the introduction of powerful mathematical techniques into economic theory when the concept of a large set of small agents was formalized by means of measure theory by Robert Aumann in 1964 and by means of non-standard analysis by Donald Brown and Abraham Robinson in 1972. It also led to the definition of a distance between two preference relations giving a precise meaning to the notion of their similarity by Yakar Kannai in 1970. The idea sown by Edgeworth in 1881, and long dormant, had suddenly entered a phase of explosive growth, and the solutions of several problems of economic theory progressed rapidly. An insight of fundamental importance was made clear by the measure-theoretical framework when integration of a family of arbitrary sets over a space of insignificant agents was seen to yield an aggregate convex set. In several results central to economic theory, convexity was needed only for aggregate sets. In large economies made up of small agents, convexity assumptions on their individual characteristics could therefore be dispensed with. Karl Vind, also in 1964, presented that aggregation property as a direct consequence of Lyapunov's theorem on the range of an atomless vector measure.

The question of determinacy of general equilibrium had received partial answers in the form of various existence theorems. A more complete solution would have been provided by additional conditions implying that there is exactly one equilibrium. But the requirement of global uniqueness revealed itself to be excessively demanding. Requiring only that every equilibrium be locally unique was not a sufficient weakening since one can display in Edgeworth's box an economy having a continuum of equilibria, even though each one of its agents is mathematically exceedingly well behaved. Taking a generic viewpoint, however, one could show that almost every differentiable economy has a set of locally unique equilibria. The basis of the proof was Sard's theorem on the set of critical values of a differentiable function, of which I learned in the late sixties in a first encounter with Steve Smale, whose path had remained separate from mine during the period of campus turbulence that began in September 1964. Differentiability assumptions that had been expurgated earlier from economic theory when they were irrelevant were essential now for the generic discreteness of the set of equilibria. One of the by-products of the scrutiny of those assumptions was a reconsideration of the problem of representation of a preference relation by a differentiable utility function. An alternative to the usual approach via the Frobenius integrability conditions was proposed in an article of 1972 in which I defined a differentiable preference relation by the requirement that the indifferent pairs of commodity vectors form a differentiable manifold.

Basic to the theory of general equilibrium are the concept of the aggregate excess demand function of an economy and its properties. In an exchange economy, the individual excess demand of a consumer is a function f of prices obtained by subtracting his endowment vector from the commodity vector that he demands. Under customary assumptions on his preferences, (1) f is continuous, and (2) for every price vector $\mathbf{p}$, the value $\mathbf{p} \cdot f(\mathbf{p})$ of $f(\mathbf{p})$ relative to $\mathbf{p}$ vanishes. Since these two properties are preserved by summation over a set of consumers, the aggregate excess demand function F of the economy also has properties (1) and (2). In 1972 and 1973, Hugo Sonnenschein conjectured that, conversely, any function F satisfying (1) and (2) can be written as a sum of individual excess demand functions generated by traditional preferences, and made the first attack on the problem he had posed. The proof given by Rolf Mantel in 1974 was based on differentiability assumptions. It was followed, in the same year, by another proof in which I dispensed with differentiability and characterized the aggregate excess demand function of an exchange economy by means of an additive decomposition with the minimal number of consumers. The paucity of properties enjoyed by the aggregate excess demand function, expressed by this result, threw a hard light on several aspects of general equilibrium models. But it also suggested endowing them with a richer structure by imposing restrictions on the distribution of the characteristics of agents. A significant step in this direction was taken by Werner Hildenbrand in 1983 in his study of the Law of Demand.

Leaving the Cowles Commission for the University of California at the end of 1961, I had made a move to a new environment that proved to be more than another powerful research stimulant. It also expanded a teaching experience that had been limited to specialized graduate courses. Essential dimensions were now added by an exceptional succession of doctoral students and of younger colleagues, and I discovered that there was pleasure in lecturing to undergraduates.

IV

In the phase of exuberant growth that mathematical economics entered in 1944, close scrutiny of its details sometimes blurred its dominant features. Bringing them into focus in the analysis of general equilibrium stresses, as one of its central themes, the study of the multiple function of prices – notably their roles in the efficiency of resource allocation, in the equality of demand and supply, and in the stability of allocations with respect to coalition formation. Explaining these functions raises major scientific questions. Any attempt at answering them must take into account the large number of agents, the large number of commodities and prices, and the interdependence of the many variables involved. Only a mathematical model can deal with these characteristics. Once such a model is formulated, appeal to deductive reasoning requires an explicit set of assumptions as its foundation. Those assumptions delimit the domain of validity of the theory that is based on them. At a given moment in the development of economic analysis, they are the outcome of a continuing cumulative weakening process.

From that perspective, engaging in controversy over the merits and demerits of the theory of general economic equilibrium has low priority in contrast to participating in its construction. In this task, mathematical form powerfully contributes to defining a philosophy of economic analysis whose major tenets include rigor, generality, and simplicity. It commands the long search for the most direct secure routes from assumptions to conclusions. It dictates its aesthetic code, and it imposes its terse language. Another tenet of that philosophy is recognition, and acceptance, of the limits of economic theory, which cannot achieve a grand unified explanation of economic phenomena. Instead, it adds insights to the perception of the areas to which it turns its search. When they are gained by accepting mathematical challenges, those insights are the highest prizes sought by a mathematical economist.

Gerard Debreu is University Professor, and Class of 1958 Professor, of Economics and of Mathematics, University of California at Berkeley. He is also the 1983 winner of the Nobel Memorial Prize in economic science.

EVSEY D. DOMAR

How I Tried to Become an Economist

I

If the city of Harbin, lost in the middle of the North Manchurian plain, lacked a few cultural amenities when my family arrived there in 1916, successive waves of Russian émigrés, fleeing the Communist Revolution and the civil war, quickly created them. With a Russian population of about 100,000 (my estimate), the city had four or five dailies, several journals and publishing houses, two polytechnic institutes, a Faculty of Law (with an Economics Department), numerous schools, and at least one impressive library. The city enjoyed frequent visits by Soviet opera and operetta troupes and concerts by musical and vocal celebrities on world tours. Lectures by local luminaries, even when not free, were well attended.[1] In a quest for culture, a circle of my friends, between the

---

[1] These are my own recollections. For a more authoritative and entertaining cultural history

ages of seventeen and twenty, met every Saturday afternoon to hear a serious paper by one of the members, followed by poetry readings, piano recitals, and tea with cookies. On some anniversary related to Spinoza (probably his birth), three formal lectures were offered (on his philosophy, his political views, and on something else); they were well received by a number of invited guests, including several adult intellectuals.

To the future economist, Harbin could offer valuable lessons, particularly in the field of money. The city had been built by the Russians in 1897 (or 1896) at the intersection of the Chinese Eastern Railway (an extension of the Trans-Siberian Railway) and a large navigable river (the Sungari). They forgot to provide the city with waterworks and a sewer, but not with their army, police, courts, and, of course, their paper currency, which circulated freely. After the February Revolution (1917) but before the October one, new notes appeared, called "Kerenki" in honor of the then head of the provisional government (A. F. Kerensky). The civil war gave birth to several White (anti-Communist) regimes, which promptly printed their own money. In time, these notes reached Harbin and were accepted at par. But as the fortunes of the White regimes waned, the populace became suspicious: Chinese merchants and peddlers still accepted the notes, provided that they looked absolutely perfect when held against the light; even a pinhole caused a rejection. (Why they applied this particular test I don't know; I have never heard of a similar case.) Anyhow, soon enough all these notes became worthless; in our downstairs closet, where firewood was stored, I found whole stacks of them.

Around 1920 the Chinese took over the city and established their own administration. They also introduced a local paper dollar that was supposed to equal and to be convertible into the Chinese silver dollar, but in reality it was neither; it circulated at some 25 percent below par. The Russian population preferred the Japanese yen notes issued by the Bank of Chosen (Korea, then belonging to Japan) because the local dollar commanded little faith. To increase the demand for it, the Chinese authorities eventually outlawed the yen. In retail trade they won, but for contracts of even a few months' duration everyone preferred the yen. Since its use was illegal, contracts were made in "silver dollars," although both parties meant the yen. Evidently, this implicit agreement worked.

In the meantime, we lived with two currencies. On graduation from high school in 1930, I became a private tutor. To safeguard my fortune (about ten yen per pupil per month) from monetary disturbances, I asked for payment in yen, which I had to convert into local dollars before

---

of Harbin, see a book review published by Simon Karlinsky in the *Slavic Review*, 48 (1989), pp. 284–90.

spending them. With the exchange rate between the yen and the local dollar fluctuating daily, if not hourly, the timing of this conversion required hard thinking. Except for a correct prediction of the devaluation of the yen in 1931 – a prediction on which I could not act because of lack of funds, and my relatives would not because of lack of faith in me – I do not recall any other financial feats on my part. But my intellectual efforts were not wasted: when I took my first course in economics at UCLA in 1936, I found the chapter on international trade the easiest in the book.

Not everyone in Harbin was satisfied with only two currencies (or even three, if the silver dollar is included). The Chinese Eastern Railway, then under joint Soviet–Chinese ownership but actually under Soviet management, trusted none of them and invented a currency of its own, which it called the "gold ruble." It was neither gold nor a ruble, but an average of several respectable currencies, such as the U.S. dollar, the pound sterling, the Swiss franc, and a few others. (What a modern touch, and in Manchuria of all places!) Expressed in this imaginary currency, the railway tariffs were said to have been exorbitant; horses and wagons were alleged to be cheaper, at least for transporting grain. Much of this was Japanese anti-Soviet propaganda: after Manchoukuo (that is, the Japanese) took over the railway in the early thirties, it was revealed that the actual tariffs had not been as high as listed because of a system of discounts.

Two more influences pushed me toward economics: my father's business and my school. My father was a small-scale importer with more or less insolvent customers whose notes he had to discount at a local bank to finance letters of credit. The customers seldom paid on time, and the arrival of a shipment (from Europe) frequently caused a crisis. Interest rates, prices, rates of exchange, custom duties, and the like were common items of discussion at the supper table.

Harbin was probably the only place on earth where old Russian (that is, pre-revolutionary) weights and measures were still in use and tsarist-type schools still existed. Ours was a so-called commercial school, which excluded Greek and Latin from its curriculum, but included English and German (for a while), accounting, commercial arithmetic, economic geography, industrial processes, and political economy. This subject was taught by an old lawyer; the course consisted of a long list of definitions that we were supposed to memorize, even if their meanings remained obscure. He probably used his own lecture notes taken when he had been a student at some Russian university. I believe now that they were based on the labor theory of value that our teacher – or more likely his own teachers – had taken from Adam Smith. Smith was the real hero of the course. When I asked for his biography (on a bet with another student), my A (a *Five*) was assured. It is a wonder that this teacher and this course did not kill my incipient interest in economics.

Accounting was the most practical course taught in our school. The teacher was a Georgian, who did not look like one but who did not lack his people's well-known temper. He was not popular, but he taught us so well that, after graduation, I was able to practice this trade with little additional instruction.

All this suggests that I was fated to become an economist. Indeed, I even took a semester at the Economics Department of the State Faculty of Law. But – sorry if this will disappoint you – the first love of my youth was, and now of my old age is, history. It all started with historical novels. How can one put down *Ivanhoe* without looking up the history of the Crusades, or the *Three Musketeers* (and its continuations) without finding out why D'Artagnan was fighting the Spanish on the Netherlands border, or admire Tolstoy's *War and Peace* without reading up on the history of the Napoleonic Wars? So one thing led to another, and to this day history remains my favorite reading.

Why, then, did I not become a historian? For several reasons. First, there was no faculty of history in Harbin. Second, in our narrow-minded and practically oriented atmosphere one did not enter a university to get an education but to qualify for a job. And what could a historian (of what?) do in Harbin? I did make an attempt, though, by writing an article on the history of the Hundred Years' War (or was it on the Magna Carta?) and took it to a local newspaper (Russian papers used to publish scholarly articles from time to time), only to get fatherly advice from the editor to seek another occupation. And he was right (even if for a wrong reason). Much as I love history, I cannot imagine myself poring over Byzantine manuscripts and Venetian accounts. Whenever I attend meetings of historians, I bless the Fates who have made me an economist. Surely, anyone who wants to learn how history is made – my lifelong aim – should begin with economics. It is the key to history.

II

I never gave up the hope of going abroad to study. When the opportunity came, six years after my graduation from high school, it was the result of a chance encounter with an old classmate on a street in Dairen (where I spent my last two years in Manchuria). He was on his way to the University of Minnesota. His family had means, but he thought that working one's way through college was not impossible in America. When this was confirmed by another friend, then a student in Los Angeles, I went to the American consulate the very next day. I was lucky. If all American consular officials were as pleasant and as helpful as the junior consul who was in charge of visas in Dairen at the time, American popularity would know no bounds.[2] My visa arrived in thirty-three days: during the Great Depression there were very few applicants.

Working one's way through college was indeed possible (I claim to have become the best dishwasher on sorority row), but coming to the Department of Economics at UCLA in 1936 (because of my Los Angeles friend) was quite an anticlimax. To be fair, they treated me very well and gave me work and scholarships, for which I remain grateful to this day. But 1936 was the year of *The General Theory*. It was hotly debated in the journals, and yet all that I had learned about Keynes by my graduation in 1939 was that such an economist existed; and even this information came not from my professors but from a fellow student. The worst course was Intermediate Theory. It made so little sense to me that I decided to turn to empirical studies. For this statistics was needed, and for statistics – mathematics. In the end I did not become an empirical economist, but for the mathematics I have been eternally grateful to that inept theorist who, unwittingly, pushed me in that direction. As a Russian proverb says, "In the absence of luck even misfortune can help." I only regret that I did not take more math.

In this spirit I went to Michigan (in 1939) to study mathematical statistics under Harry Carver (the founder of the Annals of Mathematical Statistics), the most amazing person I have ever met.[3] I did earn a master's degree and learned a modicum of relevant statistics (econometrics was in its infancy then), but my enthusiasm for statistics and empirical work began to cool off, and my interest in theory blossomed. This conversion I owe to Arthur Smithies, who taught straight Keynesian economics from the Text. For the first time, economics began to make sense to me. I became and have remained a lifelong Keynesian, even though I have plenty of bones to pick with Keynes. (Fortunately, we have not followed the Marxist example of making a saint out of him.) I wish, however, that he had been clearer in explaining which classical assumptions he had rejected: this would have saved a lot of time, paper, and ink. I wonder if he ever realized that it was perfect competition that he had put aside.

---

[2] The junior consul was John M. Allison. He became internationally famous around 1939 for having been slapped by a Japanese soldier in Hankow. Later, he enjoyed a distinguished career in the State Department, becoming our ambassador to Czechoslovakia (around 1959) and an assistant secretary of state.
[3] It was rumored in the Math Department that Carver used to offer his students an exemption from the final examination if they could beat him in six out of ten contests, including billiards and chess. I wonder if they ever won.

Under it, changes in demand fall, first of all, on prices and wage rates; under monopolistic competition, they fall on quantities – output and employment – as in fact they do.

With Smithies' blessing, I moved on to Harvard in 1941. My main interest at the time was in fiscal policy and full employment. (To remind the reader, our unemployment did not disappear completely until the end of 1942, long after our defense program had begun and almost a full year after Pearl Harbor.) Naturally, I found myself in Hansen's orbit, to Schumpeter's strong disapproval. He regarded Keynesian economics as a rather shallow doctrine born out of the Great Depression and having little value beyond it. He failed to appreciate the important role that Keynesianism played in the development of macro-economics. Schumpeter was one of my three great teachers (the other two being Jacob Viner at Chicago and Nikolai Ustrialov, a professor of law back in Harbin), but he had little influence on me and on my fellow students at the time.[4] It was difficult to accept his view that the Great Depression was merely a part of a business cycle, and to wait patiently for it to pass away, when industrial countries were acutely sick with unemployment that, among other things, gave rise to the Nazi movement in Germany. Much later I began to appreciate him. His dismissal of perfect competition and static equilibrium as the ideal objectives and his emphasis on technological and institutional change as the very essence of capitalism certainly appeal to me now. If I had to choose between perfect and monopolistic competition, I would join him in taking the latter.[5]

---

[4] Ustrialov was a leader of an intellectual movement among Russian émigrés that can be rendered into English as "Changing Landmarks." It called for cooperation with the Soviet regime, not because it was Soviet but because it was Russian. He took out a Soviet passport.

 In Harbin, besides lecturing at the State Faculty of Law, he occupied the important position of director of the Central Library (the largest in the city), which belonged to the Chinese Eastern Railway. Sometime after the railway had been sold to Manchoukuo, he returned to the Soviet Union and, to the best of my knowledge (which may be incomplete), he was never heard of again.

[5] As a teacher at Harvard, Schumpeter was a law to himself. He administered the final examinations himself, but did not read the papers. Most of the boys received A – 's, the girls A's, and the students whom he particularly liked A + 's. I was told that in his recommendation letters every student was described as a genius or, at least, close to one. A certain midwestern university was said to have hired a person on the strength of Schumpeter's recommendation. You can imagine the results.

 His office hours were on Wednesday afternoon. When you arrived, you found several students already sitting in front of his office. As soon as you sat down, Schumpeter involved you in the conversation he was having with one of them. You were flattered that your opinion was asked for, and you had a great time. Only after you left did you realize that you had never had a chance to ask the question you had come for. The next Wednesday was a repetition of the first. But you really did not mind. Schumpeter's showmanship was superb. Alone in the department, he at least pretended that he liked to see students.

Much as I loved to sit in Schumpeter's class and catch the ideas that he generously tossed at his students, the highlight of my stay at Harvard was the Fiscal Policy seminar given by Alvin Hansen and John Williams. Unfortunately for me, most of its bright stars had left for Washington before my arrival, but Paul Samuelson used to drop in from MIT, and Lloyd Metzler was still in residence. It would be hard to find two persons more different intellectually then Hansen and Williams, but they complemented one another beautifully. Williams was then, if my memory is correct, a vice-president of the Federal Reserve Bank of New York and Hansen was a special adviser to the Federal Reserve Board. Hansen always advocated bold action; Williams, caution. They brought in a number of outside speakers, including those involved in practical governmental work, a most welcome whiff of reality in our academic life.

Before I end the story of my education, I should mention the three sojourns at Chicago. The first two took place in the summers of 1940 and 1941; the last in 1947–48. In 1940 I took correlation analysis from Oscar Lange and theory from Viner. Lange was the nicest, the most beloved, and the best organized of all my teachers. I still have the notes I took in his class. His explanations were so clear that there was no need to read the text or even to think about the subject. This was the main weakness of his teaching. (After Schumpeter's class I took long walks around the Harvard Yard thinking about what he had said.) A teacher is much more effective if he leaves his students in a state of "healthy confusion," as one of my professors put it.[6]

Viner was superb because he was extremely nasty. He would write a statement on the board, challenge us to comment on it, and then make fools of those who tried. To fight him back became my greatest ambition. I spent hours getting ready for the fight; fortunately, I knew some math. Did I ever win an argument? Perhaps a couple of times during that summer quarter. But what a joy that was, the sweet feeling of revenge! Can you think of a more effective teaching method? But can you be as nasty as Viner?

I returned to Chicago in the summer of 1941 as Theodore Yntema's research assistant. He had been hired as an expert by the tobacco companies who were being prosecuted under the anti-trust laws. Yntema was nice and intelligent; working for him would have been a pleasure if my sympathies had not been on the other side. I was supposed to write a

---

[6] After World War II, Lange gave up his U.S. citizenship and joined the Polish communist government, which sent him back to the United States as an ambassador. When he addressed the Federal Reserve seminar at that time, I recognized my old teacher, even if more conservatively dressed, whom we all loved so much. He gave an interesting talk. But later, at a presentation at Harvard, he justified every measure undertaken by the Polish regime. For the first and the last time, I felt ashamed for him.

paper on the origin of profits that would help Yntema explain away the high profits of his clients. I went through a good deal of literature, while hoping to discover nothing. I should not have worried: there was little in the literature to discover. And I swore never to accept such a job again.

My education at Chicago was resumed during 1947–48, when I came there as an assistant professor. This time my (informal) teacher was Milton Friedman. We argued in every place we met: in the lobby of the Social Science Building, in elevators, at social gatherings, in the street. I doubt that he got much out of these arguments, but I learned a lot. If the devil is already here, why not partake of his wisdom?

It was time to look for a thesis topic. (We are back in 1943 now.) Once, I had stumbled (in the Chicago library) on Martin Bronfenbrenner's thesis. It threw me into a panic. It looked so technical, so high-powered, and learned that I could not even imagine ever being able to write anything like it. And what was I going to write about? Many graduate students at MIT (and probably elsewhere) waste months trying to find a topic, a problem that could be solved quickly by a chat with a friendly professor. Many professors have more topics in mind than they have time to work on and are delighted to pass them on to their students. But the students are embarrassed to tell the professor that they don't know what to do – hence the waste of time.

I was, or at least I thought I was, lucky again. Hansen asked me to join his staff at the Federal Reserve Board (where he was a special adviser) to prepare a scheme of post-war federal taxation that I could submit as a thesis and he could use for his own purposes. To write a thesis in an air-conditioned marble palace on Constitution Avenue and to be paid for it at the same time sounded too good to be true, and so it turned out. I spent some nine months helping Hansen finish a book (with Harvey Perloff) on state and local finance. The book was eventually finished, but my contribution did not look like a thesis at all. Worse than that – I lost interest in the subject. Ever since then I have warned my students – graduate and undergraduate alike – *never* to attempt research on a subject, even for a mere term paper, of no interest to them. I hope the advice has helped.

I stayed at the Federal Reserve until June 1946, working first for Hansen and then for Musgrave. Actually, I worked for myself most of the time. The Federal Reserve people were very kind to me and let me work on my own topics – growth models at the time – and bothered me very little. My direct contribution to the work of the Federal Reserve Board was almost nil. Gradually, I developed a guilty conscience and decided to return to academia. (The same situation developed later at the RAND Corporation in Santa Monica, where I was to spend a number of summers.) I did not realize then that a good research organization should contain one or several persons who are not directly involved with its work but who can stimulate those who are, because the latter miss the broadening experience of teaching graduate courses. (RAND has encouraged its people to teach from time to time and now runs a real graduate school.) So I could have stayed at the Federal Reserve longer, though the re-emergence of monetary policy in later years gave the Board plenty to do and would have made it more difficult for me to remain an outsider.

III

Before I begin describing my research, I should record that I have never had a long-term research plan. While public concern has undoubtedly affected my choice of topics, my main motivation has been curiosity, particularly about widely accepted opinions and conclusions. In economics (and probably in other social sciences as well) such acceptance is a sign of danger: it often suggests that the topic has not been researched recently and that each economist or historian merely repeated what the others had said. (A foundation for the promotion of heresy should be most welcome.) Doing research of this kind is sheer joy, but once the research is done, my curiosity is satisfied and my interest dissipates; I then have a very hard time writing up the results. I have always looked for a partner who would let me do the research and then write up the results, but have never found one. Evidently, good people prefer to do their own research.

My first published paper, with Richard Musgrave, was on the effect of a proportional income tax on risk taking (1944). It was written in response to an assertion by Abba Lerner in his famous-to-become article on functional finance that income taxes do not discourage risk taking because of the availability of loss offsets. To Musgrave and me this statement sounded preposterous, and we decided to disprove it. Eleven months later we established that not only had Lerner been right, but that he had not gone far enough: with a complete and immediate loss offset, a proportional income tax would *encourage* risk taking because the taxing authority bears a part of it.

Abba Lerner, one of our most original thinkers, stated his conclusions without ever worrying about their practical application and the damage that his radical proposals might do to his reputation. I have always admired his courage.

If the reader recognizes my name it must be in connection with growth models. I cannot explain why I became interested in economic growth, but I can describe how it all began. While still at Harvard, I found on page 272 of Hansen's *Fiscal Policy and the Business Cycle* a diagram showing the effect of a constant stream of investment on national income. At first, income rose, but presently its growth slowed down and it approached a horizontal asymptote. There was something strange about this process: the stock of capital was increasing, but its product – national income – was not, so that the capital–output ratio would increase without limit. Suppose investment was growing at a constant *absolute* rate (linear); would the ratio still rise? It would, but at a slower rate. What about a constant relative rate (exponential)? Depending on initial conditions, the ratio might fall or rise, but eventually it would approach a horizontal asymptote. Now all this looks obvious. It did not then.

The first application of this idea was to the so-called burden of the debt. A young or even a middle-aged reader who has survived eight years of Reagan's deficits without losing either his appetite or his sleep may find it difficult to imagine the debt hysteria created by the Republicans during the Roosevelt administration. Now that they themselves have indulged in a deficit orgy, their hypocrisy has been revealed for all to see: the debt issue was and is being used to frighten Congress and the public into eliminating from the federal budget the expenditures for which our owners of wealth have no use. Perhaps the Republicans have achieved more than they have bargained for: after Reagan, public fear of deficits will be gone.

In my paper on the debt burden (1944) I showed that the ratio of the debt to national income was a direct function of the fraction of income borrowed and an inverse function of the income's rate of growth. Thus the problem of the debt was reduced to the problem of economic growth. This was my first growth model.

Subsequently, similar models were applied to the old problem of capital accumulation raised by Keynes and his underconsumptionist predecessors. Keynes was concerned with the possible shortage of investment to absorb the intended savings of today; this would create unemployment now. His predecessors had in mind a deeper problem: if savings were invested, there would be no unemployment today, but the increase in productive capacity resulting from this investment would require even more investment tomorrow. So the trouble of today was solved by creating even greater trouble for tomorrow.

The reader knows, of course, that the answer to this problem lies in growth. To demonstrate this, my models were probably adequate, as they were for the introduction of growth into the main body of economic thinking (with the participation of many others and particularly with the help of Simon Kuznets' empirical work) – their main achievement. They were criticized, however, for the use of only one factor of production – capital – and for the exclusion of labor and of technological progress (everyone forgets land). I trust no one believes that I regard capital as the only factor of production; qualifications and explanations to this effect abound in my papers, but to paraphrase an old saying about a horse and water, one person can make them, but ten persons cannot force others to read. The very fact that I employed a constant capital–output ratio implies quite a hefty technological progress, as can be ascertained by using a Cobb–Douglas production function. I chose capital because only investment appears on both the supply and the demand sides of the equation (as labor does not); for the problem in hand, other inputs were not needed and therefore were omitted.

But as guides to economic development, these models could be wrong. That a good part of income should be saved and invested is good advice; that investment should be directed to sectors with low capital–output ratios, such as services, makes little sense. Already in December 1951, in a paper presented to the American Economic Association, I suggested the use of the Cobb–Douglas function in a growth model. I did not follow up this suggestion myself, but it has been put to good use by Robert Solow and others. That it emphasizes the role of technological progress as a major source of growth is all to the good, but that this progress, calculated as a residual, appears from the outside (like the fall of heavenly manna) is not satisfactory either. Perhaps the use of Leontief's method (the Index of Structural Change), which is mathematically equivalent to the residual but expresses it in a disaggregated form (from a comparison of two or more input–output tables), will show the way.

I wrote several papers on comparisons of technological change in time and in space and even one paper on index-number theory, a dismal subject that caught my eye because of the nearly unanimous condemnation of the Soviet Index of Industrial Production. It turned out that, in its pure form, the Soviet index was not any worse than the eminently respectable Federal Reserve Index. But in the meantime my interest had shifted to economic history and socialism.

As I said at the beginning of this essay, history was my first love. My first attempt to do research in it took place in the 1950s when my wife gave me five volumes of Kliuchevskii's *A Course of Russian History*. Kliuchevskii, whom I regard as the greatest Russian historian, gave a masterful description of the development of Russian serfdom – the central institution of Russian history whose influence has not yet disappeared – but, being a historian and not an economist, he constructed no model to explain its cause. This is what I tried to do. The model could be applied to the development of serfdom and slavery in other countries as well, of course with proper allowance for local conditions. To my surprise, the model turned out to be quite durable: after more than twenty years (since 1970) it is still alive.

This venture into the history of serfdom led to two others, both written to disprove some widely accepted views, but I have to confess that, judging by the number of requests for reprints, they have attracted very little attention. As a certain journal editor explained to me, the set of persons interested in Russian history and able to handle mathematics and statistics is almost empty. This, however, has not discouraged me. I believe that the application of analytical models to history has a great future. If the Fates are kind to me, I hope to construct some more.

To a person of Russian background, socialism has a significance that an American reader may not appreciate. In tsarist Russia, being a socialist made one an automatic opponent of autocracy; it was almost required for maintaining a minimum degree of self-respect. My father, too preoccupied with his semi-insolvent customers to read up on Marx and socialism, regarded himself a Menshevik (a social democrat), as did my aunt, an owner of a furniture store in a small Minnesota town, who kept worrying that all her employees — two to be exact — might join a union. To my relatives, as to many millions of others, socialism was a secular religion, the great hope for a better world.

Harbin was too close to the Soviet Union to escape its influence. After my graduation from high school, I made good use of the socialist collection that our modest library possessed. My interest in socialism never disappeared, but my serious work also dates back to the fifties; it culminated in a lengthy paper that, believe it or not, was put into final form only in the summer of 1988.[7] I called this paper "The Blind Men and the Elephant: An Essay on Isms" to underline the fact that different people find different aims in socialism: instead of the usual ones, such as greater economic equality, avoidance of cycles, internalization of external effects, etc., I emphasized the protection of workers from what the socialists call the "tyranny of the market." Even if not absolutely necessary, public (i.e., government) ownership of the means of production helps to achieve this aim by eliminating the danger of bankruptcy, but the real protection of workers is created by the presence of excess demand, which deprives consumers of all the power that they enjoy under capitalism. It is obvious, of course, that under these conditions a firm need not strive for greater efficiency, nor the workers for higher quality of the goods and services they produce.

Herein lies the great dilemma facing Mr. Gorbachev now: the Soviet economy needs the market mechanism to improve its performance in every way; the market, however, cannot function properly in the presence of excess demand; its elimination could bring back that tyranny of the market that socialism is meant to avoid. Is it possible that "market

---

[7] It was published in a collection of my essays, *Capitalism, Socialism, and Serfdom* (Cambridge University Press, 1989).

socialism" will turn out to be a contradiction in terms? Or will Mr. Gorbachev be able to find a happy compromise?

There is no doubt that by the 1980s socialism had fallen on evil days. Even a cursory survey of recent developments and pronouncements in the Soviet Union and China confirms this. It is also confirmed by the long-term decline in the number of students specializing in this field: the study of failures (except in love) is usually not enticing. This, I think, is most unfortunate. As everyone who has tried to do something new knows, the first step in a learning process is finding out how *not to do* things. Here both the Soviet Union and China have much to offer.

It was a real tragedy for socialism that its greatest experiments took place in two backward countries, which, according to standard Marxism (put by Lenin on its head), were far from ready for it. It is difficult not to project their experience into the future. But this is not a reliable method of prediction: witness the sad prognosis that Oscar Lange and so many others made for capitalism in the 1930s. Evidently, history dislikes monotonic functions. But before socialism gets another chance, I hope it will have solved its basic contradiction between the role of the State as the employer of the people and its role as their servant.

In the meantime, let us not gloat over socialism's misfortunes. There is no shortage of problems and contradictions in our own capitalism.

On re-reading the editor's instructions I realized that I was supposed to describe my "life philosophy." Some bits of it are scattered in this essay; to dwell on it longer would be an imposition on the reader's patience and time.

Evsey D. Domar is Ford Professor of Economics, Emeritus, at Massachusetts Institute of Technology.

NICHOLAS GEORGESCU-ROEGEN

Nicholas Georgescu-Roegen about Himself

Two things fill one's conscience with increasing wonder and awe, the stars in heaven and the moral law in oneself.

Immanuel Kant

PROEM

It would be superfluous to tell the reader how high my spirits were lifted by Michael Szenberg's invitation to write an account of my life philosophy. But as I started to think about the task, a fear came to me, the fear that my acceptance would be taken as an implicit presumption that I am a philosopher like Plato or John Dewey, for example. Even though I have not been a professional philosopher, I certainly "have done philosophy." One does philosophy, I think, not when one reasons about the practical problems of a community or the mathematical structure of quantum mechanics, but only if one treats in a thoroughly free inquiry issues that cannot be tested at a workbench. It is in this sense that I claim to have done philosophy, probably more often than I have exercised any other intellectual expertise. However, although like all who have done philosophy I have asked questions about things, their nature, and their relations among themselves and with the human mind, I have gone further: I have also asked questions about questions.

Everyone's way of thinking is influenced by the events of his or her life. As some have maintained, it was Einstein's experience at the Berne Patent Office that developed his interest in how to test our ideas about things. Not ignoring the considerable difference of proportions, the observation has been especially true to my shattered life. In the country in which I was born and spent the most informative part of my life, Romania, I lived under four dictatorships and three wars, all in my backyard. That history instilled me with a kind of Paretoan view of human societies. Romania was at that time a struggling, overpopulated, peasant-dominated culture and economy. And as I came to learn the economics professed in the capitalist world, I was struck by the claims of that discipline that it was a representative guide not only for capitalism but for absolutely all economic conditions. It was evident to me that standard economics could not represent an agrarian economy, and hence could not be a guide for it. I thus acquired a special eye for issues ignored by the standard economic persuasion or by ordinary economic analysis. I learned "philosophy" from many consecrated philosophers, but my own philosophy sprouted from two great teachers of mine: Karl Pearson and Joseph A. Schumpeter. From Karl Pearson's splendid *Grammar of Science* and from my listening to him for more than one year, I reached two philosophical tenets. First, contrary to the old epistemology, the stochastic form is not the peripheral but our only possible representation of natural laws. By implication I came to hold further that randomness, not just haphazardness, is an essential ingredient of phenomena. Second, given the human cosmological condition, I construed that for us nature consists of just what we can perceive. Beyond, there are only hypothesized abstractions about which a metaphysician may say anything with complete certitude, since nothing is controllable. Our laws of nature aim not at explaining phenomena, but at saving them, as Pierre Duhem calligraphed the philosophy initiated by Ernest Mach and embraced by Wilhem Ostwald and Karl Pearson. Even Albert Einstein's philosophy was largely Machian: in 1936 he explicitly stated that "physics consists of a logical system of thought [that] can only be arrived at by free inventions." Not one word about "reality." My philosophy is in spirit Machian: it is a particular kind of epistemology that is little concerned with the science of knowledge, or with the cognitive process itself, but mainly with the problem of valid analytical representations of the relations among facts.

What stirred me mainly in this direction was a frequent sin in mathematical economics. Choose any formula used by a physicist and ask him what it represents factually. He may invite you to his laboratory to witness the actual phenomenon described by that formula. However, in economics there is a vast and growing literature of purely mathematical exercises that correspond to absolutely no facts, not even to physical ones. If one starts only with mathematics, one is trapped inside it and cannot even think of the epistemological issues in my own sense.

A STATISTICIAN TURNED INTO AN ECONOMIST

For my statistical dissertation at the Sorbonne, I followed the line of the smallest effort for a mathematician and thought up a mathematical method for discovering the hidden periodicities of time series. Since economic time series were then, and still are, enjoying great consideration, I felt (as I still do) that economic phenomena are not governed by a mathematical network. If the stock exchange market were governed by a mathematical system, I reasoned, no one would have thought of setting one up. I thus applied my method to the annual rainfall in Paris.[1] After learning later about the three time series used by the famous Harvard Economic Barometer, I became curious to see it applied to them. I was overjoyed when the Rockefeller Foundation gave me an opportunity to visit that organization. But before I reached the United States, it had closed shop. Seeking some scope of activity, I naturally thought of contacting the professor who taught business cycles, whoever he might have been. This is how, quite unintentionally, I met Joseph A. Schumpeter, the man who directly and through his writings was to have an even greater influence on my thinking than Karl Pearson. Every one of his distinctive remarks were seeds that inspired my later works. In this way Schumpeter turned me into an economist – the only true Schumpeterian, I believe. My only degree in economics is from Universitas Schumpeteriana.

Because of my mathematical preparation, I naturally had to plunge first into the writings of Vilfredo Pareto, whom I learned to value as the greatest mathematical economist ever (with great accent on the noun, for Pareto's mathematics were not laudable: my first paper on mathe-

---

[1] I should mention that my method was communicated to the French Académie des Sciences by Emile Borel, and the full version of my dissertation filled the whole October 1930 issue of *Journal de la Société de Statistique de Paris*.

matical economics was on one of his missteps). Being especially concerned with the valid represention of facts analytically, I felt that the neoclassical utility theory needed a fundamental postulate, listed as Postulate A in my 1936 *Quarterly Journal of Economics* essay: on a continuous move from nonpreference to preference with respect to a given basket, we must pass through a place indifferent to that basket. I affirmed for the first time the necessity of postulating the binary indifference (an idea that has been tacitly adopted by many later writers). But some immediately assailed me: "The postulate is totally superfluous. How can you move from nonpreference to preference without passing through indifference?" That objection helped me later move toward dialectics.

At that time an object of great agitation was a paradox created by a criticism of Pareto by Vito Volterra. As is well known, on a second round, Pareto argued that the same map as that based on binary choices could be derived from the reports of a sleuth who followed the individual in a great number of market situations. Clearly, those data serve to establish a total differential equation in the commodities space:

$$\Sigma \, a_i(x) \, dx_i = 0, \qquad 1 \le i \le n. \tag{1}$$

It was about this point that Volterra committed a gaffe by countering that equation (1) is *necessarily* integrable if and only if it involves only two variables. The paradox of why Pareto's second method is valid in an economy of only two, but not in one of three, commodities was still undefeated. After searching through my box of mathematical tools, I concluded that Volterra and all who after him worked on the issue of integrability completely ignored the real snag. I prided myself on having cut a Gordian knot by proving in the 1936 essay that, contrary to what Volterra and everyone else held, even when the integrals of (1) exist, they cannot be identified with the indifference varieties without some additional *factual* reasons. To explicate this point, I considered the integral curves of (1) on a particular two-dimensional space, namely, the budget plane with three commodities. Under simple conditions, those curves always exist (Volterra's point). Two diagrams proved my contention: in one, the integral curves were logarithmic spirals around a singular point, a focus; in the other, they were ovals around a center, also a singular point. The first corresponded to the nonintegrability case in three dimensions; the second, to the standard utility map. In the first case, *even though the integral curves were there, no preference scale can be constructed on their basis.* Fourteen years later (1954), on these two pictures Paul Samuleson based a parable, highly pleasing like all others of his pen.[2]

---

[2] It does not seem at all strange to me that Samuelson was prompted to reread carefully

I further observed that, whether a utility map exists or not, the consumer always tends toward a point of saturation, either absolute or relative to the possibilities of the budget. The budget equilibrium, therefore, is always a point of saturation. Next, I pointed out that, whether or not equation (1) is integrable and whether or not saturation is at infinity, the direction from any point toward the saturation point is always one of preference. On this basis, in place of the principle of decreasing marginal utility or of decreasing marginal substitution I proposed the *principle of perseverance of nonpreference directions*; that is, once a direction becomes one of nonpreference, no good can come from persevering in it.[3]

Because of my tenet that random is an essential element of phenomena, I also initiated the idea of stochastic choice. That study led to several novel by-products, the most salient being that indifference is not necessarily transitive.

ROMANIAN "EXILE"

If my literary activity during the two short Harvard years (1934–36) seemed rather unusual, it was probably because, as Schumpeter once said, being a novice I was "able to see aspects that trained economists refuse to see and unable to see others that they took for granted." Be this as it may, that performance together with what I had published earlier must have been responsible for Schumpeter's intention to write a treatise on theoretical economics with me, which in turn led to an offer to join the economics faculty. I am now unable to say exactly why, but I simply turned my back on the fantastic chance of being a co-author with Schumpeter and becoming "Georgescu-Roegen of Harvard." I left for Romania.

I looked forward to helping my native land become a happier place for all. The Parcae, however, had decided differently; for being an economist and a statistician as well, I was given the undistinguished, tedious task of organizing the economic statistics at the Central Statistical Institute, followed by that of colligating the daily statistics of foreign trade. (At the time even orthodox countries had foreign trade clearings.) But a truly great wringer was lying in wait for me at the end of the war, the arduous job as general secretary of the Armistice Commission. For about six months it meant long, tedious, and stressful discussions, often lasting

my 1936 essay by an article of H. Houthakker in which, independently of my paper, Houthakker argued that no indifference curves may have a spiral form.
[3] I expressed the perseverance principle by an inequality on which, before long, Paul Samuelson based his epochal idea of revealed preference.

the whole night, with the representatives of the USSR Control Commission.

Since the Yalta and Potsdam conferences ultimately shattered all my hopes of seeing the world reorganized on the principles for which Great Britain and the United States had entered the war, I had to flee Romania before I was thrown into a jail from which no one has ever come out alive. According to the Communists' precepts, I was indeed guilty of three capital crimes: (1) being the servant of capitalists as a Rockefeller fellow and then president of the Romanian Association for Friendship with the United States, (2) being a "member" of the National Council of the Peasantist Party, and (3) being an ardent defender of Romania's rights as the secretary general of the Armistice Commission. Since the safest way of escape seemed to be stowing away on freighter, together with my wife I stealthly entered the Constantsa harbor in the middle of the night of February 13, 1948, surrounded by bribed smugglers. I then felt as if the past twelve years in Romania were scooped out of my life.

Before too long, my Harvard friends Edward S. Mason, and especially Wassily Leontief, found a means of bringing me back again. I arrived at Harvard in early July 1948 and what I found boggled my mind for days, for truly great avenues had been opened in economics during my "exile."

A DISENCHANTED NEOCLASSICAL ECONOMIST

Soon after my return to Romania in 1936, I entered into a wonderful friendship with Andrew Edson, the secretary of the U.S. legation in Bucharest. One day Andy said softly: "Romania is economically undeveloped because your institutions are silly. The legion of doormen who just sit at the door of every high functionary, public or private, produce nothing to motivate their pay." Andy, a strong believer in the neoclassical dogma, then opened my eyes to a violation in my own backyard of the sacrosanct neoclassical principle of marginal pricing. That icy shower on my religious confidence in mathematical economics started me worrying and thinking and thinking. The solution, when it hit me, was that marginal pricing does not maximize the national product proper — an idea that would undoubtedly strike a standard economist as a ridiculous product of some economic ignoramus. Yet the fact is that only in the lands of plenty does the marginal principle maximize a complex of product proper *and* chosen leisure. In the lands of scarcity, however, people must work as long as they can, to the point of zero marginal productivity of labor, as illustrated by the splendid institution, not too old, of the gleaners. In conditions of scarcity, income distribution is made not according to marginal pricing, but according to some institutional rules (as within most families, yours too, I think). Even in the advanced countries, we should note, the consumer is not guided only by a quantitative set of commodities as standard economics claims. Individual behavior is also affected by how one can realize one's want: work for a dollar, beg for it, or pick the cash register, actions judged according to the corresponding social matrix, not affiliated with a quantitative scale.

Another bestirring lesson also came from Romania. Because the peasants always looked to the townies for what to do, the Communists wanted to bring the urban masses to their knees. The plan was to provoke a runaway money inflation so that the decreased value of the bills would stop the peasants from bringing food to the towns. From what I then knew of standard economics, I judged the plan flawless. I cannot describe my surprise when, at a meeting of the National Council of the Peasantist Party, another member, a former village school teacher and an old Peasantist, smugly shot at me, "You do not know the peasants, my friend; they will still sell for any money because money has always been *summum bonum* for them." Nor can I describe my public shame when the developments proved him correct. The Communists then resorted to an unparalleled trick in history: they declared that, on August 15, 1947, all old money was no longer legal tender. Each person (supposedly) received new money of about one U.S. dollar in exchange value.

I had never felt any attraction for monetary theory, and the Romanian peasants convinced me to steer away from its unthinkable quicksands. Yet later, rubbing myself against the disturbing facts of the monetary conditions of Brazil, I reached another heretical conclusion to which I still cling firmly. Contrary to the general tenet of the professional establishment that inflation is the best strategy for economic development, inflation is the most perverse way of governing. Another invisible hand, a Keynesian this time, picks the pockets of the masses who cannot borrow at a privileged interest rate now and pay later.

EPISTEMOLOGY OF ECONOMICS

Science without epistemology is – in so far that it is thinkable at all – primitive and muddled. (Albert Einstein)

Shortly after my return to the United States I completed several papers consisting of significant results. I am saying this not to boast but to illustrate the special usefulness of epistemology in general.

Why include only one structural component in the analytical representation of a process when we know that there are many?

This was the epistemological question that struck me first when approaching Leontief's system. I then proceeded to find out what would happen if each industry could choose from a set of recipes satisfying Leontief's basic assumptions: labor is the only primary factor of production, and return to scale is constant. The theorem that I presented at a seminar of the Harvard Economic Project (March 22, 1949) became known as the "substitution theorem." It states that in equilibrium each industry must operate with only one particular recipe out of its own technological horizon. As I showed by the transparent diagrams reproduced in a paper presented at the December 1949 meeting of the American Economic Association, there are also some singular cases in which, for the equilibrium recipe, the ratio of labor to output is in the limit zero, the catalytic labor that represents the futurists' dream of unlimited technological progress.

An analytical representation of business cycles by nonsymmetrical waves

Through discussions with Professor Schumpeter about my idea that business cycles are not "cyclical," another epistemological question began pressing my mind: how can we represent them analytically? My answer was presented at another seminar (April 1949) in the paper "Relaxation Phenomena in Linear Economic Models." In it I debunked the idea that decumulation is the reverse process of accumulation and proposed that the business turning points are relaxation phenomena when the law of one phase suddenly changes into the other. To represent this conception of business cycles, I used a sequence of two alternating phases, F_1 for the upswing, F_2 for the downswing. Schumpeter, who always attended those seminars, left me breathless when he asked with which of the two phases the process began. He used this sort of question against the theories that explain depression as the product of prosperity and prosperity as that of depression. One must then know, Schumpeter used to say, whether business cycles began with an overproduction or an underproduction of apples in the Garden of Eden.

Vicit *Pareto*

Because Paul Samuelson believed that a Houthakker axiom that assumed away spiral formations provided the definitive liquidation of the non-integrability puzzle, he keenly endorsed it (1954). Yet the snag of the singularity was still overlooked. To prove the ineffectiveness of the new axiom, I countered with an analytical example (1954) in which the integrals of (1) involved a singular point – a node, later renamed pole – which naturally impeded the establishment of an ophelimity index. Within such a map the consumer could move around the node and arrive at the same subjective state as the initial one, a possibility not denied by Houthakker's axiom. A feeling that Pareto was right in a deeper sense than I had shown until then began pressing me. But it was only at the symposium in Pareto's memory (1973) that I presented the ultimate analytical example in which (1) is derived from *community* demand schedules and is nonetheless completely integrable without any singularity whatever. Those integrals do look like the usual indifference map, but we know only too well that they cannot be associated with it. Therefore, to identify integrals with the indifference varieties we must know beforehand that an ophelimity index exists, as Pareto did. This conclusion vindicates Pareto (and by the same coup exposes the behaviorists' folly of rejecting all subjectiveness).

DIALECTICS VERSUS ARITHMOMORPHISM

Science began as a trove of propositions describing some observed phenomenon. It still consists of such a trove, though restructured under the continual pressure of the limit of human memory. At first, some propositions were classified in groups, as in the Hammurabi Code. Later, some great relief for memory came with writing and the convenient materials for doing so. Taxonomical classification of the kind we find in biology and even in chemistry was the next advance. Ultimately, some ancient land surveyors on the Nile discovered that if one has memorized

(A) The sum of the angles of a triangle is two right angles,

one need not also memorize

(B) The sum of the angles of a convex quadrangle is four right angles.

That was the germ of the *theoretical* science (not of every science). In a theoretical science all descriptive propositions must be filed, not alphabetically (as in a directory), or taxonomically, but in a *logical order* as in geometry. Through an intricate logical sorting all known propositions can be divided into two classes:

(α) Every α proposition follows logically from some β propositions,
(β) No β proposition follows from any β propositions.

All we have then to memorize is the set (β), for by simple ratiocination we can rediscover all the others. The greatest advantage of logical filing is thus the economy of thought, a point brought up by Ernest Mach and Karl Pearson. For many, though, memorizing is much easier than ratiocinating; many a student prefers courses based mainly on memory. Why are there such sciences?

It was this question that set me on the path to dialectics, for I observed that logic, though a marvelous accessory for our thinking, has its limits set by its own power. Logic works only with a restricted class of propositions, such as

(A) The hypotenuse is greater than a leg

but is totally impotent when it comes to propositions such as

(B) Culturally determined wants are higher than biological needs.

Worthy of special note is that all concepts in proposition (A) are as *discretely* distinct as any clear symbol, say, m, 2, or ∞. Discrete distinction is the specific property of real members; a number retains its distinct individuality even within the arithmetical continuum. This is why I have proposed to call such concepts *arithmomorphic*. No arithmomorphic concept overlaps with its opposite. The boundary between the two is vacuous: *tertium non datur*. A vast number of concepts, however, overlap with their opposites. That is, A and non-A may be both true (which does not mean *tertium datur*). As Max Rheinstein once remarked, "Even the dictatorship of Hitler ... had democratic features, and in the democracy of the United States we find certain dictatorial elements." Proposing to refer to concepts of this kind as *dialectical*, I have obviously followed Hegel, yet only for a short while. In my view concepts are means of expressing our thoughts, not legislators of nature and society as Hegel and Marx (in a switched way) claimed.

Arithmomorphic concepts are absolutely invariant: "square" meant the same thing to Euclid as it does to us today. If in our imagination we alter an angle of a square no matter how little, it is no longer a "square." But we can squeeze an "oval" a great deal before it is no longer an "oval." Dialectical concepts, though not discretely distinct, are distinct. They are separated from their opposites by a dialectical penumbra that is in turn delimited by other dialectical penumbras. A baby will be old when he will be ninety; but no one can say when he will just become old. On this point as well as on similar others, Bertrand Russell argued that one can determine that event by associating it with a convenient number. What he proposed was to define a particular democracy as that of the United States at, say, March 15, 1896, at π o'clock p.m. But my epistemology faults him. In relation with facts we cannot use paper-and-pencil numbers, 1 or π. A pointer-reading belongs to dialectics. This issue recalls one of Schumpeter's incisive protests: "There is no sense in our case in asking: 'Where does that type [of entrepreneur] begin then?' and then to exclaim: 'This is no type at all!'"

Entities that change qualitatively are necessarily dialectical. The epitome is "species," which is dialectical because, as Charles Darwin put it, "it includes the unknown element of a distinct act of creation." The present temper that insists that "species" is an arithmomorphic concept is tantamount to a return to Lamarck, to species created once for all. Diehard logical positivists naturally would forever insist on exclusive arithmomorphism. Yet these apostles are utterly mistaken, for not even they could plead any case without using more dialectical concepts than arithmomorphic ones. Is "a sufficiently large sample" or "verifiability," for instance, arithmomorphic? Eminent scholars – like Bertrand Russel and Percy Bridgman – who made a point of honor in combating vagueness offered us the best proof that reasoning with dialectical concepts is not only quite possible, but also indispensable.[4] Only it is far more difficult than doing algebra when, as it often happens, the tip of the pencil may move faster than the writer's mind.

This brings to mind Blaise Pascal's immortal dichotomy – *esprit géométrique* and *esprit de finesse* – of which the widespread arithmomania of our epoch would rather not hear. Even the bland way in which I put it at a 1955 symposium – "There is a limit to what we can do with numbers, as there is to what we can do without them" – was anathema to the worshipers of the Almighty Arithmomorphic Concept. At the famous David Novick symposium organized by Seymour Harris (1954), Lawrence Klein proclaimed that "nonmathematical contributions to economics [are] fat, sloppy, and vague." A verdict on Adam Smith, Schumpeter, or Simon Kuznets? And because at that time crime and drug addiction were not on the rise, Robert M. Solow could get off unscathed for having reasoned that mathematical economics must be really good because everyday there is more, not less, of it. But the actual crux was exploded later when Salim Rashid produced the document of the time: because of the views of the economic establishment, junior economists, he said, must grind papers by the mathematical engine, lest they perish.

Dialectics and similes

There is justice in the positivist objection that communication with dialectical concepts cannot be precise. With this point in mind, I tried to mirror dialectical concepts by some analytical pseudo-images to which I have appropriately referred as *similes*. While struggling with modern utility theory, my epistemology took offense at the absence of any mention of wants or dislikes – the real movers of our actions. I was thus delighted to discover that wants of all forms had formed the pillars of the older consumer theory propounded by T. C. Banfield and Carl Menger, now fallen from favor. Standard economists have chosen just to putter with the second differential of a nominal, opaque blanket named

---

[4] For completion, I should add that a still greater economy is achieved by introducing some thought-up propositions (ω), which added to (β) propositions shift many more of these to the (α) set.

"utility," a term with which Jeremy Bentham himself was unhappy to the end. The neoclassical rationalization was that want cannot be defined precisely. To be sure, want is a dialectical concept. If want had been a rigid arithmomorphic element, the human species would not have been able to survive under the radically different environments of its long past. Wants even form a dialectical hierarchy: above those that respond to biological needs (which are common to all human) come those that correspond to social propensities (common to all members of the same community), and above these, the purely personal, disordered whims. On the basis of this hierarchy, we can justify two of the most essential propositions about us. First, the principle of marginal utility is just short-hand for the law that any human satisfies his wants in their hierarchical order. And, second, contrary to the most unfortunate fallacy of standard economics, most wants are interpersonally comparable. All humans − the Rothschilds and Hollywood stars included − will spend their *only* taler for quenching thirst and assuaging hunger. Of course, interpersonal comparison between the upper wants of two rich people, one enjoying a motorboat, the other a villa, makes no sense. Since standard economics is a discipline of the lands of plenty, Lionel Robbins' famous theses of interpersonal noncomparability fits in place there, but only there.

After seeing that Carl Menger's table of wants cannot explain how one distributes a given income with given prices among one's various wants, I proposed a simile diagram in which to every want there corresponds a domain delimited by ordinary lines and located according to the general hierarchy. It was by this factual analysis that I proved for the first time the necessity of lexicographic order for economic theory.

Similes had been occasionally used earlier in other respects. One of the most interesting cases is the theory of probability. The Laplacean, the frequentist, the betting coefficient, and all other definitions tried out are all arithmomorphic similes of probability, which is a dialectical notion in the truest Hegelian sense: it starts and ends with itself. It is because of this dialectical nature of probability that all the mentioned similes have ended in contradictions. The probability associated with natural phenomena is dialectical because its backbone, randomness, is a dialectical notion, for randomness implies irregularity, yet unlike the desultory haphazardness that irregularity is regular. I have captured all this in the following proposition:

> If A is a random event and f_n is an observed relative frequency, there exists an associated number p such that, for any positive ϵ and δ, there is an integer N such that
> $$1 > \text{Prob}[|f_n - p| < \epsilon] > 1 - \delta \qquad (2)$$
> is true for any number of observations $n > N$.

That p is the probability of A.

THE DOUBLE-BARRELED PRODUCTION FUNCTION

In another paper at the Harvard Economic Project (March 22, 1949), I pointed out a serious epistemological discrepancy between the two production models in vogue at the time, Neumann's and Leontief's. Because the first takes into account only stocks, it hides what may have happened between the beginning and the end of the process. Because Leontief considers only flows, he does not allow one to know which of two processes is more efficient. Intrigued, I turned to the standard production function, the definition of which (very strange) has remained in the same vapid form in which Philip Wicksteed introduced it almost one hundred year ago (1894): "*The product being a function of the factors of production we have P = f(a, b, c, . . .)*." He said nothing about the kind of "function," or about the nature of the "factors," and no economic luminaries have ever questioned that diction. Some just said that the representation of a process involves only quantities:

$$Q = F(X, Y, Z, \ldots); \tag{3}$$

others, that it involves only rates of flow per unit of time:

$$q = f(x, y, z, \ldots). \tag{4}$$

Yet no one seems to have been bothered by this double-barreled view, not even Ragnar Frisch, who used both definitions on the same page (*Theory of Production*, p. 43). Using the elementary *identities X = tx*, $Y = ty$, $Z = tz, \ldots$ for any t, I proved that if both (3) and (4) are equivalent representations of a process, the two functions must be identical, $F \equiv f$, and, moreover, homogeneous of the first degree. Hence absolutely *all production processes are indifferent to scale!* I presented this astounding result in a formal paper at a 1965 conference of the International Economic Association. According to their rules, only the contre-rapporteur should present the highlights of the author's paper. My contre-rapporteur, Don Patinkin, stated that he could not introduce a paper vitiated by a "fundamental mathematical error" and simply sat down.[5] This high-handed attitude of an asservative economist was an emphatic proof of how incredible my theorem could then be judged by standard economists. Did not Joan Robinson claim with her usual feeling

---

[5] While writing on this issue for my *Analytical Economics*, I said in passing that a new Aristotle might set dialectical reasoning on as solid a basis as the traditional logic. By a strange coincidence, L. A. Zadek ("Fuzzy Sets," *Information and Control* 3 [1965], 338–53) had just claimed to have achieved this. But the claim, endorsed by legions, is spurious. The entire construction, beginning with the membership function $f_A(x)$, is purely mathematical; hence, it has nothing to do with dialectical concepts.

for what economics should be that standard theory of production is an economic miseducation?

ANALYTICAL PROCESS: FLOWS AND FUNDS

"Process" is one of the most frequently used, and also the most abused, term in science. We find no definition of it even in Alfred North White-head's famous opus *Process and Reality*. Its detailed description runs against several paradoxical tangles that are circumvented by a jump in the dark, from dialectical to arithmomorphic (or analytical). What it involves epistemologically is, first, that an analytical process is *identified* by a vacuous boundary of double nature: a spatial boundary and a temporal boundary that must not begin or end at infinity. Second, even though *inside* the boundary things happened in every location – too many to be listed – in analysis what a process does is described only by what crosses the boundary. The definitions "input" equals what you put in, and "output" equals what is put out can now be made analytical: input is what crosses the spatial boundary from *outside*; output is what crosses it from *inside*.

There are only three distinct and exhaustive cases: (1) factors that go in and never come out, (2) factors that come out although they have never gone in, and (3) factors that come out unchanged just as they have gone in. There is also a fourth logical category – factors that do not cross the boundary at all. They are *internal* flows illustrated, say, by "payments of business to business," which smuggles a dialectical concept into analysis. This confusion, also committed by Karl Marx, necessarily ends in errors if not in a paradox.[6]

The three production factors just described correspond to the classical Ricardian land, capital equipment, and labor power. According to my epistemological view, they are the *agents* that transform the inflows into the outflows. I have proposed to refer to them as *funds*, conceived as agents of constant efficiency.[7] Clearly, excepting Ricardian land, everything changes with time. For the purposes of analysis, however, capital

---

[6] To be sure, shortly after the conference Don Patinkin realized that he had been wrong (probably because he was not aware of the difference between *identity* and *equation*) and requested that his criticism not be published in the *Proceedings*.

[7] When Leontief first presented his input–output system, he repeatedly insisted that all diagonal coefficients should be zero, which meant that the matrix should include no internal flow. However, in his later applications he did include them. To make the absurdity of the internal flow clearer, I devised a multiprocess matrix in which there is no empty box into which one could inscribe a coordinate for internal flow. That matrix also enables us to dispense with the helplessly intractable flow diagrams that overlay the recent ecological monographs (in which the frequent use of the "loop" should have exposed the limp concept of internal flow).

may be assumed constant, as Karl Marx first proposed. A separate process, the household, aims at maintaining the vital ability of people in
order.

What a process does is then analytically represented by a set of functions of time t from $t = 0$, the beginning of the process, to $t = T$, the
end of the process. Each such function represents the cumulative amount
up to time t of a flow, entered or exited, or of *service* provided by a fund.
This new way of representing a production process is a vector of functions, that is, a functional,

$$[R_i(t),\ I_i(t),\ P_i(t),\ W_i(t);\ L_i(t),\ K_i(t),\ H_i(t)]_0^T, \tag{5}$$

where the alphabetization indicates in sequence: natural resources, intermediate products, products, waste, and next, land, capital, and labor
power. Each production process is thus represented not by a timeless
vector in the commodity space as in standard theory, but by a *curve* in
the same space. A critical difference that I thus introduced is the inclusion
in (5) of natural resources and waste, inevitable but totally overlooked
factors of any process.[8]

Standard theory makes intensive use of isoquants – *geometrical* curves
– to represent the substitution of factors without changing the output.
But since neither capital equipment nor laborers can be quantified as
needed for the isoquant, if anybody uses an isoquant, one must inevitably
admit that one's own framework is essentially dialectical. Some have
indeed likened capital to clay or to putty. *I know of no other scientific
discipline in which dialectics is as indispensable as in most sectors of
mathematical economics.*

PATTERNS OF PRODUCTION PROCESSES

My epistemological search has also led me to the new fact that production
takes place in several and entirely different types of processes. The simplest type is that which not only is represented by (5) – all are – but can
be represented only by it. It is the process of a single craftman's workshop,
where at any time work is applied to only one unit (or one batch) of the
product and units are produced *in series*. And if we tease out any other
kind of process, we find that all consist of some arrangement of such
simple processes, which I called *elementary* processes. For an agricultural
product within a uniform climate, the elementary processes are arranged
in parallel.

---

[8] My concept of fund should not be confused with that of stock. The role of stock is to
receive or to generate flows. And contrary to some opinions, the flow-fund model is
essentially different from the flow-stock models encountered in the economic literature.

One point now deserves unparsimonious attention: in any elementary process virtually all funds are idle over certain periods, and this idleness cannot be completely eliminated by technology. Think of the plough in the temperate zone or of the saw of a cabinetmaker. If in the latter's shop an additional craftsman is brought in, the two could use the same tool alternately and thus decrease the idleness of each fund. The production would thus be speeded up many times more, which would require an equally increased intensity of the demand, a finding that analytically vindicates Adam Smith.

In the industrial sector we also find that production – of one spacecraft, for instance – is an elementary process. But that sector is dominated rather by the factory system, so common a view, yet so totally disregarded. Like money, that process is a purely economic invention, not a technological discovery. A theorem I proved states that any set of commensurable tasks that would constitute an elementary process can be arranged in a pattern that would eliminate all idleness, a commonplace illustration of which is any assembly line. This is the superiority of the factory system, which has still another economic advantage. Its production needs no waiting. If Bali Island (where uniform climate would permit it) agriculture used the factory system, it could be said that the Balinese eat the rice sown that very moment. This peculiar property is due to a specific capital item, goods in process or *process fund* (my preferred term).

Production by factories, though, needs waiting too: building the plant itself and priming it may take years. Contrary to Piero Sraffa's celebrated thesis, production of commodities in general needs not only commodities as such, but factories too. And because there is no factory to produce factories, some waiting is irreducible in the case of growth.

Curiously, the simplest analytical representation is that of the factory process for which the arguments of functional (4) are simple linear homogeneous functions of t. We may thus put in a generic form $A(T) = aT = A^0$ for every element of (5), the notation A^0 standing for quantities and the lowercase a for rates with respect to time. For the representation by quantities, there is a hitch: one hundred pounds of nails says nothing about T, which might have had almost any value. For this reason, in passing from the functional to its degenerated form – the quantitative vector – we must include T in the new form

$$(R^0, I^0, Q^0, W^0; L^0, Q^0, H^0: T). \tag{6}$$

By contrast, the representation by a vector of rates need not explicitly contain the time coordinate:

$$(r, i, q, w; l, k, h). \tag{7}$$

Formulas (6) and (7) dissolve immediately the paradox of the double-barrelled production function. The epistemology of the propounder of production function (2) failed to realize that quantities are not time dimensional. Another common epistemological fumble is the indiscriminate use of "flow" in saying, with Marxians and the legion of energetists, that the sewing needle, not only the cloth, flows into the pants.

After examining the blueprints L, K, H of a factory, specialists could say (1) how large would be the output q and (2) what production flows would be necessary for it. The factory process must be portrayed by two similes:

$$q = \phi(L, K, H) \quad \text{and} \quad q = \psi(r, i, w). \tag{8}$$

Factory production, therefore, is affected by a strict limitationality: it cannot produce more shirts by increasing only the sewing machines or only the input of fabric. A production function of only funds and flows, therefore, is total nonsense. Yet with the recent discovery of resource scarcity, numberless economists have used the function $q = F(H, r)$ for selling the newest economist's conjuring trick. If that formula were epistemologically valid, we could at whim substitute capital equipment for iron ore while increasing even the production. Another fictional function is $q = F(K, H; t)$, where t supposedly represents technological progress. Several standard economists have used the partial derivative of F with respect with t, completely ignoring when they were trapped the fact that neither the function F, nor the arguments K, H, are the same in 1980 as in 1960: $F_{1980}(K^{'80}, H^{'80}) - F_{1960}(K^{'60}, H^{'60})$ is not a difference on which the derivative is based. This fumble proves that even in mathematics we cannot do without epistemology.

GROWTH VERSUS DEVELOPMENT

Ever since John Maynard Keynes' *General Theory*, growth has been conceived as a purely monetary phenomenon sustained by the century's monetary witchery: if government spends more for itself, all people will grow economically. For the simplicity of the diagram with the 45° line, Keynes became the darling of economists and, before long, of the politicians, who could now rationalize moving mountains without increasing taxes.

In spite of my uneasiness in approaching monetary facts, my epistemological penchant found, nonetheless, some delight in the problem of growth because of Neumann's and Leontief's models of production. The mathematics of even the generalized Leontief system are rather simple (and I thought to have them all included in my article "Some Properties of a Generalized Leontief System" presented at the memorable conference in Chicago [1949] by the Cowles Commission and reproduced in my *Analytical Economics*, Chap. 9). They tell us that Leontief's system in which labor is the only primary fund needs only a definite amount of labor power, L^i, for the production of an additional unit of commodity C_i. Is this not a secret of growth? Reluctantly, I must disappoint the adherents of this viewpoint: the principle is true mathematically but not operationally.

A point I can hardly overemphasize is that *in the initial Leontief system, just like in Marx's labor theory, labor is necessary but not sufficient for production.* A pesky question therefore confronts would-be planners: given that coal is necessary to produce iron and iron is necessary, too, to produce coal, where does any growth plan based on Leontief's system get the necessary amounts of these commodities? An authentic story pinpoints this antinomy: a cookbook advised cooks to prepare stock A with some of stock B and the latter with some of the former. Even the king's cooks could not prepare anything.

It is very simple to calculate the matrix in which all net outputs are increased, yet how to pass from the initial to the last matrix is one of the most stubborn economic problems. Even Karl Marx, who considered both a stationary and an expanding state, never showed how to pass from the former to the latter.

Of course, instantaneous growth can be achieved at will if we increase the working hours of the shift. But this trivial solution is inapplicable in Leontief's system, which ignores that coordinate. And it would also be unacceptable to the temper of this era, which refuses to recognize the primary truth upon which I have repeatedly insisted: the economic progress of the West was fostered by a very long working day.

On paper, we may start by saving some of one commodity and, by ramification, stage by stage reach a higher net income for all commodities. In Leontief's dynamic system even growth by stages is beset by several snags. In that system, because growth also requires increased funds, an awful snag is that either bulldozers are consumption commodities or yogurt is a producer good. The morale: cling to the idea that all facts involve irreducible structure.

Another strong epistemological uneasiness of mine concerns the use of differential equations to show how growth can be inplanted in a poorly growing economy by fitting it to a growing differential system. Of course, this is the acme of self-deception.

For a final word, we should not delude ourselves that mere accretion poses no intricate epistemological issues. Remember that biologists had long been tormented by the problem of how the accretion of simple cells occurs. Only the double helix, by being its own negative template, cleared the mystery. Yet notwithstanding the claims of eminent biologists, development has still not been explained. My epistemology prompted me to dissent: the DNA of a zygote warrants only its identical self-reproduction, not its metamorphosis into, say, a nerve cell. How much more mysterious, then, should economic development be? I was taken to task for having said that the most valuable clues for that issue come only from economic history, but Professor Schumpeter saved my soul by avowing his own confidence in history in *History of Economic Analysis*.

FEASIBLE RECIPES VERSUS VIABLE TECHNOLOGIES

I came to realize the indissoluble dependence of the survival of humankind on scarce resources by the combined influence of two sources: Emile Borel's monograph on statistical mechanics (alias thermodynamics), which as a student of statistics I read in the 1920s, and the problems of an overpopulated agrarian economy, of which I became fully aware during my Romanian exile. I then became convinced that nothing can solve the problems of an exploding population except, as Malthus argued, the population itself. The thought that, even if the population stopped growing, its predicament would still remain came to me one day as I watched a big Romanian river running in its bed furiously and with a chocolate color. There goes, I said, our daily bread of tomorrow.

Homo sapiens, *the exosomatic animal*

As a witness of the political events during my Romanian exile, I realized that Romania could not remain neutral (as virtually everybody wished) in World War II. From history I also learned that this was true for World War I. The only impediment was Romania's possession of great reserves of oil, which neither Germany nor Russia was willing to let the other control. Other animals, however, do with just what they have. The quintessence of this view was recently expressed by Andrew Rooney, who watching a chipmunk at work observed that it never stopped to go to the hardware store to buy a tool, as humans must do. In all activities of life, all animals (humans included) use their organs with which their somata have been endowed by birth – the *endosomatic* organs, a term coined by the unusually perceptive biologist Alfred Lotka. And it is through changes of the endosomatic organs that every animal becomes better (or even less) adapted to life. But this mode of evolving is extremely slow. The human species alone found a far speedier way. Even some ancestors of *Homo* began using and finally making detachable *exosomatic* organs: first, stone hammers to hit harder; recently, airplanes to fly higher and faster than any bird. This does not justify the popular definition of humans as the only toolmakers. But as Henri Bergson first observed, humans are the only animals to use tools to make tools or, as Schumpeter used to say, to make machines, to make machines, to make machines, on end. The exosomatic human can do things that could not be done before. But exosomatism, I should stress, is not an unadulterated blessing. It is the root of inequalities within the same society as well as among societies. Because the production of exosomatic organs has to be planned and supervised, human societies have been divided into those who work (the ricksha men) and the governing individuals (the mandarins). And, not to forget, exosomatism has also made us thoroughly addicted to the exosomatic comfort – hence almost completely dependent on the finite mineral dowry of our abode.

Thermodynamics and economic scarcity

While men of science were still interested in celestial affairs and in explaining them by the laws of mechanics, Sadi Carnot, a young French officer, published in 1824 an immortal memoir on the efficiency of the steam engine, the seed of the science of thermodynamics. For these reasons I argued that Carnot was the first genuine econometrician and that thermodynamics is in essence a physics of economic value.

Thermodynamics has had an agitated history, and its theoretical structure is now beclouded by a swarm of mathematical fantasies. My own struggles with the vacillating literature have led me to a very simple and clear conception of it. One of its four laws, the entropy law, has engendered endless controversies. Yet its content boils down to a commonplace known from the time when man was not yet *Homo sapiens*. It simply states, as Rudolph Clausius put it in 1856, that heat always goes *by itself* from the hotter to the colder body, never in reverse. Or as I put it in a more homely way, it is the hand touching a hot stove that is burned, not the stove. Since such transfer of heat cannot be prevented between bodies in contact, it follows that everywhere in the universe hot things *continuously and irrevocably* become colder and cold things, hotter. Clausius cast this fact into "The entropy of the universe tends toward a maximum." But what exactly is entropy?

My view is that the entropy law, like other thermodynamic laws, reflects basic limitations of all living creatures. Let me begin by noting that a formulation of the entropy law that denies the possibility of converting the energy from a single source of uniform temperature into work, although well established in the literature, is not true; a piston and cylinder, by absorbing heat from such a source, can do it, as happens during the first expanding phase of a Carnot cycle. Yet we cannot take advantage of this splendid "engine" because of our limitation *in space*. Even after a small course, the piston must be brought back to its initial position. For this we must spend the same amount of energy as the work gained when the piston moved forward. There remains no surplus work for us.

The solution to the impasse is one of Carnot's keen propositions: bring the piston back by a colder route than the first and you will get some surplus work. All steam engines must therefore work in cycles between a hotter and a colder temperature. In general, we can obtain work only from a source that involves a difference of temperature, of electrical or chemical potential. Only such energy is *available* (useful) to us as humans, homogeneous energy is *unavailable* (useless) to us. These fundamental thermodynamic concepts are clearly anthropomorphic. They justify my earlier contention that thermodynamics is a physics of economic value.

Any direct conduction of heat from hot to cold therefore robs us of available energy. Another robber is friction. However, friction does not produce heat if the motion is infinitesimally slow, in which case any movement would take a virtually infinite time. That possibility is off bounds for us, because we are limited *in time* as well.[9]

Those who have an unrestrained confidence in the power of science to fix anything keep preaching that science would help us get rid of even the entropic degradation. As a simile for the entropic degradation, I once used an hourglass assumed not ever to be turned upside down. Paul Samuelson followed with the remark (*Economics*, 11th ed.) that "science can temporarily turn the glass over." Yet I would not advise anybody to settle in an aentropic world (if one existed); for if one took a bath there, one might have the neck scorched and the toes frostbitten by a redistribution of heat. Nor would I enjoy living in a frictionless world where I could not write or walk in the direction I wanted.

I have further argued, and very strongly, that matter, too, is subject to entropic degradation, that available matter in the bulk (say, the rubber of automobile tires) degrades irrevocably into the unavailable form of the rubber particles dispersed by friction on the pavement. We delude ourselves if we trust the popular belief that matter, unlike energy, can be completely recycled. What we can recycle is only *available* matter that is in an unusable form: broken glass, old papers, worn-out motors, and the like. I have stated this as the impossibility of perpetual motion of the third kind, defined as a closed system that could exchange only energy and would perform work at a constant rate forever. I have referred to it as the Fourth Law of Thermodynamics. The reaction to it has been thin and also very strange, for some have simply asserted that the law has long been known, while others have objected that it is not true. The latter critics have committed the same error as Galileo in claiming that the air offers no friction to the flying arrow on the ground that its existence could not be detected by any instrument of that time.[10]

---

[9] These results were presented twenty-five years ago when pollution had not yet hit us in the face, nor had the embargo of 1973 made us aware of nature's niggardliness.

[10] A few critics, typically, represented by Carlo Bianciardi, Paolo Degli Espinoza, and Enzo Tiezzi, "Ma la materia ha una storia," *SE Scienza Experienza* 4 (July 1986), 40–1,

The root of economic scarcity, hence of economic value as well, lies in the entropic degradation of energy and of matter in bulk. A different kind of scarcity is represented by Ricardian land, which is scarce because it sets a limit to the daily carrying capacity of the earth. The scarcity of mineral resources sets no reasonable limit to how much of them we can use during one day, but it sets a more dreadful limit, a limit on the survival of the human species on this planet. This was my message of twenty years ago, which, though pessimistic, did not spring from a pessimistic *Weltanschauung*, but from known facts. Yet a tidal wave of writers, new and old, have sought public admiration by opposing an ultra-optimistic battle cry to my pessimistic message.

THE PROMETHEAN DESTINY OF HUMANKIND

Confronted with the recent symptom of the scarcity of our environmental dowry, the 1973 oil embargo, economists in particular have reacted according to Disney's First Law, "Wishing will make it so," as William Miernyk aptly put it in his piercing contributions to the problem of the exhaustibility of fossil fuels. Economists have authoritatively advised us to go home and sleep tight in our beds assured that "come what may, we shall find a way" as we have done ever since the time of Tutankhamen. Robert M. Solow even declared in his Richard T. Ely Lecture that "the world can, in effect, get along without natural resources, so that exhaustion is just an event, not a catastrophe." And legions have argued that "solar energy is here, we can use it now," as Denis Hayes, a very sound student of the problem, proclaimed in the *Washington Post* a few years ago. Standard economists have made a defensive circle around the dogma that the market knows best, that prices will take care of any economic turnabout. I have strongly dissented from this economic fantasy. Its advocates have completely ignored that we could not let the polluting driver pay: instead, we have enforced the use of the catalytic converter by law. Are not the whales on the way to extinction precisely because the price of their meat is right? The same also goes for the deforestation of all time, especially of that in Brazil now.

There now rages a fashion to fancy one or another alternative to the current technology. None (yes, none) is worth anything because none has taken account of the fundamental condition of a viable technology, to which I now turn.

argued that with a magnet it is possible to reassemble all iron filings into the original piece. But they did not specify the instrument that would guarantee that the iron particles dispersed during the proposed experiment, and *only these*, would be picked up by their proposed magnet. Naturally, I think my law is true, yet I would not oppose any scientific denial of it. As I told Ilya Prigogine during a symposium sponsored by the U.S. Department of Transportation, we must know whether my proposed perpetual motion is feasible or not; we have answered this question for other perpetual motions.

The number of production recipes used by humans ever since they became exosomatic animals is so enormous that even a lifetime would probably not suffice to compile a complete list of them. However, surprising though it may seem, only three of that vast number have effectively pushed on our exosomatic progress. In chronological order they are husbandry, the mastery of fire, and the steam engine. I have called these recipes *Promethean* on remembering the old legend that Prometheus, a Titan, stole the fire from the gods and gave it to humans. With just the spark of a match we can set on fire a whole forest, nay, all forests. This property, although not as violent, characterizes the other two Promethean recipes. It is a commonplace that a seeded grain of corn will normally yield a surplus of a handful of grains.

The steam engine, however, needs further discussion along with the prodigious story of its invention. Helped by the Promethean fire, humans were able to keep warm, cook food, bake ceramics, and above all smelt metals. An era of vigorous technological progress thus began. But given human impatience, any recipe that increases our power over things is self-defeating. We would normally use it oftener and oftener so that its technology would spread at a fantastic speed. In this way, by the middle of the seventeenth century the technology based on Promethean fire ran out of its fuel: wood. Deforestation was advancing so fast that even in Norway legal restrictions onto cutting trees had to be introduced. Coal had been known as another source of heat ever since the thirteenth century. But the energy of coal, *though available*, was not profitably accessible. Below even a moderate depth, underground water floods any mine and must be drained off, which requires an appreciable amount of energy. At the time, this posed an insuperable problem. Operators of mines asked even Galileo for help. He advised them to use a pneumatic pump; nature, he explained, abhors vacuum. But after they reported back that, no matter how hard they pulled out the pump, the water would not rise above some ten meters, Galileo reflected that perhaps nature abhors a vacuum only up to that height. The situation was in all respects like that of today. Fate had it, then, that Prometheus II – two mortals, Thomas Savery and Thomas Newcomen – saved the day by inventing the steam engine. This engine, too, is a Promethean recipe: with just a little coal under it we can drain the water completely from a mine and also bring out far more coal than that used by the engine, nay, enough to operate other mines as well. Yet the steam engine has its entropic limitations, too. What the energetist tyros seem to ignore is that absolutely no recipe can produce additional available energy or available matter. From what? I would ask. Let us assume that another earth would possess vast reserves of bituminous coal located 10^7 feet below the surface. Since it would take more than the energy of one pound of coal to mine one pound, no steam engine could then be Promethean for that coal. The object lesson of this parable for the self-styled energetists is that a recipe that works well in the laboratory (as many do) may not necessarily support a viable technology.

From what I have said in this section, it is obvious that no viable technology can exist unless it is supported by a Promethean recipe. A new Promethean recipe, not just any fancy contrivance, is what the present crisis needs (a point totally ignored by those who exalt, individually or within the ever-growing number of global associations, one's own alternative solution). The stern question now is: will Prometheus III come in time to save our souls by a new Promethean recipe? Some claim that two Promethean recipes are already at hand. One is indeed: the breeder that produces more fissionable fuel than it consumes – hence its uniquely alluring name. Its hitch is the genetic danger of its waste. The second (alluded to earlier) is the *direct* harnessing of solar energy. With sanguine hopes but with accomplished technological knowledge, a serious attempt was made by Solarex, Inc., to construct a solar "breeder." The result of that experiment was categorical: the amount of solar energy captured by a number of silicon cells does not suffice to reproduce them all even if all the necessary materials are obtained gratis from elsewhere. Automobiles and airplanes have been propelled by solar cells. But as my epistemological obsession forces me to observe, the energy that produced the cells, the automobiles, and the planes came from nonsolar sources. At this time, harnessed solar energy is, like electricity, a parasite of other energies.

Faced with the present hovering crisis, what could humankind do? In strictest logic the answer is: practice "conservation," which, not to remain just a word, must be examined epistemologically. Two important factors emerge. The first is the necessity of reducing consumption so as to slow down the depletion of our vital resources to the minimum compatible with a reasonable survival of our species. A prominent economist challenged me to set a number for the reasonable consumption rate, an inept challenge. Are there numbers *set* for the rates of taxation, hospitals, schools? Undoubtedly, we must adopt some austere program (not to go back to nature, as some have wrongly read into my writings). Besides renouncing all kinds of instruments for killing ourselves, we should also stop overheating, overcooling, overlighting, overspeeding, and so on. Most important, we should cure ourselves of the morbid craving for extravagant gadgetry, such as the contradictory golf cart and two-garage cars. I think that we could stop following fashion, that disease of the human mind, as Abbot Fernando Galliani described it in 1750.

The austerity program should, of course, apply primarily to the lands of plenty, certainly not to economically wanting people, say, to Bangladesh. But nations with a growing overpopulation should make all efforts to stop growing in numbers. In a facile way we all speak of overpopulation without realizing that, if the United States were as densely populated as Bangladesh, its population would be just over 6 billion, the present population of the world! This is what overpopulation is.

Conservation would also allow more time for Prometheus III to emerge, and should he or she fail to come in useful time, we will be capable of sliding without social convulsions into a technology not identical with, but very much like, the old one based on wood. Unfortunately, two obstacles rise against this plan. First, no human would voluntarily give up luxuries or even conveniences to help some future generations have plowshares. The human species seems determined to have a short but extravagant existence. Second, conservation is not a program for a club, a town, or even a whole nation. It requires the participation of all in a world organization that would administer the use of the worldized (a word I coined after the manner of "socialized" and "nationalized") resources. But perhaps the human race will pass into extinction segregated economically. It cannot be ruled out that some of the last people should die in penthouses, the others in hovels. *Chi vivra verra.*

BIOECONOMICS AND EVOLUTION

Economic life is a unique process that goes in historical time and in a disturbed environment. (Joseph A. Schumpeter)

After learning of Alfred Lotka's idea that the role of our tools is analogous to our biological organs, I began thinking that a greater analogy exists between exosomatic and endosomatic organs. On that trail I saw that exosomatism was the fountainhead of the economic process. Since the exosomatic organs offer unique advantages to their users and also are detachable, they began being traded and being produced for trade. Production for trade ultimately led to large social organizations. This development brought down upon humans the irrevocable predicament alluded to earlier: the social conflict. Societies of other species do not know such a conflict. The periodic killing of drones by worker bees is a biological, natural action, not a civil war. The reason for the difference is the fact that the role of the individual in the latter societies is decided at birth. The ant doorkeeper, for instance, has a flat head with which it blocks the entrance of any foreigner to the gallery, and he would not like (as we can judge from experiments) to do anything else. But in our case would not a ricksha man, for example, prefer to be a mandarin? And would he not struggle to become almost one?

The exosomatic organs evolve just as the biological ones do, though much, much faster. And just like the latter, they may be deleterious to the species: enormous deer antlers and the automobile that "attains one hundred miles per hour before the cigarette lighter gets hot," as a topical advertisement praises it. Our incurable addiction to even futile exosomatic organs complicates further our existence with problems that belong to *bioeconomics*.

Bioeconomics reminds us of Alfred Marshall, who first envisioned the sisterhood of economics and biology. Although he repeatedly preached that biology, not dynamics, is the Mecca of the economist, he himself hardly practiced that teaching. The economist who developed a general framework to represent evolution everywhere, not only in economics, was Professor Schumpeter. Let me explain this great contribution of his to science, for it still needs to be explained. Schumpeter's vision of development, as he termed it for the first time in opposition to accretionary growth, anticipated by some thirty years a salient idea thought up in 1940 by a prominent biologist, Richard Goldschmidt. Schumpeter's view was that economic evolution is constantly fostered by discontinuous innovations, the product of the continual inventing faculty of the human mind, whereas Goldschmidt contended that biological evolution fares primarily through successful monsters. Inspired by Schumpeter, in my bioeconomics I assimilated the emergence of palpable endosomatic changes with his chain of innovations. Both are essentially unpredictable, not even randomly regulated, a point that exposes the fantasized attempts, such as Trygve Haalvelmo's, to equate evolution with an arithmomorphic mechanism.

In a firmer way than the biologists, Schumpeter maintained that economic evolution is irreversible just as the biological one is. But several biologists who believed in the supremacy of mechanics argued against irreversibility by pointing out that the color of the drosophila's eye changes back and forth constantly, like a pendulum. In this opposition there lies Schumpeter's piercing idea, which he relegated to a footnote (p. 81). There, Schumpeter excluded from innovations small changes, reversible changes akin to drosophila's changes of eye color. It was at that point that Schumpeter was confronted (for the first time, I believe) with an issue of a dialectical nature: What change is small? And there, as on other occasions, his answer was that you and I know when a change is small, although neither of us is able to say exactly when. By taking this position, Schumpeter implicitly opposed the neo-Darwinism account of evolution; for as he splendidly put it, "Add successively as many coaches as you please, you will never get a railway engine thereby." The railway engine compared with the horse cab is a monster, but such a successful one, as Richard Goldschmidt might have put it thirty years later. Of course, in an ocean of Darwinists and neo-Darwinists, Goldschmidt's thesis could not be accepted. Yet very recently, Stephen Gould, one of the most active minds in biology, has rehabilitated Goldschmidt's theory, adding, interestingly, that no explanation of evolution can dispense with dialectical reasoning. Economists, however, have failed to pay any attention to the greatness of the conception of evolution first thought up by one of them.

AGAINST SOME CURRENT?

Don't be modest, you are not that great. (Golda Meir)

The question brings up the relativity of motion; for one may feel one is moving against a current although one just stays put, as many men and women did because they could not do anything else to oppose the Nazi onslaught. And there is the symmetrical case in which one may feel movement against a current even though one is just moving in a placid milieu, in which one might hear the whisper *"Sh! vous reveillez Monsieur,"* as happened to me on a few occasions.

To try to ascertain whether I have ever moved against an objective current is not smooth sailing, for it inevitably entangles me in what, in line with my epistemology, I prefer to call the *sociology of scientists*. This term correctly describes the discipline now known as *sociology of science*, as Karl Mannheim called it first; for sociology necessarily refers to living individuals: humans, chimpanzees, bees, horses. It would be nonsensical to speak of the sociology of books or of differential calculus. As the unorthodox sociologist Florian Znanieki argued, we can speak only of the role of people in acquiring and spreading knowledge. It is by reorienting Mannheim's view that Robert K. Merton set the "sociology of science" on a better track. There is, in particular, Merton's magnificent studies of the Matthew effect, of the multiple discoveries, or of plagiarism, topics germane to what scientists do rather than to what science is.

We may not *all* be aware of the most striking illustration of the Matthew effect; *"E pur si muove"* is ordinarily attributed to Galileo, although those words were the last ones uttered by Giordano Bruno on the burning stake! To descend to common people, my theorem of substitutability of Leontief's static system is usually not connected with my name but with Samuelson's, although Samuelson himself has always acknowledged my priority. (Maybe, Samuelson can be modest.) In the economic literature we also encounter a veiled plagiarism when an author lists only very recent works, two or three years old, avoiding any reference to Adam Smith, Karl Marx, Vilfredo Pareto, John R. Hicks, or others just as great. The aim is to place oneself within the tidal wave of pseudo-innovators. Newton thought this practice to be an academic crime of which he accused Galileo for failing to mention Kepler. When I receive one elegant flier after another about future large congresses organized by energetists who have never referred to my contributions, I always ask, "Why do they send these fliers to me?"

I should list now some of my strange ideas that have a connection with the question of my running against a current. For a start, I thoroughly deny that money is an economic factotum. By itself, it creates impediments for the customary international aid consisting only of money. More often than not, such aid has filled the pockets of the privileged with still more money and has developed the industry of luxury goods instead of much needed wage goods. This wrong is aggravated by the fact that the wanting people usually are toilers of the soil, using either inadequate methods or inappropriate tools. We could train industrial workers by bringing them in successive groups to a huge teaching workshop, but we could not do the same with people occupied in husbandry. Northeast Brazil is the strongest case in point. With this idea in mind, after a 1965 meeting on subsistence farming I declared to a Honululu newspaper that the best way to help the undeveloped countries was to send not gushers of money, not a peace corps, but a peace army. Would sending a peace army instead of one fully armed be an inept idea?

When the UN General Assembly met in Stockholm in 1972 to consider the problems of the environment, I participated in the meeting of the Dai-Dong Association, the sole organization acknowledged by the UN. As Tom Artin tells in his *Earth Talk*, a delectable report about the general events of that occasion, I offered several motions that immediately upset the other members. One motion was that all natural resources should be worldized. My aim was to preclude increasing scarcity from accentuating the extant international inequalities and from eventually fomenting wars. In an interview with the *New York Times* (December 1979), I insisted that, if the use of resources is still to be at the whim of the market, missiles will fly for the possession of the last drop of oil. What recently took place in Kuwait was, fortunately, only a rehearsal, but a rehearsal in full dress. My second tabled motion was to abrogate all passports for international travel. It was another bioeconomic idea to aid the people of undeveloped countries by allowing them to move freely where there is a much greater opportunity for the use of their hands, instead of resorting to the conventional, but extremely difficult operation of bringing capital equipment into their native countries. These ideas certainly were utopian, but I would plead guilty and with pride to that incrimination. There is hardly any social or economic practice of which we are proud now that was not a distasteful, though fully sensible, utopia once. Yet I did not feel that by the foregoing thoughts I was running against a current; there was no current opposing me. I just made my interlocutors conscious of their latent opinions, which happened to oppose mine.

In my earliest contributions I even ran with the current, which was then to expand the legitimate use of mathematics in economics, a program in which I have never ceased to believe and for which my exemplar is Sir John Hicks. My opposition is to the abuses of mathematics, although they have not caused the greatest harm. The greatest harm could come from the prevalent orientation that allowed as a leading item in the *American Economic Review* a paper about rats (which compelled me to resign from the American Economic Association).

If I finally realized that I was running against one current or another, it was not from any crossing of intellectual swords with my fellow economists, who have systematically shunned such an encounter, but from their personal attitudes toward me. I was a darling of the mathematical economists as long as I kept contributing pieces on mathematical economics. Several things radically changed their mood, especially that of the econometricians.

First, there was my contention that marginal pricing is the worst policy for an agrarian overpopulated economy. Soon after returning to the United States, I informally presented that idea at an after-dinner chat at the University of Chicago. How well I remember that there were absolutely no questions at the end! Those good friends wanted to spare me the embarrassment of being exposed as a neoclassical ignoramus. My position in the profession worsened irreparably when, owing to the grace of George B. Richardson, my agrarian paper appeared as a leading item in *Oxford Economic Papers* (1960), not only for having thus touched the sacrosanct neoclassical dogma, but especially for pointing out that the much lauded proof by Kenneth Arrow and Gerard Debreu of the existence of a solution of the Walrasian system was irrelevant in practice because it was based on a fantastic premise; that every individual already had an income sufficient for life. My disclosure was hardly mentioned by subsequent writers, *et pour cause*. Yet it must have succeeded *in sotto voce* to alert others to the danger of breaking intellectual bread with Georgescu-Roegen. When quite recently I proposed collaboration on a significant agricultural project to a colleague, he turned me down explaining that he could not renege on his neoclassical testament.

Second were another series of irritating blunders. In *Analytical Economics* (1966) I stated that not all things can be made with the aid of numbers. And in a paper read at the meeting in honor of Corrado Gini (also in 1966), I dared to expose the ineptitude of predicting economic futures by econometric models. That was like signing my death sentence as a fellow of the Econometric Society (to which I had been elected in 1950 when election to fellowship was extremely selective). It was after expressing those anticurrent ideas that I received identical treatment from two coeditors of *Econometrica*, E. Malinvaud and J. Dréze. Each sent me a paper critical of one of my articles. In their letters, both stated categorically that they *had decided* to publish those papers and that I might, if I so wished, write a small reply (which I did). To my great surprise, both later sent me new versions with notes saying that, after seeing my reply, my critics had modified their initial versions. From Malinvaud I received even a third version together with a pronouncement that I had no proper right to a reply since my critic's paper was not aimed at my own work. After I pointed out that even in that relatively small third version my name appeared not less than twenty-two times, the strange tug of war had to end with the publication of my last reply, but, probably a unique case in the scientific literature, with an additional *replique* by that critic (1963). I am completely correct, I think, in believing that those two coeditors decided to publish the first critical versions because they thought that (without much care) they represented irrefutable blows to my scholarly reputation. But the greatest message of ostracization on the part of my fellow econometricians came on the occasion of my Richard T. Ely Lecture entitled the "Theory of Production" (1969). The Fellows of the Econometric Society scheduled their annual meeting at exactly the same hour as my lecture, a machination that I dissected as a prelude to the lecture. This is just one symptom of the modern sociology of scientists.

Third, my idea that has irritated not only the immense new crop of energetists, but especially most of the economists, was made known at a Distinguished Lecture at the University of Alabama (1970). It was then that I raised my voice against the neoclassical dogmatic belief that the free mechanism of prices is the only way to ensure rational distribution of resources among all generations. One pillar of that belief was (and still is) that the interests of future generations are taken care of by the fact that we care for our children, our children for their children, and so forth and so on. Our economic interests have been taken care of (so it seems) by this algorithmic sequence from the time of, say, Julius Caesar – nay, much earlier. Yet none of those propounders thought of asking whether the relation "take care of" is transitive.

I firmly believe in the philosophical idea that our understanding in any domain (including, yes, mathematics) needs both dialectical and arithmomorphic concepts. I cannot even get near the irascible reductionism – everything can be reduced to numbers – that especially dominates the thought of this century. Naturally, I cannot see in a computer anything other than a device to *calculate with numbers* (please, mark those words well) much, much quicker than our brain. About the time I was writing *The Entropy Law and the Economic Process*, a big din was being made about a computer that calculated 1 million decimals of π in eight hours.

As I was writing the present essay, another computer printed out 1 billion decimals! Besides greater speed, nothing has fundamentally changed. In both cases, I believe, the computers used Leibniz's infinite series for $\pi/4$. And as I said in my volume, if Leibniz had had to calculate by paper and pencil just 1 million decimals, it would have taken him thirty thousand years. How much ink, how much paper, how many quills? Now I wonder whether even the presupposed life of the universe would have sufficed Leibniz for calculating 1 billion decimals. But I am certain that the discovery of any new important theorem, Gödel's, for example, will remain the appanage of the human brain.

Today, "artificial intelligence" is a name so dressed up as to make us easy believers in the fantasy. In my 1971 volume, in considering the claim of that marvelous brain of A. M. Turing, that one day we will no longer be able to determine whether an interlocutor hidden by a screen is a human or a computer, with the proper apology I said that reading Turing's paper convinced me that it may have been written by a computer, that Turing only signed it. I recently sent the same punch to the editor of *Scientific American* in connection with an overenthusiastic article by a staff member. They naturally did not publish it: apparently, the press is free but only for those who own it.

I also contend that the impossibility of relating every function of the brain to some digital or chemical phenomenon is salient proof that we cannot do everything with numbers. The extraordinary experiment by the famous brain surgeon W. Penfield pinpoints the mystery. When Penfield told a patient under brain surgery not to raise his arm if Penfield touched his brain with an electrode, the patient just used the other arm to keep the impulsed one down. Surprised, Penfield then asked what electrode caused the second arm to move. We still wait for a nonfantasized answer.

My epistemological addiction is the reason I am against arithmomorphia. I have only words of protest for the typical assertion of a physicist that it is not necessary to explain phenomena before dealing with them mathematically. If one starts only with mathematics, one is likely, as I said, to be trapped inside it. A superb illustration is the theorem of some mathematical economists that the market tends to an equilibrium even if the traders are more numerous than the continuum power. Being trapped, they could not even dream of asking what actual space could have room for so many actual traders.

This has been the story about my claim that I have indeed run against a current, why and how. Other scholars and philosophers have also run against a current. To my knowledge they are Isaiah Berlin, Paul Feyerabend, and Gunnar Myrdal. By comparing their conditions with mine, after long years I have concluded that for the results of one's struggle the place from which one runs against a current matters enormously.

Nicholas Georgescu-Roegen is Distinguished Professor of Economics, Emeritus, Vanderbilt University.

RELEVANT CONTRIBUTIONS

"Leontief's System in the Light of Recent Results," *Review of Economics and Statistics*, 32 (August 1950): 214–22.

"Toward Partial Redirection of Econometrics: Discussion," *Review of Economics and Statistics*, 34 (August 1952): 206–211.

"Mathematical Proofs of the Breakdown of Capitalism," *Econometrica*, 28 (April 1960): 225–43.

"Measure, Quality, and Optimum Scale," *Sankhya*, Ser. A, 27 (March 1965): 39–64.

Analytical Economics: Issues and Problems, Cambridge, Mass.: Harvard University Press, 1966.

The Entropy Law and the Economic Process, Cambridge, Mass.: Harvard University Press, 1971.

Energy and Economic Myths: Institutional and Analytical Economic Essays, Elmsford, N.Y.: Pergamon Press, 1976.

"Methods in Economic Science," *Journal of Economic Issues* (June 1979): 317–27; (March 1981): 188–93.

"The Measure of Information: A Critique," in J. Rose and C. Bileiu, eds., *Proceedings of the Third International Congress of Cybernetics and Systems*, New York: Springer Verlag, n.d., 3: 187–217.

"Feasible Recipes Versus Viable Technologies," *Atlantic Economic Journal* (October 1983): 21–31.

"Hermann Heinrich Gossen: His Life and Work in Historical Perspective," in *The Laws of Human Relations and the Rules of Human Actions Derived Therefrom*, R. C. Blitz, tr., Cambridge, Mass.: MIT Press, 1983, 11–140.

"An Epistemological Analysis of Statistics: The Science of Collective Description and of Rational Guessing," in M. C. Demetrescu and M. Iosifescu, eds., *Studies in Probability and Related Topics*, Montreal: Nagard, 1983, 221–59.

"Man and Production," in M. Baranzini and R. Scazzieri, eds., *Foundations of Economics*, Oxford: Blackwell Publisher, 1986, 247–80.

"Interplay between Institutional and Material Factors," in J. A. Kregel, Egon Matzner, and Alessandro Roncaglia, eds., *Barriers to Full Employment*, London: Macmillan Press, 1988, 297–326.

"Closing Remarks: About Economic Growth – A Variation on a Theme by David Hilbert," *Economic Development and Cultural Change*, 36, Suppl. 3 (April 1988): S291–S307.

FRANK HAHN

Autobiographical Notes with Reflections

This is an opportunity for self-indulgence, and I propose to take it. I am not much in the habit of reflecting on my life, let alone on so weighty a matter as my philosophy of life. Certainly I have never done so in public. But as a Borgia pope memorably remarked, "God has given us the papacy, now let us enjoy it"; I shall approach my task in the same spirit.

I was born into an intellectual Central European family but in Berlin. My father, a chemist by profession, had decided early on that chemistry was not really what he enjoyed, and in any case it involved exposure to unpleasant smells (he was a notable hypochondriac). By the time that I came to know him, he had turned into a rather well known literary person. He wrote a weekly column for the *Simplicissimus*, and published novels and popular science books. He was also a very good poet, and in the middle of the Second World War published in England a book of sonnets in German. He was formidably learned and tried to impart something of his learning to my brother and myself at an early age. German

160

classics and the Bible were read to us and Greek myths recounted. When we left Berlin I was six years old, and we spent the last two weeks visiting every conceivable museum. When we got to Prague, both my brother and I were sent to English schools, but we also had to learn Czech. My parents soon established a fortnightly salon at which a talk was given and heated arguments were the rule. My father wrote for the German papers and dabbled in chemistry. Toward the end of our stay in Prague (1938), my parents were distinctly short of money. My mother, a beautiful and rather pleasure-loving woman, continuously urged my father into somewhat crackpot projects for making money that invariably failed.

I suppose that the first thirteen years with my parents left a permanent mark. Thereafter I never lived with them. They were in London (later Oxford) and I at school in Bournemouth, later separately in Oxford and in the air force. Reflecting on what that mark might be, I conclude that it is a rather voracious appetite for reading and intellectual speculation. In fact, over the years I have become somewhat wary of intellectuals, especially when they are French or educated above their intelligence. But I fear that, willy-nilly, I am of that ilk. I find myself irritated when so many of my economist friends whose work I admire turn out to have no appetite for anything but economics. But when that much is admitted, it remains overwhelmingly true that "England made me."

Quite early after my arrival I fell in love not only with the English countryside and the wonderful purity and understatement of early English Gothic, but also with the intellectual tone of the place. This was serious without being frantic. But above all I detected a fastidiousness of expression that I had not found in Prague. This was not so much "understatement" as avoidance of pomposity and of extremes. It made a great impression on me, although now that I am older I am no longer an unqualified admirer.

I thought I ought to become a chemist. My father knew me better and actually suggested economics. (I do not know whether he had any notion of the subject.) My real love was mathematics, and that is what, in due course, I set out to study. The war had broken out and I had only a short time of such study before I joined the air force. Kalecki, whom my parents knew, urged me to read some economics while in the forces. It was, he said, "easy." I took his advice and, after the war, went to the London School of Economics (LSE) rather than back to mathematics. Although I would never have made a good pure mathematician, I have, unlike Samuelson, some regrets about my decision. I lack some of the attributes of an economist that Keynes thought necessary; in particular, I have only a weak interest in the practical end of the subject. Astrophysics, for instance, might have allowed me to work with a clearer conscience than I now have in a subject that Keynes once urged should be "like dentistry."

One of the first books in economics that I read was Hicks's *Value and Capital*. I do not now know how much of it I understood, but it made a deep impression because I was able to discern a vital element in it. That was the reductionist project of going from the "atom" to the whole. Nowadays, people speak of micro-foundations of macro-economics as if the necessity for this were a new insight. My early Hicksian experience had never led me to think otherwise. In any event Hicks was a lasting influence, and my later absorption in General Equilibrium Theory a perfectly natural consequence.

At the LSE I was fortunate in many ways. I met my wife (also an economist) whose intelligence exceeds mine by an order of magnitude and whose good sense has been invaluable to me for more than forty years. William Baumol was a fellow student, and we became firm friends. He also taught me a great deal. Seminars presided over by Lionel Robbins were great and exciting events. Robbins, we students believed, would not understand the "highbrow" papers that were delivered. We were always proved wrong by his masterly summing up. Kaldor, Coase, and Hayek attended the seminars, as did Lewis and Radomysler. We were suspicious of Hayek because of *The Road to Serfdom* (which I now believe to contain much good sense) and his anti-Keynesian stance. (His cycle theory is to this day mysterious to me.) Kaldor was always of much value but not always serious. (He would sometimes invent "facts.") Coase we undervalued because he was so much less colourful than the other personae. In any case I learned a great deal in these seminars and from the endless discussions they gave rise to between sessions. Harrod delivered his famous growth lectures and expounded the theory in one of the seminars. At the time it seemed less momentous than it turned out to be.

I wrote my Ph.D. on distribution. Kaldor was my first supervisor (I saw him only twice before he left for Geneva) and thereafter Robbins. I then went to my first teaching post in Birmingham. It was there that my real education in economics began, for by great good fortune Terence Gorman was my colleague. He had by far the best and clearest mind I had yet come across. His speed of comprehension and his ability to get to fundamentals was and is formidable. Combined with a splendid unworldliness, he proved irresistible and I did not resist. Birmingham in those years was one of the first British universities where mathematical methods in economics flourished, largely because Gilbert Walker (the head of the department) allowed us to teach and practice it.

We were all much inspired by some of the books that were then published: Samuelson's *Foundations of Economic Analysis*, Lange's *Price Flexibility and Employment*, and Arrow's *Social Choice and Individual Values*. No comparable coincidence of great books in economic theory has occurred since that time. These books, rather than Keynes's *General*

Theory, set the agenda for some of us young theorists. Gorman quite early on found the "dual" formulation to Samuelson's micro-theory, but characteristically never published it. Lange's book led me to a lifelong concern with monetary theory in a general equilibrium context. Arrow's result set a standard of rigour and elegance that we attempted to emulate.

In 1956 I received an invitation to be visiting professor at MIT. It was then that the second phase of my economics education began. Solow at once became a model and a friend, and we collaborated on some stability theory. Not only was Samuelson by far the cleverest and most versatile economist I had ever met, but he disposed of a wide and vast intellectual capital. He taught me the great economist's art of how to reduce a messy and difficult problem to manageable size. In this visit also, a one-page proof of a theorem on gross-substitute matrices earned me an invitation from Arrow. Thus started a lifelong friendship and apprenticeship. Since that time frequent visits to America have been essential since it is there that one can find the best practitioners of the kind of economic theory that interests me.

I have now come to the "philosophy" part of this essay. I begin with what separates me from many American economists rather than with what unites me with them.

Very many American economists regard economics as a "science" and often refer to themselves as "scientists." This is not just a semantic matter. Behind the words there is a *Weltanschauung*, and that is the nineteenth-century view that what was achieved in the physical sciences can be achieved by the same means by the social sciences. This view, for all I know, may turn out to be correct. What is striking, however, is that so far economics has provided no evidence that it is. For instance, it is hard to think of any economic proposition that all reasonable economists regard as either conclusively falsified or verified by the world. There are vast and quite fundamental gaps in both theory and empirical knowledge. The basic assumptions of much of our theory are often of low descriptive merit, and our success in prediction has not been such that we can adopt the cavalier attitude to assumptions that Friedman advocates. And so on. In the first instance, then, I regard the claim that economics is a science as not only premature and not very honest but also, perhaps worse, pretentious.

And yet I strongly hold the view that economics even now is both useful and important – but not in the way that engineering is. What economics delivers at present is a route for grammatical argument and methods for usefully summarizing such economic data as there are. The "grammar" I take very seriously. Economic theorists can speak to each other and not past each other. For instance, whether or not one holds the view that Competitive General Equilibrium is an accurate enough description of the American economy, both sides of the argument understand not only the claim, but also what would have to be observed if the claim were false. For instance, the sizeable fraction of GNP spent on non-informative advertising needs explaining. Equally important is the shared knowledge that the theory is incomplete, as when there are many equilibria or when one is reluctant to take the variety of goods and the number of firms as data.

Economic theory at its best is a powerful aid to thought about the world, not because it provides a very satisfactory description, but because it provides clear limits to understanding. It also weeds out genuine nonsense, since many actors on the economic stage (e.g., politicians and bankers) start with the same assumptions but cannot think their way through to entailed conclusions. Nonetheless, this leaves us with a whole set of possible worlds. Indeed, economists who understand what they are doing will have this fact always before them, and in this realization will be a good part of their usefulness, for "practical" people want certainties and despise "on the one hand" and "on the other." One of our functions is, I believe, to teach them otherwise and so give a helping hand on the road of humanity away from magic.

This is not the place to give a detailed defense of my view (see Hahn, 1984). But I can say that I have found this confirmed by recent happenings in macro-economics. I am sure that many of the "new" macro-economists regard my disapproval of their work as stemming from Keynesian pieties. Nothing could be further from the truth. My ire is aroused by the "scientific" pretensions and the quite inadequate command of the theory that they wish to invoke. They are proud of the lack of rigour and the lack of sophistication, because they believe that this is the mark of the "true" scientist (see Lucas, 1987). Tell that to Schrödinger et al! Their views have percolated to politicians who believe the "scientific" claims. In this way, like other magicians in history, they have done real harm to the project of using reason in human affairs. I believe all of this stems from the urge to ape science and above all from the desire to attain the same certainties.

This leads me to a confession. A number of other contributors to this volume have described how their wish to better the world brought them to the study of economics. Of course, I have not been free of such desires. But I cannot say that they played a major role in making me an economist. As I have already said, *Value and Capital* whetted my intellectual and not my moral appetite. I was certainly stirred by my first reading of Keynes and by the promise of more sensible policies. But what in the end proved most exciting was the prospect of studying whether the claims made *could* be true and under what assumptions. I am not particularly proud of this excessively cerebral approach to the subject; indeed, it is surely a failing and presumably explains why I am not a better economist. But that is how the cookie has crumbled, and I cannot pretend that questions of economic policy can engage me to the extent that theoretical questions can.

Indeed, I have worked very little even in welfare economics. This is also partly due to my reluctance to start from the thoroughgoing utilitarianism that this branch of the subject entails. There is no doubt that utilitarian thinking is essentially humane and also of a kind that allows one to reach conclusions. But I shrink from its rather all-embracing claims as I do from economics as a science. Utilitarian arguments seem to me to be always relevant, but I do not find them decisive. For instance, an egalitarian argument based on comparisons of marginal utilities of income seems to me both less compelling and interesting than one based on the change in preferences that might result from life in an egalitarian world. It is true that the utilitarian approach can lead us to precise statements concerning "optimum" income taxes while the other argument, by comparison, is "hand waving." But here precision and definiteness are bought at the price of a mechanical morality that carries some, but not sufficient, conviction. Nonetheless, I often find myself on the utilitarian side. For instance, I am impatient of the view that one cannot place a value on human life, especially since we are by our actions continuously doing so.

Marx and Marxian economics I have for the most part found uncongenial. This may be because I have not understood them. I have been baffled by such phrases as the "innate laws of history" and bored by what passes for technical Marxian economics. The modern manifestations of this approach have also for the most part left me unmoved.

This leads me to my last confession, and once again I am not proud to make it. While I am passionately interested in history, I have no interest in the history of my subject. A study, say, of the influence of classical economists on nineteenth-century poor laws in England engages my interest; a study of what Ricardo means by "value" does not. Whenever I have tried, I have felt that I am wasting my time. What the dead had to say, when of value, has long since been absorbed, and when we need to say it again we can generally say it much better. To work through the arithmetical examples of Marx, or Ricardo, or Böhm-Bawerk is not work that I am willing to undertake. I am prepared to believe that those who passionately believe that we need to know our predecessors before we can know ourselves have some truth on their side. But even if the flesh were willing, the spirit is weak.

In politics I have undoubtedly moved to the right, a movement that I like to think is not just a function of elapsed time since birth. Of course, this does not mean that I support, say, Mrs. Thatcher or have a sympathetic ear for Alan Walters. Rather it is an increasing scepticism – occasioned, I believe, by a better understanding of both my subject and the past – of "blueprints" and radical programmes for the improvement of the human condition. I might still find myself supporting such programmes, but not with much hope of success.

Frank Hahn is Professor of Economics, Cambridge University.

REFERENCES

Hahn, F. H. "In Praise of Economic Theory," Jevons Lecture published by University College London, 1984; reprinted in *Money, Growth and Stability*, Blackwell, 1985.

Lucas, R. E., Jr., *Models of Business Cycles*, Blackwell, 1987.

CHARLES P. KINDLEBERGER

My Working Philosophy

One day a fairly long time ago – long enough ago that the Department of Economics at MIT was the Department of Economics and Social Science and housed political scientists, psychologists, sociologists, and that ilk as well as economists, but not so long ago as the days when janitors, or I suppose custodians, washed the blackboards between classes, I came into a classroom and found a Latin square left on the board by the last class. It read:

	Things Known to Self	Things Not Known to Self
Things Known to Others	_____	_____
Things Not Known to Others	_____	_____

My class was diverted from international-trade theory long enough to fill in some of the blanks. In the upper-left quadrant is the material in one's curriculum vitae, familiar and boring. In the lower-right quadrant I suppose are the hidden depths known only to God and to one's psychiatrist, those doctors that play god in the here and now.[1] The upper-right-hand corner is the scary one. Bobby Burns was concerned about it:

> Oh wad some power the giftie gie us
> To see oursel's as others see us!

I suppose that an assignment to write about one's philosophy – one that I interpret to cover one's professional philosophy and not the relation with the cosmos – calls on some filling in of the lower-left-hand box, things known to self but not, perhaps, to the rest of the world if to one's wife, one's children, one's valet to whom one is not a hero, and to the more perspicacious of one's students. In the course of trying, I may slip a bit and produce some material for the upper-right-hand box.

Let me go back to footnote one and spend a moment on temperament before getting to philosophy. I suppose that in the taxonomy published by a team of California doctors studying susceptibility to heart attacks, I am a Type A. The *New York Times* account (August 7, 1984, pp. C1, C4) lists 25 Type A characteristics of which I am guilty of perhaps seven.[2] The fetish of being on time is unpleasant. I frequently turn in papers a month or two ahead of the deadline, and then have to wait, sometimes for years, while the other participants in the symposium or *Festschrift* ultimately turn their attention to the overdue assignment. In one case – a paper for the eighth volume of the Cambridge Economic History of Europe, not yet published in 1986, I turned in my essay in February 1976. Editors are notoriously cowardly in refusing wildly overdue papers, or in some cases are themselves overcommitted or dilatory.

It may be that in retirement I glamorize my working rules, rules that I think I adhered to, more or less, and in some cases still do, but a few may be worth stating:

---

[1] On one occasion in the 1950s when a prominent professor died of a heart attack, the Medical Department at MIT thought it useful to test the faculty for stress and included in the annual physical check-up a half-hour's interview with a psychiatrist. This produced one sentence in the ultimate evaluation. Mine read, "You are high strung but adjusted to it." I found this amusing and repeated it to my colleagues. With characteristic wit, Robert Solow multiplied through by −1 and said, "That's better than being low strung and unable to stand it."

[2] "Walks fast, eats fast, and leaves the table right after eating. Makes a fetish of always being on time. Has trouble sitting and doing nothing. Hurries or interrupts the speech of others. Always plays to win, even in a game with children. Explosive, staccato speech pattern; hostile response to verbal challenges." On the first, in a term at the University of Texas at Austin, I was told that one student said, "You can tell he comes from New England: he wears tweed jackets and walks fast."

1. Be available to students. That is what you are paid for.
2. Be honest in writing letters of recommendation, book reviews, citing references.
3. Do not be a perfectionist, fussing and fussing over a paper or book until it is watertight. Two or at most three drafts are enough.[3]
4. Cultivate *Sitzfleisch*, the capacity to put your tail in the chair and leave it there for hours at a time while you read, write, calculate, take notes, chase illusive references. Outputs have pride of place in the objective function, but require copious inputs from all of us but the geniuses, and from some of them too.
5. Review any book you are asked to, unless there is compelling reason to the contrary (you think it is likely to be poor and the author is a relative or intimate friend). This is part of one's duty to the profession; it is also good discipline in forcing one to widen one's horizons (slightly). This rule self-destructs when it becomes known, as reviewers will pile on the dogs and the thousand-pagers.
6. Accept rents, but avoid rent seeking or accepting outlandish allocations of your time and interest because the price is right. This means that if you are invited to do something over the phone, try to decide whether it is a good scholarly undertaking, or not, before you have heard whether there is an honorarium and how much it is. This applies to conferences, commissioned research, substantial commitments in consulting, and the like, but not of course to casual speeches or writing for profit-making organizations. Most of us, however, do not get so many competing and worthy demands on our time that it makes sense to use the price system to allocate that time.

Perhaps a few words on each of these rules (except book reviewing, to which I have nothing to add) may not be amiss, despite the risk of sounding pharisaical.

AVAILABILITY TO STUDENTS

The corruption of the academy which is threatened if it has not already arrived comes from demands on the academician's time that tempt him

---

[3] Not perhaps enough to make the paper perfect, but before strongly diminishing or even negative returns set in. Perfection and certainty are illusive. I had the great fortune during World War II to meet John von Neumann and to have a brief discussion of probability with him. We were discussing bombing. Two squadrons of B-26 bombers were enough to have an 80 percent chance of knocking out a bridge of a certain size, but to get the probability up to 85, 90, 95, or certainty, at 100, would increase the necessary number of sorties enormously. Von Neumann explained certainty like this: "Assume that you want to be certain that your living room floor does not fall through. Calculate the strength of the construction needed to support a grand piano with a dozen fat men gathered close around it, perhaps singing. Then multiply the result by three."

or her to work on the outside. Allocating time between academic work and one's own family is difficult enough, especially for women who cannot be said to share the work of the household and family evenly with their spouses. I see that issue facing my children but had my career when women for the most part did not work outside the household. The problem of dividing professional time between the university or college and the outside is difficult enough. For two years I was chairman of MIT's Committee on Outside Professional Activities and was struck with how difficult it is to maintain the proper balance between involvement in the world in order to keep in touch with the problems of one's profession and one's primary duty to teaching and the advancement of knowledge.

I used to try to stay out of the office one day a week, Friday, at home to write or read, free from interruption by students. I taught Tuesdays and Thursdays, but came to MIT on Mondays and Wednesdays to be available to students, especially during the string of years when I was graduate registration officer and adviser. The office door was kept open so that students could see me and I could see them and wave them in. When a rearrangement of furniture in the outer office put three secretaries there, with a persistent babble of conversation, I shut the door but only after a glass window had been put in it. I must not exaggerate. In my first years at MIT, when I had taken a substantial cut in salary on leaving government – from $9,000 to $7,500 – I did a certain amount of moonlight teaching, one year even commuting to Columbia University in New York, and for several years driving in midafternoon on Tuesdays and Thursdays to the Fletcher School of Law and Diplomacy. It may be worth mentioning that all this moonlighting was on courses not given at MIT and from which I derived some professional broadening.

One rule, very difficult to follow, is to refuse trips out of town on professional missions of prestige or high-paying assignments when they interfere with regularly scheduled classes. On rare occasion, the scholarly interest of the occasion, or the public interest in such a matter as testifying before Congress, but not the financial reward, leads one to break the rule. It is then mandatory to make up the class at an hour convenient to the students. Too many of the more prestigious professors in major universities cancel classes without qualms and are not punctilious in making them up. Perhaps I am saying nothing more than one should have abundant qualms. A shallow defense of cutting classes by the professor is that the students learn more in the library than in class. When this is true, there is little value added in one's teaching and it verges on swindling to take money for teaching.

An especially difficult problem arises in universities with the supervision of doctoral theses and leaves. Neglect of doctoral students at one and another university is widely rumored, although I see no way to collect adequate data on the point. One thesis is said to have been turned in at a major university with a number of pages pasted together at various places, and that when it was returned, after acceptance, it was clear that the pasted pages had not been pried apart. In 1936–37, I was lucky enough to have had a supervisor who wrote me three- or four-page single-spaced letters on chapters finished after I had left the campus. I have tried to balance that account multilaterally.

Sabbatical leave is highly useful for advancing knowledge and refreshing teaching, but it constitutes a severe interruption of thesis supervision. More, the two-platoon system that was followed in some universities with huge departments, half expected to obtain foundation grants to substitute for teaching, while the other half stands up in front of classes, interferes with the slow cooking that seems to me to be the recipe for dissertation writing.

Preparation: it varies. I never quite believed the history teacher, not at MIT, who claimed that he spent two hours of preparation for every hour in class. At the same time, the doubtless apochryphal story that students could tell in class whether Professor X had come by the stairs or the elevator because when he chose the stairs he was prepared suggests that all is not always well. New courses take more time, old less. Handouts outlining what the class is to cover both save the student time in taking notes and lets him or her concentrate on substance, and if redone frequently freshens the teacher's attack on the subject. They can even end up as a book.

A teacher should grade him- or herself after every class, and wonder what went wrong when it did, or right, when that was the outcome. The best teaching is done, as is well known, in the leading undergraduate colleges – Amherst, Oberlin, Reed, Swarthmore, Wesleyan, and Williams, to name but a few. Adam Smith said that emulation is a more pervasive drive than making money, and the value system in such colleges values teaching in a degree not known in the universities. A book by Robert Frank suggests that the secret to contentment is *Choosing the Right Pond* (New York: Oxford University Press, 1985).

It may be more cookbook stuff than philosophy but other teachers may be interested in a few suggestions about grading that I have been slow to learn and which I wish I had caught on to earlier:

1. Instead of one long term paper, better require three minipapers, spaced a month apart, each focused on a different aspect of the course. The advantages are many: first, the student escapes the trauma of a 20-page paper due at the end of the term that so often does not get finished in time and results in an "Incomplete"; second, it forces the

student to spread him- or herself more widely through the subject matter; third, by spreading, say, three five-page papers through the course, the link between research and reading is strengthened.

2. Grade all quizzes and examinations blind. (I have not figured out, or worked out, a way to do this for the mini-papers.) At the exam, the student signs his or her name on a sheet of paper against a number which is all that appears on the bluebook. It helps the grader not to have a face in view, or a personality. Grading is easier, more objective, fairer.

3. Comment on all papers and examination questions, if only in a few words. The simple grade with no indication of where the work fell short or excelled is niggardly teaching.

4. Get term papers and examinations back rapidly while the student still has the subject in mind. A professor from another university shocked me by saying: "I prefer teaching graduate students. They know our research is more important than their class work, and don't press you to get their papers back fast." The man gets an "A" for frankness, but a "D" for dedication.

HONESTY IN RECOMMENDING, REVIEWING, CITATIONS

Letters of recommendation are a problem, especially whether to judge by one's own standard or by the standard you think appropriate in the place to which the letter is to go. Some instructors write a different letter for the same student, depending on whether he or she is applying for a position at a major university, an outstanding college, a middle-level university or a run-of-the-mill college. This is to play god to a certain extent. On the one hand, to enter a single letter in the word-processor or in the career center, and send it out to all and sundry, without emendation, has serious drawbacks. The letter tends to be bland and without much information.

There is a strong temptation to assume that all other recommenders are being friendly to their students, and that to try to describe your student honestly is to condemn him or her. Inflation sets in, and if one is not careful half of all students are judged to fall in the top 5 percent. Truthful weighing may be hard on the one weighed. With luck and persistence, however, one can cultivate a reputation for honest appraisals which has external economies for the system.

I happen to believe in hard-hitting reviewing and refereeing, and in learning to take it as well as to dish it out. I continue to wince under some reviews and some rejections. Namby-pamby book reviewing is pleasant for the author, easy for the reviewer, but fails to produce the external economies the profession needs. One can overdo the hard-hitting, as I suppose I am as guilty as anyone of that sin. What I sanctimoniously have in mind, however, is a towering figure in the field who has on at least three occasions viciously criticized works which he has later, in each case, come around to accept into the corpus of doctrine. My private psychological interpretation (amateur division) was that the vehemence of the denunciation had its origin in each case in the fact that the reviewer was more an expositor of the ideas of others than an original thinker, and that he was repelled in the first instance by highly original ideas that had not occurred to him.

As for high ethical standards in the research process itself, I have some confessions to make. The most heinous scholarly crime on my conscience refers to a period more than 35 years ago when I was commuting weekly to Columbia to teach a class that met at 10 AM. Arriving on the sleeper, having breakfast, and getting uptown, I had about 45 minutes each week between the time the Butler Library opened at 9 o'clock and the time to go to class. I wanted a great deal of data available conveniently in the *Annuaire Statistique de la France, Partie Pétrospectif,* not available at MIT, nor accessible to me from Widener at Harvard then. There were no copying machines. To my present and abiding shame, I slit a page out of the book – a premediated crime as I had to bring the concealed weapon into the library – took it back to Cambridge, copied it there, and returned the next week to replace it in the book, fastened with scotch tape. The burden of guilt has eased some after the statute of limitations ran its course, but is still there.

On citations: if I remember correctly there have been two or perhaps three occasions when I had failed to provide a page number for a reference that was demanded hurriedly as a manuscript was going to print, could not find it in my notes, or in the book in the library, which was, let us say, out. On these two or three occasions, I made up the page number, or perhaps could say I estimated it. The defense, weak to be sure, was that speed was of the essence, the chance that any subsequent researcher would need the number was low, he or she might think it was an honest, instead of a dishonest mistake, and anyway I had the book right. Still, shameful.

More cookbook stuff instead of philosophy. In reading for note-taking I put pencil tick marks in library books by passages or ideas that I later transcribe by typewriter into notebooks, but erase all ticks after transcription. The slight damage done to public property is compensated, I believe, by the fact that I erase all other marks in pencil left by earlier malefactors, and leave the books, on balance and as a whole, better off.

The notebook technique is more suitable perhaps for economic history than for economics in general, but it may be worth saying something about it. First, I detest cards. I have visited a professor of law who has over a million 3 × 5 cards in his office, on tables, file cabinets, the floor, everywhere. The 5 × 8 card is somewhat better, but not much. Ordinary typing paper, 8½ × 11, organized in loose-leaf notebooks typed single space on both sides of the paper are best for easy handling and information retrieval. Napoleon's armies marched on their stomachs. I do research in economic history with a three-hole punch. In working on a paper or book, I go through old notebooks and reassemble the relevant readings in a separate notebook, the pages of which can be flipped. On the floor behind my desk I have some 25 or 30 binders, some by countries – three broadbacked ones each for France and Britain – some by subject where the books deal with more than one country, some left over from an old project after the easily classified notes had been broken out and returned to their long-term position.

There are drawbacks. If you have five or six pages of single-spaced pages of notes, on both sides, you think you no longer need to look at that book again. Not true. When the focus of your interest changes, you need a new set of notes, although there is lots of overlap. A friend in economic history tells of reading a book, taking detailed notes, losing the notes, reading the book again five years later and taking more notes. He then found the first set and compared the two. The overlap was only about 50 percent as his interests had shifted. In the case of big massive books, I have some sets of notes that are marked on top: manias only, or financial history only, to underline that the reading was limited and for a special purpose.

A small twinge about my notes. They are worthless to anyone but me, but I hate to tell my heirs and assigns to take all those man-months of reading and typing to the sanitary land fill that used to be called the dump.

Back to honesty for one point. A free-trade economist friend used to take pleasure in smuggling purchases through customs on the high moral ground that tariffs were evil. That would trouble me. I resent a remark in the *New York Times* of December 18, 1985 ("Big Numbers Game in Capital") that mentions the "underground economy" made up of billions of dollars of income from legitimate business activities that are not reported to the Internal Revenue Service. "It includes flea market operations, *the honorariums that professors or politicians collect for speeches*, tips for waiters and parking attendants" (my italics). On behalf of academia, I resent the writer associating professors with flea market operators, waiters, and parking attendants, perhaps even politicians, but especially I object to what appears as a common belief that academics cheat on income taxes. I do not, in fact, take priggish pride in reporting untraceable small sums such as $11.25 for writing a book review for an

Indian journal, or the (wholesale) cost of my wife's travel to a conference that is paid for by the inviting institution. To be sure I exceed the 55 mile an hour speed limit on long trips and used to drink bootleg liquor in the few years between late adolescence and repeal.

NO PERFECTIONISM

This is another question of temperament. In a contribution to my secondary school fiftieth reunion notes, I expressed thanks to Mother Nature for a well-functioning digestive tract, and that I have not been beset by the anal affliction of perfectionism. On the contrary, I may be safely accused of logorrhea. As between the person of brilliance and perfectionism and him or her of normal intelligence with an easy capacity for delivering work I'll take the latter. The geniuses of the profession are blessed with both very high IQs and a relaxed delivery mechanism. Many an economist, including contemporaries and friends, are unable to let the paper go so long as there is a tiny chance of improving it. A set of lectures of mine from 1980 is in the hands of an editor with a trade-off function in which he is pleased if he catches two errors at, say, the bibliographical level, per year, and justified in keeping the work out of print. I am sloppy, but mind it only a little.

The first edition of my textbook, *International Economics*, in the first printing had so many errors that one or two instructors wondered whether I had introduced them purposely to advance the student's thinking. Not so. I was humiliated by that degree of sloppiness, and think I have not descended to that depth again. But there are gains from working with dispatch. The prose tends to be less heavy, more conversational. Faster work makes faster reading.

In *A Financial History of Western Europe* I begged one specialist friend to read the manuscript for slips, and induced the publisher to hire an expert in a different area to catch any mistakes there. All this helped. The friend, as it happens, takes a sort of *Schadenfreude* (joy at the troubles of others) when he finds me erring. But I have never been sure that I agree with the boilerplate passage in book introductions that thanks A, B, and C for correcting errors and then assumes responsibility for those that remain. To be sure if A, B, and/or C finds one that the writer persists in, the claim is justified. But if a prepublication reader misses one that he or she undertakes to pounce on, for love or money, surely the blame should be shared.

It is intolerable, however, to have good economists produce third, fourth, and fifth drafts of brilliant work but be unwilling to let it go into print because improvement is still possible. Sometimes, some of us should never let it rest, until our good is better, and our better best. At other times and for other analysts, the best is the enemy of the good. But there is probably little that most of us can do about it since temperament decides and is not readily altered.

SITZFLEISCH

Cultivate *Sitzfleisch*, but not compulsively. Good work habits are important to good work. One can have a grasshopper mind, moving from one subject to another – in my case international capital movements, foreign exchange, balance of payments, international trade theory, economic growth, the multinational corporation, economic history, financial history, financial crises – but one must spend long hours with each. The message of writers in fiction and non-fiction echoes the same refrain – regular and prolonged work. It is tempting to interrupt oneself when the muse is recalcitrant and ideas or words are shy about coming forward, or when one fails to see the solution to the problem. Time and again one feels that a given paper is not working out – the order is all wrong, or it is obvious, or it has all been said before, or is wrong, or should be said differently – but changing the subject, going to the bathroom, for a walk, reading a magazine, seldom help.

Among the work habits that I have found productive is to keep a file of "research ideas," and to add to it when things occur to me, either on a new sheet for a new idea, or snippets of this and that to fill out an old subject. When a new paper is commissioned, it helps to put a piece of paper in the typewriter and let the stream of consciousness process operate. I recommend to students planning a major project, and sometimes follow the procedure myself, to write a one-page outline first, and then a one-page outline of each of the sections or chapters in the first. If the project is large enough one can go on expanding the sections of the outlines until the whole is written. This preserves overall shape. But often one lacks a clear idea at the beginning where it is all coming out, and this may call for a number of drafts as the overall shape of the exercise takes form slowly.[4]

Hard work and sustained work are efficacious, but the compulsive workaholic is not very attractive. He or she may produce external economies for the profession in a bounteous stream of papers, valuable editing, and the like. Many have to guard against tendencies to excess in one direction or another. I gave up chess in college because it took too much

---

[4] On one sabbatical my wife and I rented a house in Oxford from a don who had gone to the United States for the year. One day early in the term came a knock on the door from the landlord's friend, another don, who had been asked to go to his college, find a certain key, then come to his house, open a file and pull out a folder marked "Ideas." The landlord had gone to the United States for a year without his ideas.

time to do well, and in adult life I have stayed clear of tennis and bridge for fear they would be too absorbing. But moderation. One famous American economist defended his childlessness by saying that he had calculated that each child cost a scholar two books. I have a vivid memory walking along the train platform at midnight in Pittsburgh to the sleeping car, coming back from an American Economic Association convention, and asking a well-known professor climbing into a coach why he was not headed with the rest of us for the sleepers. He answered that he was planning to work on the trip home. Noncompetitive skiing and sailing provided recreation in middle age and now yard work, gardening, sawing wood, and shovelling snow, all with the technology of about 1930.[5]

RENTS

I know it is priggish but I am troubled that the economics profession seems to be getting corrupted by success, and greedier. Money is needed for research where equipment is needed, or computer time, or travel, or to free time for teaching so as to enable scholars to concentrate more fully on research. Freeing up time from teaching is of course a greater need in colleges and small universities where instructors have three or four courses a week, than in the major universities with normally two courses, a schedule that already is presumed to leave half time for research. Competition for stars, both established and in embryo, takes the form of more and more time for research and less and less for teaching, subverting a major, perhaps the major, purpose of the university. In grants for these purposes, the income of the recipient is supposed not to be increased.

Many academicians in economics routinely seek support for summer research on the ground that they could otherwise add to their income by working for a salary in business, teaching summer school, consulting, or writing textbooks. If income is needed, and summer grants reallocate resources to economic research, they can be approved. But if the research would be done without the grant, asking for it approaches rent seeking and is questionable. More and more, it seems to me, scholars get grants for what should be their ordinary research. I confess to shock at the initial footnote of one recent article by a professor teaching at two universities, and head of a private consulting firm on the side, thanking four separate institutions for support in doing research for a paper written in commemoration. It is possible that there was expensive travel involved,

---

[5] In visiting a Belgian friend who had just moved from Brussels to the country, I asked his wife whether H _____ liked to work outside, meaning yard work. "Oh yes," she said. "H _____ loves to take his chair, his table, his books, and his papers and to work outside."

and that the four institutions divided it. It seems ironic, however, that it is the most successful professors of economics who seem to need the most support in doing research that does not seem to involve extra expense.

As one who has written two textbooks, and a third volume which has been viewed as such by others, though not be me, I should perhaps say something on that thorny subject. There is of course a useful scholarly purpose in writing a textbook – organizing and even improving one's knowledge of the subject, and keeping up with the progress in the field. There is the important task of dissemination of knowledge. Too often, however, the groves of academe risk corruption, aided and abetted by the publishing industry, as together they gamble to produce a best seller.

The project that led to my *International Economics* started out in a folder marked "Five C's," or five hundred dollars a year that I hoped to earn to educate my children. (It did better than that.) Planned obsolescence on the part of textbook publishers, and, as indicated, the progress of the field, led me to revise one textbook four times and the other once. Since then I have not been averse to collecting rents on a declining basis, after turning over the work to others and freeing time for more scholarly pursuits.

Apart from best sellers, it has been suggested, on the analogy of the theorem that all commuting roads to the city have the same congestive delays, that writing textbooks, consulting, or working as an employee all produce about the same amount of income.

But I run on too long. Nonetheless, one more priggish thought comes to mind. A letter today (the day of the first draft) from a young Austrian scholar to whom I corresponded about a paper of his in 1983, and asking for criticism of a new paper, mentioned that he had sent the earlier paper to 20 other economist authorities in the field asking for comments, and received only one acknowledgement and that without comments. In retirement, I have more time than most, and I have frequently indulged in the defensive game of acknowledging a book on receipt, promising to put it on the list of those to be read when my hopes of getting back to it are low. Occasionally I do get back to the book and write again. Looking up a book recently, a letter fell out which indicated on the top that I had acknowledged receipt on May 19 and on the bottom "did follow through July 23." In *Candide* they cut off the head of one general "to encourage the others." That is one device. Collegial intercourse and encouragement are another.

Economics teaches competition, and too often practices it in dysfunctional ways. At one university, not MIT, is was said that the graduate students deliberately misshelved books on reading lists before examinations to ensure monopoly returns for the practicing individuals. That is saddening if true. Learning and teaching are cooperative endeavors at all levels, among students, among instructors, between instructors and students, and in the wider world among scholars with similar interest, exchanging papers, reprints, ideas. Micro-sociology is important. Individuals in a given culture will behave as do their peers, working hard if those about them do, or taking it easy if that is what is done. I have been lucky in landing into a hard-working, highly collegial, and loving academic environment. I wish the same for all.

Charles P. Kindleberger is Ford International Professor of Economics, Emeritus, Massachusetts Institute of Technology, and Visiting Sacher Professor of Economics, Brandeis University.

L. R. KLEIN

My Professional Life Philosophy

It is difficult to deal with this subject under a single heading. To contain the discussion and lend form, I shall deal only with *professional* life. The personal biographical details about my entry into the study of economics have been taken up in other publications.[1] Obviously personal, family, social, and other aspects of life interact with professional life, but I shall try to stick as closely as possible with *professional* life and treat it under four main headings: (1) teaching, (2) research, (3) policy, and (4) other professional activities of an economist. Before I get into the life philosophical aspects, let me first clarify and spell out the meaning of the selected categories.

---

[1] See *Les Prix Nobel*, 1980 (Stockholm: Almqvist & Wicksell International, 1981), 269–72; Lawrence Klein, "An Autobiographical Research Commentary," in *Economic Theory and Econometrics*, ed. by Jaime Marquez (Oxford: Blackwell Publisher, 1965), 5–22; "Lawrence R. Klein," *Lives of the Laureates*, ed. by William Breit and Roger W. Spencer (Cambridge, Mass.: MIT Press, 1986), 21–41.

Teaching, of course, means meeting with classes, but teaching goes far beyond that specific activity. We teach members of our research staff or policy makers with whom we consult. We teach when we are called upon to lecture before audiences all over the world, sometimes in classrooms and sometimes in general halls. We teach when we write. This is obviously the case with textbook writing, but it is also the case with popular or semipopular writing too. Teaching, in the present context, is to be understood as general pedagogy.

Research can be theory spinning, working out explanations for users of economic ideas, or delving into the statistics of the real world to describe, discover, or analyze economic hypotheses. Research can be quantitative or qualitative, although it will become clear to the reader of this essay that I have distinct leanings to the quantitative side. Since I work in the mixed field of econometrics – mixing statistics, mathematics, and economics – what might seem like applied research is actually basic research in econometrics if it is trying to do something original and abstract in any or all parts of the mixture. I must state that I have considerable difficulty in making this point clear to some of my colleagues in econometrics, who often imply that pure theoretical research in econometrics can proceed without any economic content and that, if economic content is brought to bear on the issue, it must involve applied econometric research.

Economic policy, whether reached through the medium of econometrics or otherwise, is usually associated with prescriptions for public officials. This is often, but not always, the case. There are many groups who try to formulate policy even though they do not act in any official capacity. They are merely "friends of society." Also policy decisions may be made by executives in the private sector. Policy means, to me, the formulation of decision making in economic life.

An economist does not solely teach, do research, or work in an office for others. I, and many colleagues, simply use our professional position – for me, my university base – for operating throughout the world, undertaking many activities, as a professional, simply because they are thought to be good for society. They may or may not generate extra income, but often they do. We might be called upon to endorse something, not a commercial product, but an idea, a report, a proposal. We might engage in some enterprise activities that are professionally based. We might try to establish professional contact in areas where there has been a period of isolation, as in the Third World or the socialist world. There are countless activities, committee assignments, or appearances that have no direct bearing on teaching, research, or policy but that are deemed important enough for me or my colleagues to want to be professionally involved.

TEACHING

For instruction in general economics, nothing unusual fits into my life style, except possibly the use of the computer as a visual teaching aid. Many, if not most, of our students at both graduate and undergraduate levels are now computer literate. By using the computer in classroom examples, it becomes possible to do more things – to be more exploratory by way of economic conditions and hypotheses – but the most important aspect of the computer approach to teaching is that it enables and encourages the student to work out problems from basic data and other building blocks. In this way, students obtain a better understanding of the subject.

For my main interest, my first love, *quantitative economics* is best taught along the lines of "learning by doing." This is easiest at the advanced graduate level, where students have already acquired a number of quantitative tools, not only the use of the computer, but also statistical methods and an ability to reason in an economic way. Learning by doing consists of working out realistic economic patterns and making quantitative analyses from them. Estimation of elasticities, productivities, reaction effects, and many other general concepts should be made by the students and then used for the analysis of economic issues. If these issues happen to be burning questions of the day, so much the better, because student interests are then heightened.

I grew up searching for data that are relevant to economic inquiry. Since we cannot "create" data in our subject through designed and controlled experiments, we must use whatever data are available through observation of life's economic laboratory. Data are scarce and elusive in economics; therefore, every student needs a solid stint at serious data preparation – searching, transforming, and using data for inferential purposes. I want my students to appreciate the data problem and acquire experience in working with source materials. It is much like assigning great books in the history of economic ideas. Students should read Smith, Ricardo, Marx, Mill, Walras, Marshall, Wicksell, Keynes, Schumpeter, Viner, Knight, and others, *in the original*. Also, they should learn how to use the library, even though they now have the luxury of drawing on large data banks, available at the touch of keys.

Findings in quantitative economics, particularly econometric findings, should be brought to bear on teaching at all levels, from the most elementary to the most advanced. It is a general practice in the teaching of economics to sketch out classroom diagrams in a purely casual way, sometimes for pure aesthetics. The curves are smooth, have many nice properties, and interact or shift in a way that often suits the expositor more than the real world. I believe in the use of realistic diagrams. Careful methods should be used to develop demand, supply, production, expenditure, trade, price formation, and other relationships in such a way that they are calibrated to the world in which we live, or to one that can be documented, historically or geographically. The intensive use of the computer, brought right into the classroom, makes this possible. Computer-generated diagrams that depict actual markets or economies should be at the base of diagrams. For my tastes, teachers do not have poetic license for teaching the subject in a purely personal way. There should be objectivity and, above all, realism in economic teaching, and this should be effective at the level of visual aids.

At all levels of teaching, for both undergraduate and graduate students, there should be close touch with daily news. The stock market crash and its monitoring provide more insight into the workings of financial markets and the economy than ordinary textbook paragraphs. As I write these lines, such things as Soviet restructuring, the depreciation of the U.S. dollar, and commodity price signals for the conduct of monetary policy are contemporary news items that should be followed by all students. Even the most abstract lectures in econometrics can draw interesting material from the data on dynamics of commodity price signals.

RESEARCH

Good research needs motivation, and the researcher must be completely wrapped up in the method or substance of his inquiry. Tastes vary a great deal among academic scholars, but, for me, the blends of methodology, real-world relevance, and the quantitative approach came together with the philosophical side. They pointed at an early stage to the then-budding field of econometrics. Although some rudimentary thoughts about this subject were germinating in my mind as an undergraduate, once I found out that there was a formal subject just being established in the field of econometrics, I knew immediately what my calling would be.

Econometrics rests on three legs, and I find it hard to get enthusiastic about research in any limited subset. The research that has always caught my fancy was in all three together. The typical problem should consist of

statement of the issue to be investigated (economics),
specification of the models (mathematics and economics),
preparation of the data base (quantitative economics and method),
estimation of the model (statistical method),
validation of the model (statistics and economics), and
use of the model for policy and other forms of analysis (statistics and economics).

Sometimes, especially for particular audiences or users, research may be concentrated on only parts of this list, but my own econometric investigations have usually tried to encompass all the steps sequentially in order to fashion an entire research project.

It bothers me that people will devote a great deal of attention to general linear models. It may be very much worthwhile for gaining insight by analogy, but the mathematical system representations for the general linear case could be anything – a problem in psychology, engineering, demography, or whatever – and it generally lacks economic specificity. Also, economic life does not follow a linear model. Linear systems yield elegant closed-form results, but not truly economic results, and are but indications of results that we should be seeking. In some sense they provide approximations to reality, but econometrics should, especially in the computer age, seek to deal more directly with the problem of nonlinearity.

Econometric research is necessarily concerned with model specification. Drawing on scientific analogies, many econometricians have followed the rule of *parsimony*. They seek a transparent, easily manageable, and elegant model. The smallest or most compact system that is capable of generating the results that interest them is the preferred system.

I disagree fundamentally with this point of view for our subject. Given that economics is a nonexperimental discipline resting on a sparse data base, we cannot be sure that the parsimonious system that appears to work well in an environment of limited experience will continue to work well when put to extrapolative use. I have watched one simple theory after another break down in predictive applications during the past 45 years of active economic research operations.

In contrast with the parsimonious view of natural simplicity, I believe that economic life is enormously complicated and that the successful model will try to build in as much of the complicated interrelationships as possible. That is why I want to work with large econometric models and a great deal of computer power. Instead of the rule of parsimony, I prefer the following rule: the largest possible system that can be managed and that can explain the main economic magnitudes as well as the parsimonious system is the better system to develop and use.

An aspect of research that has always intrigued me is team research. This fits well with my view that good econometric research should focus on the use of large systems. The lone scholar can, of course, be productive, but my first job, after leaving graduate school, was as a recruited member of a research team at the Cowles Commission, and that was an unforgettable experience. Given that I think that the true economy is large, detailed, and complicated, it is only natural that a team approach be used. In the development of the Brookings Model, the successive generations of the Wharton Model, the organization of Wharton Econometrics, the forming of Project LINK, not to mention work at such research centers as the National Bureau of Economic Research, the Survey Research Center, and the Oxford Institute of Statistics, the team approach worked very well for me, and I do believe that a good part of the world's economic problems can be treated in this manner.

In other fields of inquiry team research appears to work very well, but is not necessarily recommended exclusively. Laboratories group principal investigators, research assistants (many at the postdoctoral level), and laboratory technicians. This mode of research has proved to be very productive. In economics and other social sciences, there is certainly room for lone scholars, many of whom make the best contributions, but there is also an important place for team research, and I personally have always functioned in the latter kind of environment.

In teaching, it makes me feel good to find that students have gone on to make recognized achievements in later professional life. In research, the good feeling comes when things work out the way that received doctrine says that they should. When we find that Marshall–Lerner conditions hold or do not hold, that demand functions satisfy the fundamental equations of value theory, that our macrodynamic models are capable of generating documented characteristics of business cycles, that growth models satisfy von Neumann conditions for an expanding economy, then I get a good feeling that the laborious efforts have paid off. Similarly, when we have learned to harness the computer *now* for problems that seemed to be out of reach *some years ago*, I have a warm feeling inside.

ECONOMIC POLICY

Whether a professional economist should get involved in policy is a matter of taste and personality. There is much to be said for remaining detached, independent, and purely scholarly or academic. Also, there are degrees of involvement in policy making for an economist; some may be directly and formally involved by virtue of official appointments in both the public and private sectors. Others may be only informally involved through giving advice, if requested, and writing on policy issues. Some have to be actual policy makers; I prefer to have a sense of detachment and serve only informally as a policy person when requested. As far as public policy is concerned, I believe that we have duties and responsibilities to act in *pro bono publico* servicing of the economy.

There is obvious self-satisfaction in seeing one's own efforts being put to use. That, in itself, should be a motivating factor in bringing economists into the policy arena. In addition, some economists want to be involved in a public policy process because they support the general notion of activist, interventionist decision making in order to guide the economy on a good path, i.e., a path of stable equilibrium growth along which economic improvement takes place. Others may want to be involved in order to block activist policy, but that is definitely not to my tastes. I do encounter such activity frequently.

Philosophically, I do not believe that the market system, in even its purest form, provides adequate self-regulatory responses. The economy definitely needs guidance – even leadership – and it is up to professional economists to provide public policy makers with the right information to deliver such leadership. As for the methods of doing this, I see no alternative to the quantitative approach of econometrics, but I do realize that all policy issues are not quantitative and measurable. At times, subjective decisions must also be made.

In the field of macroeconomics, policy decisions, mainly at the public level, are confined to such broad categories as fiscal, monetary, and commercial policy, but decisions in the aggregate are not sufficient to guide the complicated modern economy. Supply-side policies, sometimes called structural policies, are needed. These encompass agriculture, energy, R&D, industry, income distribution, social welfare, naturally regulated sectors, demography, job training, and many other fields. In the present context, supply-side policies mean those that draw on the economic relationship of production, cost, technology, and efficiency of organization. These concepts are not to be confused with the popular notions of supply-side economics that have come to be associated purely with tax cutting and deregulation, to a large extent for their own sake.

Econometric information, to be useful in policy formation, must be detailed. In many instances partial analysis of specific industries, markets, or decision processes will fit the policy need, but in general we need to move in the direction of preparation of large-scale complex systems in order to help policy makers. In this respect, significant advances in computer technology and the provision of detailed information through associated telecommunications processes are making it ever more possible to push econometrics in the direction of serving policy makers.

OTHER PROFESSIONAL ACTIVITIES

Organizations of economic or a broader range of scholarly activities need direction from interested members who are willing and able to devote time to such activities. Administration, committee work, and special assignments can be time consuming but rewarding and important. For me, a day spent in committee meetings is not necessarily a day lost, but committee work can be overdone. In many cases, however, I have stumbled on some of my best research leads as a result of participation in committee meetings. I have always felt that it was proper to devote a fair amount of time to such activities. Universities and professional organizations depend heavily on committee input. That is effectively how they are run, and at least a large number of persons have to be willing to contribute; otherwise, we shall all be the worse for it. Service of this sort extends beyond the narrowly conceived professional body and extends to community, social, religious, and other organizations that need economic input.

SOME VIEWS ON ECONOMIC SUBSTANCE

In this essay, I do not want to take up discussion of particular economic issues such as specification of models, or strategic parts of them, the explanatory power of certain relationships (Phillips curve, production functions, demand systems), or matters of doctrine such as classical vs. neoclassical vs. Keynesian vs. Marxian vs. monetarist. I do, however, want to close with some general thoughts about what might be useful or not in organizing thinking about the economy.

Consider first micro- and macroeconomics. Which is more important or more fundamental? In awarding credit for two semesters of economic principles, my departmental colleagues clearly favor microeconomics over macroeconomics in the sense that a term's credit for the former can stand alone, but in order to obtain credit for successful completion of a semester in macroeconomics, the student must also complete a semester's requirements in microeconomics. I have worked at various times on the technical problems of building a bridge between micro- and macroeconomics in terms of index number construction, but I do believe that macroeconomics stands on its own as a separate subject and cannot be entirely derived from microeconomics. The overall business cycle, the overall rate of inflation, and other concepts are peculiarly macroconcepts that are integral parts of macroeconomics with their separate explanations. I strongly disagree with the idea that the beginning student should not get credit for a semester of macroeconomics without a semester's credit in microeconomics. There is much more, in a very deep sense, to macroeconomics than the pure summation of results from microeconomics. Also, there is a misconception, in general, as to what constitutes macroeconomics, because there are two dimensions to aggregation – over commodities and services, and over economic units (firms and households). Specific and narrow market analyses, which involve intricate aggregation over economic units, are important in price determination, yet they are not purely microeconomic since they involve aggregation in at least one of two dimensions.

Where does fundamental understanding about the working of the economic process lie, in the real or in the monetary sector? In a true sense, both are important, and one cannot meaningfully exist without the other. At an earlier stage of my career, I thought that the real sector was, by far, the more important and that a good understanding of the economy could be achieved without careful reference to the monetary sector.

Over the years, particularly in studying the macroeconomy, I have come to appreciate, more and more, the role of money and of the whole monetary sector. I think that *monetarism* is fundamentally flawed, and dangerous when used as a doctrinaire policy approach, but I do believe now that *money matters*; it is not everything, but it does matter. That is perhaps the chief outcome of the debate between the monetarists and the rest of the economics profession.

The sensitivity of housing, consumer expenditures on durables, and business investment to fluctuations in interest rates convinced me of the significance of the monetary sector to the above-mentioned activities of the real sector. Similarly, exchange rate determination is significant for understanding exports, imports, and trade balances.

During the 1960s, I became increasingly interested in international economic issues. That was the time when I shifted many of my interests toward international model building. The planning meetings for the establishment of Project LINK took place in 1968. I was impressed, as were many of my colleagues (not only Pennsylvania colleagues, but associates from around the profession), that the U.S. economy could not be properly analyzed without much more careful attention being paid to the international sector. There was an early recognition that the U.S. economy was no longer *closed*.

Textbooks of economic principles generally treat the United States first as a *closed* system and then introduce, almost as an afterthought, some modifications to deal with international trade and payments. I find this misleading, even to the point of being incorrect. I believe that exporting, importing, determination of currency rates, and capital flows should form an integral part of the teaching from the first day of class and that U.S. economics should be taught as an *open* subject. That is certainly the way that I teach freshman economics.

While I do concede the importance of getting the monetary sector right, I have not lost my confidence in the importance of research, development, innovation, and their roles in the dynamics of the economy. As I have said, both the money and real sectors are important but, for me, science, technology, and production function changes are real processes of extreme interest at the present time. Supply-side economics has a great deal of meaning handed down from successive generations of economists, after

1776, but this interpretation of the supply side is far different from the simplistic and populist approaches through tax cuts.

Since econometrics itself is interdisciplinary, it should not be surprising that I hold interdisciplinary studies in high esteem for developing our ideas about the economy. Very serious collaboration with scientists, engineers, and general technologists can be very important for advancing our understanding of the functioning of the real economy. A full supply-*and* demand-side economics must have a great deal to say about these related disciplinary activities, as well as others in the social sciences.

L. R. Klein is Professor of Economics at the University of Pennsylvania and the 1980 winner of the Nobel Memorial Prize in economic science.

RICHARD A. MUSGRAVE

Social Science, Ethics, and the Role of the Public Sector

I have been asked to lay down my philosophy of life and its bearing on how I view social science. Why should this be of interest to the readers of this volume? Surely not because it proved appropriate for my own purpose, but perhaps because the findings of one life's journey may enrich the map for another. At the outset and at the risk of what some may consider lack of imagination, let me admit that my philosophy of life has followed a rather linear path. Though shaped by the tumultuous events of the decades, the essentials have remained intact: how to create a social environment which serves the dignity of the individual, not in splendid isolation but bound and enriched by membership in a community of shared rights and obligations. Liberty, as I understand it, involves both these dimensions. What constitutes a good society, to be sure, is open to more than one formulation and science does not offer the final answer.

It may tell us what can or cannot be accomplished, but the choice between feasible options must in the end be a matter of how values are judged – note that I do not use the suspect term of "value judgment" – and this is for each individual to decide.

Note, however, that value sets are one thing, and how they can be implemented is another. It is in the latter context that scientific discipline takes over. Thus, it is the function of economic analysis to tell us what rise in prices will be associated with what reduction in unemployment. More generally, and reaching beyond economics, it is the function of social science to define the available opportunity frontier, be it regarding the simple choice between hamburgers and hot dogs or that between complex states of social organization and the individual's place therein. Given this "best" set of trade-offs, the choice among outcomes has to be made in line with one's social values.

Beginning with such a normative view, so my hard-headed friends will respond, offers a dangerous path. As history tells us, so they hasten to note, human weakness only permits second, third, or nth best solutions. Perhaps so, but a third best result cannot be identified without knowing what would be second, and second best cannot be identified without reference to what would come first. I have thus never been troubled with linking a normative view of outcomes with a positive analysis of how to reach them. On the contrary, it has been this interaction between what should and what can be that has been my major fascination with economics and the social sciences.

When exploring the interaction of social variables (from relative prices to birth rates), the task of the social scientist differs little from that of the botanist who wishes to explore the variety of plants in the Amazon region or the astronomer who follows the movements of planets. The social scientist, unhappily, may be confronted with a more complex and ever-changing set of relations, but the essential task is the same: to learn the interaction of cause and effect and to obtain a basis from which to predict how X will (or will not) respond to a change in Y. Here it is objective analysis that matters. This becomes problematic, however, when choosing among hypotheses that may be tested. Time and research funds are limited and such a choice must be made. As other scientists, the economist in so choosing will be driven by a desire to increase the understanding of his particular universe and to tackle its most intriguing analytical problems. But the social scientist's choice of hypotheses may also be directed at implementing what are viewed as desirable goals. Here, quite properly, the researcher's value set may enter, provided an effort is made to let it cease where analysis begins. It would indeed be foolish to let analysis be distorted by a value bias. Such bias not only leads to a misreading of how social variables do in fact interact, but also to faulty policy conclusions that will not obtain the desired results.

VIEWS FROM THE ROAD

All this, however, runs ahead of my story. To begin at the start, I was born in 1910, grew up in the Germany of World War I and its struggling Weimar Republic of the 1920s. Childhood memories of political reality include the return of beaten troops, the revolution of 1918, and the French occupation to follow. Then came the murder of Walter Rathenau, my symbol of what a democratic Germany might have been, and not the last such tragic event which my years would experience. My teens, during the 1920s, stressed literary interests – Goethe, Dostoevsky, Hesse, and especially Rilke, rather than Adam Smith and Karl Marx. This combined with the outdoor romanticism in the tradition of the German youth movement, a precursor, though stern and quite different, to that of the U.S. in the 1960s. Also, there were political concerns, rallies, and bicycle flags, extended if unsuccessfully so, on behalf of Germany's first and futile attempt at democratic rule.

After completing school I turned to the study of economics, as this seemed to promise, as in retrospect it did, the best entry into how society functions. The broader interests of my earlier years thus had to phase into the background, at least temporarily so, but they were not lost. My first year of study was spent at the University of Munich, and the next two at Heidelberg, where I obtained my first degree in 1933. Following the curriculum of those years, more time was spent on law than on economics, and academic pursuit was disturbed by the rising tide of Nazi unrest, especially on the university campus and in its lecture halls. The major intellectual impact of these early years came from neither economics nor law, but from the tradition of that great sociologist Max Weber. While Weber had died in 1920, his spirit was still extant in the Heidelberg setting, kept alive by seminars held in Marianne Weber's house and by his brother, Alfred Weber, also a sociologist, whose seminars I shared. Here was a sweeping vision of social forces, at the scale of Karl Marx, but interacting along many dimensions, from the impact of Calvinist ethics on capitalism to the role of market and of bureaucracy as forms of organization. All this was to be explored, synthesizing a value-directed choice of hypotheses with objective analysis in exploring their merit.[1] This Weberian dualism, permitting the scientist to be human and the human to be scientific, has stayed with me as a guiding principle (aimed

---

[1] See Max Weber, "Science as a Vocation," *From Max Weber, Essays in Sociology*, Gerth and Mills, eds., Oxford University Press, New York, 1946.

at, though not necessarily met!) in my professional work. Also to be remembered from the Heidelberg days was Jacob Marschak's seminar on the Appendix in Keynes' *Treatise*, which had just appeared.

In 1932, thanks to my father's guiding hand, I applied for and received a fellowship from the International Student Exchange for a year's study in the United States. I thus left Germany in the fall of 1933, escaping Hitler's holocaust that was to follow. My first year here was spent at the University of Rochester, followed by a move to Harvard in 1934. Once more, it was my good fortune to be there for my graduate work during these very years. Pointing back, Schumpeter's sweeping history of economic thought was a highlight, linking scientific advance in economic analysis with the intellectual and political movements of their time. Pointing forward, the debate over economic policy was ripped wide open as the New Deal experiment got under way. Moreover, two momentous breakthroughs in economic analysis, so at least they appeared at that time, entered the stage. First, there was the emergence of a new theory of imperfect markets pursued by Joan Robinson and Edward Chamberlin on their two sides of the Atlantic respectively, offering a major departure from the classical doctrine and its competitive model. Then, and even more exciting, came the Keynesian revolution. The saving–investment balance, the concept of underemployment equilibrium, the multiplier and accelerator were novel and puzzling concepts which had to be explored. How to overcome the depression through expansionary fiscal policy offered a startling challenge. Alvin Hansen's Fiscal Policy Seminar was the center of the new economics, and we as students felt ourselves the pioneers in crossing a new frontier. Many of the great names which led the profession in later years, from Paul Samuelson and Lloyd Metzler on, were members of our group, and it would indeed be hard to repeat so ideal an environment for enthusiastic graduate work.

This then was also a fertile setting in which to advance my interest in the public sector, even though its focus was in micro rather than macro terms. Having done my early work in Germany, I had the comparative advantage of familiarity with the early contributions of continental authors, Italian, Austrian, and Scandinavian, but especially Wicksell and Lindahl. As yet unknown to the English-speaking profession, these contributions together with Samuelson's later efficiency conditions for public goods became the basis of public sector theory. My dissertation became a first attempt to develop a model of a normative public sector, trying to combine the Wicksellian tradition with the welfare economics of Pigou. While I did not get very far, as few dissertations do, it laid the basis for my subsequent work twenty years later.

After completing my Ph.D. and a few years of teaching, I left for Washington to join the Research Division of the Federal Reserve Board in 1942. Dealing with fiscal matters and security markets, this offered a splendid opportunity to observe how the economy functions and to witness policy formation. Once more I had the good fortune to be at the center of economic activity, focused now on the tremendous wartime expansion of the American economy and the fiscal contribution thereto. An ongoing Board seminar brought visitors such as Hicks and Keynes, viewing the postwar world and planning for a new international order at Bretton Woods. In time, I came to serve as personal assistant to Marriner Eccles, the brilliant Chairman of the Board and architect of the New Deal banking reform. This also offered an opportunity to gain an insight into operations "on the Hill," with many a night spent in preparing testimony for the boss.

But splendid though the Washington experience was (no young economist should be without it!), I had always viewed this as a temporary departure from academic work. When invited to join the University of Michigan in 1948 I gladly accepted, staying there for the next decade. These years, with a wonderful set of colleagues and an enthusiastic group of graduate students to work with, permitted me to return to my earlier work on modeling the public sector. My *Theory of Public Finance,* which appeared in 1958, tried to model an efficient and equitable public sector. This included its three-fold task of providing for social goods, adjusting the distribution of income, and contributing to macro stabilization. Though differing in objective, these goals could be achieved in an integrated and non-conflicting fashion. Much water has gone over the dam since then, and many parts of the analysis have been improved upon. Yet I still like the structure of that model and its underlying proposition that a well-functioning public sector can be designed so as to offer an essential complement to the market system.

After a productive decade at Ann Arbor, I left for Johns Hopkins in 1958, where Simon Kuznets was the major figure, and then in 1962 proceeded to Princeton and its newly created Woodrow Wilson School. Once more, this offered a congenial environment but I could not withstand the temptation to return to my point of departure, when Harvard invited me to do so in 1965. The appointment was doubly attractive, as it was offered jointly by the Department of Economics and the Law School. In the former, my major teaching was in the courses and seminars on public finance offered jointly with Martin Feldstein. In the later years there was added a seminar on "Economics and Society." Entitled in Weber's image, it dealt with a wide sweep of problems, ranging from distributive justice, a hot topic following Rawls' treatise, to issues in economics and law, explored in association with Law School colleagues. At the Law School, my primary activity was a seminar on federal taxation, offered jointly with Stanley Surrey, that brilliant guardian of honest tax reform, as well as a basic course on economics for lawyers and some early work in "Economics and Law."

In addition to these academic pursuits, there were many side trips over the years into Washington to consult with the Treasury and other agencies, including especially the Kennedy years, testifying before Congress, and direction of tax reform missions to developing countries. All this offered prime opportunities to mix academic analysis and research with practical applications in the field, a combination which I found most enjoyable and indeed essential to productive academic work. After retiring from Harvard in 1981, we left Cambridge for Santa Cruz, where my wife Peggy had joined the UCSC faculty. Here I continue to do a bit of teaching, including a seminar on equity and efficiency in legal rules. I also continue with my writing, taking some time off now and then to go sailing or fishing on the side.

WHY PUBLIC SECTOR: (1) SOCIAL GOODS

The preceding sketch of my experience has been offered in the hope that it will contribute to an understanding of my approaches to the role of the public sector in a healthy democratic society. To begin with, why is there a need for a public sector? In posing this question, I accept the proposition that, over a wide range of economic activity, private enterprise and the market mechanism are indeed the most efficient way of producing and delivering economic output. It would be absurd for government to prescribe how much consumers should spend on meat and fish, or what color dresses should be produced. These things, which involve the bulk of economic activity, are well handled by the market process. Nevertheless, there also arises a need for public sector activity, simply because the market fails in dealing with certain problems.

To begin with, there are certain goods (referred to as social or public goods), the nature of which is such that A's partaking in their consumption will not diminish what is available to B and C. National defense or a warning system against earthquakes are cases in point. If a city is given a protective umbrella against air attacks, the benefit will accrue to all residents. No one could be excluded even if desired. In the case of the warning system, particular individuals might be excluded by not permitting their TV set to receive signals or do so only if a fee is paid. The market mechanism can then be put to use, but exclusion would be wasteful as the total benefit would be reduced. In short, there are certain goods and services with regard to which exclusion is impossible and/or inefficient. As a consequence, such services cannot be provided by private firms selling to individual consumers. Individuals have no reason to reveal their preference by bidding, as they will obtain the benefits in any case. The mechanism of voluntary payment, so essential to the functioning of the market, breaks down. Such goods must therefore be paid for and provided through the budget, and be made available free of charge to their users. It does not follow, however, that they need be produced by government. Like most private goods, they can be produced by private firms which then sell their output to government rather than to individual consumers.

In order to determine when public provision is needed and how much, consumer bidding at the market must be replaced by a political process: voters guided by their preferences must decide what should be provided and how it should be paid for by taxation, including what their own contributions should be. Efficient provision of public goods thus requires a political process, operating side by side with consumer choice of private goods at the market. This process is needed also to meet external costs (e.g., environmental pollution) which result as a byproduct of private activity. Efficiency now requires that such costs be rendered explicit and be curtailed, though not eliminated, by imposing a tax on the damage-producing activity or by regulatory restraint. In either case, the public sector has to take corrective action because a market failure results.

The question then is how the political process of public choice can be designed so as to best approximate what individual consumers want. As critics of the public sector quickly note, this is a difficult process and public as well as private sector failure is a contingency that must be allowed for. The political process may generate choices which are not representative of what consumers want, be it because of defects in the process of majority rule or of action by the administrative organs of government. These organs, now referred to derisively as "bureaucracy" and formerly as "civil service," may have a will of their own, be it based on self-interest (as the critics hold) or because they feel entitled to an input into policy formation. These, to be sure, are problems which need be considered and have received increasing attention in recent years.

Unfortunately, much of this attention has not followed the Wicksellian tradition of seeking more efficient procedures, but has yielded to ideological bias, desiring to demonstrate a preconceived and inherent inefficiency of the public hand. Some may view this as a matter of historical justice, offsetting a perhaps opposite tendency in earlier years. But matching one bias with another is hardly a route to progress. There *are* areas where public provision is needed, and it *is* important that they be served as efficiently as possible.

Let me here return once more to the Weberian dichotomy between objective analysis and value judgment. Public provision (or "purchase" as referred to in the GNP statistics) now accounts for about 20 percent of GNP. Excluding defense, the ratio is 13 percent, with provision almost entirely at the state–local level. Is this too much or too little? As I have argued before, this should be answerable in objective fashion, but the matter quickly becomes subject to political debate. Proponents of the market system like to discount the need for public provision, while supporters of the public sector tend to stress it. The reason of course is that the existence of social goods flaws the rule of the "invisible hand" and thus carries broad ideological implications. Hence the difficulty in separating (1) the objection question of how much in social goods is needed (i.e., how large the purchase part of the budget should be) to meet the preferences of consumers from (2) whether or not the finding of such need is pleasing or displeasing to a particular observer. As to (2), I find the existence of such need to be a happy feature, as it requires a mixed form of social organization, including consideration of shared concerns via the political process, as well as self-interested choice via the market. As to (1), my finding is that the 13 percent and all that they contain (from roads to police, the administration of justice and education to public health) is not excessive although, based on what I just noted with regard to (1), the reader may suspect me of failing to properly separate (1) from (2).

WHY PUBLIC SECTOR: (2) DISTRIBUTION

So far I have viewed the rule of the public sector in the efficient use of resources, i.e., the provision of social goods. This provision, as that for private goods, was to depend on the preferences of consumers, albeit now recorded via a political process rather than individual market purchase. For the premise of consumer preference to be rendered effective, we must also assume a given distribution of income to prevail, on the basis of which demands can be recorded. This state of distribution as determined by the market process reflects the pattern of earnings, be they on labor, land, and capital, the ownership of resources, and the acquisition of property via gifts and bequests. Factor earnings in turn may reflect the marginal product of their contribution to output, as well as market imperfections and institutional arrangements which can have no sanction on efficiency grounds. The market thus generates its own pattern of distribution. In the United States, over 40 percent of disposable income (earnings plus transfers minus income tax) goes to the top quintile of the income scale and 5 percent to the lowest. This prevailing degree of inequality would be even larger if viewed prior to allowance for taxes and transfer payments. It exceeds that of most industrialized countries and has been increasing in recent years. However one views these facts, some standard of distributive justice has to be applied thereto. While some economists have held that our concern should be with efficiency only, I find it evident that our analysis cannot bypass this crucial issue.

How this standard of justice is to be defined is not given by scriptures or natural law, but involves considerations of value on which tastes differ. This is evidenced by the history of moral philosophy and its divergent views. Thomas Aquinas and the scholastics held the return to labor as deserved, but were skeptical regarding entitlement to capital earnings. Locke thought there to be a natural right to the fruits of one's labor, but not to that of land, which was to be seen as a common resource, a pattern followed later by Henry George. Adam Smith, in *The Wealth of Nations*, took entitlement to factor earnings for granted, but his *Theory of Moral Sentiments* takes a more complex view. While the impartial observer counsels to consider the welfare of others, the promise of gain induces economic effort, and thus creates wealth. People in turn are enticed thereby, not knowing that in the end little is to be gained, as the beggar on the side of the road – so Smith held – is left no less happy than the lord who passes by in his carriage.[2] Some decades later, Bentham and the utilitarians departed from the entitlement premise. Instead, they applied an efficiency criteria and argued that welfare would be maximized by an equal distribution of a given income total. Such would be the case because marginal utility declines when income rises. However, this finding is qualified since inequality is again needed to provide the necessary incentive for the creation of output. More recently, the debate over distributive justice was rekindled in the 1970s when John Rawls advanced his criterion of distributive justice. Fairness would require an impartial judgment (reached under a veil of ignorance) and would call for earnings to be adjusted by a tax-transfer scheme so as to maximize the welfare of the lowest.[3]

Bypassing the issue of how to define *the* just distribution, economists have used the policy instrument of a social welfare function. This function expresses the value which society places on incomes at various points on the scale, or, putting it differently, its inequality aversion, while leaving

[2] See Adam Smith, *The Theory of Moral Sentiments*, Liberty Classics, Indianapolis, 1969, pp. 303, 113. Also see my "Adam Smith on Public Finance and Distribution," in *The Market and the State, Essays in Honor of Adam Smith*, T. Wilson and A. Skinner, eds., Clarendon Press, Oxford, 1976.

[3] See John Rawls, *A Theory of Justice*, Harvard University Press, Cambridge, Mass., 1971. While I agree with the principle that distributive justice need be based on a rule of fairness, I have some difficulty with the Rawlsian solution. If individuals are to choose in a disinterested fashion, i.e., are willing to place themselves under a veil so as not to know what their particular position will be, why would they then wish to choose a pattern based on their own risk aversion? Would it not be more direct for them to partake in the choice of an acceptable tax-transfer scheme, knowing what their position before and after adjustment will be? See my "Maximin, Uncertainty, and the Leisure Trade-Off," *Quarterly Journal of Economics*, 1974.

it to society to determine the specific shape of that function. In my view, this function should reflect the Rawlsian premise that the issue of distributive justice is not settled by innate entitlement to market earnings, but calls for a rule of fairness to be reached by social consensus. My voice in that consensus would reflect a view of the good society in which excessive inequality is avoided.

In practice, society does not begin with a de novo distribution of income along what are considered just lines. Rather, it begins with a distribution as determined by the market and then applies an adjustment. The citizen is entitled to his/her property as acquired under the rules of law (e.g., for exchange of services, exchange between properties, gifts, or bequests) and cannot be derived thereof without due process of law (Bill of Rights, Amendment XI). But this due process then permits majority action for budgetary taking by taxation (Bill of Rights, Amendment XVI) and transfers (or services in kind) to lower income groups so as to adjust the market state of distribution. How far such action should be carried depends on the views of the voters, and they may change over time. Observing the history of the income tax over recent decades, there has been first a movement toward and then a withdrawal from progressive taxation. The sharp reduction in upper bracket rates under the Tax Reform Act of 1986 testifies to the latter, even though offsetting measures of base-broadening left effective rates largely unchanged.[4] This development has been accompanied, however, by a steady spread in the redistributive impact of the expenditure side of the budget, primarily through the growth of transfer payments, so that the scope of redistribution has risen on balance. Concern, it appears, is more with expenditure measures to alleviate distress at the low end of the income scale (whether adequately or not is a different question) than with reducing inequality at the upper end via progressive taxation. The Tax Reform of 1986 sustains this judgment.

However this may be, it is evident that our society recognizes that market-determined distribution of income is not inherently just. A problem of distributive justice thus remains, calling for a degree of correction. To some extent, this may be provided voluntarily through charity, but its scope is limited and bypasses the entitlement issue. There thus remains a role for the public sector. How far such activity is to be carried depends on (1) one's value-based view of distributive justice and (2) the cost of adjustment. Income decline and dead weight losses that result in the process need be weighted against the social gains from reducing inequality. Once more, we arrive at a distinction between a hopefully objective finding on the level of cost and on the value to be placed on

[4] See my "Short of Euphoria," *Journal of Economic Perspectives*, A.E.A., Vol. 1, 1987.

resulting gains in distribution. As noted before, I find extreme inequality inappropriate for a healthy democratic society. It is hardly necessary to add that distributional goals in the end are best achieved not via transfer-type redistribution, but by policies designed to raise productivity and to assure adequate earnings opportunities.

WHY PUBLIC SECTOR: (3) MACRO STABILITY

It remains to note the role of the public sector in maintaining macro stability. A market economy needs money to serve as a medium of exchange and as a source of liquidity. The bulk of this money is in the form of bank credit, and the level of credit does not regulate itself. Thus a monetary authority is needed to regulate the money supply, i.e., to avoid an excess which causes inflation or a deficiency which induces recession and unemployment. Economists may disagree on the precise rules which the monetary authority should follow, but such an authority is obviously needed. My years at the Federal Reserve made this an evident lesson.

The problem of regulating the money supply, moreover, is not simply one of letting money grow in line with a steady growth of real output. Nor is adjustment to a given rate of steady growth the only problem. The level of economic activity, as generated by the private sector, is subject to fluctuation, and economic efficiency as well as considerations of social welfare require that there be no substantial periods of under-utilization of resources with extensive unemployment, nor that there be sustained inflation. Monetary policy can play a vital role in this, but the cooperation of fiscal policy is needed as well. During the earlier stages of Keynesian economics, when the problem was one of reviving a highly depressed economy, primary stress was placed on fiscal policy as a means of economic expansion. By increasing expenditures, so the argument went, aggregate demand might be raised, while increasing the money supply was considered relatively ineffective. The vast expansion of output during World War II validated this case. In the 1950s and 1960s, when the economy showed sustained strength, monetary policy was reinstated as an effective policy tool, with an appropriate mix of monetary and fiscal policy set in inducing expansion or restriction. The Kennedy tax cut of 1964, in which many of us were actively involved, showed that expansionary action could be taken as well on the expenditure side. It proved the high point of fiscal stabilization.

Since then, confidence in the ability of macro policy to stabilize the economy has suffered under the course of events. Excessively expansionary fiscal policy during the Vietnam War was followed by rising oil prices during the 1970s, leading to successive waves of inflation and culminating in a sharp price rise at the close of the decade. Monetary restriction, undertaken at the cost of a severe recession, brought inflation to a halt but only to be followed by a new macro dilemma. An excessive deficit matched by monetary restriction produced a lopsided policy mix. While successful in maintaining price stability and reasonably high employment, it did so at the cost of a widening trade deficit. Financed by an inflow of foreign capital to sustain the rising U.S. debt, a high-consumption economy has been sustained at the cost of future generations. A tax increase with monetary easing is called for on macro grounds, but has been frustrated by the administration's use of tax cuts to force reduction in the non-defense budget. But though policy has been misguided, it does not follow that the economy can do without macro measures or that stabilization based on the earlier framework of monetary-fiscal analysis cannot be made to work. What follows, rather, is that we need to learn how to do better.

CONCLUSION

An unprejudiced view of the social scene tells us that the conduct of economic affairs calls for cooperation between and interaction of a public and a private sector. This interplay has several dimensions, three of which, pertaining to the operation of the public budget, have been noted here. Unnecessary to say, there are other respects in which the invisible hand of the market need be supplemented by the visible hand of public policy. Imperfect markets require measures to maintain competition, financial institutions need supervision to protect investors, protection is needed to safeguard the environment, and so forth. Beyond such rules of economic conduct, public policy is needed in setting the very framework within which society can operate, ranging from its broad mapping by the Constitution to an array of specific rules, such as contract and liability law, the criminal code, and the rights and obligations set down by family law. In short, a modern society cannot operate by a principle of anarchy. The miracle of the invisible hand by which self-interest yields the common good only goes that far, as Adam Smith in his *Theory of Moral Sentiments* well knew. Visible cooperation is needed as well. In my view, this is not a defect in the nature of things. As noted before, it is a happy circumstance, as it requires cooperative action, reaching beyond the principle of self-interest in the market. Strange though this may sound in the 1990s, recall Justice Oliver Wendell Holmes' reference to taxation as the price of liberty.[5]

---

[5] More precisely, he rebuked a secretary's query of "Don't you hate to pay taxes?" with "No, young fellow, I like paying taxes, with them I buy civilization." See Felix Frankfurter, *Mr. Justice Holmes and the Supreme Court*, Harvard University Press, Cambridge, Mass., 1961, p. 71.

As with all good things, however, the need for cooperation and government also carries its own risks. Some form of majority rule is needed to decide on common action, but a balance must also be struck between individual rights and majority wishes. Government should reflect and serve the interest of its citizens, but not permit ruling groups to impose their wishes. Public policy, no less than the market, thus carries its own risk of failure. To make democratic society function, both need be made to operate properly in their respective spheres, and do so in a coordinated fashion. To contribute thereto is the challenge which to me has made the social scientist's task so fascinating.

In concluding, I once more return to my earlier theme that the social scientist's work permits a combination of (1) objective analysis, searching for an unbiased understanding of how social variables interact with (2) the application of such findings to the pursuit of goals which reflect his/her image of how a good society should be shaped. Objectivity in analysis is all-important, but so is a vision of social ethics and the values which underlie human interaction, including their all-important application to the economic sphere. Our challenge in the end is to determine and combine what can be with what should be done.

Richard A. Musgrave is H. H. Burbank Professor of Political Economy, Emeritus, Harvard University, and Adjunct Professor, University of California at Santa Cruz.

AUSTIN ROBINSON

My Apprenticeship as an Economist

I

What made me begin to study economics? What made me devote the rest of my life to studying, teaching, and writing economics? Within the broad field of economics, what have been my special interests and what has dictated my choices? These are questions that, busy with day-to-day business, one seldom asks oneself; but after seventy years as an economist I find it fascinating to try to answer them.

I must start, I think, with some background. My boyhood, more than eighty years back, belongs to a period before the welfare state. Son of an impecunious parson, I depended for my education on being able to win scholarships, first at a school and later at a university. The examinations were in Latin and Greek – the classics. I was lucky enough to possess a capacity to get scholarships in the classics; thus, I could desert them only at my peril and to the age of nineteen remained a competent but not, in retrospect, very enthusiastic student of them. This phase of my life ended with a scholarship to Christ's College, Cambridge. If the world had been normal, this road might have led on to the Home Civil Service or the Indian Civil Service – the very competitive prize careers for a clever boy at that time.

But the world was not normal. When I got my scholarship in December 1916, we were two and a half years into the great war of 1914–18. Military service was by now compulsory. In the modern world, deeply concerned with the dreadful threat of a nuclear war, it is too often forgotten how terrible was the mortality of that pre-nuclear conflict. Of the twenty senior boys in the "house" into which I had gone at Marlborough School in 1912, thirteen were dead before I got to Cambridge in the summer of 1919.

I myself had gone immediately after the scholarship exams in December 1916 into the Royal Naval Air Service. After some seven months of flying training, I had about ten months of active service and then nine months of testing and delivering new flying boats. I had gone into the RNAS a schoolboy. I came back to Cambridge in the summer of 1919 a very different person. Of the sixteen who reported at the training centre with me, more than half – including many of my closest friends – were dead. But it was a young man's war in which, before reaching the age at which one then acquired the right to vote, one had carried heavy responsibilities, such as I was not allowed to carry for another twenty years.

Quite inevitably, all this had profound effects on almost all of my generation of Cambridge undergraduates. We were not, in the technical sense of the word, pacifists. Indeed, we rather despised those whose consciences had not permitted them to face the possibility of dying for their country. But we were determined that the problems of the world should never again have to be settled by war. Naive we may have been, but we were nonetheless sincere.

In my own case I arrived in Cambridge in April 1919, having tested my last flying boat forty-eight hours before. I was quickly defeated by my college, which was unsympathetic to my view that I should use a classical scholarship to be taught the more professional aspects of designing aeroplanes. I found myself back on the classical treadmill, reading Homer, Aeschylus, and Plato for my own pleasure and Livy and Demosthenes to please my tutor. In fifteen months I duly acquired my "first." But my heart was not in the classics. Like many of my friends with classical scholarships, I was looking for an alternative occupation for my final two years.

My decision that it was to be economics was the consequence of two pieces of singular good fortune. First, one of my friends took me to hear one of a course of lectures by Maynard Keynes that were to be published as *The Economic Consequences of the Peace*; to anyone hungry for relevance to the state of the world, it was a revelation. Second, I got to know Ryle Fay, then teaching economic history in Christ's; he did his utmost to encourage me to tackle economics and persuaded the college to let me.

Fay, to start me off, lent me Tawney's *Acquisitive Society*, with its dogma that one cannot have rights without obligations, and the little elementary book by Alfred and Mary Marshall called *Economics of Industry*. Fay hero-worshipped Marshall, from whom he had acquired a tremendous enthusiasm for the subject but singularly little understanding of theory.

With Fay's list of books, I went off for the summer of 1920 to help a friend of mine run the "University Settlement" in Liverpool, built in the midst of the slum area where the dockers lived who were taken on, if they were lucky, in the early morning for a day's work. The settlement was run by a half-dozen young men, chiefly from Cambridge, who gave their evenings to supervising some activity involving the people of the neighbourhood. My own responsibility was running the "poor-man's lawyer." Some of the lawyers working in Liverpool spent their evenings providing free legal advice to the poor of the area. My job was to listen to the incoherent outpourings of their grievances and scribble down for the lawyer a short summary of what the basic problem was – rental problems, marital problems, or whatever. It was a remarkable education regarding the life and problems of the poor. And during the day I had the library to work in and, while there, was able to read for the first time and absorb, first, the fat volumes of Taussig's *Principles*, and then Alfred Marshall's *Principles*, normal pabulum of my generation.

By the time that I came back to Cambridge in October 1920 and attended for the first time lectures in economics, I had almost inadvertently acquired a view – a set of prejudices if you like – regarding the sort of economics in which I was interested. My economics was concerned with improving the state of the world – with making it a somewhat better place for the poor as well as for the rich. I was well on the way to becoming an applied political economist. These initial preconceptions were reinforced by the lectures I now attended. Pigou, the complete Marshallian, always regarded economics as a subject one studied not for itself but for the benefits it might bring. And this was the prevalent outlook of virtually the whole of the Cambridge staff of the period.

I was lucky again in that Fay was impressed by something that I had written and told Keynes about it; I was quickly absorbed into Keynes's Monday night "Political Economy Club" and thus very early in my career got to know him. It was from Keynes that I learned the very important lesson that good intentions do not justify woolly thinking – that, faced by an economic problem, one's first duty is to think it out absolutely clearly and rigidly and to think out equally clearly and critically the limitations of any solution that one might wish to suggest.

In the Oxford–Cambridge system of those days, one "read" a subject: the emphasis was on reading a half-dozen or so outstanding books, nearly all of them written in Cambridge. One acquired one's capacity as an economist from them. One read other books for information. But there was a happy orthodoxy. We had not yet learned to look around the world for disagreement. And one had a "supervisor," as Oxford and Cambridge undergraduates still do, for whom each week we had to write an essay, which we discussed with him. When after my months in Liverpool I got back to Cambridge, I had the good luck to have Fay as a supervisor.

Being taught by Fay was an unorthodox route to mastering economics. He was full of enthusiasms and excitements. He knew all about obscure groups and movements. But he was completely innocent of any real understanding of Marshallian economics. He would propound some wholly ridiculous theory. To defend myself I had to read and reread Marshall. Thanks to Fay, but not through Fay, I sufficiently mastered what passed for the orthodox Marshallian economics of the 1920s. By my second year of economics, Fay had gone off to a professorship in Toronto. I had the much more orthodox supervision first of Gerald Shove and then of Dennis Robertson. It no doubt taught me a great deal. But I missed the inspiration of those furious arguments with Fay. It was those that set me on fire and made me the sort of economist that I have since remained.

I duly collected the "first" that was necessary for an academic career. I cannot remember debating with myself whether that was what I wanted. It was Keynes who told me to take the examination for the Almeric Paget studentship. With its help I had sufficient money to do a year's research. It was certainly Keynes who decided that my subject should be "foreign investment." But getting the Almeric Paget had far more important long-term consequences. It was attached to Corpus Christi College. That college was dominated by its tutor, Will Spens – by origin a scientist, in practice a high-church tory theologian – who, before I knew what was happening, had me rethinking the traditional liberal economics of Cambridge, reading Disraeli and the tories, and asking myself whether Adam Smith and the long line of liberals down to Marshall had established an incontrovertible truth.

II

After a little more than a term of this, I found myself being elected to a fellowship and starting to teach economics before I really knew what I myself thought. The problems of high-church toryism and of the limitations of Adam Smith laissez-faire that were imposed on me by Spens were not, of course, new to Cambridge. Pigou, good Marshallian that he was, was already actively thinking about them. Indeed, any young economist who had been brought up, as I had been, both at home and at school as a Christian could not but be aware of the apparent conflict between the argument of Adam Smith that, by acting selfishly, you could benefit the human race and the commandment to love your neighbour as yourself. I had been brought up in a manse and had been educated at a school that had been founded for the principal purpose of teaching the sons of the country clergy. I was not a crusading Christian. But I had retained the essentials of my Christianity. And, think what one might, one could not fight a war without thinking about one's obligations to sacrifice oneself if necessary for the benefit of others.

I cannot remember whether I tried seriously to sort out my thinking at that stage in my life. I was certainly conscious of the severity of the transition from the student's obligation to understand and be able to reproduce what other people think to the adult teacher's obligation to know what he himself thinks. Thinking out and deciding what I myself think has always been made more difficult by the fact that I keep my schizophrenia in the wrong place – or perhaps I should say in an inconvenient place. There are some lucky people who, when they are convinced that something is seriously wrong, can be satisfied with having reached that conclusion. There are others (and I am one of them) who, when they are convinced that something is wrong, feel a compulsion to do something about it; the unfortunate implication is that, if one does not feel prepared to go to battle, one tends to deny that things are so bad that one should.

But one must remember the very different intellectual background of the 1920s. My high-church tory colleagues were conserving the principles of Disraeli. The Tory Party had not yet been taken over by the Gladstonian liberals. Adam Smith's *Wealth of Nations* was not then the Bible of the Tory Party; indeed, it was anathema, and a good tory economist, if there were one, would be looking for reasons for distrusting its oversimplifications. The gap between the sincere tory and the intellectual socialist, such as Richard Tawney, was (as Will Spens told me) much narrower than that between either of them and an orthodox liberal disciple of Adam Smith. I was not living among colleagues who discouraged critical thinking about the basics of my subject.

At that stage in my life I think in retrospect that I was, despite the intellectual pressures of my colleagues in Corpus Christi College, nearer in my outlook to Tawney and the intellectual socialists of that day than to the more self-seeking tories. It is more difficult to say where I stood vis-à-vis the liberals. I think it would be true to say that in the 1920s

almost all Cambridge economists would unhesitatingly have called themselves liberals. But it was a private liberalism of their own. It was not
yet fashionable to be "labour." Their liberalism did not exclude a considerable element of socialism.

III

In the four years that I spent at Corpus I grew up. But I had not found
a lifetime career. I was not happy trying to lecture on monetary theory
– a branch of economics in which I am interested in listening to others
but to which I do not think that I myself have anything much to contribute. More important, I happen to have a realistic and pragmatic mind;
I can analyse and seek ways of improving only those things in which I
have practical experience and detailed working knowledge. I was not cut
out to become a monetary expert. And this was the moment at which I
was offered a quite fascinating job in India as tutor to the young Maharaja
of Gwalior, then about ten years old.

I learned much in India. I had to stand up for my own convictions
both against the intrigues of the coterie of the palace and against the
constantly changing policies advocated by the eternally changing residents supposedly representing the government of India. I had come to
know India, not only as did some of my contemporaries in the enjoyable
cold weather, but also in the searing heat of the hot weather. I had
acquired a lifelong interest and concern with what has since become
development economics and some capacity to distinguish practicable
from wholly impracticable proposed solutions and the limitations imposed by sheer distance, by the magnitude of problems, and by the eternal
uncertainty of rainfall. Above all, I had acquired a lifelong capacity to
make close friends among Indian economists.

IV

By the beginning of 1929 I was back in Cambridge. They were still short-
handed. I quickly accumulated as much college teaching as I wanted and
settled back into a familiar routine. But in one respect I was very lucky.
They were short of someone to lecture on industrial economics, and I
acquired a job that was very congenial and for which I think I had a
capacity.

In the period from 1929 to 1939, I was able to make something of a
modest position for myself in England. I had, as I said, quickly fallen
into the routine of university lecturing and college supervision. I was
elected a fellow of Sidney Sussex College; it has been the centre of my
life for the sixty years since then. But it was Pigou, then professor and

chairman of the faculty, who did most to start me off. A faculty teaching a given subject was administered by a chairman and a secretary. There were no rules as to which of them did what. At the end of a few months in Cambridge, I was made secretary of the Faculty of Economics. Pigou hated administration. He was an excellent chairman, determined that justice should always be done. But the whole running of the faculty was left to me, with Pigou always ready to descend on me like a ton of bricks if anything went wrong. This meant that I knew very well and worked closely with my senior colleagues, planned the lecture list, collected and paid the lecture fees in the ways of that time, and generally carried a great deal of responsibility.

Among those with whom I had to work was, of course, Keynes. When I had been doing this for about four years, Keynes invited me to become review editor of the *Economic Journal*, of which he was editor, and thus began in 1934 the fifty-odd years of association with the Royal Economic Society that still continues.

Being a review editor was a wonderful education. I had through my office nearly all the books published on economics; fortunately, they were then numbered in tens rather than hundreds. I made it my rule to dip into any serious book for an hour or so. One could quickly discover whether a book was just restating the orthodoxies or was rethinking parts of the subject and if so, what. This was a necessary stage in thinking who would be the right reviewer. But as a by-product, I read very widely.

Teaching undergraduates and being review editor of the *Economic Journal* during those ten years were only a part, and in retrospect a rather small part, of my life as an economist. I still regard the decade of the 1930s as the most creative period in which I have lived as an economist. There were at least four revolutions going on at the same time in Cambridge. In some, Cambridge was playing a critical part; in some, we were one of a number of participants. These theoretical revolutions were separate. But there were only about a dozen of us teaching economics in 1929 and only one or two more by 1939. We almost all knew one another intimately and had a foot in other people's revolutions besides our own. And because we were supervising undergraduates over the whole field of economics, we needed to know what was going on throughout the subject.

The various revolutions were going on in parallel and one cannot give one or another precedence. Pigou, in curious isolation from all the rest of us, was revising and rerevising his life's work on welfare economics. Keynes, when we came back from India in 1929, was in the last stages of writing the *Treatise on Money*; Dennis Robertson was still his chief Cambridge ally and was himself still developing the ideas envisaged in *Banking Policy and the Price Level*.

Those men were for us the older generation. For the younger of us, the major involvement was in the rethinking of value theory that was inspired by lectures given by Piero Sraffa, who had been brought to Cambridge by Keynes a few years before. He was so irreverent as to analyse, criticize, and refine Alfred Marshall's *Principles,* on which I had been brought up by Pigou as equivalent to holy writ. I unfortunately could not myself hear the lectures. But my wife Joan and Richard Kahn, then Keynes's young pupil at King's, retailed them to me. In an important sense Sraffa's lectures set us free to rethink even the basics of our subject.

The rethinking of value theory advanced another stage because of an essay that Charles Gifford, a very bright pupil of mine, wrote for me early in 1931. He used a concept, I think derived from something that Yntema had written, that I subsequently suggested naming "marginal revenue." It so happened that Richard Kahn was lunching with us that day. I passed on to Joan and him the idea that Charles Gifford had produced, and they started playing with it. Gradually the game became more serious. It became substantially easier to tackle a number of problems. And out of this grew Joan's first book, *The Economics of Imperfect Competition.* It was very much Joan's book. But like most work in Cambridge at that time, others of us saw drafts, made suggestions, proposed topics, and in my own case invented many of the now very familiar names for concepts.

I myself was at work at this time on what subsequently became two elementary books. Dennis Robertson had asked me to write a book for the Cambridge Economics Handbook series on the subject of monopoly. I quickly found that one could not tackle monopoly without a theory of the size of the firm, and I set out to provide it. Like most inexperienced authors, I quickly overran my limit of words. Thus *The Structure of Competitive Industry* became a book on its own, and I had in effect introduced to Cambridge the study of the theory of the firm. But this meant that I had a rather special interest in what Joan and our friends were doing in relation to oligopoly.

I have left till now, because in our lives it followed a little later, the greatest of our Cambridge revolutions of that decade – that which resulted in the *General Theory.* Keynes had published the *Treatise on Money* in the autumn of 1930. We of the younger generation of Cambridge economists had not been involved in it, though Richard Kahn had produced the index. Remember, however, that we were supervising very able undergraduates who would expect us to be able to help them understand the *Treatise.* Apart from that, we younger economists wanted to understand it ourselves.

Our very natural solution was collaboration. Five of us tackled it together. Richard Kahn, Piero Sraffa, Joan and myself, and James Meade, who was having a year away from Oxford with us in Cambridge before beginning to teach in his own university. We were not being deliberately exclusive. But this was for the moment a group of younger dons wishing to discuss at their own level. This was not Pigou's sort of game. Robertson was not interested.

This is not the place to discuss what contribution the "circus" may or may not have made to the genesis of Keynes's *General Theory*. Keynes knew of our meetings and asked Kahn what we were discussing, and Kahn conveyed to him our problems and difficulties. There gradually emerged a two-way flow. I do not want to argue that we contributed more than marginally to the *General Theory,* though we did in fact come to visualize many of its ultimate constituents. What I do want to emphasize is that we had the interest and excitement of living in a very creative world and were almost certainly among the irritants that made Keynes move forward from the *Treatise* to the *General Theory*.

The last of the revolutions that I have always regarded as having belonged to that period is the quantification of economics. Nineteenth-century economics was almost wholly non-quantitative. So was the economics that I had learned in the early 1920s. It was only in the 1930s that it became axiomatic that one must measure all phenomena and the relationships of one phenomenon to all the factors that were affecting it. Cambridge was not particularly early in this field. Manchester, London, and Oxford were all ahead of us in developing serious statistical work. But with Keynes's help, we acquired Colin Clark and were quickly outstripping others in brave comparisons and long-term projections. I was particularly interested and involved in this because I had found myself repeatedly handicapped in my own work by a lack of statistical evidence and was an avid user of all of Colin Clark's output.

But during those ten years I was not just sitting in Cambridge, looking on at other people's work and doing the review editing of the *Economic Journal*. I still retained my human interests, and though my religious motivations were modest, they overlapped constantly with the activities of the church and the missionary societies. May I confine myself to two major enterprises? The first of these came when William Temple, by then archbishop of York and president of the International Missionary Council, approached Pigou and asked him to suggest an economist who might be one of a team that was to go out to study conditions in what was then Northern Rhodesia (now Zambia), where a copper industry was being developed. In those days all education and health services were the responsibility of missionary societies, which worked all over the world and had competing claims on their limited funds. Pigou suggested my name to Temple. I got a term off teaching and set off for Cape Town (this was before the age of air transport) in the weekly Union Castle liner. In the fortnight or so of the voyage I was able to read and absorb such limited literature on African development as then existed.

In due course we landed at Cape Town, joined up with our other colleagues, and started off on a drive that ultimately took us to Abercorn at the southern end of Lake Tanganyika. On the way we stopped for a day or two in numerous places and rather longer in Johannesburg and in Elisabethville, then the capital of that part of the Belgian Congo and full of valuable lessons derived from their earlier development of a copper industry and urbanization of a rural population.

Our visit to the copper mines taught us much. I myself learned almost more from nights spent with lonely missionaries at isolated mission stations and with equally lonely members of the Colonial Service, who were delighted to have someone to talk to about the disastrous results of the migrations of their male tribesmen to the highly paid work at the mines and the break-up of the traditional authority of the tribal chiefs.

I came back from that trip with a picture of the realities of Africa, with its endless miles of scrub, of the loneliness of those then trying to develop it, of what it means to be a scattered white minority governing a potentially hostile black world, and equally what it means to be a black majority denied its democratic rights. I had added Africa to India as one of the continents that I had a personal duty to try to help.

My second major undertaking of this kind grew out of this first one. I had met Lord Hailey (as he was later to become) when I was still in India and he was governor of the Punjab; he was in London in 1933 as secretary of the round-table conference on the future of the Indian constitution and asked me to see him. He told me that he had been invited by Chatham House to do a survey of the whole administration of Africa, south of the Sahara, and asked me if I was prepared to be one of his team, responsible for the economic aspects. There was only one possible answer. Hailey was the greatest of a great group of Indian administrators. There was no question that the Colonial Office and the officials all over Africa would open all doors to him and that his recommendations would lead to action. I quickly said yes.

The Hailey Survey kept me busy during all of my Cambridge vacations from 1934–37. Working with Hailey was an education in itself, though I certainly did not so regard it at the time. Hailey was an administrator. Writing a report was a preliminary to action. Action required infinite care and accuracy in preparation. There was no scope here for the academic's light-hearted kite flying. Every word I wrote had to be criticized and justified. I have learned to admire his splendid thoroughness. I did my best to acquire quickly the capacity to live up to it. It has left me with a contempt for the academics who do not themselves apply similar standards to their quantitative estimates.

I find it fascinating to look back and try to assess myself as I was in 1939 when war broke out. I was by then a little over forty. I was an experienced and confident junior administrator. I had more down-to-earth practical knowledge of Africa and India and the underdeveloped world generally than anyone else in Cambridge. But I was not, and made no claim to be, a pure theorist. In retrospect I think I give myself a little more credit now than I did then for starting off the development of the theory of the firm. Development economics and the theory of growth were still in the distant future; I would then have regarded what I had done and written in relation to Africa and India as the normal activities of a competent applied economist. Looking back fifty years later, I feel a little kinder. The advance of economics comes from asking new questions and then trying to answer them. It is not infrequently the applied economist who finds himself confronted by a new question. Too seldom do the theorists move on to tackle the new question. I give myself in retrospect a little more credit for having asked unanswered questions. I have asked more in the subsequent fifty years.

V

When war broke out in September 1939, I, like most of the population of the United Kingdom, found myself wondering what I ought to be doing, wondering indeed whether the RAF might have any use for a twenty-year obsolete flying boat pilot. That period did not last long, however. Keynes got hold of me and asked me whether I would be interested in a job in the Cabinet Office that involved both the ordinary Cabinet Office responsibilities and working with Stamp, Clay, and Henderson on the survey they had been commissioned to do of departmental war plans. The job was fascinating and of course the answer was yes.

When I arrived in Whitehall I found that my ultimate boss was Edward Bridges, son of the poet and immensely competent secretary of the Cabinet; the task of secretary of the Cabinet itself belonged exclusively to him, but the Cabinet handled only the major and debatable issues. There was a vast amount of minor business that was left to be settled by smaller committees of ministers or by interdepartmental committees of civil servants representing their ministries. It was the task of us juniors to act as secretaries of these ministerial or interdepartmental committees, summarize the problems and arguments, and record the decisions. If you were lucky and had a good chairman who summed up the discussion and formulated the decision, this was an interesting and straightforward task. But not all chairmen were good and clear. Sometimes a committee went on to the next business without having reached a clear and unambiguous decision. It was then the very difficult task of the Cabinet

Office secretary to record what he believed to be the decision of the committee.

My own chief contribution at this time had a much more lasting consequence for British economics. While in Cambridge I had heard Keynes give a talk entitled "How to Pay for the War." I could see that this involved having an up-to-date series of accurate estimates of the national income. Keynes, for his own purposes, had got Erwin Rothbarth to make a working estimate. But it was obvious that, if we were to run the war economy efficiently, we needed a continuous series of quickly available and consistently defined national income estimates, produced with all the data and information available to a government. When I was back in London I told my immediate boss all about this and persuaded him to let me talk to Bridges about it. I can still visualize our talk with Bridges across the fireplace of his office. He agreed to give us authority to recruit two experts to tackle the job. I was allowed to choose them. My choices were James Meade, our Oxford friend from the days of the pre-*General Theory* circus, then working in Geneva, to get the logic right and a then-unheard-of youngster called Richard Stone, who was showing extraordinary ability to organize statistics. They arrived, in Meade's case after an adventurous journey, and we had the beginnings of the subsequent nearly fifty years of official national income statistics.

More generally, one could not conduct a war economy efficiently without a steady flow of more micro-economic statistics. It was Eli Devons who with Harry Campion was principally responsible for the first issue of the then-secret *Statistical Digest*. But we all had a share in determining its contents.

I remained with the growing Economic Section of the Cabinet Office until 1942, engaged in a wide variety of tasks ranging from a study of war controls to the problems of our primary producing colonies and ending, at Keynes's suggestion, with an estimate of the necessary increase of exports to balance our post-war payments.

VI

By 1942, however, a new group of problems had emerged. We had expanded the three armed services. We had built and were manning the munitions factories. The United States was now at war with Germany, and we were frantically building aerodromes to meet the needs of their aircraft as well as our own. We had quite definitely reached full employment, and more effective war planning had become imperative. One contribution to this was the creation of a Ministry of Production, with responsibilities for allocations of manpower and materials for war purposes. I was invited to become chief economic adviser and head of statistics. It was what I was most interested in, and without hesitation I accepted.

We had already decided to use manpower allocations as the chief instrument of economic control, with raw material and machine-tool allocations fitting in, so far as possible, to the resultant pattern. My main task for the rest of the war was to agree, with those responsible in the ministries concerned, on the manpower requirements of their programmes and then, with those responsible in the Ministry of Labour, to find what manpower might be available and, with a representative of the chiefs of staff, to find what intakes the armed forces wished to have for their proposed activities. There was always a very large gap between what was demanded and what was available. The next task was that of cutting munitions programmes, cutting proposed military operations, cutting civilian consumption until a balance was achieved. This operation, which was repeated every few months, could never be finally settled at our level. We collected all the data and worked out a possible solution. Some minister, usually Sir John Anderson, was authorized to submit to the Cabinet his proposed solution, and the final decision was made in the Cabinet.

This was not, of course, the sole activity of the Ministry of Production. There was a stream of minor problems and bottlenecks and of discussions with the U.S. authorities of the forms that mutual aid should take. There were the problems of making sure that absolutely all the necessary equipment would be ready for D-day. There were the problems of making it possible for the railways to carry all the men and equipment to the ports of embarkation. We had on our plate, that is to say, all the macroeconomics of war. To handle this we had various divisions, and in my own were four of us at my level; I had a staff of some six or eight statisticians, most of them young women who had been my wife's brightest pupils.

Since we were deeply involved in lend-lease, mutual aid, and the constant flow of decisions as to what should be produced in the United States and what we should produce ourselves, there was a constant flow of missions to Washington, sometimes ministers, sometimes very senior civil servants, more often people like ourselves, and on major occasions all three. I usually found myself holding the fort at home. My turn to go to Washington came only in the fall of 1944. After the Quebec Conference, it was necessary to get into more concrete form what had been agreed about mutual aid for what we called Stage Two – the war against Japan whenever Germany was defeated. None of us knew about the atom bomb or that it was a potential war finisher. We were expecting two or three years of very severe island-to-island fighting with very formidable casualties.

The negotiation had a two-fold basis. We had to agree on the munitions requirements and sources for our participation and activities in that war. We had to agree on the rules that would govern mutual aid in that war. For the German war we had agreed, very reasonably, that we would not export any British production of anything we were receiving as lend-lease. But this had meant that our exports were less than a third of those before the war. We were anxious that we should be able during the Japanese war to begin the first stages of making ourselves solvent again.

The machinery for settling the lend-lease munition arrangements already existed. The revision of the rules governing our exports was very much more difficult and was the responsibility of Keynes and a small number of Treasury experts. We had never hitherto told the U.S. authorities all our worries about the post-war world or the full extent to which we had mortgaged the future in order to fight the war. It was now necessary to do so. The task of preparing the case was entrusted to the Ministry of Production and in practice fell to Otto Clarke, then one of our small group, and myself, getting all the help we needed from the Board of Trade and other ministries. I find it the best record I know of how we then saw the problems confronting us.

Keynes, with his troublesome heart, was not allowed to fly. I was sent with him by sea on a fast liner, sailing independently; to avoid German submarines we had to go south of the Azores and then north to Halifax, followed by a glorious railway journey to Montreal and then to Washington.

We had a straightforward negotiation regarding munitions. Keynes had a much more difficult task. But we left the United States much better informed, and most of their officials were much more sympathetic about our difficulties and needs. After a short visit to Ottawa to discuss the same problems, I recrossed the Atlantic with Maynard and his wife, this time in a large Dutch liner crowded with American troops.

VII

I got home amidst the temporary anxieties of the Ardennes attack by the Germans, much relieved to find how little worried were my friends on the Chiefs of Staff Committee, and thereafter it was only a matter of a few months to the end of the German war.

I had been involved during the previous year or two in planning for the post-war administration of Germany and the associated problems of reparations. Now I found myself one of a group of three or four who were sent off to Paris to join up with as many American economists who were to travel around Germany, evaluate the state it was in and the extent of possible reparations.

My still-vivid memory of Germany in the summer of 1945 is of the contrast between the wreckage of the big cities and the bright freshness, lively new paint, and colourful girls' dresses in the country villages, contrasting so extremely with their drab counterparts in the England of that time.

We went back to England and then were sent to Moscow as members of a larger delegation to follow up with the Russians the preliminary discussions of reparations at Yalta. We did much work among ourselves and with our American counterparts, saw a lot of Moscow, and attended the victory celebrations in Red Square, but had little effective discussion with the Russians.

From Moscow we were called back to the Potsdam Conference, flown this time by a Russian pilot along the railway lines by which he navigated. After various adventures we finally arrived in time to see the strange change that occurred when the Churchill administration was succeeded by that of Attlee. I found the conference terrifying. Major problems regarding the future of Europe were being settled after a few minutes' discussion. One might or might not be able to catch one's minister and brief him during the lunch break. Much of the work we had done in Moscow on post-war populations and the viability of different areas was immensely relevant but unknown to the ministers concerned. I was too careful and rational to be an international diplomat.

With Potsdam finished, I was sent to Berlin to negotiate reparations with the other three allies. We made some progress, but it was, from a British point of view, very limited progress. Before I started for Berlin, I had a talk with Keynes. He said to me, "See that we do not pay the reparations." Our fear was that the Russians and possibly the French would take so much out of Germany that we should find ourselves paying for the imports necessary to maintain the people living in our zone. My clearest memory is of trying to construct a minimum input–output table for Germany and of the fierce arguments with the Americans, who were somewhat influenced by Morgenthau's idea of ruralizing Germany. Our meetings with the Russians as well as the Americans and French were few, and one was never certain whether they would turn up.

One of my clearest memories of that period in Berlin is of relearning what I had half-learned previously in Washington – the extraordinary difficulty of negotiating between countries with different constitutions. A British negotiator knows that, provided that he stays within the instructions given him by his minister or permanent secretary, he can make an offer or accept an offer. An American would negotiate toughly, extract concessions from you, and then tell you that he did not know whether he could persuade Congress. The Russians in the same way would bargain, extract your concessions, submit them to Moscow, and come back demanding more concessions. I learned the hard way that one must not play one's final card until a very late stage in the game.

VIII

Interesting as this was, I was glad to be called back to London. After the Japanese war had ended sooner than we had expected and the Attlee government had taken over, the Ministry of Production had been absorbed into the Board of Trade, and our permanent secretary had been moved to the Board of Trade. He wanted me back as economic adviser to the Board.

My next few months were a welcome change from Berlin. I found myself acting in effect as personal assistant to the permanent secretary and as such was in close touch with Stafford Cripps, the political president of the Board. We were in the midst of the post-war transition from the war economy to a peacetime economy consistent with a balance of payments and the promise of full employment. Life was not made easier by the fact that four ministers were responsible for parts of the policy: Morrison nominally in charge but ill-equipped in practice, Dalton at the Treasury, and Isaacs, a poor successor to the splendid Ernie Bevin at the Ministry of Labour, in addition to Cripps. Our immediate problem was to manage with about three-quarters of pre-war imports while making 50 percent more exports, overtaking wartime arrears of maintenance, doing something to deal with war damage to housing, and above all doing the expansion necessary to provide exports in the forms that importers were wanting. It is obvious that the central problem was to get the priorities as right as we could. It is equally obvious that, whatever one did, a very large number of people would be maintaining that what they regarded as their objectives were being frustrated by controls. Without the controls, there would have been chaos and extreme inflation.

It was after a few months of this that I had to make up my mind whether I wanted this to be my life or whether I really preferred to be an academic. Dennis Robertson, now back in Cambridge and head of the faculty, was insisting that I return to help with the post-war flood of pupils or resign and become a civil servant. I was fascinated by my job. I enjoyed being at the very centre of making applied macro-economic policy in actual practice. But for seven years I had had no family life. I wanted to be a civil servant only if I could be at the centre of things. I knew that I was not tough enough to carry on indefinitely under the pressure that I had worked during the past four years. The verdict was that I would return to Cambridge.

That was not, however, the end. After I had been back in Cambridge lecturing, supervising, and examining for some six months, there came the two-fold crisis of 1947 – the cruel freeze-up of that spring and the exhaustion of the limited dollar resources that Keynes and others had negotiated in Washington. Attlee moved Cripps from the Board of Trade to a new position as minister of economic affairs. When the unfortunate Dalton who made the mistake on his way into the House of Commons of telling a friendly journalist the essentials of his budget, was betrayed by him and obliged to resign, Cripps also took over as chancellor of the exchequer.

Before this Cripps had already created a Central Economic Planning Staff and had made Plowden his principal economic adviser. Cripps urgently needed a staff that he knew and could trust. He demanded of the Cambridge vice-chancellor that I come back for another year. The university could not refuse him. I was allowed to recruit three assistants. I was lucky to find in Cambridge three very able youngsters who have greatly distinguished themselves subsequently – Ken Berrill, Robin Marris, and Patricia Brown. During the year I was in Whitehall, our principal tasks were to draft and get agreement on the *Economic Survey for 1948* and the long-term *Economic Survey for 1948–52*. In effect these were a short-term and a longer-term national economic strategy, reflecting the strategies of Cripps, Plowden, and Robert Hall, now head of the Economic Section of the Treasury. But they had also to satisfy the criticisms of all the ministries concerned. It was the first stage in working out a realistic and co-ordinated national economic strategy.

When this was done I was all set to return to Cambridge. But meanwhile General Marshall had made his great speech. The future of Europe depended on our satisfying Congress that we had effective individual and collective plans for survival. The future of Europe had been entrusted to the Organization for European Economic Cooperation (OEEC) in Paris. I was asked to play a part in criticizing and co-ordinating the various long-term plans in Paris and defending the British plan. An increasingly reluctant Cambridge faculty again conceded to the pressures from Cripps. I spent six months in Paris working very hard as one of the small British delegation. But the staff of the OEEC under Robert Marjolin was composed largely of English friends of my own; I found myself an honorary member of the secretariat as well as a member of the British delegation and ended by being chairman of the committee that drafted the collective report to Congress, showing that we collectively had plans that would make us viable. When that was finished, I was free to return to Cambridge and my academic life. I had finished my apprenticeship. I was on the threshold of a subsequent forty years as an academic.

IX

What did I learn from this long apprenticeship? I think the first and most important thing is that the responsibility of an economist is to use his brains and capacities to benefit humanity, not only within his own nation, but throughout the world. And to achieve that he must look ahead. Parliament, or whatever the national body may be called, is perpetually concerned with the problems of the short term. A civil service may try to persuade ministers to consider the longer-term effects of their policies, but they are involved in the short-term limitations. The individual industrialist, considering long-term investment policies, can see them only in terms of his own firm and is inevitably ill-informed about the trends of national and world markets. It is these longer-term trends that the academic economist is best equipped to study and, within his limitations, to forecast.

I have learned the great difficulties of doing this. I know the uncertainties. I know that one cannot predict with precision the political events or technical developments that may affect the trends. But I know also from experience that decisions must be made and that the decision to do nothing may be the most damaging decision of all. In a world with long periods of design, authorization, construction, and running in, it is in many cases necessary to plan ten years ahead. With modern technological progress, today's output may be produced ten years hence by some 30 percent fewer workers. How, where, and in what form will the liberated resources be employed? What skills will be required?

My own feeling is that the current work of this generation of economists on this immensely important problem is second rate and inadequate. It is almost wholly macro-economic where it ought to be both macro-economic and micro-economic if it is to provide any guidance to the "where" or to the "skills required." Progress is being impeded because no one has properly studied the long-term income elasticities; thus housing, roads, materials, and trained labour with the relevant skills have not been adequately provided in the right places. If governments cannot or will not provide rational foresight, then I think that economists individually and in their institutes should be undertaking the task. It is ridiculous to talk about rational expectations if there are no adequate ways of forming them.

I have learned from experience that these are not questions that can be answered with precision, that one cannot foresee all the political changes or the technical developments of the next ten years. But, more important, I have learned that an estimate 10 percent wrong is immensely better than nothing at all, for this implies the need to make decisions wholly in the dark. But equally I have learned that no economist is more dangerous than the pure theorist without practical experience and instinctive understanding of the real world that he is attempting to analyse, seeking precision in a world of imprecision, in a world he does not understand.

Sir Austin Robinson is Professor Emeritus of Economics, Sidney Sussex College, University of Cambridge.

W. W. ROSTOW

Reflections on Political Economy: Past, Present, and Future

COMPLEXITY, HUMOR, AND CREATIVITY

I have rarely received an invitation to which my initial reaction was more negative than Mr. Szenberg's gracious suggestion that I set down my philosophy of life. He was good enough to send along essays by four distinguished contributors to this volume. I found all of them illuminating, but still, the notion of pronouncing solemnly on my life philosophy made me reach out for some properly deflating *bon mot* of Mark Twain, Mr. Dooley, Will Rogers, or Groucho Marx. It was only when I began to understand the dual sources of my instinctive resistance that I concluded the enterprise might be doable.

First, I regard human beings and their behavior as too complex to be governed by a philosophy of life. David Hume, one of the wisest of men, put it memorably: "These principles of human nature,

222

you'll say, are contradictory: But what is man but a heap of contradictions."[1]

The great philosophers and theologians, in most cultures, have tended
to begin with some version of this complexity. For example, those two
great scientist-poets of the human condition – Plato and Freud – simplified their systems to three similar, interacting forces in human beings:
the spirited side, appetite, and reason; the id, ego, and super-ego. And
both elevated the triad, which Plato called the state within us, into their
analyses of politics – a continuity in moving from micro- to macro-
analysis economists have never been able to achieve.

It is this kind of perception about people – the marvelous "diversity
and paradox in their... natures," to use a phrase of Elting Morison's[2]
– that leads the best politicians to conduct their business, even their most
solemn business, in a context of humor. Humor conveys without cant
the inherent disparity between the scale of the problems they confront
and the capacities of mortal individuals.

In the Kennedy Presidential Library you can buy a coffee mug with an
inscription from Aubrey Mennen that President Kennedy had inscribed
on a silver beer mug he gave to his friend David Powers on his birthday
in April 1962:

> There are three things which are real;
> God, Human Folly and Laughter.
> The first two are beyond our comprehension
> So we must do what we can with the third.

I take that to be part, at least, of the truth about the human condition.

Second, and following from this perspective, an individual is unlikely
to be the best judge of his life philosophy. But the observed style of an
individual in action over a sustained period of time may provide an
approximation of what his operating philosophy of life, in fact, is. And
it may differ a bit from what he quite honestly believes it to be.

The problem here is not unlike the difficulty we sometimes get into in
our profession when trying to explain where our ideas came from. Historians of economic thought often try to construct time sequences. With
whom did the subject talk and what did he read? And when? But time
sequences tell us nothing definitive about causation. Besides, as Winston
Churchill is reported to have once remarked: "Men often stumble over
the truth, but most manage to pick themselves up and hurry off as if

---

[1] David Hume, *Philosophical Works*, T. H. Green and T. H. Grose (eds.), London: Longmans Green, 1912 edition, Vol. 3, p. 238.
[2] "The National Style," in Elting E. Morison (ed.), *The American Style, Essays in Value
and Performance*, New York: Harper, 1958, p. 321.

nothing had happened."[3] And when the truth firmly grips us, it may emerge from some quite unlikely process. Keynes, for example, explained how Isaac Newton made his discoveries: through intuition operating in periods of uniquely sustained concentration – the mathematical rationale for which he did not bother to write down until much later when pressed to do so.[4] Or the process may be as messy as Watson's description of finding DNA. With the rise of artificial intelligence we may learn to call creativity the interaction among parallel super-computers with large idle capacity; but, in the end, creativity is the bringing together of strands never brought together before – like a good joke. And thus far, impenetrable human capacities like intuition continue to play a large part.

Mennen is right. There is an ample supply of folly in the world. But there is also magic.

To return to my assigned theme, it turned out that the two sources of resistance to the invitation, once identified, were, after a fashion, the beginnings of a response. This was the case because I do believe these reflections bear not only on how I have gone about my business as an economist, but, more importantly, on the abiding schism in our profession and the crisis that many perceive economists must try to resolve if we are to serve humanity well over the next century.

NEO-NEWTONIANS AND BIOLOGISTS

At the risk of considerable over-simplification, it is fair to say that economists have for long been divided between what might be called the neo-Newtonians and the biologists. I belong with the biologists.

The distinction was never more vivid than in the moving effort of Ricardo and Malthus – polar representatives of the two schools – to establish why they disagreed so profoundly and could not resolve their differences. Here were men engaged for twelve years (1811–23) in intense dialogue, focused on essentially the same issues, their friendship suffused with an authentic mutual affection and the kind of respect that comes when two human beings know each is striving with total integrity to find answers to large questions. But their endless exchanges, face to face and in a correspondence of 167 known letters, remained almost – not quite – a dialogue of the deaf. Malthus explained their differences as follows:

The principal cause of error . . . among the scientific writers on political economy, appears to me to be a precipitate attempt to simplify and generalize. . . .

In political economy the desire to simplify has occasioned an unwillingness to

---

[3] Quoted in Alexander B. Trowbridge, *Private Leadership and Public Service*, Washington, D.C.: National Academy of Public Administration, 1985, pp. 14–15.

[4] J. M. Keynes, "Newton the Man," in *Essays in Biography*, London: Rupert Hart-Davis, 1951, pp. 310–23.

acknowledge the operation of more causes than one in the production of particular effects. . . . The first business of philosophy [science] is to account for things as they are.[5]

Ricardo found "one great cause of our difference in opinion" in Malthus' concern with "immediate and temporary effects," whereas he (Ricardo) put them aside and fixed his "whole attention on the permanent state of things which will result from them. Perhaps you estimate these temporary effects too highly, whilst I am too much disposed to undervalue them."[6] But, of course, Ricardo did not bring about this reconciliation. He continued, in Schumpeter's phrase, with the Ricardian Vice, piling up abstract assumptions until "the desired results emerged almost as tautologies."[7]

Marshall did seek a reconciliation. Despite his great neo-Newtonian gifts, mathematical appendixes, and short-term equilibrium formulations, he was a convinced biologist. For example, probably in 1881 he formulated in mathematical terms a quite recognizable approximation of a neo-classical growth model, vintage 1960s.[8] He then specified the determinants of the variables. For example, the rate of increase of the working force and its efficiency he viewed as dependent on six sub-variables, including the "evenness of income distribution," the strength of family affections, and the willingness to sacrifice present for more distant enjoyment as it determines both age of marriage and willingness to invest in a good education. Faced with such complexities, the neo-Newtonian tends to bundle them up in a black box, shove the box into an equation, and get on with often meaningless, elegant manipulations. Marshall put aside his model and wrote Book IV of the *Principles*.

Which way we go is determined, I suspect, like W. S. Gilbert's Liberals and Conservatives, by the time we are born into the world. In my case, although the outcome may well have been pre-determined, the decision was made in my sophomore year at Yale, where I majored in history. I wrote my freshman and sophomore term papers on aspects of the French Revolution and the English Revolution of the seventeenth century and was much impressed by the gross inadequacy of Marxist or any other single-cause explanations. As a sophomore, I was taught my first serious economics by Richard M. Bissell, just back from a year at the London School of Economics, at work on his doctorate, and a man with extraor-

---

[5] T. R. Malthus, *Principles of Political Economy*, 2d ed., New York: Kelley, 1951 (reprint), pp. 4–5.

[6] Piero Sraffa (ed.), with the collaboration of Maurice Dobb, *The Works and Correspondence of David Ricardo*, Cambridge University Press, 1952, Vol. 7, p. 120.

[7] See, e.g., Joseph A. Schumpeter, *History of Economic Analysis*, New York: Oxford University Press, 1954, pp. 472–73.

[8] J. K. Whitaker (ed.), *The Early Economic Writings of Alfred Marshall, 1867–1890*, London: Macmillan Press, 1975, Vol. 2, pp. 305–16.

dinary gifts of exposition. He laid out both micro- and macro-theory in mathematical terms to four of us in a kind of black-market seminar on Thursday evenings. It was an exciting experience. I decided then, at the age of seventeen, that I would try to combine economic theory and economic history in just about the way I have done for the past fifty-five years.

By the spring of 1934 I had conducted my first experiment as an economist-historian: a paper of ninety-seven pages on the British inflation during the French Revolution and the Napoleonic Wars, the subsequent deflation, and the return to the gold standard. I began believing that the theoretical structures incorporated in current monetary theory would provide a sufficient framework to explain what happened to prices. The beginning of my education as an independent economic theorist was the discovery that conventional monetary theory was incomplete and, on occasion, significantly misleading as a tool for explaining why prices moved as they did from 1793 to 1821. In the course of the exercise I came to understand the shrewdness of Wicksell's description of quantity theorists: "They usually make the mistake of postulating their assumptions instead of clearly proving them"[9] – a phenomenon that persists but surprises me less than it did.

The lesson of this first experiment was systematically reinforced with the passage of time. I found mainstream economics, including the so-called neo-classical synthesis, an incomplete framework for a serious economic historian or analyst of the current scene; and, as I learned more, I judged it increasingly necessary to introduce as systematically as I could political, social, cultural, and other non-economic forces as they bore on economic behavior.

We all know what kind of theory neo-Newtonians produce. But what about the biologists? What kind of theory can we produce if we feel impelled, in Malthus' phrases, "to account for things as they are" – and were – and to look for "more causes than one"? Marshall knew all too well what happens to the use of differential calculus when one introduces increasing returns: there is no unambiguous equilibrium position and no reversibility. One is confronted with "organic growth" in all its complexity, much as contemporary physical scientists are being forced to face up, in Ilya Prigogine's words, to "instability, mutation, and diversification where irreversible processes are constantly at work, and non-equilibrium is itself a source of dynamic order."[10] The economist-biologist answer,

[9] Knut Wicksell, *Lectures on Political Economy*, Vol. 2, *Money*, E. Classen (trans.), Lionel Robbins (ed.), New York: Macmillan, 1934, pp. 159–60.
[10] The words are drawn from Professor Prigogine's "Order Out of Chaos," a public lecture delivered at the University of Texas at Austin, November 18, 1977, on the occasion of the announcement of his Nobel Prize award.

I believe, is to discern and try to inter-relate recurrent dynamic patterns operating in the past and at present.

I suggest five examples: the demographic transition; the occurrence over the past two centuries of four identifiable periods when major innovations clustered; the recurrence of major cycles of about nine years in length from a peak in 1782 to one in 1937; the existence from 1790 to the present of four and a half cycles in the prices of basic commodities relative to manufactures; and the existence of a definable period of discontinuity in economic growth that I call the take-off and that Kuznets, with virtually the same dates, called the beginning of modern growth.[11] And I would argue that, beyond take-off (or the beginnings of modern growth), there are distinguishable stages that can be defined in terms of (1) the degree to which the pool of (then) modern technology has been absorbed and (2) the operation of the income elasticity of demand.

Three of the patterns are the result of lags of different lengths and other imperfections in the investment process leading to systematic over-shooting and under-shooting of dynamic optimum sectoral paths with wide-ranging macro-consequences.

There is a hard scientific core to these related patterns. Something like this system with all its components brought together, rendered endogenous, and linked to more or less conventional macro-economics is what is required to fulfill Allyn Young's vision of a "moving equilibrium" and Schumpeter's unfulfilled dream of dynamizing the Walrasian model. It is also the clue to rendering the Leontief matrix authentically dynamic. I have used this system for more than thirty-five years – since I wrote *The Process of Economic Growth* (1953, 1960).

THE ILLUSORY TRIUMPH OF THE NEO-NEWTONIANS

I evoke this enterprise here not to argue its merits but to underline how profound a minority position it reflects at this stage of the history of economic thought. In his essay for this volume, Paul Samuelson says, I believe correctly, that it is not a virtue for economists to nurture their originality in isolation and not read their colleagues' work. And so I read the papers and books of my mainstream friends as Samuelson counsels. I am simply as unimpressed in 1989 as I was with the quantity theorists of the period 1793–1821 when I read them in 1934.

Let me cite an example. The great boom in the world economy of 1951–72 is conventionally presented as a triumph of modern macro-

---

[11] For reference to Kuznet's dating and analysis of discontinuity in relation to mine, see W. W. Rostow, *The World Economy: History and Prospect*, Austin: University of Texas Press, 1978, pp. 778–79.

economics, a unique combination of low unemployment, rapid growth, and low rates of inflation brought about because effective demand was held at an appropriate level (at least to the mid-1960s) by a skillful combination of fiscal and monetary policy. Three critical forces have no place in this demand-side story on which we are now bringing up the young. First, a sharp movement in relative prices granted the advanced industrial countries a favorable shift in their net barter terms of trade of about 20 percent between 1951 and 1964, when the absolute decline in basic commodity prices bottomed out. Second, the existence of a large backlog of automobile and durable goods technologies for Western Europe (an enormous backlog for Japan) proved easy to absorb and diffuse because of the rise in real wages after 1951, which, in turn, partially reflected the favorable shift in the terms of trade. Third, in a perfectly natural process, the leading sectors of the boom began to decelerate in the mid-1960s, yielding a slowdown in the rate of productivity increase and a tendency of the capital–output ratio to rise.

I would argue that we cannot understand what happened in 1972–74 and subsequently in the world economy without introducing these factors plus the gathering tension in commodity markets as grain stocks fell in relation to world consumption levels and U.S. dependence on oil imports rose with oil and gas production topping out in 1970–71. These proved to be macro- not simply micro-phenomena when the explosion of grain and oil prices came in 1972–74. I submit that this image of the great post-1951 boom coming under progressive strain from the side of basic commodity supplies and relative prices as well as from a reduced technological backlog requires considerable modification in the theoretical structure we now teach our students.

But if all this came to rest simply in a debate on the causes of the great boom of the third quarter of the twentieth century, its attenuation, and demise, Mr. Szenberg could legitimately take the view that I hired the wrong hall. But if, against this background, we look ahead to the problems of political economy over, say, the next fifty to one hundred years, I believe issues of how we view the world and our fellow humans emerge, as does the need for quite fundamental changes in our methods of analysis.

THE CENTURY AHEAD

The first century of political economy – from, say, Hume and Smith to J. S. Mill and Marx – centered on economic growth, its potentialities and limits, and their implications for relative prices and distribution. But Mill and Marx, while rooted in the older tradition, also opened the second century of political economy. They assumed that an ongoing system existed on the basis of more or less regularly expanding technological possibilities. They identified its inequities and elements of harshness. Although Marx might not be happy with my formulation, they both asked, in effect, how the system could be rendered humane and civilized in terms of the abiding values of Western culture and its religions. Mill, a passionate environmentalist and designer of the democratic welfare state, provided, of course, quite different answers than the bloody revolutions counseled by Marx; but they and their contemporaries launched a century and more in which the central question of political economy became a kind of zero-sum struggle for the allocation of resources from a pie that, except for the inter-war traumas, could be assumed to be expanding. The revolutionary rise of welfare outlays from an average of about 14 percent to 24 percent of GNP in the major countries of the Organization for Economic Cooperation and Development between 1960 and the mid-1970s brought that phase to a rather dramatic close.

The central question for political economy in the presently advanced industrial countries during the third century of modern growth already is – and will be – the question David Hume posed in 1758, a quarter-century before the first wave of modern industrial innovations began to assert itself. He asked what would happen to front-runners who first develop the skills of large-scale trade, the specializations that go with the exploitation of comparative advantage, including improvement in the "mechanic arts," when their success stirs a "fermentation" in less advanced societies that proceed to imitate the more advanced but with the advantage of lower wage rates.[12]

Hume's answer, in response to the mercantilist instinct to throttle the latecomers in the cradle, was that the front-runner could enjoy the advantages of expanded two-way trade with the aspiring country if it maintained an open trading system; but to sustain the inevitably intensified competition, it would have to remain "industrious and civilized."[13]

Hume provided a quite explicit description of the structural adjustments implicit in his notion of "industrious." In our day, of course, these structural adjustments require the generation and diffusion of the fourth great wave of innovations in the past two centuries, which emerged commercially around the mid-1970s: micro-electronics, genetic engineering, a batch of new industrial materials, the laser, robots, and a communications revolution combining several of the other new tech-

[12] See, notably, Istvan Hont, "The 'Rich Country–Poor Country' Debate in Scottish Classical Political Economy," in Istvan Hont and Michael Ignatieff (eds.), *Wealth and Virtue: The Shaping of Political Economy in the Scottish Enlightenment*, Cambridge University Press, 1983, chap. 11.

[13] David Hume, *Writings on Economics*, Eugene Rotwein (ed.), Madison: University of Wisconsin Press, 1955, p. 80.

nologies. The implications of these and no doubt other major technological innovations will unfold over the decades ahead and offer to the
more advanced industrial societies an opportunity to maintain themselves
near the front of the queue if they bestir themselves.

But there is no cause for complacency if we are to fulfill Hume's
conditions. At the moment, we tend to focus on Japan as the great
challenger; but behind Japan are South Korea, Taiwan, and other vital
states of Southeast Asia gearing up to go high tech; India and China,
despite their enormous problems, will not be far behind, nor, I predict,
will Brazil and other Latin American countries.

I hold this view because of a virtually unnoticed revolution in the
technologically more advanced developing countries. Over all, the proportion of the population aged twenty to twenty-four enrolled in higher
education in what the World Bank calls "lower-middle-income" countries
rose from 3 to 10 percent between 1960 and 1982; for "upper-middle-
income" countries the increase was from 4 to 14 percent.[14] The increase
in India, with low income per capita but a vital educational system, was
from 3 to 9 percent. To understand the quantitative meaning of these
figures it should be recalled that in 1960 the proportion of the United
Kingdom was 9 percent and that of Japan 10 percent.

Even discounting problems of educational quality, the potential ab-
sorptive capacity for the new technologies in the more advanced developing countries is high. Their central problem – like that of most
advanced industrial countries – is how to make effective the increasingly
abundant scientific and engineering skills they already command. This
requires, in turn, an ability to generate and maintain effective, flexible,
interactive partnerships among scientists, engineers, entrepreneurs, and
the working force. For the United States, the outcome will depend not
only on the pace at which we generate the new technologies – at which
we remain fairly good – but on the pace at which we diffuse them to old
basic industries, agriculture, and the services – at which we are spotty
but improving.

WHAT IS TO BE DONE: POLITICS

If my view of the challenge posed by the new technologies in the world
economy is roughly correct, a radical change in the contours of politics
is required in the United States and Western Europe. The change, put
simply, is from primary emphasis on a zero-sum conflict over the allocation of what has been assumed to be an automatically expanding pie

---

[14] *World Development Report*, New York: Oxford University Press, 1984 and 1985, Table
25, pp. 266–67 and 222–23, respectively.

to sustained communal cooperation to ensure that the pie will, in fact, continue to expand.

A quick glance at national politics in the United States would not appear to justify a high degree of optimism. At first sight, we give every sign of preferring to go down in the style to which we have become accustomed rather than face reality. But that is not quite the way it is. Beneath the surface, some fifty high-tech highways, all of which will not flourish, have nevertheless been built by intimate cooperation among the private sector, state and local governments, the universities, and quite often representatives of labor. Large segments of labor and management are aware that they have come to a new phase in their history, and new kinds of cooperation will be required if the American industrial structure is to continue to flourish and sustain both constituencies.

Similarly, successful governors in the states, Republican and Democratic, as well as successful mayors in hard-pressed cities, reach out to damp confrontation and unite their communities. Often in American history national political trends and styles are foreshadowed in the states; and I believe this is happening, although no national political figure or party has yet found the terms and defined the agenda that would rally the nation for the long test of our viability as a society that has already begun.

This is, evidently, an extraordinary historical interval of restructuring for all the advanced industrial societies – and others as well. In its great continental society, with multiple centers of initiative and responsibility, the American *peristroika* is moving along quite well – certainly more briskly than that of the USSR and more rapidly than the Japanese response to the Maekawa Reports.

WHAT IS TO BE DONE: POLITICAL ECONOMY

If we Americans take our objective from Hume, it comes to this. We must sustain a civilized and industrious society capable of remaining viable in an open trading system in a world undergoing a powerful multi-dimensional technological revolution that will diffuse rapidly to lower-wage-rate developing regions as well as to the advanced industrial countries, affecting, in the end, virtually every sector of each of the world's economies. Clearly, this objective has a good many implications for the future shape of political economy, of which I shall cite only a few examples.

First, mainstream economics should, at last, concern itself in a serious, sustained way with the generation and diffusion of technologies. An inability to deal with this process as part of the central body of economic theory has been a characteristic of our trade since 1870 at least.[15] The Schumpeterian insights on innovation were basically correct, but never absorbed into mainstream economics. Models were designed so as to split investment between the endogenous operation of the accelerator and something called exogenous investment coming along from time to time at random or at the stochastic will of drunken gods. The highly aggregated models generated in modern macro-economics had no place for an R&D investment sector out of which inventions were generated in response to more or less conventional market calculations, or for a dynamized Leontief matrix that would track out their impact on other sectors and the aggregates. Nor do economists clearly distinguish the tasks of entrepreneurship in maximizing profits under Marshallian short-period assumptions and under conditions of rapid discontinuous change in production functions – a major flaw in mainstream economic theory, an almost fatal flaw in the curricula of our business schools.

There are, of course, differences between the investment process in the R&D sector and that in more conventional sectors. Serendipitous results are perhaps more frequent and Murphy's Law somewhat more active. But, at least since the mid-eighteenth century in Britain, R&D should be accounted an investment sector and the flow of inventions into the economy viewed as an endogenous aspect of the growth process. Clearly, there is a long and quite revolutionary theoretical and empirical agenda before us if our craft is to be rendered relevant to a world economy in which the generation and diffusion of new technologies are, and will remain, a central phenomenon.

Second, building not only on Hume's suggestive observations but also on Folke Hilgerdt's classic League of Nations study, *Industrialization and Foreign Trade,* economists should extend our understanding of the positive and negative impact on front-runner A as latecomer B learns to exploit the hitherto unexploited backlog of technologies and narrows the gap in real income per capita. This kind of analysis should include all the factors – economic as well as non-economic – that are required for a successful dynamic structural adjustment of both parties.

Third, as already suggested, a new definition is required of the appropriate role of labor in the transformation ahead and of the widened area of authentic mutual interest in labor – management cooperation. Labor has, for a century, by and large concentrated on maximizing its short-run gains in each sector in a zero-sum struggle over the expected spoils in that sector. Now, new issues have asserted themselves – for example, the long-run level of employment in particular sectors, the increase in

---

[15] See, e.g., my "Technology and the Price System," in *Why the Poor Get Richer and the Rich Slow Down*, Austin: University of Texas Press, 1980, chap. 4.

sectoral and overall rates of productivity, the intensity of international competition in particular sectors, the international value of the dollar, and the appropriate role of an incomes policy. And one can detect a parallel changing agenda under discussion among thoughtful business leaders. In redefining their objectives in the new international setting and the appropriate relations between them, business and labor could be helped by fresh thought from first-rate economists.

This, of course, is not all. There are other difficult problems that evidently deserve sophisticated attention. How do we avoid yo-yo oscillations in the world energy markets? How do both advanced industrial and developing countries work their way out of their different but equally pathological agricultural policies in ways that are politically acceptable? How do we deal with the developing nations that have not yet moved into takeoff or beyond in, for example, Africa south of the Sahara and the small Pacific islands? What is the appropriate relation between the industrial countries and the more advanced developing countries in, for example, the Pacific Basin and the Western Hemisphere? And, of course, what lessons are to be learned about the possibilities and limits of fiscal and monetary policy since the end of 1972 and the optimum form for incomes policies at a time when the vitality and flexibility of the private sector are also of critical importance?

Without laboring the point, it is clear that contemporary mainstream economics is not now coming to grips with some such array of palpably urgent and relevant problems. Our graduate students are, by and large, taught to respect the primacy of method and technique, and problems are cut down to the size the chosen techniques can handle.

I suggest it might be wholesome for all of us to look back and recall what our discipline was like in its classic origins and, indeed, down to a half-century ago, from, say, Hume and Adam Smith through J. S. Mill, Alfred Marshall, and Knut Wicksell to D. H. Robertson, Keynes, Myrdal, and the others who fought to use political economy to save democratic societies from destruction in the Great Depression. They took the problem, as they perceived it in all its complexity, and made it their discipline, bringing to bear insights from every direction. Their efforts included, but were not limited to, the refinement of the concepts of economic theory as they inherited them cumulatively from the past. They acknowledged that they were driven by moral objectives, abhorred the human degradation imposed by poverty, and looked to economics and economists, in the phrase of Keynes' famous toast, as the "trustees not of civilization but of the possibility of civilization." And they would have all, I believe, signed on to the dictum that appears on the first page of the preface to all the editions of Mill's *Principles*: "Except on matters of mere detail, there are perhaps no practical questions, even among those which approach nearest to the character of purely economical questions, which admit of being decided on economical premises alone." Our generation has deviated radically from the best in the tradition of our profession — at great cost.

A BIT OF "LIFE PHILOSOPHY"

There is a reason for urging this course that transcends any I have thus far evoked. Modern political economy arose in Western Europe, in both its French and British branches, in opposition to the mercantilists. The physiocrats argued powerfully for the critical importance of agriculture — even overdoing it a bit — in opposition to mercantilist neglect. Hume argued boldly for the British interest in the prosperity of France. Smith argued against a regime of colonies. In Britain their arguments gained ground; but the fact is that Britain was at war for just about forty years during the eighteenth century. In such an age there was a considerable logic to mercantilist doctrine.

If my view of what lies ahead is broadly correct, the world economy and polity face an adjustment familiar in character but unprecedented in scale over the next century. The advanced industrial countries (including the USSR and Eastern Europe) now constitute about 1.1 billion people, or, say, 24 percent of the world's population. At least 2.6 billion people, or about 56 percent, live in countries that will, I would guess, acquire technological virtuosity by the middle of the next century. Moreover, population in the decades ahead will increase more rapidly in the latter than in the former group. We are talking about a great historical transformation.

There can be important economic advantages for the early comers as the latecomers move toward technological equivalence. But, evidently, the process could generate all manner of mercantilist frictions and dangers — as did the belated rise to technological maturity of Germany, Japan, and Russia. It will take strength, unity, poise, and inner confidence for the presently advanced industrial nations to maintain their vitality and play a constructive part in helping the world community, as a whole, gracefully through this complex and potentially explosive adjustment.

For just about forty years I have committed a good deal of time and thought to economic development in Latin America, Africa, the Middle East, and Asia. I have come to know as colleagues and brothers-in-arms a great many of the development economists, planners, businessmen, and administrators in these regions. And I have gone out from the capital cities to many villages in a good many countries from the Peruvian Andes to Iran and Korea and seen in the faces of men, women, and children the terrible dehumanizing burden of poverty not quite overcoming the magical determination to live, love, and laugh.

The associations that arose from this commitment were among the most rewarding of my professional life. They reinforced a lesson that is the one we shall most need in the generations ahead if we are to come through the dynamic transition we confront in reasonably good order, a lesson to which I have often been driven back, incorporated in the lines of the poet after whom I happen to be named:

> One thought ever at the fore —
> That in the Divine Ship, the World,
>   breasting Time and Space,
> All peoples of the globe together sail,
>   sail the same voyage,
> Are bound to the same destination.

W. W. Rostow is Professor of Economics, University of Texas at Austin.

PAUL A. SAMUELSON

My Life Philosophy: Policy Credos and Working Ways

ETHICS

Many economists – Alfred Marshall, Knut Wicksell, Léon Walras,... – became economists, they tell us, to do good for the world. I became an economist quite by chance, primarily because the analysis was so interesting and easy – indeed so easy that at first I thought that there must be more to it than I was recognizing, else why were my older classmates making such heavy weather over supply and demand? (How could an increased demand for wool help but lower the price of pork and beef?)

Although positivistic analysis of what the actual world is like commands and constrains my every move as an economist, there is never far from my consciousness a concern for the ethics of the outcome. Mine is a simple ideology that favors the underdog and (other things equal) abhors inequality.

I take no credit for this moral stance. My parents were "liberals" (in the American sense of the word, not in the European "Manchester School" sense), and I was conditioned in that general *Weltanschauung*. It is an easy faith to adhere to. When my income came to rise above the median, no guilt attached to that. Nor was there a compulsion to give away all my extra coats to shirtsleeved strangers: my parents would have thought me daft to do so, and neurotic to toss at night for not having done so. Some personal obligation for distributive justice liberals do expect of themselves: but what is far more important than acts of private charity is to weight the counterclaims of efficiency and equity, whenever public policy is concerned, in the direction of equity. As my University of Chicago teacher and friend Henry Simons used to say, "Any *good* cause is worth incurring some *costs* for. Everything should be pushed beyond the point of diminishing returns (else, why desist from pushing it still further?)."

Persons who will not volunteer to serve in the army can with good logic vote to pass a fair conscription law that will entail their being drafted with the same positive probability as any other persons. I have generally voted against my own economic interests when questions of redistributive taxation have come up. The fact that I have favored closing tax loopholes has not precluded seeking some advantage from those left in the tax code. But too avid an effort in that direction would seem not only unaesthetic but also a source of some discomfort and self-reproach.

Without exception all the economists I know regard themselves as humanitarians. This includes communists who toe the Stalinist line and Chicago-school zealots for laissez-faire. Yet we all pretty much know what to expect of each other when it comes to policy recommendations and judgments. It is not unanimity. If political economy were an exact, hard science, then more agreement on probable outcomes would occur. If economics were no science at all, only a tissue of value judgments and prejudices, then soliciting an opinion from an economist would tell the Prince or Parliament nothing about the merits or demerits of the proposal under deliberation but only give a reconfirmation that Economist Jones is a bleeding-heart liberal and Economist Smith a selfish elitist.

Political economy as we know it falls in-between. Economists do agree on much in any situation. Where Milton Friedman and I disagree, we are quick to be able to identify the source and texture of our disagreements in a way that non-economists cannot perceive. The disparity of our recommendations is not an unbiased estimator of the dispersion of our inductive and deductive beliefs. With my *social welfare function* (or, in Waldian statisticians' terminology, my "loss function") concerning the relative importance of unemployment and business freedoms, I could disagree 180° with his policy conclusion and yet concur in diagnosis of the empirical observations and inferred probabilities. Yet such is the imperfection of the human scientist, an anthropologist studying us academic guinea pigs will record the sad fact that our hearts do often contaminate our minds and eyes. The conservative will forecast high inflation danger on the basis of the same data that lead the dogooder to warn against recession. (Conscious of this unconscious source of bias, as the subsequent discussion will elaborate on, I make a special effort toward self-criticism and eclecticism – with what success, the record must testify to.)

An economist who has been preoccupied over the years solely with *Pareto optimality* wrote me long ago that I would be surprised to know how liberal he is. Indeed I would be. Reflecting on his writings, I wondered how he knew he had a heart: it had been so long since he had used it. Organs atrophy without exercise. "Use it or lose it" is nature's law.

It is not only the arteries that harden with age. Economists are said to appear to grow more conservative as they rise in seniority. This they often deny.

In my own case, I do not perceive that my value-judgment ideology has changed systematically since the age of 25. For a decade now mainstream economics has been moving a bit rightward. But I have not been tempted to chase it. What does tend to change with the accumulation of years and experience is one's degree of optimism about what is feasible and one's faith in good intentions alone. My enhanced skepticism about government ownership of the means of production or the efficacy of planning is not a reflection of ossifying sympathies and benevolence, but rather is a response to the testimony of proliferating real-world experiences.

I am conscious of one occasion in which my respect for the market mechanism took a quantum leap upward. This change had nothing to do with improved performing of the market system. Nor was it related to any new arguments brought forward by Hayek about generating and utilizing information, or to any old arguments about market efficiencies and freedoms by Adam Smith, Frederic Bastiat, or Frank Knight. Rather my changed viewpoint came from observing the communist witchhunting episode of the 1950s.

The McCarthy era, in my judgment, posed a serious threat of American fascism. I knew plenty of people in government and the universities whose civil liberties and careers came into jeopardy. I observed at close hand the fears and tremblings that the Harvard and MIT authorities experienced, and these were the boldest of the American academic institutions. As Wellington said of Waterloo, it was a close-run thing that Senator McCarthy was discredited: the Richard Nixon "enemy list" was a joke in comparison, and my being named on it only added to my fading credentials as a New Dealer. What I learned from the McCarthy incident was the perils of a one-employer society. When you are blackballed from government employment, there is great safety from the existence of thousands of anonymous employers out there in the market. I knew of people who got some kind of work in private industry, usually smaller industry since large firms tend to try to keep on the safe side of government. To me this became a newly perceived argument, not so much for laissez-faire capitalism as for the *mixed* economy.

How did free-market advocates among the economists score as defenders of personal freedoms and civil liberties? This was a subject of great interest to me and over several years I kept a quiet tally of the behavior and private utterances of scores of the leading American and Continental libertarians, almost all of whom I knew intimately. Like a visiting anthropologist I would ask innocent questions designed to elicit relaxed and spontaneous views. If it was churlish to keep a record of private conversations, then I was a churl. The results surprised and distressed me. Worshippers of laissez-faire à la Bastiat and Spencer were insensitive and on the whole unsympathetic toward the rights and personal freedoms of scholars. Alone among the members of the Mt. Pelerin Society the name of Fritz Machlup stood out as one willing to incur personal costs to speak up for John Stuart Mill values. It is not the failure of people to be heroes that I am speaking about. There is little of the heroic in my own makeup and I have learned not to expect much of human nature. What my research found was a sad lack of genuine concern for human values.

I was taught at the University of Chicago that business freedoms and personal freedoms have to be strongly linked, as a matter both of brute empirical fact and of cogent deductive syllogism. For a long time I believed what I was taught. Gradually I had to acknowledge that the paradigm could not fit the facts. By most Millian criteria, regimented Scandinavia was freer than my America — or certainly at least as free. When I used to bring up these inconvenient facts to my conservative friend David McCord Wright, he would warn: "Just you wait. British and Swedish citizens, it is true, have not yet lost their freedoms. But it cannot last that the market is interfered with and people remain politically free." We have all waited for more than thirty years now.

Friedrick Hayek wrote his bestseller, *The Road to Serfdom*, at the end of World War II, warning that partial reform was the sure path to total tyranny. Cross-sectional and time-series analysis of the relationship between politics and economics suggest to me important truths.

1. Controlled socialist societies are rarely efficient and virtually never freely democratic. (There is considerable validity then for the non-novel part of Hayek's warning.)
2. Societies which resisted partial reforms have often been those overtaken by revolutionary change. If it is the free market or nothing, often it has then had to be nothing. Indeed, after midcentury the finest archetypes of efficient free markets have often been quasi-fascist or outright fascist societies in which a dictatorial leader or single party *imposes* a political order – without which imposition the market could not politically survive. Chile with its military dictatorship cum-the-Chicago boys is only one dramatic case. Taiwan, South Korea, and Singapore are less dramatic but more representative cases.
3. I can nurture a dream. Like Martin Luther King, I have a dream of a humane economy that is at the same time efficient and respecting of personal (if not business) freedoms. Much of producing and consuming decisions involve use of the market mechanism. But the worst inequalities of condition that result from reliance on market forces – even in the presence of equality of ex ante opportunity – can be mitigated by the transfer powers of the democratic state. Does the enhancement of equity by the welfare state take no toll in terms of efficiency? Yes, there will be some trade-off of enhanced total output against enhanced equality, some trade-off between security and progress. I call the resultant optimizing compromise *economics with a heart*, and it is my dream to keep it also economics with a head.

MY METHODOLOGY

It is some relief to move from the exalted realm of philosophical ethics to the mundane realm of scientific methodology. However, I rather shy away from discussions of Methodology with a capital M. To paraphrase Shaw: Those who can, do science; those who can't prattle about its methodology.

Of course I can't deny that I have a methodology. It's just that there seems little appeal in making it explicit to an outsider. Or for that matter, in spelling it out to my own consciousness.

I am primarily a theorist. But my first and last allegiance is to the facts. When I began study at the University of Chicago, Frank Knight and Aaron Director planted in me the false notion that somehow deduction was more important than induction. This was a confused tenet of Austrian methodology at the time, and I certainly do not mean by the word "Austrian" the logical positivism of the Vienna Circle. Rather, such direct and indirect disciples of Carl Menger as Ludwig von Mises, Friedrich Hayek, and Lionel Robbins seemed to put on their own heads the dunce caps of the classical Ricardians who believed that by thinking in one's study one could arrive at the basic immutable laws of political economy. I remember believing Director when he pooh-poohed Wesley Mitchell's empirical work on business cycles, claiming instead that the greatest breakthroughs in the subject were coming from Hayek's a priorisms on the subject.

I grew out of this phase fast. Once Lionel Robbins explained lucidly in the first edition of his *An Essay on the Nature and Significance of Economic Science* his claims for Kantian a priorism in economics, his case was lost. Logical positivism is now judged to be an oversimplified doctrine, but it was enormously useful in deflating the pretensions of deductionists. If one had to choose between the methodologies of the warring brothers – Ludwig the economist and Richard von Mises the mathematical physicist – Richard would win hands down.

Let me not be misunderstood. I abhor the sins of scientism. I recognize that, as social scientists, we can have relationships with the data we study that the astronomers cannot have with the data they study. I am aware that my old friend Willard van Orman Quine, one of this age's greatest logicians, has cast doubt that anyone can in every case distinguish between "analytic" a priorisms and the "synthetic" propositions that positivists take to be empirical facts. Furthermore, Wesley Mitchell's empiricisms on the business cycle do seem to me to have been overrated – not because they are empirical, but rather because his was an eclecticism that never had much luck in discovering anything very interesting, as the lifecycle profile of his post-1913 career sadly reveals. Some of the skepticisms of Knight and Jacob Viner concerning the empirical statistical studies that their colleagues Paul Douglas and Henry Schultz were attempting, I readily admit, were well taken – just as some of Keynes's corrosive 1939 criticisms of Jan Tinbergen's econometric macromodels were. But it is on *empirical* grounds that these empirical attempts have to be rejected or accepted, and not because deductive syllogisms can claim a primacy to vulgar fact grabbing. What was wrong with the German Historical School was not that it was historical, but rather that its sampling of the facts was incomplete and incoherent. The facts don't tell their own story. You can't enunciate all the facts. And if you could, the job of the scientists would just begin – to organize those facts into useful and meaningful gestalts, into patterns that are less multifarious than the data themselves and which provide economical *descriptions* of the data that afford tolerably accurate extrapolations and interpolations.

Whatever logical positivism's faults and superficialities are in science at large, it gets an undeservedly bad name in economics from being confused with Milton Friedman's peculiar version of positive economics. Much of what is in Friedman's 1953 essay on this topic is unexceptional and a story so old as to seem almost platitudinous. But what is novel in his formulation and commands most attention is that which I have called "the F twist" – the dictum that a scientific theory is none the worse if its premises are unrealistic (in the usual meaning of "unrealistic" as stating hypotheses that are false and/or far-from-true assertions about what obtains in the actual world), so long as the theory's "predictions" are usefully true. Thought suggests, and experience confirms, that such a dogma will be self-indulging, permitting its practitioners to ignore or play down inconvenient departures of their theories from the observable real world. A hypothesis's full set of predictions includes its own descriptive contents: so, literally understood, an unrealistic hypothesis entails some unrealistic predictions and is all the worse for those false predictions – albeit it is all the better for its (other) empirically correct predictions. We are left then validly with only the prosaic reminder that few theories have all their consequences exactly correct; and it can be the case that a scientific theory is deemed valuable because we have reason to give great weight to those of its predictions that happen to be true and to give little weight to those that are found to be false. In no case is unrealistic falsity a virtue; and there is danger of self-serving Humpty-Dumptyism in letting the theorist judge for himself which of his errors he is going to extenuate or ignore.

Unpopular these days are the views of Ernst Mach and crude logical positivists, who deem good theories to be merely economical descriptions of the complex facts that tolerably well replicate those already-observed or still-to-be-observed facts. Not for philosophical reasons but purely out of long experience in doing economics that other people will like and that I myself will like, I find myself in the minority who take the Machian view. "Understanding" of classical thermodynamics (the archetype of a successful scientific theory) I find to be the capacity to "describe" how fluids and solids will actually behave under various specifiable conditions. When we are able to give a pleasingly satisfactory "HOW" for the way of the world, that gives the only approach to "WHY" that we shall ever attain.

Always when I read new literary and mathematical paradigms, I seek to learn what descriptions they imply for the observable data. The paradigm's full set of entailed descriptions is what is of interest and forms the basis for a complete judgment on it. My work in revealed preference, in *Foundations of Economic Analysis*, and in the several volumes of *Collected Scientific Papers*, consistently bears out this general methodological procedure.

I dislike being wrong. Long before knowing of Karl Popper's writings, I sought to be my own strictest critic. Why give that fun to the other chap? All this explains why I am an eclectic economist. It is not because of inability to make up my mind. I am eclectic only because experience has shown that Mother Nature is eclectic. If all the evidence points to a single-factor causation, I have no internal resistance to accepting that. But there is a big "if" involved in the previous sentence.

Being prepared to be eclectic does not have to inhibit bold theory building. One creates boldly knowing that this does not commit one to exaggerated belief in the sole potency of one's brain child.

We all have secret vanities. He prides himself on his good looks. She takes satisfaction in her sense of humor. I do delight in producing still another beautiful model that illuminates important terrains of economics. But in my heart of hearts I nurture the claim that I have good judgment. Be wise, sweet maid, and let them who will be clever. My theories must run the gauntlet of my judgment, an ordeal more fearsome than mere peer review. (Of course one can have one's cake and eat it too by presenting a theoretical gem as an unpretentious mirror of some aspects of some corner of the economic terrain under observation.) Why let sagacity degenerate into well-informed nihilism? The mindless naysayer is no better than the mindless yeasayer. Neither adds anything to the silent scientist's cipher.

Joseph Schumpeter, who all his life whored after beautiful theories, just before he died testified at the 1949 National Bureau conference on business cycles: If he had to choose between mastery of mathematics and statistics, or of economic history, he would have to choose mastery of economic history. I won't disagree. But I deny the need for dichotomous choice. Give apes in the Widener Library a data bank of all that's there and you don't get a master economic historian. What you get back is the data bank and a curator.

Let me make a confession. Back when I was 20 I could perceive the great progress that was being made in econometric *methods*. Even without foreseeing the onset of the computer age, with its cheapening of calculations, I expected that the new econometrics would enable us to narrow down the uncertainties of our economic theories. We would be able to test and reject false theories. We would be able to infer new good theories.

My confession is that this expectation has not worked out. From several thousands of monthly and quarterly time series, which cover the last few decades or even centuries, it has turned out not to be possible to arrive at a close approximation to indisputable truth. I never ignore econometric studies, but I have learned from sad experience to take them with large grains of salt. It takes one econometric study to calibrate another; a priori thought can't do the job. But it seems objectively to be the case that there does not accumulate a convergent body of econometric findings, convergent on a testable truth.

Does this mean that I belong to the camp which regards truth as in the eye of the beholder? Which denies the existence of an objective truth out there, in political economy as well as in astronomy and biochemistry? Which recognizes in the truth of mainstream economics only the class interests of the bourgeoisie, and in the truth of Marxian economics either the class interests of the nascent proletariat or the objective truth of the final classless and universal society?

No. Observing myself over fifty years and a vast number of scientists in various disciplines, I do recognize that truth has many facets. Precision in deterministic facts or in their probability laws can at best be only partial and approximate. Which of the objective facts out there are worthy of study and description or explanation depends admittedly on subjective properties of the scientists. Admittedly, a given field of data can be described in terms of alternative patterns of description, particularly by disputing authorities who differ in the error tolerances they display toward different aspects of the data. Admittedly, observations are not merely seen or sensed but rather often are perceived in gestalt patterns that impose themselves on the data and even distort those data.

But still, having admitted all of the above, as you observe scientists and study the developments of disciplines when schools evolve and paradigms are born and die, it is forced upon you that *what ultimately shapes the verdicts of the scientist juries is an empirical reality out there.* When a Marxist scores a triumph it is not by employing a useful alternative to $2 + 2 = 4$ logic, or cultivating a different Hegelian dialectic. We esteem a Pavlov, Lysenko, Haldane or Bernal, Landau or Baran for what they can or cannot accomplish with respect to animal experiments, plant breeding, hydrogen-bomb explodings or phase transitions, or insights into the observable paths of economic development.

When Thomas Kuhn's book, *The Structure of Scientific Revolutions,* came out in 1962, I made two lucky predictions: one, that in the physical and life sciences its thesis would have to be modified to recognize that there is a cumulative property of knowledge that makes later paradigms ultimately dominate earlier ones, however differently the struggle may transiently look; two, that Kuhn's doctrine of incommensurability of alternative paradigms would cater to a strong desire on the part of polemical social scientists who will be delighted to be able to say, "That's all very well in your paradigm, but your white is black in my paradigm – and who's to say that we'uns have to agree with you'uns." Kuhn has correctly discerned the warts on the countenance of evolving science. His readers must not lose the face for the warts.

HOW I WORK

As a theorist I have great advantages. All I need is a pencil (now a ball pen) and an empty pad of paper. There are analysts who sit and look vacantly out the window, but after the age of 20 I was not one of them. I ought to envy the new generation who have grown up with the computer, but I don't. None of them known to me sit idly at the console, improvising and experimenting in the way that a composer does at the piano. That ought to become increasingly possible. But up to now, in my observation, the computer is largely a black box into which researchers feed raw input and out from which they draw various summarizing measures and simulations. Not having access to look around in the box, the investigator has less intuitive familiarity with the data than used to be the case in the bad old days.

I have been blessed with an abundance of interesting problems to puzzle out. Many artists and writers run into long fallow periods when new creative ideas just will not come. Luckily, that has not been my experience. Perhaps I am insufficiently self-critical to recognize when problems of lower quality are involved. In any case mine has never been the Carlylean view of Schumpeter that only the greatest ideas count, and only a few great men are important in history and in the development of science. One tackles the most important unsolved problem at hand. Then the next one. If that leads down the path of diminishing returns in the absence of dramatic new challenges and breakthroughs, so be it.

"What are you working on now?" This is a question I have been asked all my life. And never in my life have I known how to answer it. At any one time I have several balls in the air. And always there is an inventory of questions just below the threshold of my explicit attention. Some of these slumber in that limbo for two decades. There is no hurry; they will keep. Some morning (or at night in a dream) the evolving wheel of chance will turn their number up.

Poets testify that often their lines gush up from within. They merely write down what their muse is dictating. That sounds rather highfalutin, but there is something in it. When I was young I used to explore a topic; write down equations and syllogisms dealing with different aspects of it; then outline the final work. After that the final draft could be written out. Perhaps what I am describing is the optimal way to write a paper.

Increasingly after the age of 35 that is not how I have in fact operated. Instead I have often let the paper write itself. A problem is posed. One begins to solve it, writing out the steps in the solution. One development leads naturally to another, as one exposits in writing. Finally, what can be solved of the problem has been solved. The paper is finished. What has been finished is not something that has ever been envisaged, waiting only to be written down. All this is reminiscent of Franklin Roosevelt's dictum, "How do I know what I think until I hear myself saying it?"

This means that some articles might be composed in half a day. Of course the first draft need not be the final draft. There may follow many hours of revisings, involving additions, deletions, rearrangements, and corrections. Perhaps it would be better to follow the first draft with a completely new rewrite. But that is not my usual practice, as I trade some perfection against more time for new topics. This means I am a prisoner of my first drafts, and it is a source of exquisite pain if a manuscript is lost: my mind rebels at having to reconstruct a lost argument, and impatience is likely to make a recollected version abridge some essential matter.

Prolific scholars are addicted to writing. A day spent in committee meetings is for me a day lost. After an interval of fasting, you are hungry. After an interval of doing no analytical research, there is so to speak a fluid inside you that wants to get free. I used to think that the unconscious mind, which Henri Poincaré described so beautifully as working away at specific puzzles the mathematician is interested in, was accumulating findings on the particular problems that routine duties prevented me from dealing with. But I have come to think that not to be quite correct. For *any* new topic can capture one's enthusiastic and fruitful attention after a period of deprivation. One snowy day in New England I was told at the airport gate that Washington was snowed in. A friend hearing me inquire, "Can you go to New York?" asked, "Are you just bound to go somewhere this day?" That's exactly what it's like with the creative urge: It doesn't have to spend itself on the theory of capital that has been engaging the scholar's recent attention; it just wants to go about doing something creative, and its motors seem revved up to be effective in whatever direction it is pointed.

Reporters used to speak of a nose for news. What is important in scholarship is an aesthetic sense for what is an important problem. Otherwise the facile mind can spend itself on patterns that are merely pretty. For recreation I would rather play tennis than play chess, or read pedestrian detective stories than solve the mathematical conundrums that appear in the back pages of learned journals. My unconscious motivation, I suspect, is that chess and problem-solving involve the same energies as innovative scholarship does. They will usurp some of the limited supply of precious brainpower that might better go toward learning something new; and, involving use of the same workday muscles so to speak, those recreations do not provide as refreshing rest periods. I daresay that the powerful pure mathematician faces a different problem from the applied scientist. A great mathematician is only as great as his greatest deeds. The revolutionary idea that might lead to great deeds comes very rarely.

One marks time in between and one might as well mark time while keeping the brain tuned up in chess or bridge as in any other way. However, I do not have too much confidence in the distinction that I have just made. For it certainly does not cover the case of prolific mathematicians such as Poincaré or Euler. A mathematical snob like G. H. Hardy might judge that much of Euler and Poincaré could just as well have never been written. But even from the snobbish viewpoint, we must reckon with the fact that some of their best work would not have gotten done if it had not been an outgrowth of some of their less transcendental achievements.

I said that my working tools are only pen and paper, and that an airplane cabin provides as good an environment for research as a library study. That is true as far as analytical creativity is concerned. On the other hand to stay well informed on what it is that is important to be done, a scholar must have access to books and to learned journals. In this regard I have always been very lucky. Whatever works the MIT libraries have not had, the neighboring Harvard libraries can be counted on to provide. There are very few great scholars working off by themselves with paper and pen far from the centers of creative economic thought. Those who pride themselves on being most autonomous usually end up most idiosyncratic.

Long ago I set myself the grandiose challenge of not being merely subjectively original. More useful to science – and more truly fulfilling if you can bring it off – is to try to stay informed on what other scientists have done and to advance the frontier by your own quantum jumps. In terms of the old song: "Good work if you can get it. And you can get it if you try."

Paul Samuelson is Institute Professor, Emeritus, Massachusetts Institute of Technology, and 1970 winner of the Nobel Memorial Prize in economic science.

TIBOR SCITOVSKY

My Search for Welfare

The advantage of being asked to write your life philosophy is that it may provide you with one. It forces you to review your professional and private life, makes you conscious of the principles, interests, passions, appetites, vices that have shaped it, and then compels you to try to integrate them into a coherent whole that deserves being called a style of life.

I was born in semi-feudal Hungary, the only child of a higher civil servant. My father was that by training, by temperament, and during the first part of his life also by occupation. I had an early glimpse of what the good life means to non-puritans, partly in my parents' example, partly in the life I shared with them. My father knew how to enjoy both a very successful career of hard work and his many leisure activities; at the same time, his exceptionally high principles and great integrity made him an imposing figure. My mother was a different kind of person and exceptional in very different ways, one of which was her extraordinary generosity. She enjoyed the role of great lady and fairy godmother and played it to the hilt, helping servants, former servants, their fiancés, workmen she knew, impoverished friends, relatives, both financially and otherwise; lavishing presents on nieces, nephews, her more than 70 godchildren, and the inmates of a small veterans' hospital, whom she regularly supplied with Christmas feasts and packages, wine, cigarettes, Easter cookies, and warm sweaters.

Between such openhandedness, their shared passion for interior decoration and antiques, and their know-how for enjoying everything life has to offer, my parents managed to uphold their pre-capitalist tradition of spending every penny of my father's very considerable income. They led a very active and varied life, with much travel and many wonderful parties in and out of our beautiful home, which was full of relics of the artistic splendor of eighteenth-century France. I shared in much of that and went to many more countries, places, museums, art exhibits, antique stores, plays, concerts, and operas in my teens than during any period in later life.

At the same time, however, being an overprotected, oversupervised, privately tutored only child who never went to school, I was quite lonely and matured late. My early interests were solitary: voracious reading of fiction, biography, and popular science; building radios, which then were in their infancy; and learning both how to maintain and repair cars and about socialism from our chauffeur.

As soon as I entered adolescence, I revolted: against the society around me and the banking career my mother wanted to ease me into. I resented not only the gulf between our luxurious house with its platoon of servants and Budapest's miserable slums, which I often passed, but even more the rigid social system that locked people into their places by making every job, every advance, almost every achievement depend on connections and pull. I was fortunate to experience all that from above rather than from below, but resented it nonetheless. To mention just a minor aspect of the social atmosphere, although I was an almost straight-A student when presenting myself for the annual examinations, I was frustrated because I wanted to know and prove my own worth but could never be quite sure that I had fully earned my excellent grades or just owed them to my father's or uncle's place in the cabinet.

When in revolt, one fights one's environment or flees from it. I fled, lacking the aggressiveness and ruthlessness of the revolutionary, foreseeing far worse to come in the shape of fascism, and also hoping to minimize the shock to my parents, for whom I retained great respect and affection.

In 1935, therefore, against my parents' wishes but with their reluctant blessings, I left Hungary for good and enrolled in the London School of Economics (LSE) to prepare myself for life in the West and a career of my own making. I developed into a "premature antifascist," to use the words of the State Department official who so described me nine years later when he wanted to have me deported from the United States.

Beyond the desire to stand on my own feet and develop whatever abilities I might have, I felt no special vocation for any particular subject and chose economics because the world's main problems at the time seemed to be economic. I had already gained a nodding acquaintance with the subject years earlier, from Dennis Robertson, Maurice Dobb, and Joan Robinson during a short stay at Cambridge University, but studied it in earnest only at the LSE. Those were the depressed 1930s; and I found myself fascinated by the model of a self-equilibrating system of markets but greatly bothered by the gulf that separated that beautiful theory from the ugly reality of great misery and mass unemployment. We students were shocked by the faculty's helplessness in the face of pressing problems and suspicious of the bitter and cruel remedies some of them advocated.

I felt that something was crucially wrong with or missing from economic theory and that rather than use an imaginary model of perfection and try to bring reality closer to its unreal assumptions, it would be better to develop a realistic model that showed up the economy's shortcomings along with its virtues and thereby might point the way to dealing with the shortcomings while retaining the virtues. In my youthful conceit, I resolved to devote myself to trying to develop such a model and worked terribly hard to prepare myself for that formidable task.

Then, in 1936, Keynes's *General Theory* appeared and seemed to provide not only the kind of theoretical framework I was wishdreaming of, but also the remedial policies that logically followed from it. Together with my fellow students and most of the junior faculty, I became an ardent Keynesian overnight. In my first flush of enthusiasm, I believed that Keynes had resolved all the economic problems that really mattered and left little for the rest of us to do, beyond clearing up a few obscurities, explaining and preaching his message to the unbelievers, and helping to put his policies into practice.

That seemed a worthy task, and my first two articles tried to explain difficulties in the *General Theory*. One dealt with what I considered the book's crucial point: that no single price can be expected to equate two sets of supply and demand at the same time, so that the price of any commodity used partly as a store of value will tend to equate the demand for holding it as such to its accumulated stock and so cannot at the same time also equate the flow of its output with its flow of absorption. The second article discussed the role of price rigidity in employment theory.

Soon, however, my preoccupations changed. I discovered that I was a bad salesman and could be more useful by exploiting my comparative advantage in often seeing the flaw in an old established argument or the possibility of a better approach to a newly encountered subject. That partly explains why I never stuck to a single field but worked on many subjects in a variety of fields, including development, which is a catchall for all other fields. I also began to realize that Keynes's exposing the falsity of Say's Law, however important, left standing plenty of other questionable assumptions that the profession, blinded by the beautiful theories built on them, seemed hardly to notice, but that made me uncomfortable because I continued to feel uneasy about elegant models based on unreal assumptions. I therefore went back to what I originally wanted to do: look out for blatantly unrealistic economic models and try to put better ones in their place, or at least pave the way for the construction of better models, in the hope of creating a more usable framework for policy. I felt especially unhappy about the idealized, unrealistic nature of the perfectly competitive model and the narrowly crude motivation that economic theory attributed to people.

While I left Hungary to escape the injustice of the ingrained extreme inequalities that the country retained from its feudal past, I now realized that capitalism too had its substantial, if lesser, inequalities. Those based on inherited wealth may have been feudal relics, but the rest must have been created by economic power. That to me seemed an unavoidable and all-pervasive feature of capitalism and as such ought to form an integral part of any theoretical model of its laws of behavior. Accordingly, I deemed it wrong and misleading for economists to relegate economic power to the status of an exception or imperfection of the market system and close their eyes to its very existence in the centerpiece of economic theory, the model of perfect competition.

The challenge was to fit power into a model of the economy in a way that would show its presence to be the rule rather than the exception. The main answer to my problem, once I found it, was simple: the main source of economic power turned out to be the superior knowledge of one of the parties to almost every market transaction – an unavoidable state of affairs in every market economy based on the division of labor; for when people specialize and concentrate on their respective specialties, every economic activity becomes the preserve of its specialists – with the all-important exception of market transactions. Since people must go to market for everything they do not produce themselves, market exchange is the one and only economic activity in which specialists and non-specialists alike participate. Non-specialists confront specialists in most market transactions, with predictable consequences for the division of the gain from trade between them.

I developed that simple idea in my first book and tried to shift the focus of attention from perfect competition to the asymmetrical market relations between expert specialists and inexpert non-specialists by introducing the concepts of price maker and price taker and analyzing the way in which the former gain advantage from exploiting the power of their superior knowledge. That caught on, thanks to its usefulness in providing a framework for dealing with non-price as well as price competition and in explaining the temporary stability of market offers by the cost of changing them, thereby leading the way to a dynamic analysis of market behavior.

Only decades later did I see the important new light that my approach also threw on the welfare implications of capitalism and the mechanics of inflation, for introducing the power of superior knowledge into an analytic model of the economy showed two things: first, that competition in asymmetrical markets merely curbs economic power but cannot eliminate it completely; and second, that by exploiting their remaining economic power, those wielding it can still earn substantial profits but in securing them also generate such important social benefits as innovation, growth, and a buyers' market in consumer goods. Those benefits mitigate the inequities of income distribution and go a long way toward softening and hiding the adversary relations between buyers and sellers in product markets.

In labor markets, which are the mirror image of product markets, competition among employers was insufficient either to curb their monopsony power and profits or to generate the benefits of a sellers' market for workers, which would have mitigated the confrontational conflict between labor and management. That forced workers to offset employers' superior market power by organizing themselves into unions and so turning the labor market into a bilateral monopoly. The resulting difference in the power structure of labor markets, on the one hand, and product markets, on the other, explained the upward wage–price spiral and resulting inflationary bias of modern capitalism.[1]

That introducing power into a model of the economy and owning up to its influence on economic relations should not only deepen one's understanding of capitalism but also incline one to a more favorable view of it was a surprise. Yet it showed that monopolistic competition not only creates but also mitigates inequalities and is responsible for some of the economy's most valuable accomplishments. Such surprises are among the rewards of the search for knowledge.

My other concern was the economist's theory of individual behavior. I soon realized that there was not one theory but two: the theory of the utility-maximizing consumer and the theory of the income- or profit-maximizing income earner. As a lifelong believer in the equality of the sexes, it never occurred to me to look upon those as two equally valid but separate theories, applying to wife and husband, householder and breadwinner, respectively, who do not always coordinate their behavior.

---

[1] See my "Market Power and Inflation," *Economica*, 45 (1978), pp. 221–33.

Instead, I took it for granted that earning and spending money were the closely related activities of the same person or same harmonious household; one of my earliest articles exposed the conflict between the two theories by showing that to maximize profits or income is not a rational person's intermediate step toward getting the most out of life but looks more like a miser's infatuation with money, or the puritan work ethic of a Calvinist who values money as a symbol of good work and token of success.

When writing that article, I believed that the theory of the utility-maximizing consumer was more realistic; but many years of life in America made me reverse that judgment, at least as far as Americans are concerned. The average American does seem to be a puritan income maximizer at heart; and casual observation in this country belies such assumptions of the accepted theory that people have given tastes, know what they want, and make money solely to spend it, save it for future consumption, or leave it to their children. Window shopping and department store visiting are favorite pastimes, mail-order catalogs are considered interesting reading, traveling salesmen are welcome visitors as well as popular characters of American literature, all of which suggests that people earn money first and only afterward learn how and on what to spend it and what satisfactions its spending will yield. That also accounts for the great effectiveness and importance of advertising in America.

All that raised the question of consumers' sovereignty in my mind. Do market prices bring the pattern of output into harmony with consumers' preferences as economic theory teaches us, or does advertising mold people's tastes to make them conform to the pattern of output?

Once one recognizes that many tastes are not innate and genetically determined but changeable, influenced by tradition, education, fashion, and advertising, one begins to wonder: is it possible to distinguish legitimate from illegitimate influences on the formation of tastes – if so, by what criterion – and who among us is qualified to pass judgment on other people's tastes? Those are difficult questions, somewhat related to the philosophical question of what constitutes the good life, and they are shirked by most present-day economists. I felt, however, that anyone as concerned as I was with the economy's contribution to human welfare had to face up to them.

Accordingly, I set out to learn what was known about the sources of human satisfaction. That made me turn from the technically oriented writings of my colleagues to the broader and more philosophical perspective of previous generations of economists brought up on the classics and to the extensive, experimentally based scientific work on motivation of physiological psychologists. The views of those two groups seemed to complement and confirm one another and to fit well into the threefold classification of human satisfactions, which goes back to the classical Greek philosophers and which also proved to be a good framework for dealing with the questions I was grappling with.

I have in mind the distinction between appetitive desires to satisfy bodily needs, the social desires to belong and achieve distinction as well as display their symbols, and finally the need for stimuli. All of them are urgent and essential needs but differ one from another, those in the second group because their sources of satisfaction are subject to special limitations,[2] those in the third, because they are so very non-specific.

In contrast, the body's needs for shelter, warmth, rest, sex, and the various nutrients in food are quite specific, with little scope for substituting one for the other. The many forms that housing, clothes, and food can take are non-specific; but they constitute the stimulus content of shelter, warmth, and nourishment and are some of the myriad sources of active and passive, mental and physical stimulation that provide many different but equally satisfying ways of catering to the same human need for stimulus or excitement. That renders people's choice from among the many alternatives fairly arbitrary and easily influenced by advertising, though largely determined by upbringing, by education, and by having or lacking the skills and knowledge required for the enjoyment of particular forms of stimulation.

It seemed, therefore, that the economist's standard assumptions that consumers' tastes are exogenously given, unchanging over time, and best known to themselves were reasonably apt only when applied to the bodily satisfactions of visceral needs but did not fit the other two categories, and especially not the desire for stimulus, whose sources are not only easily changed but include change itself – considering that novelty is the crucial ingredient of all mental stimulation.

With the problems of distinguishing good from bad tastes and good from bad influences on tastes uppermost in my mind, I decided to concentrate mainly on the third category, because those problems arise mainly with respect to the sources of stimulus satisfaction (and also because I managed to persuade a young friend to concentrate on the second),[3] for lifestyles and national cultures differ mainly in the ways in which people obtain their stimulation. In Western societies, an important difference in sources of stimulation lies between people with a puritan and those with a non-puritan upbringing; and having been transplanted in mid-life from a non-puritan into a puritan environment, I was fortunate

---

[2] See my "Growth in the Affluent Society" *Lloyds Bank Review* (Jan. 1987), pp. 1–14. See also Fred Hirsch, *Social Limits to Growth* (Harvard U. Press, 1976, Cambridge, Mass.).

[3] See Hirsch, *Social Limits to Growth.*

enough to acquire an outsider's more discerning eye for noting their differences and respective merits and demerits.

Work has always been the main outlet for human energies, as well as its main source of stimulus, because the many different kinds of work provide different levels of strain, difficulty, hazard, and physical or mental challenge in order to meet people's need for stimulation. Most of us also engage in a variety of lesser stimulating activities, but the main need for other sources of stimulation and energy outlets arises only when and for whom work is or becomes easier, safer, less challenging, less time-consuming – or unavailable. In advanced and wealthy countries, stimulation is therefore an especially great need for rich people who do not need or want to work, and for the unemployed.

The difference between puritans and non-puritans lies in their differing attitudes toward sources of stimulation other than work. Puritans frown or look down upon them and extol the virtues of work, stressing both its intrinsic satisfactions and its worth to society as symbolized by the income it earns. Non-puritans, regarding the full development of each person's faculties to enjoy life as the ultimate aim, consider other sources of stimulus satisfaction no less valuable than work, provided that they do not harm others. Accordingly, puritan education is focused on work skills and work discipline to the neglect or detriment of all else, whereas non-puritan education puts equal weight on work skills and the knowledge and skills necessary for the enjoyment of other sources of stimulation – in short, it comes close to old-fashioned, many-sided humanistic education.

Having grown up in the non-puritanical environment of pre-war Hungary's educated circles, where sports, art, music, literature, and coffee-house conversation all made great claims on everybody's time and competence, I retained most if not all of the elements of that relaxed, easygoing attitude to life. I enjoyed work and the thrill of having and developing new ideas just as much as my colleagues did; but I refused to give up the pleasures of long walks, many daily hours of musical enjoyment, extended vacations to see new places and interrupt the routine, or any of my other leisure activities for the sake of the extra money, distinction, and intrinsic satisfaction I might have gotten from my work by a more single-minded application to it. Even in my work on economics, I moved around among half a dozen different fields because I enjoyed gaining a broader perspective, which often also proved helpful for finding new and unexpected ways of looking at or dealing with a problem that others had not thought of before.

At the same time, observing the effects of America's puritan work ethic from close quarters, I was impressed by people's great involvement in and relentless concentration on their work and amazed by their single-minded drive to maximize money income – all of that strikingly different from the leisurely European attitude. It made me understand and appreciate much more its oft-discussed contribution to rapid productivity growth and spectacular development in the Protestant countries, but it also made me aware of its drawbacks.

The main drawback of a too single-minded reliance on the intrinsic satisfaction of work seemed to be the danger of life's becoming too empty and unfulfilling when work ceases, is unavailable, or becomes too routinized and unchallenging. Keynes and Harrod, speculating on the long-run effects of continuing productivity growth, were greatly concerned about that danger and its effects on that majority of the population that is unprepared for the use of leisure. Keynes foresaw a drastic reduction in the length of the workweek within a century and predicted that it would greatly increase the incidence of nervous breakdowns.[4] Harrod, contemplating the same short workweek, feared lest war, blood sports, and violence, the favored pastimes of past leisure classes, also become the main preoccupation of a future leisure society.[5]

I took those fears seriously, because they seemed to be confirmed both by the disorientation, rapid decline, and premature death that befalls people on retirement if they fail to find a sufficiently stimulating new outlet for their energies and by the rowdyism of unemployed youths who roam the streets of our large cities because – having no leisure skills, only work skills that lie idle – they find in violence and crime the only cheap and easily available outlets for their youthful energies and need for stimulation. Another long-known manifestation of the same problem is the alienation of workers whose labor is deprived of much of its challenge and satisfaction by employer-imposed discipline. The statistics of the much longer hours worked by independents than by employees in every kind of job testify to the greater satisfaction work provides when it calls for more initiative.

Alienation has become much worse in industries whose technology of continuous-process mass production has simplified jobs to the point of utter monotony and boredom, demanding absolutely no responsibility or scope to excel and advance that would yield satisfaction along with income. Such work is worse, in a sense, than no work at all, because it is fatiguing enough to keep workers from seeking satisfactory stimulation elsewhere. The harm that alienation does to workers' mental health also shows up in their low productivity, absenteeism, sloppy work, and failure to contribute to the ongoing process of productivity growth. As a result,

---

[4] See J. M. Keynes, "Economic Possibilities for our Grandchildren," in his *Essays in Persuasion* (Norton, 1963, New York).
[5] See R. F. Harrod, "The Possibility of Economic Satiety," in Committee for Economic Development, *Problems of Economic Development* (CED, 1958, New York).

that problem has at last begun to be recognized and remedied. Something is being done already to restore and maintain the intrinsic satisfaction of work and workers' self-respect and involvement in their jobs by rendering their tasks more varied, interesting, and responsible and labor–management relations friendlier and more cooperative.

Another harmful consequence of the puritan ethic and its single-minded concentration on work and money making is that it causes people to pay much more attention to making than to spending money – a bias that would be irrational if to obtain what money buys were its only use and its function as a symbol of success counted for nothing. That, indeed, was the reason such a no-nonsense economist as Wesley Mitchell criticized what he called America's "backward art of spending money" in his book of that title. Rational or not, the careless spending of money hurts not only the person who wastes it, but society at large as well; for though the work ethic promotes productivity and growth, it is consumers' choices that determine the direction taken by that growth, whose value to society therefore is no greater than the care and wisdom consumers exercise in their spending decisions. Here, then, is an externality of consumers' choice and a potential reason for not curtailing their sovereignty.

The class societies of European capitalism used to, and to some extent still do, practice a peculiarly undemocratic division of labor between the puritan capitalist and working classes and the non-puritan remnants of the feudal leisure class. The former, preoccupied with production and money making, provided the economy's engine of growth; the latter, expert in spending money and the use and enjoyment of leisure skills, gave direction to growth by demanding high-quality products and setting an example of what leisure activities to pursue and leisure skills to acquire. That is why the leisure classes' cultivation of the arts, literature, learning, and philosophy has often been cited as the justification of their privileged position, since it gave them the education and leisure that made those activities possible.

In the United States, the art of spending has noticeably improved over the past decade or two – owing perhaps to the European travel of an ever-larger segment of the population. The public's interest in the quality of cooking and food and the design of consumer goods is on the rise, although the supply is slow to respond to demand. So far, the increased sophistication of demand has increased imports, but not yet the quality and design of domestic products, except perhaps in restaurants and bakeries, and it will take long for the change to percolate throughout the country.

The great increase in labor productivity, however, is increasing most people's free time and excess energy, which not only makes it possible for all to learn the skills necessary to practice and enjoy leisure activities and to partake of the finer things of life, but makes it imperative that they do learn them; for too much free time and excess energy are boring, demoralizing, and unpleasant if wasted in idleness. They are enjoyable and enrich life only if well used in leisure activities, most of which require no less knowledge and skill than does work.

I recount all that to show why my study of the sources and nature of human satisfactions has not only answered my questions, but also shifted my concern from the economist's model of human behavior to the behavior that it modelled. I had started out with the conviction that the economist's model was unrealistically narrow when it pictured the earning of money as people's main motive for work and the comforts money buys as their main sources of satisfaction. But I soon discovered that in our society, many people's motivation was just as narrow as the economist's theory pictured it; for their puritanical upbringing gave people the skills and discipline of work but little of the know-how needed to enjoy other kinds of stimulation, while modern mass-production technology deprived many jobs of their challenge and their holders of that feeling of accomplishment and contentment that comes from meeting a challenge. That left many workers in well-paying jobs vaguely dissatisfied with their lives, which offered them little beyond dull, unexciting work, the income that work yielded, and the comforts their income bought. This part of the economist's model of human beings, therefore, could hardly be called unrealistic.

When coming to that conclusion, I also realized, of course, that our puritanical high schools, which neglect the arts, discourage creativity, and are narrowly work-oriented, are becoming increasingly inadequate in an economy whose advancing technology is gradually reducing both the amount and the stimulus content of work, rendering it insufficient to satisfy the need for stimulation of a large segment of the population. The nature of that problem, the probable cause of so many people's increasing hunger for excitement and violence, was a new and unexpected revelation to me, an important insight gained from combining the study of economics and psychology.

The problem, though created by economic advance, was not an economic but a psychological problem, calling for a change in our educational philosophy and people's approach to life, and therefore out of my field of competence. Also, at the time it looked more like a cloud on the horizon than an actual problem, despite its already visible manifestations, certainly much less important and pressing than many economic problems. I was nevertheless concerned with it, and for two reasons. The first was that it contained the answers to my original questions, how to choose between individual preferences and how to judge the value of outside influences on those preferences. It seemed to make clear that the individual's freedom of choice should be respected only as long as it was rational and inflicted no harm on others by creating external diseconomies. Education, therefore, is essential to imparting the knowledge and skills necessary for rational decision making. The law is designed primarily to discourage and prevent choice that is harmful to others; but since it is not very effective in achieving that aim, education should also provide the aptitudes that make harmful choices easier to avoid by rendering some of their harmless alternatives accessible and enjoyable. That is the argument for broader, more artistically and culturally oriented education. In short, it is irrationality and the interdependence of individual satisfactions that necessitate abridging freedom of choice; and, like other externalities, they call for public intervention through law and education to straighten things out.

The second reason for focusing on a psychological problem was my realization of its seriousness and my abiding concern over inequality. The problem was more serious than the rather abstract economic problems I was also concerned with, and while its mental-health aspect seemed to be in the comfortably remote future, the possibility of resolving it through educational reform seemed equally remote, and therefore it was none too early to start thinking and talking about it.

At the same time, the problem had a distributional aspect. I was increasingly aware that income, beyond some minimum level, is not the only important source and condition of satisfaction. One's ranking on the social scale is just as important, and education may be more so. Educational reformers have always stressed the equalizing effect of education but had in mind mainly the equalizing of opportunities to rise on the social and income scale.

No less, or perhaps more, important would be for education to develop, at an early age, as many of people's abilities to enjoy life as possible. That would render the wider public less dependent on work as the only fully satisfactory activity, but it would be a drastic educational reform, since it calls for reversing the direction in which education is going and turning it back toward the humanities. That would require convincing our money-minded, puritan society of the equal importance of knowledge and skills required for work and for activities whose products cannot be sold for money, because their value lies in their contribution to the individual's enjoyment, society's sanity, and people's peaceful, non-violent coexistence. Fortunately, others were also advocating a broader, more culturally directed school curriculum, though for other reasons, and I was anxious to add my voice and very different arguments to theirs.

My writings on the subject, however, had little success. To begin with, I may have been addressing the wrong audience by directing my words to fellow economists, who did not know what to do with a problem that, though created by economic growth, clearly required non-economic remedies. Also, they may have failed to appreciate the seriousness of the problem, never having experienced it personally. We academics are fortunate in almost never lacking for satisfying work, not even in old age or when without a job.

Second, I have been decried as an elitist. I was, indeed, arguing for an education and approach to life that once was the privilege of a favored (and hated) elite, but the gist of my argument was that today, thanks to our higher standard of living, most people could adopt, and would be better off by adopting, that once exceptional lifestyle. Many intellectuals, however, believe that to be an unattainable ideal, because they think that intellectual activities and pleasures, which require an average or higher than average IQ, are the only sources of stimulation comparable to work in their ability to make life worth living.

I believe that to be mistaken. Sensory stimulation and the development and exercise of physical prowess, manual dexterity, a green thumb, and musical and artistic skills are just as challenging and satisfying as intellectual activity and, unlike it, some of them at least are accessible to almost everybody. Examples are the flourishing of folk art in illiterate populations; the artistic quality of young children's painting and singing; the high musical culture of U.S. blacks and Central and South European gypsies; the expertise in the culinary arts of Frenchwomen and Frenchmen alike, more than a third of whom engage in gourmet cooking as an enjoyable leisure activity;[6] and the playing of *boule* (bocce ball) as a nearly full-time occupation by old men of all nationalities around the Mediterranean. They all suggest that most of us are born with many and varied artistic and other talents and skills, which are easily developed in the young but just as easily lost when not practiced or suppressed by a work ethic that considers worthless any activity that yields no income.

Keeping up and exercising some of those talents is and will become especially important for the great mass of people with no exceptional gifts, because those with an exceptional ability can happily live a lifetime for the cultivation of that one ability alone. I myself will always be grateful for my non-puritanical upbringing that enabled me to lead a reasonably happy life in happy and not so happy circumstances alike.

Tibor Scitovsky is Professor of Economics, Emeritus, Stanford University.

[6] See Pierre Debreu, "Les comportements de loisirs des Français (Enquête de 1967) résultats détaillés," *Les Collections de l'INSEE*, Ser. M, No. 25 (Institut National de la Statistique et des Etudes Economiques, 1968, Paris).

HERBERT A. SIMON

Living in Interdisciplinary Space

A life philosophy: what is that? The phrase sounds solemn. Does one need a philosophy to live a life? Is a philosophy a book of rules to which one refers before making choices? Or is it an account (I won't say a "rationalization") of the choices one has made? In either case, it would appear to be a lot easier to have a life philosophy at age 68 than at age 18.

Or is it easier? Perhaps living confuses as often as it clarifies. Perhaps one should write down a life philosophy at 18, before the complexities have emerged, so that one can produce it, on request, when one is 68. But that is dangerous too. Readers would be tempted to compare the philosophy with the life. Safer to write it at 68.

Does one need to be a philosopher to have a life philosophy? I have long thought that a philosopher could be defined as someone who was more interested in questions than in their answers. If that is a correct definition, then probably I qualify, so let me proceed.

Still, we must distinguish two different meanings of "life philosophy." In one sense, a life philosophy is your picture of the universe in which you find yourself, including, in center foreground, your picture of the human condition. In a second sense, a life philosophy is a statement of your raison d'être in the midst of this cosmic and human environment.

COSMOLOGY

I personally would find it difficult to frame a life philosophy in the second sense except against a background provided by my views of the cosmos and of humanity. The creature of bounded rationality that I am has no illusions of attaining a wholly correct and objective understanding of the world in which I live. But I cannot ignore that world. I must understand it as best I can, with the help of my scientific and philosophical fellows, and then must adopt a personal stance that is not outrageously incompatible with its apparent conditions and constraints. I must eschew personal goals that require gravity shields or the perfection of humankind for their success. I am an adaptive system, whose survival and success, whatever my goals, depend on maintaining a reasonably veridical picture of my environment of things and people. Since my world-picture is only a crude approximation to reality, I cannot aspire to optimize anything; at most, I can aim at satisficing. Searching for the best can only dissipate scarce cognitive resources. The best is enemy of the good.

Already, you have learned something about my life-philosophy$_1$, the cosmology, and my life-philosophy$_2$, the personal one. Let me now try to describe the former a little more systematically. I am a creature of the Twentieth Century, thoroughly immersed in its science and its empiricist epistemology. My cosmos began (probably) with a Big Bang, and has been evolving inexorably ever since through astronomical, geological, biological, and anthropological ages, the time line being gradually, perhaps exponentially, magnified as we approach the present, and shrinking again, perhaps exponentially, as we peer into the future. Parts of the picture change from time to time, especially the parts that are most distant fore and aft, but not (at least in the past quarter century) in ways that have much importance for a life-philosophy$_2$.

This cosmological machine has laws, but I cannot detect in it any purposes. In this respect, also, I am a creature of my century, needing, like logical positivists and existentialists, to postulate my own goals because I cannot see that they have been given to me by any external donor. The world is vast, beautiful, and fascinating, even awe-inspiring — but impersonal. It demands nothing of me, and allows me to demand nothing of it, a little like some people's conception, today, of a house-sharing or bed-sharing "relationship."

But if the cosmos is indifferent to me, I need not be indifferent to the cosmos. I can fashion my life so as to live in peace with it, assuming that I can settle on an acceptable definition of peace. Nor need I put the matter so negatively. The cosmos can be the source of some of my deepest pleasures. Gazing at it, outdoors at night or in a forest or through a microscope, I find inconceivable variety, pattern, and beauty, beyond the competence of human artists.

Some of the beauty of the cosmos is hidden, to be revealed only by the cryptographic activity we call science. Catching glimpses of new patterns, never before seen by the human eye, bringing them into the open, provides the scientist with his most moving experiences. And though he can have such experiences directly only a few times in a lifetime, he can have them vicariously as often as he wishes by studying the work of his fellow scientists, present and past.

THE HUMAN CONDITION

I suppose that is why I am a scientist. But why a social scientist? To explain that (if, indeed, I know the reason), I must return to the cosmological stage, this time the part occupied by human beings. Neither the "featherless biped" nor the "rational animal" definition seems to capture it all, though the latter is closer if we place equal emphasis on both noun and adjective. We humans are minds (and consciousnesses) in bodies that locomote in a physical world. We are subject, without any exemption, to physical and biological laws. If we fall, our bones break; if we cannot find food, we starve.

We have become the species that we are through a long process of selective evolution. As a result, we come into the world equipped with at least some of the requisites of survival (including an environment of adults who will nurture us). The newborn child is ready to breathe, to suck, to defecate. It doesn't need a life philosophy to do those things or to want to do them. It is ready, also, to learn. And whether through learning or because of the inbuilt equipment it brings into the world with it, it is soon prepared to empathize with other members of its species: to feel their hurts as its hurts and, at a later level of sophistication, their poverty as its poverty.

I don't want to go down a full list of human traits, inborn or acquired; we all know what they are. I have mentioned some of the more positive ones. I could equally well have mentioned human propensities for predation against our own species, and the deeply ingrained selfishness that was surely one of the prime conditions for our survival.

The human condition has often been described as absurd. Surely the term is appropriate: a body shackled to a self-conscious head — or is it the head that is shackled to the body? The wants and needs of the two parts are so disparate. Can the body regard as anything but absurd the head while it is gazing at the stars – or worse, sitting wrapped in its own thought? Can the head regard the act of sex or the savoring of food as anything but absurd?

Of course it is only the head, not the body, that makes judgements of absurdity. And so, given the range of needs and wants that we human beings possess, it becomes the task of the head to create myths that reconcile it with the body; that turn absurdity into pleasure, beauty, and tenderness. The head even tries to find, from time to time, a common denominator for all of the claims that are made upon the human system by body and by mind and by the surrounding physical environment. It gives this common denominator impressive names like the Good or utility. But the single, overarching goal implied by these names is an illusion. We, the head and the body, have many needs, many desires, fortunately not all clamoring at once.[1] To stamp them all with the label of "utility" is futile. The plurality is real; there is no monolithic goal.

In this committee of urges, wants, and needs, housed in body and head, there is no consensus about *the* purpose of life. Mark Twain told a story of Siamese twins who agreed upon alternating time slots during which one or the other was in full charge. The story did not end well – both twins had reason to regret the murder one committed while he had control. But the absurdity of the story is the human absurdity. We all time-share, but we are many more than twins. So some parts of life are spent in the enjoyment of music, others in the enjoyment of sex, yet others in the enjoyment of food, leaving lots of time for the enjoyment of mountains, the enjoyment of friends, and especially the enjoyment of science.

Of course the list is not complete; I mean it only to be illustrative. Moreover, I have left out everything except the time spent in consuming. There is work, too, and obligations and duties; a great deal of them in most of our lives. And there are sorrow and grief, which we do not count among life's blessings, but which deepen our other experiences and give them meaning and sometimes a poignancy they might not otherwise have.

So – a life with many goals but without a goal. A human life. Who would want it to be otherwise? Who would want to be free of the hundred desires that are always making exigent demands on a day that will not stretch beyond 24 hours? And who is capable of fashioning that Master

---

[1] In my paper, "Rational Choice and the Structure of the Environment," *Psychological Review* 63 (1956), 129–38, I tried to provide a crude picture of how this kind of symbiosis of needs and wants can work.

Plan, that comprehensive utility function that allocates to each want precisely its proper time slice?

HOMO RATIONALIS

In these paragraphs, I have been describing my life, and also my life-philosophy$_2$. But I have also been describing the life of Everyperson, and the life of Economic Person, that creature who is the special object of our professional interest and attention. My interest in economics began in 1935 as an interest in human decision making, and especially an interest in how human beings cope with the complexities, the uncertainties, and the goal conflicts and incommensurabilities of everyday personal and professional life.

The question first struck me forcibly as I was trying to apply what I had learned in the intermediate price theory course taught by Henry Simons at the University of Chicago to the problem of how the Municipal Recreation Department in the City of Milwaukee adjudicated competing claims on funds in budget decisions. How did one measure the marginal utility of planting another tree on the playground, or the utility of more hours of recreational leadership or of a better tennis court surface? And what was the utility we were aiming at anyway? Joy through play? Less juvenile delinquency? Green spots in the city?

It is now 1991, 56 years later, and the problem has never left me. I do not mean that I feel as ignorant of the answer as I did in 1935; I flatter myself that I and others have made considerable progress toward understanding the question and providing an answer. But the allocation of individual or organizational resources – how it is done, and how it ought to be done – remains a central question about the human condition.

Pursuing the answer to the allocation question has led me on a long, but pleasurable, search through a tortuous maze of possibilities. To understand budget decisions, one has to understand decision making in general. And to understand decision making, even in its rational aspects, it is necessary to study the processes of decision making, and more generally, the processes of human thinking. To study thinking, I had to abandon my home disciplines of political science and economics (my degree was in the former, but my graduate training divided fairly evenly between them) for the alien shores of psychology and, a little later, of computer science and artificial intelligence. There I have remained since, except for occasional brief visits to the home islands. My emigration took place about 1955, with some interdisciplinary commuting for a few years thereafter.

At least that is one version of the story: a single-minded search that has persisted for a half century. Perhaps it is even the true version. Another possibility is that excitement lit the path: first the excitement, after World War II of game theory, linear programming, and the use of mathematics to solve problems of economics and operations research. Then, the excitement of the computer, the machine that taught us how a mind could be housed in a material body. What significance should one attach to coincidences? The demands of the problem and the excitement of the new tools lured me down the very same path. And so I was able to spend the large part of my scientific life pursuing a problem I thought central to understanding the human condition, while indulging myself in the mathematics, and later in the computer programming, that gave me so much pleasure just in the doing. Nor was I denied the pleasures of friendship, even in professional life, for most of my work has involved congenial and warm partnerships.

The pictures of Homo economicus and Homo cogitans that emerged from this quest have already been hinted at in my earlier description of the human condition. When, abandoning the a priorism of classical and neoclassical assumptions about human behavior, we looked at actual decision making and problem solving, we saw a creature of bounded rationality using techniques of heuristic search to find satisficing – good-enough – courses of action. And with the help of the methods of computer simulation, we were able to show that these techniques could account for the data of human problem solving in a range of both simple and complex situations.

Readers would not be deceived by the claim that economists flocked to the banner of satisficing man with his bounded rationality. The "flocking" was for a long time a trickle that is now swelling into a respectable stream. These ideas still remain well outside the mainstream of economics – but not indefinitely. For they provide a realistic picture of human choice, a picture that may instruct us about some of the most puzzling problems confronting economics today: decision making under uncertainty, business cycles with their accompanying natural or unnatural unemployment, the role of entrepreneurship in investment, and others. But economists are just becoming aware of these possibilities, and there is a long road ahead of backbreaking empirical work, for the theory of bounded rationality does not permit all one's theorems to flow from a few *a priori* truths. Fixing the postulates of such a theory requires close, almost microscopic, study of how human beings actually behave.

Science, viewed as competition among theories, has an unmatched advantage over any other form of intellectual competition I know. In the long run (no more than centuries), the winner is selected, not by its superior rhetoric, not by its ability to persuade or dazzle laymen, not by political influence, but by its agreement with data, with facts, as they are gradually and cumulatively revealed. As long as its factual veridicality is unchallenged, one can remain quite calm about the future of a theory. The future of bounded rationality is wholly secure.

HOMO SOCIALIS

I have said a great deal about pleasures, little about duties. How do you put duty in a utility function? For a satisficing theory it's quite easy: simply place it among the constraints. Of course we may also view duty as a cost we pay for society's willingness to cooperate with us. This implies that every person has a price. Possibly so, but I prefer the satisficing view.

What duties? By starting at the weak end of the spectrum, perhaps we can reach some consensus. There is the duty not to harm others unless they harm us – the negative version of the Golden Rule. A higher standard is the obligation to leave the world no worse off than it would have been without us. Since most people, even people in rather humble circumstances, can meet that one, perhaps it is not an unreasonable requirement to impose.

The heavier obligation at the social level is for our society to leave to future generations as wide and interesting a range of options as those our generation inherited from our forebears. To do that, we must accept collective responsibility for securing continuing energy sources, for preserving the environment, for stabilizing world population, and for somehow removing or dulling the threat of the Bomb. We have no obligation to solve all the world's problems (and no prospect that we can); we do have an obligation to avert irreversible catastrophe, and to oppose implacably every step toward it.

When we turn to obligations to do positive good, the road gets steeper and stonier. The economists of my generation are Depression Children, so perhaps what I shall say is not applicable to economists in general. In any event, I find that a great number of economists (including some who have contributed to this volume) came to the profession because of the poverty they witnessed or, more rarely, experienced in the Great Depression. (Perhaps President Reagan, with his cheerful indifference to the poor, will help create another strong generation of economists.) The elimination of poverty has been for Depression-bred economists a lodestar, and compassion for the poor and unlucky an admirable trait of character.

I cannot really say what role the Depression played in bringing me to economics – a relatively small role, I would guess. But I share the values and feelings of my generational siblings. And given the productivity of which human societies today are technically capable, I regard the elimination of poverty (at least poverty measured against basic physiological and psychological needs) as one of the Big Goods that is actually attainable, perhaps within a couple of generations.

Distributive justice? That's more elusive. My cosmology allows me to see quite clearly that the distribution of the world's goods owes little to virtue and a great deal to the globewide lottery that distributes genes, families, places of birth, and other forms of access by the throw of cosmic dice. Does that imply, as Rawls thinks, a norm of full equalization? Only if you believe that people's aspirations are to be guided by comparison with the well-being of others. That belief seems highly unproductive, since it turns the whole life of society into a zero-sum game in which some can win only by others losing. There must be better games; and if I were to select a research problem without regard to scientific feasibility or interest, but only in terms of social welfare criteria, it would be the problem of finding conditions under which human beings will design and play games that all can win. (Neither the USSR nor the PRC has yet invented that game, nor have we, although perhaps we are closer.)

HOMO SCIENTIFICUS

Does a life philosophy include a life-philosophy₃, a philosophy of economics? If so, you have already been exposed to most of mine, for it follows from my cosmology. The quality of a research problem or a research domain rests on two considerations: (1) the importance and excitement of the questions it addresses, (2) the availability of concepts and techniques that hold out some promise of progress. By those tests, the study of the nature of mind is one of the world's most promising research domains today. The questions it addresses have roused intense interest in humankind since the earliest times, and have given rise to the most fundamental problems of epistemology, including the celebrated mind–body problem. Moreover, understanding the nature of mind is fundamental to building viable theories of social institutions and behavior, of economics and political science. Economics dodged the problem for two centuries with its *a priori* assumptions of human rationality. But as I argued earlier, those assumptions have reached the limits of their fruitfulness; they must now be supplemented and partially replaced by a more veridical theory of the human mind.

But do we have the tools to study mind? We now have a quarter century's accumulation of evidence that the digital computer is the powerful tool that we lacked previously. It now shows us the way, both by providing a language in which we can state theories of human behavior without placing them on the Procrustean bed of real numbers, and by providing a mechanism that, by simulation, will spin out the implications of our theories. Obviously, I am not speaking of the computer as it is generally employed in modern econometrics, but the computer as it is employed in the new discipline or interdiscipline of cognitive science.

From what I have written, it should be eminently clear that my tribal loyalties are weak. I am a social scientist before I am an economist, and a scientist before a social scientist – and, I hope, a human being before either of the others. I believe (my third creation myth) that what brought me to the social sciences was the urge to apply mathematics to a body of phenomena that sorely needed it if it was to be understood scientifically. Physics was already too far along (I thought) for genuine adventure. The social sciences offered a field of virgin snow on which one could imprint one's characters.

Disciplines, like nations, are a necessary evil that enable human beings of bounded rationality to simplify the structure of their goals, and reduce their choices to calculable limits. But parochialism is everywhere, and the world sorely needs international and interdisciplinary travelers who will carry new knowledge from one enclave to another. Having spent much of my scientific life in such travel, I can offer one piece of advice to others who wish to try an itinerant existence. It is fatal to be regarded as a good economist by psychologists, and a good psychologist by political scientists. Immediately upon landing on alien shores, you must begin to acquire the local culture, not with the aim of denying your origins, but so that you can gain the full respect of the natives. When in economics, there is no substitute for talking the language of marginal analysis and regression analysis – even (or especially) when your purpose is to demonstrate their limitations.

The task is not onerous – after all, we acculturalize new graduate students in a couple of years. Besides, it may lead you to write papers on fascinating topics that you would otherwise never have encountered. For one of the nice features of the utility function (or the committee of goals I would substitute for it) is that it is capable of acquiring ever new dimensions. Perhaps that is why I started learning the Chinese language and doing psychological research on memory for Chinese ideograms at age 64. A great immunizer against incipient boredom.

Herbert A. Simon is University Professor of Psychology and Computer Science at Carnegie Mellon University and the 1978 winner of the Nobel Memorial Prize in economic science. His autobiography, Models of My Life, *incorporating a modified version of this essay (which first appeared in the* American Economist *series) as Chapter 23, was published by Basic Books (New York) in 1991.*

ROBERT M. SOLOW

Notes on Coping

As the editor of this volume can testify, I have tended to resist his invitation to contribute to it. My reluctance had two sources, one general and one specific.

The general reason was a feeling that interest in personalities had already gone further than is healthy in the literature of economics, and further still in the culture at large. I do not suppose that anyone would be crass enough to say or believe that the personal characteristics of an author have any bearing on the truth or falsity or value of her or his written work. I would not deny that the personality traits of an author have quite a lot to do with the differential success and diffusion of ideas within the profession and even more so outside the profession. But that is something to be deplored; and even if it is inevitable, it should certainly not be encouraged. I do not for a moment think that this collection of essays is intended to have such an effect. But it is a cultural artifact nevertheless, and I am put off by peeks into the hearts and minds of people who should in some important sense be anonymous. Of course, the cult of personality in economics is of no great importance. It is of great importance in politics, say, where the United States has just been through a presidential campaign that seemed not only to be devoid of ideas, but positively determined to keep them from interfering in the election.

The specific reason was rather different. I do not think of myself as having a "life philosophy." The phrase suggests something significant, aiming at least for consistency and perhaps for universality, the quality of being recommendable to others. When I asked myself about my life philosophy, I thought that its first (and last) tenet might be: Do not have one. But then I decided that I would not go so far as to offer even that recommendation. It occurred to me that what I have instead of a life philosophy are a few guidelines for coping. It can do no harm to say what I think they are. I want to emphasize that this is empirical work, not theory. These are things I think I observe in my own behavior, not rules that I have ever formulated and debated with myself or my wife. Here are some examples.

Don't take yourself too seriously. Life is full of little ridiculousnesses, including your own. It is pretty hard to recognize your own, but at least you can avoid being pompous about them. I think a lot of error comes from the intertwining of ideas and egos. The worst consequences could be avoided by a little more attention to the humor of it all. I know that I violate this guideline occasionally, but I guess the essence of the maxim is not to worry too much about that either. There is a flip side to this maxim, and "flip" is the right word. I am sure that, too often, I dismiss with a joke what I should meet head-on. If you do not take yourself seriously, it may sometimes be concluded that you are not serious. I do not have to remind my professional colleagues that there are always two kinds of error to be traded off. No recipe for coping is perfect.

If you see something that needs doing, do it. It is not easy for me to explain what I mean by this guideline, but I think it has been deeply ingrained in me for a long time. I rather believe that I was once promoted to Acting Corporal at the age of 19 because of this trait. I suppose that it entails a partial contradiction of the conventional injunction to get your priorities straight before acting. To my mind, the priorities are not so certain that one ought to pass up any opportunity to get something useful done. Perhaps it also reflects my belief that much more good is done by tinkering than by starting over from scratch. I claim for this approach that it fits in with the Hippocratic injunction to the doctor to "do no harm" and that gradient methods are a good all-purpose recipe for local optimization. What about global optimization? Good point. I suppose I worry that enthusiastic seekers after global maxima run the risk of falling off steep cliffs. On the bad side, I know I sometimes find myself doing meaningless busywork when I could presumably spend my time at something more useful. My wife reminds me that once, when we discovered that the automatic wake-up mechanism in our hotel room was not working, I spent an hour and a half trying to fix it. (I got it to work. Once.) No recipe for coping is perfect.

Don't let the team down. I hope I mean something more than a triviality here. My feeling is that most useful accomplishments are made by groups. This means not only face-to-face groups like army companies, ball clubs, and academic departments, but also, say, research communities that are interested in a common problem but interact directly only occasionally. So I regard reliably doing your share of the group's work as a cardinal virtue. Needless to say, I have spent plenty of time struggling to stay awake in boring committee meetings. Not every collective enterprise has value. But it is both exhilarating and efficient to be part of a successful, high-morale group that enjoys itself because it is productive and is productive because it enjoys itself. Of course, too much attention to this maxim would have ruined Beethoven or Proust. No recipe for coping is perfect.

Probably I could think of a couple more such maxims and defend them as ways of coping with the complexity of life. But they would be no more grandiose and no more airtight than these. I wouldn't have it any other way.

Do these thoughts have any relevance to the doing of economics? It would be absurd to suppose that any methodological rules follow literally from such generalities. But I think I could claim that they are at least peculiarly compatible with certain methodological precepts (or prejudices).

For instance, I think it does economics no good to be too ambitious. In recent years I have heard particle physicists say, only about one-quarter self-mockingly, that they may be on the verge of a Theory of Everything. I have no opinion about theoretical physics. But my view is that economics is foreclosed from a Theory of Everything, not just because it is all so complicated but for deeper reasons.

Pretty clearly, economic behavior depends on the nature of social institutions (and on culturally determined attitudes and beliefs or, better still, on these attitudes and beliefs as filtered through social institutions). Believers in an economic Theory of Everything would say, "Okay, but then we just have to include the choice of social institutions as an endogenous process." I think that response is wrong, not just hard to carry out, but wrong. Social institutions are not chosen, they evolve. No doubt this evolution is subject to selective pressure; utterly dysfunctional social institutions are unlikely to survive. Just as surely, however, a wide range of institutional arrangements and behavior patterns will prove viable. This sort of evolutionary indifference may occur because they are all more or less equivalent as far as survivability is concerned, or because they come in interconnected complexes that are very difficult to change, or because competitive pressure among such complexes is not so very great anyway. Even in biological evolution, where selective pressure is undoubtedly much more intense, there appear to be many traits that persist for no particular reason so long as they are not actively harmful. In social evolution this must be even more the case. The talk about "optimal choice of institutions" is not just metaphor but bad metaphor. The consequence is that economics must pay close attention to local institutions, because they matter for behavior.

Thus I think that economics should not take itself too seriously, but just go about doing what needs to be done. It is sometimes said that economics done in my preferred piecemeal way results in just a whole bunch of little models, connected to each other only tenuously at best. I can live with that. It is much better than insisting on a single unified model that is wrong about nearly every particular thing.

The only candidate so far for an economic Theory of Everything has been competitive general-equilibrium theory. It was once immensely valuable in showing that a system of unregulated markets could, in principle, exhibit order instead of chaos. Without that demonstration, modern economics might not have been possible at all. That is a terrible reason for sticking to the overarching model even where it is inappropriate, i.e., nearly everywhere. There are alternatives and more would be better.

To put the point differently, I think my general maxims for coping are especially compatible with an opportunistic approach to doing economics. I do not mean "opportunistic" in the sense of "amoral," but as shorthand for "unwilling to sacrifice a potentially useful insight on the altar of methodological purity." It seems to me that this preference for opportunism over formalism applies to empirical work as aptly as to theory. In that sphere I think opportunism suggests that we should gratefully exploit every bit of evidence we can find. Formal time series analysis is wonderful where it gives robust answers to interesting questions. Experience suggests that it hardly ever happens. Then we have to piece together what we can from casual observation, questionnaires, folk beliefs, historical narrative, and anything that comes to hand. Of course, it is very hard to make defensible sense of such scraps, but the alternative seems to be worse. I think the economist is in the position here ascribed to the historian: "In an historian we are not to be critical for every punctilio not relating to his grand design; yet I think 'tis but just to demand that what he doth write be true." (This is from Henry Stubbe, "The Lord Bacons Relation of the Sweating-Sickness Examined" [1671].

Of course, I am not capable of finding such gems for myself; it is quoted in Christopher Hill's *The Experience of Defeat* [1984].)

What about my peculiar belief in the importance of group enterprises? I am not sure there is any parallel or analogue in economic method. Maybe it explains why I think teaching is an important activity and itself part of the advance of knowledge, and why I sometimes have the feeling that we demand too much of a superficial kind of "originality" from our graduate students. But that would probably be stretching it.

Robert M. Solow is Institute Professor of Economics at Massachusetts Institute of Technology and the 1987 winner of the Nobel Memorial Prize in economic science.

JAN TINBERGEN

Solving the Most Urgent Problems First

MY ROUNDABOUT WAY TO ECONOMICS

My life was shaped by an unusual lot of good luck. My parents were very devoted to one another and to their children. Being the eldest of five I profited longest from their upbringing and example. Among my teachers – from elementary and high school to university – were many excellent people. On top of that I have been very happily married for over half a century. Of course, some dark shadows occurred in our life as in everybody's, but these remain stored in our hearts.

My favorite subjects in high school were the sciences and the corresponding mathematics courses; thus, at university my choice fell to those areas. At Leiden University my main teacher was Paul Ehrenfest, successor to H. A. Lorentz and a close friend of Albert Einstein's. Einstein came to Leiden to give lectures for three weeks every year. He then stayed at the Ehrenfests', where I had the privilege and joy to be present on many evenings, when physics and music were the main subjects. Of course, Einstein was the greater physicist, but Paul Ehrenfest and his equally gifted wife Tatiana Afanasjewa had the gift of translating very complicated theories into understandable terms.

This was the period when a series of Nobel Prizes of winners in the natural sciences (Lorentz, Kamerlingh Onnes, Zeeman, Van't Hoff, Enthoven) were from Holland, so the climate could not have been more inspiring. I got my doctorate in theoretical physics in 1929. I had hurried through my studies in order not to be too long a burden to my parents (who had four more children going to university), but I enjoyed every moment. In particular, I shall never forget the help and friendship of the Ehrenfests. I still think of theoretical physics as ranking high among human achievements, but Ehrenfest understood that my desire to switch from science to economics was based on my feeling that I might be more useful as an economist. Because of his own interest in economics, he had been corresponding with Schumpeter and helped me to find my way toward that subject.

In 1923 I had joined the Labor Party and its Youth Organization. At that time I came in contact with the poorer part of Leiden, not usually known by the students. Even before the Great Depression, conditions among the working classes in Leiden were about the most abominable in Holland. Unemployment was high, public assistance minimal. Many people were living in slums in utmost poverty. A postman I met and frequently talked with offered to show me the inside of this town with its famous history. I was horrified, and this certainly influenced my ultimate choice to focus on economics rather than continue in physics.

I found a job at the Central Statistical Bureau (CBS) on business cycle research, which forced me to read a number of textbooks. Presumably on the suggestion of Gottfried Haberler, I was invited by the League of Nations Secretariat at Geneva to investigate which of the theories that Haberler had set out in his famous "Prosperity and Depression"[1] had best explained the nature of business cycles. The director general of statistics gave me permission to take a leave of absence for two years, provided that I would spend two weeks every three months at The Hague to supervise the work going on at CBS.

During this period the League of Nations Financial Section and Economic Intelligence Service, headed by A. Loveday, had a staff of gifted young economists from several countries. Working with them was excellent training for me. Among my colleagues were Ragnar Nurkse, James E. Meade, Marcus Flemming, and many others. These were wonderful days.

[1] Written at the request of the League of Nations, Geneva, 1937.

I was not the only one who, in that period, switched from the physical sciences to economics. We had quite a lot of "migrants," among whom were Tjalling Koopmans, Piet de Wolff, G. Goudswaard, Dick Derksen, and Arie Bijl. Our choice was in part a reaction to the Great Depression.

MY VALUE SYSTEM

This brings me to my personal "value system." In retrospect, adding much from later experience and the course of world politics, I am inclined to regard sympathy for the suffering underdog and tolerance as the basic elements of my ethical creed. I am a member of the Remonstrant Protestant Church, which has always laid strong emphasis on tolerance and humaneness. I would not call myself religious, but I am a product of Christianity interpreted in my own way. My choice of democratic socialism, my ideal of European federalism, and my priorities for the Third World all have that source of inspiration.

Two of the biggest evils in this world seem to me to be excessive and egoistic nationalism and war. Warfare was probably necessary and even helpful in times gone by. It is now completely dehumanized by technical and organizational developments that have vastly multiplied the number of innocent victims. Nuclear weapons, as the last step, have maximized the absurd nature of wars, while mental slowness carries the danger that often the military establishment tends to fight the "previous war" with the new weaponry. If this were to happen now, it would put an end to our history.

THE SATISFACTION DERIVED FROM DOING SCIENTIFIC WORK

What is most attractive in doing scientific work, whether in economics or any other science? The happiness you feel when understanding all of a sudden something you did not understand before. For instance, the echo theory of business cycles, in its simplest form, assumes that at a time 0 there is a peak in investment, followed by zero investment in the next time units (years). Say that all investment goods have the same lifetime, for instance, eight years. Then in year 8 all capital goods will be worn out and will have to be replaced. The same things will happen in years 16, 24, 32, and so on. These are the "echoes." We know, however, that capital goods do not have the same lifetime: lifetimes are distributed rather widely. When we look at the curve, the first echo will then show that distribution, the second will be even flatter, and so on until the last echo is not perceptible at all. This seems to kill the echo theory. Can it be saved? Yes. If the moment of replacement depends on

(1) the duration of the capital good and (2) the cyclical position of the economy, early replacement will be postponed, and late replacement must be undertaken earlier. This tends to accentuate the peak character of the echo theory, and we may arrive at an undamped cycle movement (see Tinbergen, 1938).

A somewhat different, but related satisfaction is derived from the construction of a very simple, the simplest possible, model of a phenomenon under discussion. Starting at a monopoly, the simplest form of competition has, minimally, two sellers. Cournot's duopoly theorem is such a "simplest" answer.

Cycles can be found to be the solution to a difference equation. What is the simplest form then? How many lagged terms should it have? When will the cyclical movement be damped? What are the consequences of the existence of non-tradables for a Keynesian model of an open country? (Tinbergen, 1965).

For the econometrician working with carefully observed figures, considerable satisfaction is derived from finding a multiple regression equation with an R^2 close to unity. Stone (1981) found one in which $R^2 = 0.999$, using as the only independent variables for the total volume of consumption (1) permanent income, (2) transient income, and (3) wealth. I had the luck of obtaining an $R^2 = 0.9775$ (Tinbergen, 1984). The desire to obtain high correlations gave birth to a species of econometricians called correlation hunters, and this species is sometimes rightly ridiculed. Do not think, however, that hunting successfully is an easy matter!

ATTRACTIVE AND LESS ATTRACTIVE ECONOMICS

Not all subjects within economics are equally attractive. From the start of my economic research work, I liked the genesis of cyclical movements; so the cobweb theorem became one of my favorites. Just after I discovered how a lagged supply and an instantaneous demand curve could produce a cyclical movement with a period of twice the lag, Hanau's study on pork prices supplied a magnificent concrete example (Hanau, 1930). It was fun to extend this to durable goods and to find that a supply lag could then cause a cycle whose period was about four times that lag, and to apply this to shipbuilding (Meuldijk, 1940). In fact, we had here a combination of a pure durable goods cycle and an echo cycle.

Another subject I began to like increasingly was that of the optimum, socio-economic order. My feeling was that we had much to learn from welfare economics. The unknowns of welfare economics are not the quantities of goods and services consumed in an optimum situation; one should dig more deeply and consider as the ultimate unknowns a number of institutions together constituting the socio-economic order; along that line, a synthesis between market economics and centrally planned economics could be found. Of course, I was strongly influenced by Oscar Lange's work on this subject (Lange and Taylor, 1938–48). To be sure, the problem of identifying the optimum order can be solved only under a number of restrictions whose validity is debatable. Calling the objective function "world welfare" involves the necessity of studying a series of questions. Can world welfare be derived from individual welfare? Can individual welfare be corrected by the authorities for errors and short-sightedness? Do the authorities have sufficient knowledge of their citizens? Can (corrected) welfare be measured (approximately)? Do we know the production functions that are the main constraints under which world welfare has to be maximized? Can we trace the external effects of authority decisions?

The diverging answers to these and other questions reflect diverging opinions on what is the best socio-economic order and thus might hamper convergence of "capitalist," "socialist," and any forms of "mixed" societies. But they may open our eyes before we formulate our preferences. This, I think, is what makes this subject so fascinating.

ECONOMICS AND OTHER SCIENCES

A fascinating subject, too, is the relationship between disciplines, the comparing of different sciences. I cannot help sticking to my boyhood admiration for physics, in particular astrophysics. I think the most imaginative contributions to human understanding have been made by Einstein. To be faced with the fact that the velocity of light is the same when measured from a body moving toward the source of a beam of light as when measured from a body moving away from that source, and then to change the concepts of time and space accordingly so that the constancy of that velocity is the result – I cannot imagine more fundamental originality.

I think the theories about the material universe reveal the unbelievably creative working of the human mind. I feel the same about the chain we are building from single hydrogen atoms to more complicated ones with carbon at the threshold of organic chemistry and from there to protein and subsequently to cells; and gradually we are approaching the basic ideas of computers as possible models of the working of our brains.

Coming back to earth, economics takes possession of us. Economics is of human origin, in contradistinction to the universe and our environment. It reflects many of our imperfections, such as our self-centeredness, our myopia, and the lagging of our ideas behind evidence. As Keynes said: "Many people's economic thinking is based on what they were taught decades ago." But as everybody who has to operate in the economy thinks to be an expert, doctrinaire thinking abounds."

So much for the shortcomings of others. I have my own. "Trial and error" might characterize my way of working.

TRAVELS

In reviewing my work I cannot fail to mention the many times I traveled to foreign countries, as a lecturer, or as a participant at meetings and conferences, or as an adviser to governments. That last function took me to Egypt, Turkey, India, and Mexico. Most of these trips were very rewarding and provided me with excellent contacts with officials. However, the results, if any, cannot be measured: maybe some small seeds have been sown. In any case, I have seen some of the difficulties in less developed countries with my own eyes, which has made me all the more eager to do something in that field.

Most memorable among my Western European travels was our two years' stay in Geneva from 1936 to 1938. I have given lectures in many other countries also. I love and admire Italy and its contribution to architecture, music, and painting. However, the Italian contribution to social policy is negligible. I think for a good social climate the Scandinavian countries lead the way – Sweden in front. It is also the most advanced country with respect to the necessary construction of a world community.

I was invited to lecture and attend some meetings in Japan. My wife and I found these three weeks unforgettable. The countryside, the temples, and the parks are overwhelmingly beautiful, but first and foremost we enjoyed the hospitality and the friendship we met everywhere. I greatly appreciated the opportunity of meeting Saburo Okita, with whom I have shared our work in international cooperation. With many others I have made lasting and fruitful contacts.

Twice, we had a prolonged stay in the United States – once in Haverford, Pennsylvania, at the famous Quaker College. The lovely campus and the warm Quaker atmosphere, which appealed very much to my own way of thinking, and the friendship of colleagues and students were a joy to me and my family. Communicating with Gilbert White, Philip Bell, Holland Hunter, and others has been greatly stimulating. We were all very happy there.

We also spent about six months in Cambridge, Massachusetts, where I taught international trade at Harvard, during a sabbatical year for Gottfried Haberler. I profited enormously from the gatherings at Littauer Center and around MIT and thoroughly enjoyed the chance to participate in discussions with Leontief, Galbraith, Gerschenkron, Smithies, Bergson, and Samuelson, among others. For my work in developing countries, Ed Mason's school of development policy was very important. His significance can be measured by the flocks of former students who came to meet him and his wife at every airport they stopped at during their trip around the world.

At Harvard I also met Shigeto Tsuru, the famous Japanese economist. Together we gave a course on socialism. One of the "students" (an American colleague) thought my contribution to be more Dutch than socialist. He did not know democratic socialism.

HOBBIES AND ANTI-HOBBIES

Curricula vitae are not quite complete without some information about one's hobbies. I enjoy most of all, together with my wife, who was my high school girl friend, the close and warm relationship with our children and grandchildren. In these days of so much estrangement between family members, this is surely a great boon. With my wife I share the pleasure of walks in the open country, of listening to classical music, and of amateur comparing of languages. My earliest childhood, but still standing, hobby concerns streetcars. Cities without streetcars, or trams, as we call them, are incomplete. Washington, D.C., lost a good deal of attraction for me when it changed its excellent PCC cars to buses. Thanks to the oil scarcity, there has been some switching to streetcars again, which will also benefit the economy.

Anti-hobbies? Yes. I don't like sports and I dislike automobiles. I have to admit, though, that sometimes I am grateful for a lift: not a consistent attitude!

Jan Tinbergen is Emeritus Professor, Erasmus University, Rotterdam, and the 1969 winner of the Nobel Memorial Prize in economic science, together with Ragnar Frisch.

REFERENCES

Hanau, A., *Die Prognose der Schweinepreise,* Sonderheft 18 der Vierteljahreshefte zur Konjunkturforschung, Berlin, 1930 (German; *The Forecast of Pig Prices*).

Lange, O., and F. M. Taylor, *On the Economic Theory of Socialism,* Minneapolis: University of Minnesota Press, 1938 and 1948.

Meuldijk, J., Jr., "Der englische Schiffbau während der Periode 1870–1912 und das Problem des Ersatzbaues," *Weltwirtschaftliches Archiv* 52, 1940, p. 524ff. (German; "English Shipbuilding during the Period 1870–1912 and the Problem of Replacement").

Stone, R., *Aspects of Economic and Social Modelling,* Conférences Luigi Solari, I, Geneva: Librarie Droz, 1981.

Tinbergen, J., "Vertragingsgolven en levensduurgolven," in J. v.d. Wijk et al., *Strijdenskracht door Wetensmacht,* Amsterdam: De Arbeiderspers 1938, pp. 143–50 (Dutch; "Lag Cycles and Life Time Cycles").

"Spardefizit und Handelsdefizit," *Weltwirtschaftliches Archiv* 95, 1965, pp. 89–101 (German; "Savings Gap and Trade Gap").

"Allocations of Workers over Jobs," *De Economist* 132, 1984, pp. 23–9.

SHIGETO TSURU

Scientific Humanism as an Ideal

FROM JAPAN TO AMERICA

Of the three factors contributing to the formation of my life philosophy – inherited attributes, education, and the social milieu – probably the last was the strongest, followed closely by the second.

In 1929 I entered what was known as Higher School, an elite preparatory institution for university training in pre-war Japan. That period, however, had been characterized by a number of unusual events that made a strong impression on us Japanese youths. For one thing, Japan's imperialistic invasion of China was taking concrete forms, such as the deliberate killing of Chiang Tso-Lin by a railroad explosion and the incursion of the Japanese army into Shantung Peninsula, both in 1928. Almost coincidentally, the Wall Street panic in October 1929 shook the capitalist world, while the Soviet Union was launching the First Five-Year Plan with bright promises, so it seemed.

283

On the domestic scene, underground Communist activities were on the ascendant, resulting in a series of mass arrests under the newly revised Security Maintenance Act of 1928. On university and higher-school compuses all over the country, clandestine study groups on Marxism mushroomed. Already in my first year of high school, I became involved in the organized student movement known as "the Anti-Imperialist League" and participated in its various activities, including an anti-military-training campaign and the editing and distribution of the League's publication, which we called *Iskra*, as well as in intensive studies of Marxian classics.

The inevitable came in early December 1930 when I was arrested along with some forty co-students. I was apparently regarded as one of the three leaders of the Anti-Imperialist League on campus and was detained for more than three months before being released because I was a minor.

When released from prison in the spring of 1931, I followed my father's suggestion to study abroad. My choice was to go to Germany, inasmuch as my first foreign language was German. It happened, however, that the Marxist-oriented Social Democratic Party was quite strong then in Germany, and my father agreed to finance my study abroad only on the condition that I go to the United States. I agreed to this and chose for matriculation a small college in the northern part of Wisconsin – Lawrence College in Appleton – with the clandestine intention of crossing the Atlantic in due course.

In fact, I spent two well-filled years at Lawrence, with even an amateur attempt at experimental psychology, which resulted in my first published work, "The Meaning of Meaning," in an academic journal.[1] The experiment consisted in selecting about twenty-five pairs of contrasting sensorial adjectives in Japanese and having each pair pronounced twice in reverse order by subjects who were asked to identify which of the pair sounded more like which. The experiment was considered meaningful because the Japanese language had been spoken for centuries before it acquired any means of ideographic or alphabetical rendition, which could mean that contrasting sensorial adjectives, in particular, might have evolved by a certain *Gestalt* with semi-universality.

I personally regarded this research more as playful amusement than as scientific endeavor; but Dr. Horace Fries, who taught psychology and philosophy at Lawrence and guided me in this research, was quite serious and apparently found in me a potentially promising disciple in the *Gestalt* school he was committed to. Philosophically, he was a pragmatist; it was thus that I was introduced to Max Otto of the University of Wisconsin, with whom I spent two summers (1932 and 1933) studying philosophy.

---

[1] Shigeto Tsuru, "The Meaning of Meaning," *General Journal of Psychology*, 1942.

He was a great teacher. I learned two things from him, which could be succinctly described as "realistic idealism" and "scientific humanism." It was under Otto's influence that I developed an enduring philosophy of life, which, departing significantly from my earlier Marxist orientation, placed emphasis above all on the difference in the *practical results* of alternative ideas. Always to relate any policy proposal to its probable concrete consequences has become a habit of my work since then.

My original intention was, as I said, to study in Germany. But fortuitous (from my point of view) events gave a twist to my plan, that is, the Reichstag fire of February 1933 and the rise of Hitler to power in Germany, which clearly precluded the possibility of free scientific study there. The choice thrust upon me then was either to remain at Lawrence College or to move on to the big time at a place like Harvard. The longer I stayed at Lawrence, the more attracted I became to the place, especially with its proximity to Madison and Max Otto, the source of my newfound inspiration.

I was fortunate, however, in having as my mentor Gordon Clapp — later to become board director of the Tennessee Valley Authority — who was then the dean of students at Lawrence. Wisely seeing through my state of vacillation, Professor Clapp advised me to transfer to Harvard College for my junior year and to start concentrating on the subject of my career interest. I followed his advice and went to Harvard in September 1933, registering in the Department of History, Government, and Economics with the intention of majoring in economics. But again, my amateur interest in other subjects seized me during my undergraduate years. I managed to minimize my commitments to economics and took advantage of the accessibility to the great minds that shined on campus, notably Alfred North Whitehead in philosophy and Crane Brinton in history. As a term paper for the former I wrote a rather lengthy essay, "On Construction and Criticism of a Rational System of Beliefs," and for the latter I took advantage of my knowledge of Marx to write "Dialogue between Denis Diderot and Karl Marx,"[2] both of which, fortunately enough, received high commendations from the teachers. At the same time, with unexpectedly strong encouragement from Gordon Allport, professor of social psychology, I took up the experiment that I had conducted in relation to my 1932 article "The Meaning of Meaning." Professor Allport found the experiment most intriguing and insisted that I develop it further (1) by using a larger sample of pairs of words and (2) by asking the subjects to report on their introspection. I wrote a lengthy paper on the entire experiment but never felt bold enough to

[2] Shigeto Tsuru, "Dialogue between Denis Diderot and Karl Marx," reprinted in idem, *Collected Works*, Vol. 13 (Tokyo: Kodansha, 1976), pp. 200–24.

have it published anywhere; and I suspect that the report is still lying somewhere in the laboratory of social psychology at Harvard University.

FINALLY INTO ECONOMICS

Through detours of this kind, I still maintained my basic interest in political economy and somewhat hastily decided to write an honor's thesis in the field for my bachelor's degree. My tutor was O. H. Taylor, nicknamed "Nat" on account of his persistent devotion to the idea of "Natural Law." Weekly discussions with him on the philosophical basis of classical economists were stimulating enough but I apparently disappointed him by choosing to title my thesis "An Aspect of Marx's Methodology in Economics: 'The Fetishism of Commodities' " – a subject that after more than half a century still occupies a niche in my mind.

The courses in economics that I took were rather unsystematic. For one thing, I managed to persuade the department chairman to excuse me from going through the standard comprehensive course in economics on the pretext that my education in Japan had included it, which was not quite true, and I regretted in later years missing the basic training in the discipline. Memorable, however, was a half-year course, "Value and Distribution," given by Frank W. Taussig. I was fortunate in being exposed to the famed Socratic method of this indefatigable old gentleman-economist in his last year of teaching at Harvard. It was probably he, more than any other person, who inspired me to go to Harvard graduate school in economics.

I did so in the fall of 1935. Surprisingly, I was the only Harvard College graduate in the group of about twenty who started graduate economics that year. But this group, for a number of reasons, was a remarkably fortunate one. First, the group itself happened to be composed of some brilliant aspirants in the profession, such as Paul Samuelson, Robert Triffin (Belgium), and Robert Bryce (Canada), who, along with those who had come there earlier, such as J. K. Galbraith, Richard Musgrave, Abe Bergson, Paul Sweezy, and Wolfgang Stolper, created an unusually stimulating atmosphere of mutual edification. Soon to follow us in the graduate school were Evsey Domar, Sidney Alexander, James Tobin, Joe Bain, and Robert Solow, among others. The graduate student body at Harvard during the years 1935 to 1938 was of such a caliber as to have prompted Robert Triffin to write, "I ... learned as much or more, as an economist, from *student colleagues* of mine in the most brilliant class that Harvard probably ever had ... than from the professors whose classes I attended."[3]

---

[3] R. Triffin, "An Economist's Career: What? Why? How?," in *Banca Nazionale de Lavoro Quarterly Review*, September 1981, p. 254.

It is true, however, that the economics faculty at Harvard was then in a stage of transition from the patriarchal dominance of F. W. Taussig to a new golden decade with "imported scholars" like Schumpeter, Haberler, and Leontief, and slightly later with Alvin Hansen from Minnesota. There is no denying that we benefited greatly from their instructions in their prime. This is the second reason for my saying that we were a fortunate group. Related to this is the third: the presence of Schumpeter and others attracted visiting scholars from abroad on their Rockefeller fellowships to Harvard. And among them were Oscar Lange, Abba Lerner, Nicholas Kaldor, Paul Baran, Eric Roll, Fritz Machlup, Nicholas Georgescu-Roegen, Oscar Morgenstern, and Jacob Marschak. Almost every day, either at lunch, cocktail hour, or late at night, we found an occasion for heated discussions on the state of economic science. It may be said, too, that probably nowhere in the world at the time could one witness a freer and more productive confrontation between frontline modern economics and Marxian orthodoxy.

The fourth reason is somewhat fortuitous. The publication of Keynes' *General Theory* was foretold by our student colleague Robert Bryce, and the first shipment of thirty copies arrived from England in March 1936 – an occasion that marked the beginning of what Samuelson characterized as a period affecting "most economists under the age of 35 with the unexpected virulence of a disease first attacking and decimating an isolated tribe of south sea islanders."[4] Seymour Harris, the most enterprising member of the faculty at that time, immediately organized an informal study group on Keynes, to which most of us flocked to test our understanding of the new vista opened by that genius of our age.

DETOURS AGAIN

I must say that the academic year 1935–36 was the most fruitful one for me during my apprenticeship in economics. Within one year I managed to pass the general examination toward a Ph.D. degree, and by June 1936 I was ready to start writing my dissertation. However, at that point my peripatetic propensity sidetracked me again, and while I held an assistantship in the department to sustain my living, I wandered into activities little related to my field of concentration, namely, theoretical and empirical studies of economic fluctuations in capitalist countries.

---

[4] P. A. Samuelson, "The General Theory (3)," in S. E. Harris (ed.), *The New Economics: Keynes' Influence on Theory and Public Policy* (New York: Knopf, 1950), pp. 145–80, quoted at 146.

The times were such in those years of 1936 and 1937 that many a resident of the ivory tower could not ignore outside developments. The victory of the popular front group in the Spanish parliamentary election took place in February 1936, followed in May by the formation of a similar popular front in Argentina; and then in June the first Front Populaire cabinet by Blum came into existence in France. July 1936 was the month that began the Spanish Civil War, the war that, it may be recalled, drew many a literary and intellectual person onto the battlefield from outside Spain. In Asia, Japan's invasion of China, which began with the Manchurian Incident of September 1931, gradually escalated, eventually taking a blatantly undisguised form in July 1937.

It was against such a background on the world scene that a group of young Marxist scholars in Cambridge, Massachusetts, began thinking about publishing a quarterly journal with a Marxian orientation intended to be broad enough to meet the needs of the popular front strategy. I was an active member of the planning stage for this in the first half of 1936, with almost weekly meetings in Cambridge. The first issue of the journal, which was called *Science and Society – A Marxian Quarterly*, was published in October 1936 and immediately aroused a controversy over its compromising editorial attitudes toward non-Marxist scholarship. I spent a great deal of energy attempting to straighten out the editorial policy, somewhat in vain, I am afraid.

The China problem, too, occupied a substantial portion of my time in those years. I worked closely with the Institute of Pacific Relations in New York in the journalistic campaign against the Japanese aggression. I wrote frequently for a magazine called *Amerasia*, which came into existence at the time; and I also drafted for the Chinese Council for Economic Research, under a pseudonym, a lengthy pamphlet, *Japan's Economy under War Strain*, trying to demonstrate the deteriorating economic conditions in Japan with no prospect of military settlement in sight. My statistical analysis itself may not have been off the mark, but I was grossly mistaken in drawing inferences from it: namely, a large part of what I interpreted to be the war consumption in Japan's conduct in China was actually, as it turned out, nothing but stockpiling for the preparation of a much bigger war to come.

Looking back, I must say that, although my philosophical posture inclined more toward pragmatism under the influence of Max Otto than toward the dialectic materialism of my youth, I seemed to have guarded jealously the intellectual attributes I had acquired in the turbulent atmosphere of the late 1920s in Japan, especially in the sphere of social science and in international political analysis. Besides, I could not suppress my reformist zeal, which has persisted to this day.

MARXIAN CONCERN

In the state of mind I have just related, I continued defending the more or less orthodox position in Marxian economics; and along with working toward the completion of my doctoral dissertation, I engaged in a debate with Maurice Dobb on Marx's theory of value and also with Kei Shibata on the theory of the falling tendency of the rate of profit. My article in debate with Dobb appeared under the nom de plume of Alfred Lowe in the pre-war English journal *The Modern Quarterly*.[5] My contention was essentially to point out the importance of the *qualitative* aspect of the value theory in Marx, criticizing Dobb for having concentrated too much on the *quantitative* aspect and for posing questions in terms of a "general concept of value" and its *desiderata*.

The debate with Shibata I will not dwell upon here. But on the question of the falling tendency of the rate of profit I also defended the then-orthodox Marxist position. After I completed my doctoral dissertation in May 1940 with the title "Business Cycle Theories and Their Application to Japan," I wrote two articles, again from the Marxist point of view. One, "On Reproduction Schemes," appeared as an appendix to Paul Sweezy's *The Theory of Capitalist Development*, 1942, and another, "Business Cycle and Capitalism – Schumpeter vs. Marx," had to wait for public appearance until 1956, when I compiled a volume of essays on Marxian economics.[6]

The first of the two, which related the steady and expanded reproduction schemes of Marx to Quesnay's *tableau économique* and to the Keynesian aggregates, attracted some attention among non-Marxist economists as well and evoked controversy among some Marxian economists. For example, Charles Bettelheim offered a critique[7] on one of the points I made in that paper to the effect that in the expanded reproduction scheme the physical component corresponding to additional variable capital (which takes the form of wage goods) is *twice* represented in the value component, i.e., first as a part of surplus value accruing to capitalists and second as income for incremental wage earners. Bettelheim contended that my "mistake" was twofold: one, definitional, and the other, methodological. On both accounts, I remained unpersuaded, and the debate

---

[5] Alfred Lowe [Shigeto Tsuru], "Mr. Dobbs and Marx's Theory of Value," *Modern Quarterly*, 1, No. 3 (July 1938), 285.

[6] Shigeto Tsuru, "On Reproduction Schemes," appendix to Paul Sweezy, *The Theory of Capitalist Development: Principles of Marxian Political Economy* (New York: Oxford Univ. Press, 1942); idem, "Business Cycle and Capitalism – Schumpeter vs. Marx," in *Essays on Marxian Economics*, Science Council of Japan, Economic Ser. No. 8, February 1956.

[7] Charles Bettelheim, "Revenue national, épargne et investissements chez Marx et chez Keynes," *Révue d'Economie Politique*, 1948, pp. 198–211.

went on, involving a number of Japanese economists as well. To this day, after forty-five years, no one has yet given us the final word.

More or less committed as I was to the basic tenet of Marxian political economy, I could not quite fall in line with the dominant *Weltanschauung* of American society in spite of my long sojourn there during my formative years from age nineteen to thirty. Thus, I wrote in 1943[8] on the subject of the national character of Americans, stating that one of their distinctive attributes was their strong confidence in the inherent power of the individual. This confidence, no doubt, is closely related to the historical circumstances in which the United States developed. Alien to it is the following sociological insight of Schumpeter's, with which I agreed: "Things economic and social move by their own momentum and the ensuing situations compel individuals and groups to behave in certain ways whatever they may wish to do – not indeed by destroying their freedom of choice but by shaping the choosing mentalities and by narrowing the list of possibilities from which to choose."[9] The idea that a society might evolve in accordance with objective laws to which individuals may unknowingly be subject appears to escape the comprehension of representative Americans.

It was therefore a kind of revelation to me when I came across a statement in President Franklin Delano Roosevelt's message to Congress of April 29, 1938, proposing to strengthen the anti-trust law because he strongly felt that the American society had to find effective measures of control against "blind economic forces," which are distinct from blind personal selfishness.[10]

REPATRIATION AND THE END OF WAR

To go back a little in time, I married Masako Wada in Tokyo in June 1939 and brought her to Cambridge while I completed the final year of work on my degree and dissertation. After receiving my Ph.D. degree in 1940, I had a choice of either going back to Japan for an academic post somewhere or seeking a position in one of the universities in the United States. The former option was not so easy at the time because a guildlike clique prevailed in academic professions in Japan and each of the university faculties was generally staffed by an inbred hierarchy usually headed by a commanding "master of the guild." Thus, I decided to remain

---

[8] Later incorporated into my contribution to *Paths of American Thoughts*, edited by A. M. Schlesinger, Jr., and Morton White (Boston: Houghton Mifflin, 1963).
[9] J. A. Schumpeter, *Capitalism, Socialism, and Democracy*, 3rd ed. (New York: Harper Bros., 1950), pp. 129–30.
[10] See *Congressional Record*, 1938, pp. 5992–6.

in the United States at least for a while and depended on Oscar Lange and others for a possible opening on the North American continent.

I recall vividly a day – it was Friday, December 5, 1941 – when Robert Bryce, then a Treasury official in Canada, paid a homecoming visit to Harvard, and we had a special seminar with Schumpeter and many others who had been student colleagues of Bryce. The European war was going on then, and a major topic of our discussion was post-war economic problems and the issues of free trade versus "appropriate discrimination." Bryce favored the latter, and naturally a heated discussion ensued, where-upon Schumpeter abruptly intervened and asked Bryce, "When do you think the next world war will come?" "Around 1972" was Bryce's an-swer, to which Schumpeter commented immediately, "You are too op-timistic." At that time, of course, relations between the United States and Japan were close to the breaking point, and the discussion went on naturally to a possible war between the two powers. I took a strong position, saying that it would be suicidal for Japan to start a war against the United States. I was proved wrong within a mere two days, and found myself classified as an "enemy alien" subject to various restrictions on my conduct, including the temporary freezing of my bank account.

As may be recalled, the initial phase of the Pacific War was somewhat one-sided in favor of Japan. But I was convinced that eventually Japan would be defeated and began harboring an idea, as early as the spring of 1942, of returning to my home country in order to be on the scene of defeat so that I could be of some service during the period of post-war reconstruction. The first chance of repatriation came in early June 1942, in an exchange program mainly for the diplomatic corps and people classified as "international merchants," both of whom had been kept in informal confinement at luxury hotels after the outbreak of the war. Those of us who had been essentially unmolested and drawing salaries from American institutions were allocated berths only on sufferance on the exchange ship and were discriminated against in a number of ways; for example, our luggage was limited to thirty-two cubic feet per person with no paper materials allowed. Thus my wife had to surrender all her music scores as well as her cherished amulets before going aboard.

I suffered the same fate; this was the second time I had lost my library by a single stroke (the first was when I was arrested in 1930; there was a third time to come, when my room in Tokyo burned to ashes in an air raid in May 1945). To leave the country of my intellectual apprenticeship extending over eleven years, stripped of all accumulated assets in the form of books, documents, and my own writings, was painful enough for me. But apparently my sense of emergency at the time overcame all my anxieties.

We arrived in Japan toward the end of August 1942, and for almost a year I "loafed," as it were, with no sense of urgency in searching for a stable job. But as was expected, I was called to the colors in June 1944 and underwent strenuous physical training as a private in one of the infantry regiments in Kyūshū. To my surprise, however, some people in the Foreign Office apparently knew of me and worked for an exceptional discharge from military duty in order that my professional qualifications could be better utilized in the foreign service.

Thus I was discharged and returned to Tokyo, where soon after, I was appointed a diplomatic officer. It was in this capacity that I went to the Soviet Union in the spring of 1945 and escaped the severe air raids on Tokyo, only to find my library burned to ashes on my return.

OCCUPATION AND GOVERNMENT EXPERIENCE

It took exactly three years after the end of the war for me to return to my professional career as an economist. But during those three years many things happened to me.

When General Douglas MacArthur landed in Japan as the Supreme Commander of Allied Powers (SCAP), he found the Japanese economy in a shambles. Under this circumstance, the SCAP requested that the Japanese government send the Economic and Scientific Section (ESS) "a competent economist with good facility in the English language." Whereupon, Mr. Shigeru Yoshida, then the minister of Foreign Affairs, picked me from within the Foreign Office, and I became an economic adviser to the ESS starting in April 1946.

A year later, the Socialist Party obtained a plurality in the first postwar general election, and a coalition cabinet was formed with Mr. Tetsu Katayama, a socialist, as the prime minister. At this juncture, the SCAP ordered a radical reform in the organization of the Economic Stabilization Board (ESB) in the Japanese government, creating four vice-ministers and transferring some of the major administrative powers from other ministries. Now it was the turn of General Marquet, head of the ESS, to suggest to me that I go into this newly strengthened ESB as one of the vice-ministers. I did so and remained in that post until the Katayama cabinet fell in February 1948.

My experiences, first in the ESS and then in the ESB, during that hectic period of Japan's post-war reconstruction were naturally laden with battles and skirmishes often won but more often lost. One innovation I initiated in my capacity as vice-minister was to take the leadership in drafting an Economic White Paper that was intended to give to the general public the fullest available information on key aspects of the Japanese economy, while exhorting compatriots to support the government policy of combating the vicious circle of inflation and of reversing the economy's drift toward negative growth. Naturally, I mobilized all the technical staff of the office in the drafting stage, but I personally wrote the "General Introduction," in which I made full use of the macroeconomic approach, and also the concluding section, in which I said, in part:

Speaking figuratively, our difficulties are not simply that our fingers have been cut or our legs broken. It may be said that we are suffering from more serious physiological effects such as blood poisoning or dysfunction of the ductless glands. The fact that honest people find themselves fooled and that those who work sincerely suffer from losses testifies to the "physiological" malady of the economic organism of the country.... The stages in which the people, after going through conditions in which even the base of simple reproduction of the economy gets more and more restricted, emerge, with hope for the future, onto the road to rehabilitation and reconstruction shall be the stages in which those who work honestly in close relation with each other will make their livelihood easier through their own effort, though inevitably they will have to go through a temporary period of hardship and deficiencies, which they should take as a hardship imposed on them by themselves.

The general tone of the White Paper, as well as the tools of analysis it employed, were quite a departure from those of the erstwhile bureaucratic documents; and it could be seen that my training in the United States as an economist with pragmatic inclinations was visibly reflected in the document.

BACK TO THE ACADEMIC WORLD

In September 1948, after resigning from my government post, I decided to return to Hitotsubashi University, with which I had a brief association from 1943 to 1944 and which had been reorganized in the post-war period into a multi-faculty social science university. This time my association with Hitotsubashi lasted for twenty-seven years, first as director of the Institute of Economic Research attached to the university and finally as president, from which I retired in March 1975.

Upon my return to an academic post, Schumpeter wrote me a very nice letter, from which I quote a passage:

It is with particular pleasure that I welcome you back to academic activities which, as in the 5th century in Rome, are perhaps the least distasteful ones to indulge in, in the world as it is. Studies in mathematics and statistics will complement most usefully your theoretical achievements and I greatly look forward to the results. Of course, distance always beautifies, but I who am near enough to Harvard cannot say that I experience very much stimulus from my surroundings. Scientifically, Leontief is the only man who is really alive.... Fundamental ideas, methods and approaches you know, and original achievement can be built upon this in Tokyo as well as in Boston.

As I recall my Hitotsubashi days, where I had no regular undergraduate courses to give, the fields of my research shifted back and forth rather widely. Also, I was able to take extended leaves abroad frequently, as among other positions, Irving Fisher Professor at Yale (1960) and as Dyason Lecturer in Australia (1964). And on each occasion of staying abroad I was fortunate in having stimulating intellectual exchanges with colleagues and participants. Most of my theoretical papers were written during this period, among which I may mention, in particular (only those that were written in English): "A Note on Capital/Output Ratio" (1956); "Applicability and Limitations of Economic Development Theory" (1962); "The Effects of Technology on Productivity" (1965); and "In Place of GNP" (1971).[11]

This last article actually goes back, in its main thesis, to an article I wrote (in Japanese) in 1943 in critique of the market-oriented concept of national income. My main contention has become much more relevant in recent years.

Another subject that occupied my mind during those years was Marxian economics and the analysis of capitalism. Among a number of articles I wrote in English, I would single out the following as representative of my endeavor: "Keynes versus Marx: The Methodology of Aggregates" (1954); *Has Capitalism Changed?* (1961); "Marx and the Analysis of Capitalism: A New Stage on the Basic Contradiction?" (1968); and "Towards a New Political Economy." (1976).[12]

The third category of subject matter that has continued to concern me more or less since the immediate post-war period is that of environmental problems. I took the initiative in 1963 in organizing an interdisciplinary group of scientists to wrestle with this complex problem, above all by making on-the-spot investigations in the problem areas. On practically all of the major litigations concerned with environmental disruption, such as the Minamata mercury poisoning, the multiple pollution in Yokkaichi

---

[11] Shigeto Tsuru, "Applicability and Limitations of Economic Development Theory," *Informazioni Srimez* (Supplement) 12 (1962), 4238–46, reprinted in idem, *Essays on Economic Development* (Tokyo: Kinokuniya, 1968), pp. 17–38. Idem, "A Note on Capital/Output Ratio," *Keizai Kenkyu* 7, no. 2 (1956), 114–20. "The Effects of Technology on Productivity," in E. A. G. Robinson (ed.), *Problems in Economic Development* (New York: Macmillan, 1965); idem, "In Place of GNP," originally presented at the Symposium on Political Economy of Environment organized by Maison des Sciences de l'Homme in July 1971.

[12] Shigeto Tsuru, "Keynes versus Marx: The Methodology of Aggregates," in Kenneth Kurihara (ed.), *Post-Keynesian Economics* (New Brunswick, N.J.: Rutgers University Press, 1954); idem (ed.), *Has Capitalism Changed?* (Tokyo: Iwanami Shoten, 1961); idem, "Marx and the Analysis of Capitalism: A New Stage on the Basic Contradiction?" Originally presented at the Symposium on the Role of Karl Marx in the Development of Contemporary Scientific Thought organized by UNESCO, May 1968; idem, "Towards a New Political Economy," in Kurt Dopfer (ed.), *Economics in the Future: Towards a New Paradigm* (New York: Macmillan, 1976).

City, and the noise pollution of Osaka International Airport, the members of this group, including myself, actively participated in the legal battle on the side of the plaintiffs and contributed, we believe, to winning the court decisions against the polluting firms and local autonomous bodies.

In this connection, I cannot fail to mention one symposium I organized in Tokyo in 1970 for the International Social Science Council entitled "Economics of Environmental Disruption."[13] This was the occasion when the famed "Tokyo Resolution" was adopted, which urged "the adoption in law of the principle that every person is entitled by right to an environmental free of elements which infringe on human health and well-being and nature's endowment, including its beauty, which shall be the heritage of the present to the future generation." Besides a paper that I contributed on this occasion to the symposium entitled "Environmental Pollution Control in Japan," I may mention another paper I wrote in English for the Columbia–United Nations Conference, "Economic Development and Environment," held in New York in April 1972, entitled "North–South Relations on Environment."

WHITHER JAPAN?

In rounding out this essay, I should like to summarize my views on the direction I think Japan should take. Most of my published writings on various aspects of this broad question are in Japanese; but there do exist a few articles of mine in English to which I can refer for interested readers.

In 1955 I contributed an article to a special issue of *The Atlantic* on Japan[14] in which I discussed broad political, economic, and social aspects of post-war Japan with the then-justified apprehension concerning the probability of Japan's economic viability. Clearly I failed to discern the potential growth power that existed in our economy, for Japan's "miracle" actually began around 1955 and lasted without letup until the first oil crisis of 1973, with a cumulative average annual growth rate of more than 9 percent in real GNP. Naturally, this called for a reappraisal on my part of my erstwhile analysis; and I wrote a booklet for the Atlantic Institute for International Affairs in 1976[15] in which I attempted to explain, at least to my own satisfaction, how and why such sustained rapid growth was possible, at the same time indicating that a turning point was in sight.

Essentially this was the same analysis I had made in one of the two

---

[13] Proceedings of this symposium were published by *Asahi Evening News* under the title "A Challenge to Social Scientists," 1970.
[14] Shigeto Tsuru, "A New Japan?" *The Atlantic Monthly*, 195 (January 1955), 103–7.
[15] Shigeto Tsuru, *The Mainsprings of Japanese Growth: A Turning Point?* (Paris: Atlantic Institute for International Affairs, 1977).

lectures I gave in Australia in 1964 as a Dyason Lecturer.[16] But there I pointed to the importance of looking at the negative aspect of rapid economic growth also, the concern that I have already spoken of in a previous section.

And in another of my lectures in Australia[17] I offered a discussion of a broader issue regarding the future of Japan, stating the framework in which my life philosophy is more clearly revealed. I used there an old Japanese parable to illustrate the nature of alternatives that Japan could follow. This parable is a story of three brothers, Strong, Rich, and Warmhearted. At first, Strong ruled the family with his muscular power. "Might makes right" was the rule. As the years passed, however, age began to tell on Strong, and he could not assert his authority as before. By that time, the second brother, Rich, had amassed wealth, having built a number of warehouses. Now it was Rich who could assert authority in the family. In other words, the criterion of excellence had changed from strength to wealth. One day there was a fire in the village, and it burned all the warehouses that Rich owned. Overnight, he became penniless. In the wake of the fire there was an epidemic. The third brother, Warmhearted, had studied medicine and could tell immediately what kind of epidemic it was. He proceeded to take the necessary measures and saved many lives in the village. As the story goes, if you visit the village today, you will find a statue of Warmhearted standing in the center. Warmhearted triumphed over Strong and Rich.

After relating this parable, I stated in my lecture:

The transition of the criterion of individual excellence has more or less followed such a course in the history of mankind. As for the criterion of national reputation, however, we may still be in the era of Strong and Rich. But I am certain that the time will come when the criterion for nations also will shift. Japan is not, cannot, and should not be one of "the powers" as judged by the criterion of Strong. Japan is not, though she could be, one of "the powers" as judged by the criterion of Rich. But I should like to see Japan become one of "the powers" as judged by the criterion of Warmhearted. The era of Warmhearted will inevitably come to this world. For, if the criterion of Strong and Rich is encouraged still further, I have a sneaking suspicion that this globe will not be a fit place for humanity to live.

That was in 1964, and since then, the sentence that would require revision is "Japan is not, though she could be, one of 'the powers' as judged by the criterion of Rich." It may be agreed now that Japan is a first-rate economic power.

[16] Shigeto Tsuru, "The Economic Problems of Japan: Present and Future," idem, *Collected Works*, Vol. 13, pp. 370–99.
[17] Shigeto Tsuru, "The Future of Japan in the Modern World Including Relations with the United States and China," *Collected Works*, Vol. 13, pp. 400–25.

What do I propose, then, by way of making Japan a country respected not for its military strength but for its beauty, culture, science, and other qualities of human excellence? I wrote a lengthy article[18] on this subject some eleven years ago, itemizing concrete proposals that are in accord with the tenets I learned from Max Otto in my youth, i.e., realistic idealism and scientific humanism. Let me summarize those proposals here:

(A) Japan should strive, as part of her policy of placing emphasis on human lives and health, to become the "health care center" of the world, expanding and improving her medical personnel and medical facilities while putting greater effort into the development of medical technology.

(B) Japan should work to develop more facilities for use at places of scenic beauty (and hot spring areas) which can be visited by many people, both native and foreign, for tourism and health.

(C) Japan should exert its full efforts to promote international exchange in the spheres of cultural and aesthetic activities.

(D) Japan should take long strides in increasing its aid to the United Nations University, making it a world center for education, research, and technical innovations that contributes to the social and economic development of the Third World countries.

(E) Japan should raise the level of its aid for developing countries and refugee relief so that as a percentage of GNP it becomes the highest in the world.

To these I hasten to add that our nation's position of renouncing the "criterion of Strong" is clearly stated in the basic law of the land, the Japanese Constitution, in particular, in its Article IX, which reads:

Aspiring sincerely to an international peace based on justice and order, the Japanese people forever renounce war as a sovereign right of the nation and the threat or use of force as means of settling international disputes.

In order to accomplish the aim of the preceding paragraph, land, sea, and air forces, as well as other war potential, will never be maintained. The right of belligerency of the state will not be recognized.

In addition, the so-called Three Non-nuclear Principles (not to produce, not to possess, and not to have nuclear weapons brought in) was proclaimed by the Japanese government in 1960, on which occasion then Prime Minister Kishi explained in the Diet: "Under no circumstances, whether threatened or attacked, will Japan use nuclear weapons. American forces in Japan will not use nuclear weapons either."

These constraints, it is true, have been rendered almost powerless in the course of the thirty-year rule of the conservative party (Liberal Democratic Party), which, on the pretext of Japan's dependence on the United

---

[18] Shigeto Tsuru, "Whither Japan? A Positive Program of Nation-building in an Age of Uncertainty," *Japan Quarterly*, 27, No. 4 (October–December 1980), 487–98.

States for military protection and deterrence under the terms of the U.S.–
Japan Security Treaty, has kept on expanding Japan's defense forces and
has acquiesced in the logistic disposition of nuclear weapons in and
around Japan by American forces. Nevertheless, public opinion in Japan,
especially as evidenced by grass-roots groups, is becoming increasingly
critical of the subservience of the Liberal Democratic government to U.S.
pressures, and even some members of the party are apparently impor-
tuned to pay lip service in public to the letter of the Constitution and
the Three Non-nuclear Principles. The tug of war between Article IX of
the Constitution and the U.S.–Japan Security Treaty appears to be fa-
voring the latter at present, but the contest is by no means over yet. At
least, the proposal that Japan take the lead in pressing for world disarmament is becoming an urgent issue transcending political and ideological
differences among a broad spectrum of the Japanese people.

A Japan that took the lead in pressing for world disarmament, that
was assiduous in the fight against disease by making Japan the health
care center of the world, that provided tourist facilities at sites of natural
scenic beauty, that was active in international cultural exchange, that
was willing to increase radically contributions to the United Nations
University, and that worked hard to eradicate the poverty of the Third
World would be a Japan in which the people felt assured of holding in
common positive values worth defending and would also be a Japan in
which an attack from abroad would patently appear meaningless and
inhuman.

When we consider the future of Japan in this way, we are naturally
led to feel that things such as the U.S.–Japan Security Treaty must lose
their raison d'être. It is most likely that public opinion will then gradually
come around to supporting the eventual liquidation of the Security
Treaty, in the same manner that the sun, not the north wind, may make
the traveler take off his coat. The age of the Warmhearted is certain to
come, for this is the only road to survival for Japan.

Shigeto Tsuru is Professor of Economics, Meiji Gakuin University.

Index